Metaverse, MetaIntelligence and Infinite Worlds with AI

Edited by Jane Thomason, Meltem Huri Baturay, Ritesh Jain and Ferdi Çelik

Published in London, United Kingdom

Metaverse, MetaIntelligence and Infinite Worlds with AI
http://dx.doi.org/10.5772/intechopen.1009489
Edited by Jane Thomason, Meltem Huri Baturay, Ritesh Jain and Ferdi Çelik

Contributors
Adam Szalach, Alberto Camarero-Orive, Aleksandar Šević, Andrii Diak, Baijun Chen, Barbara Buljat Raymond, Dominik Mirosław Piotrowski, Fabio Oliveira, Fei Zhao, Feng Liu, Ferdi Çelik, Harun Serpil, Ilona-Elefteryja Lasica, Ilona Nowosad, Ingvar Tjostheim, Jaime Gallego Vila, Javier Vaca Cabrero, Jesus Casal Martinez, John A. Waterworth, Junji Ohyama, Liudmila Bredikhina, Mingze Zhang, Monica Storss, Nan Xiang, Nem Samejima, Nevenka Popović Šević, Nicoletta González-Cancelas, Pranavsingh Dhunnoo, Sana Jamshaid, Sarah Katz, Stavros Pitsikalis, Tomasz Gross, Veslava Osinska, Viktorija Diak, Volkan Duran, Weronika Kortas, Yihong Wang, Zihan Deng

First published in London, United Kingdom, 2026 by IntechOpen
IntechOpen is the global imprint of INTECHOPEN LIMITED, registered in England and Wales, registration number: 11086078, 167-169 Great Portland Street, London, W1W 5PF, United Kingdom

For EU product safety concerns: IN TECH d.o.o., Prolaz Marije Krucifikse Kozulić 3, 51000 Rijeka, Croatia, info@intechopen.com or visit our website at intechopen.com.

British Library Cataloguing-in-Publication Data
A catalogue record for this book is available from the British Library

Metaverse, MetaIntelligence and Infinite Worlds with AI
Edited by Jane Thomason, Meltem Huri Baturay, Ritesh Jain and Ferdi Çelik
p. cm.
Print ISBN 978-1-83635-551-9
Online ISBN 978-1-83635-550-2
eBook (PDF) ISBN 978-1-83635-552-6

Meet the editors

Dr. Jane Thomason is a global thought leader in emerging technologies, including AI, Blockchain, Web3, Metaverse, and MedTech. She holds distinguished roles on the editorial boards of peer-reviewed journals and is an Industry Associate at University College London, Center for Blockchain. She is the author of "Blockchain for Global Social Change," "Applied Ethics in a Digital World", "Advancements in the New World of Web 3: A Look Toward the Decentralized Future", "Infinite Playgrounds - Gaming as the Architecture of the Future" and "Stablecoins and the Future of Financial Regulation " (forthcoming). She has published widely on MedTech, Web3, Blockchain, AI, and Metaverse, and is at the forefront of the impact of emerging technologies on industry and society.

Dr. Meltem Huri Baturay is the founding leader and president of Türkiye's international learning organization LET-IN R&D and serves as the Education Sector Leader of the World Metaverse Council. She is a globally invited speaker and has published extensively in SSCI- and Web of Science-indexed journals. Baturay has worked as a researcher in international projects, including a COST action supported under the EU Horizon 2020 Program, as well as TÜBİTAK and Erasmus+ KA2 projects. Her research focuses on innovative educational technologies, including XR applications and Artificial Intelligence in Education, Distance Education, Technology-Assisted Language Teaching, the design of multimedia-enriched instructional materials, and Human-Computer Interaction.

Dr. Ritesh Jain is a global fintech and technology leader known for advancing AI-driven innovation, open banking, and digital transformation. An advisor to the World Bank, he is also a Fellow at the Digital Euro and Global Blockchain Associations and a founding member of the World Metaverse Council. Dr. Jain has held senior roles at HSBC, VISA, and Maersk, where he led the launch of Apple Pay in Europe. As an entrepreneur, investor, and board advisor to private equity and venture capital funds, he helps scale ventures across fintech, sustainability, and emerging technologies, bridging policy, capital, and innovation to shape the future of finance and immersive economies.

Dr. Ferdi Çelik is a Turkish educator-researcher with a Ph.D. from Ondokuz Mayıs University. His work explores the intersection of emerging technologies, such as AI, AR/VR/MR, the metaverse, and language learning, with a specific focus on learner psychology. His research has been published in leading journals, including the British Educational Research Journal, BMC Psychology, and the Journal of Computer-Assisted Learning. He has served as editor for special issues in multiple prestigious journals. He has received the Research Article of the Year Award (2024) from Ondokuz Mayıs University, alongside nominations for the Cambridge Dedicated Teacher Award and the eTwinning National Quality Label.

Contents

Preface

Metaverse has been somewhat maligned and confused since Facebook appropriated the term. This book clarifies this confusion and provides a valuable resource for those seeking to expand their understanding of what the Metaverse is and how it is shaping the future. The book aims to open readers' minds to the opportunities of the Metaverse for all aspects of life in the future and to outline a future vision for immersive worlds.

Metaverse is an Internet-based ecosystem of virtual worlds that utilise virtual (VR), augmented (AR), and extended reality (XR), Artificial Intelligence (AI) and blockchain to: generate new types of digital experiences; enable people to perform their digital transactions with other people or with digital agents; improve efficiency of digital transactions with new immersive environments; enable new digital product development and new digital service delivery; and generate new monetary, social, and public value opportunities.

This book offers the reader a wide-ranging insight into the current state of the art in the Metaverse. The chapters in this volume chart the evolution of immersive, intelligent environments. They explore how extended reality (XR), digital twins, decentralized systems, and AI coalesce into dynamic ecosystems where humans and machines learn, build, and evolve together. The chapters cover adaptive human digital twins, AI-based meta-universities, embodied presence and trust, digital travel as sustainable experience, gamified learning systems, and AI-enhanced healthcare and wellbeing.

Intelligent, immersive worlds have the potential to democratise education, expand access to healthcare, and enable inclusive participation in digital economies. Yet they also raise difficult questions about identity, agency, and digital labor. Collectively, these chapters illustrate how the Metaverse is a new social, educational, and ethical landscape. It serves as a general reference for students, practitioners, and the intellectually curious, outlining how immersive realities will change our world.

Who Should Read This Book

This book is designed for those who want to understand and shape the intersection of AI and the Metaverse, including: researchers examining immersive learning, AI ethics, and digital transformation; educators exploring virtual, gamified, and adaptive environments; healthcare practitioners seeking to leverage immersive tools for clinical care, training, and wellbeing; innovators designing responsible and sustainable virtual ecosystems; and students and professionals preparing for emerging roles in digital economies.

Domain Coverage

Across its chapters, the volume presents research on: education through AI-based curricula, immersive classrooms and gamified learning, redefining how to teach, learn, and credential knowledge; health and wellbeing including use of XR, avatars, and AI agents to deliver remote therapy, medical training, and personalised health ecosystems; human identity and presence, exploring trust and authenticity in avatar-based interactions and digital labour economies; sustainability and digital travel as alternatives to physical travel; ethics and governance, through digital rights, inclusion, and accountability; and creativity through understanding the aesthetic and philosophical dimensions of immersion, emotion, and meaning in virtual worlds.

A Research Agenda for the Future

The emerging AI Metaverse frontier requires scholarly attention across several critical frontiers:

- Interoperability and Standards: developing shared infrastructure for identity, data, and assets across virtual worlds;
- Ethical AI Design: embedding transparency, explainability, and fairness into immersive systems;
- Digital Wellbeing: assessing the psychological, cognitive, and cultural impacts of prolonged immersion;
- Decentralized Governance: creating inclusive models of co-creation and accountability in digital economies;
- Sustainable Digitalization: whether VR/AR can support environmental and sustainability goals.

This agenda invites collaboration across disciplines, including computer science, philosophy, education, health, and social policy, to ensure that the future Metaverse is equitable and improves human existence.

Looking Ahead

The chapters in this book show that the Metaverse is not a distant horizon. It is already a place where AI, creativity, and human values intersect. The challenge now is to steer this transformation with wisdom and foresight. As we build the intelligent worlds of tomorrow, our most significant task is to imagine and design virtual spaces that extend empathy. This book invites readers to join the journey toward a more ethical, inclusive, and intelligent Metaverse.

Dr. Jane Thomason
Industry Associate,
UCL Centre for Blockchain,
Australia

Meltem Huri Baturay
Konya Food and Agriculture Universit,
Konya, Turkey

Ritesh Jain
University of East London,
London, UK

Ferdi Çelik
Ondokuz Mayıs University,
Samsun, Turkey

Section 1

Meta-Learning Frontiers: AI, XR, and the Reinvention of Education

Chapter 1

AI-Based Meta-Universities and the Smart Curriculum

Volkan Duran and Ferdi Çelik

Abstract

The rapid advancement of artificial intelligence (AI) is reshaping higher education, giving rise to AI-based meta-universities—decentralized, digitally augmented institutions without a physical campus. These meta-universities leverage AI to personalize learning, optimize educational delivery, and facilitate real-time international collaboration within a global knowledge network. Central to this transformation is the development of smart curricula—adaptive, data-driven learning pathways tailored to individual learner profiles, curricular goals, and societal challenges. This paper examines the theoretical foundations, design principles, and implementation strategies for smart curricula in AI-based meta-universities. Drawing on interdisciplinary insights from educational technology, cognitive science, and data analytics, it highlights the role of AI in enhancing curriculum flexibility, enabling competency-based assessments, and promoting lifelong learning. The paper also addresses key ethical, pedagogical, and infrastructure considerations, providing strategies for institutions to transition toward intelligent, equitable, and sustainable higher education systems. In an era dominated by the metaverse and pervasive digital technologies, the integration of smart curricula will be crucial in fostering responsive, learner-centered educational ecosystems.

Keywords: artificial intelligence (AI), meta-universities, smart curriculum, adaptive learning, personalized education, digital transformation

1. Introduction

The rise of artificial intelligence (AI) in higher education represents a shift toward intelligent, adaptable, and integrated learning environments, fundamentally changing the higher education model. AI-centered meta-universities envision a new reality for higher education, where digital infrastructure, smarter curricula, and virtual learning ecosystems come together to create personalized, adaptable, and globally connected educational experiences for students across different levels, industries, and backgrounds. This technological change is reshaping higher education through smart curricular design, expanded student engagement, and alignment of expected educational outcomes with progressive industry expectations and advancements in technology, facilitated by AI-led platforms using adaptive learning and real-time analytics [1, 2].

The use of AI technologies has emerged as a significant practice for enhancing knowledge acquisition and career readiness, especially when trusting AI [3]. AI tutor-supported immersive virtual environments have demonstrated success in engaging learners and improving skill development, showcasing the potential of AI-derived virtual learning ecologies [4]. Successful implementation of AI technologies will need to be prepared at the institutional level and developed using structured organizational models, including ethical oversight and collaboration among various stakeholders [5]. Smart course development is only just emerging, as AI will play roles in automated assessment, personalized learning, and intelligent teaching support. While AI-driven cloud infrastructures will support institutional change, the future of education systems may become more equitable, ethical, and scalable [6].

The rapid evolution of AI-enabled smart curricula in virtual learning ecosystems is allowing universities to curate personalized learning pathways that incorporate the demands of the twenty-first-century skills holistically [7]. Cross-cultural education projects, such as the HyDe model, are examples of how students from different countries can cocreate virtual learning spaces through AI-enabled design thinking [8]. The emerging technologies' constructivist principles – blockchain, generative AI, and NFTs – support accessibility and personalization, democratic governance affordances, and drive a new economic paradigm for global virtual learning environments [9]. These rapidly evolving systems are adjusting their digitally persistent curricular elements dynamically, evolving to meet industry demand and improving workforce readiness and academic significance, thereby transforming postsecondary education into a digitally integrated ecosystem capable of real-time adjustments [Melnyk and Pypenko, 2025; 10].

The role of educators in this transition is significant; however, digitally literate teachers, as leaders in curating curriculum content within AI-powered Smart Learning Management Systems (SLMS), are a game-changer and represent a shift toward better alignment of educational processes with organizational culture [11]. Blended and web-based learning processes with AI can foster and curate student-centered learning environments that support and promote personalized, flexible, and collaborative learning [12]. However, there are challenges to implementation, which raise questions about sustainability, equity, and relevance, especially in an authentic world context [13].

AI-powered adaptive learning platforms have brought significant advances to university education, transforming the education domain with adaptive algorithms and real-time data analysis to customize the delivery method, pace, and student feedback in real time for each learner. These platforms have reported significant increases in student learning performance and learner motivation compared to traditional or standard methods [14, 15]. Technologies, including reinforcement learning and deep analytics, are supporting curriculum design by developing smart technology to adapt to learner behaviors, positively impacting learner satisfaction and mastery-level performance [16]. In addition, these platforms provide benefits to students requiring disability support, particularly in terms of providing diverse accessibility, equity, and inclusion to enhance cognitive outcomes [17].

Smart universities are increasingly utilizing AI-based systems to provide collaborative, data-driven educational ecosystems, which enhance instruction and educational administration [18, 19]. Automated functions, such as grading and providing feedback, permit education to be scaled and made more accessible [Aggarwal et al., 2023; 20]. Overcoming obstacles such as data privacy, algorithmic bias, and infrastructure deficits is essential so that such innovations can be adopted without undue harm [21, 22].

AI's personalization capabilities are not limited to what content is sent to learners but encompass entire learning pathways and intelligent curricula. AI-supported systems can facilitate adaptive learning by dynamically profiling and adjusting content for learners. This type of AI-enabled learning results in students experiencing overall academic performance improvements, as well as students completing tasks more quickly and learners being more engaged [23].

Universities have begun using AI systems to enhance the curriculum of academic learning by aligning it with industry-requirements as they occur in real-time, thereby developing work-ready graduates. The integration of data is only possible with the intervention of analytics and predictive modeling [24]. Procedural advice systems enabled by AI provide better student support, course and career decision-making, and may also lead to improved student satisfaction and retention [25].

Examples of innovative tools like SocratiQ highlight the potential of generative AI in personalizing instruction via Socratic questioning strategies, back-trained on student responses [26], and smart campus systems that can analyze the actions of learners and provide real-time feedback and learning materials to capitalize on those behaviors for better learning outcomes [2]. These tools are being used effectively across disciplines such as statistics, STEM, and higher education as a whole, providing scalable models of individualized instruction and advancing the evolution of curricula [27].

This paper addresses the dawn of AI-based meta-universities and smart curricula as a disruptor in higher education by exploring how they deliver personalized, adaptive, and job-attuned learning ecosystems, transforming university education in response to the challenges and opportunities associated with adopting digital systems.

2. AI-driven curriculum design: Smart curriculum

AI-enabled curriculum design marks a significant paradigm shift in higher education's approach to developing educational experiences to adapt to the changing workforce demands of the twenty-first century. This revolutionary paradigm utilizes advanced AI technologies, including predictive analytics, knowledge graphs, and real-time analysis of labor markets, to enable educational institutions to design more adaptive, personalized, and industry-informed learning experiences that respond to both individual student learners and generalized changes in the economy [28]. The power of these new technologies transforms educators' approaches from the existing one-size-fits-all curriculum design to more complex, data-saturated approaches that highlight emerging skills gaps, predict future industry needs, and automatically update educational materials to ensure students graduate with relevant, job-ready skills and competencies in line with current and anticipated workforce demand.

Nevertheless, the successful enactment of AI-laden curriculum design plans is highly contingent upon the advancement and technological literacy of the faculty members, who are the main enactors of these enhanced learning experiences. Research has demonstrated that comprehensive professional development programs allow educators to increase their AI literacy, teaching confidence, and effectiveness in fulfilling pedagogical technology-enhanced approaches [29, 30]. These professional development programs provide both the technical capabilities to navigate AI educational tools and the pedagogical frameworks for effectively implementing the technologies into their teaching practice and processes, while maintaining the human elements that are crucial to quality education.

In addition, collaborative curriculum codesign practices with multiple stakeholders (i.e., university researchers, teachers, industry-specific professionals, and, in some instances, students) show enhanced promise to be inclusive and relevant with respect to broader AI education initiatives. Collaborative forms of codesign allow for many perspectives to be enacted into curriculum development, examining more inclusive, culturally responsive educational programs [31, 32]. A thorough international study of published global research on AI-curriculum highlights that the global exploration of AI-curriculum is fraught with variation across regions with respect to the emphasis on implementation priorities, focusing on both AI curricula and approaches. The international trends around AI-curriculum focus on developing personalized learning experiences facilitated through new pedagogical approaches, while institutional reform and structural integration of AI technology throughout the entirety of the educational system are more prominent in some regions than others [33]. Implementing comprehensive AI-learning ecosystems at the organizational level is complex. As an emerging example, the University of Florida has revealed how AI can be adopted holistically across disciplines to prepare all students for the emerging demands of a future world where AI technology is prevalent through comprehensive literacy representations that engage all actors well beyond computer science and engineering [34].

Intelligent tutoring systems (ITS) and AI-infused smart curricula are fundamentally changing the university landscape through personalized, adaptive learning, while also increasing institutional effectiveness and administrative efficiency. These systems utilize powerful algorithms and computational technologies, including Bayesian networks, machine learning models, and case-based reasoning systems, to collect student behavior data on performance constantly and dynamically, and to adapt content, pacing, and delivery of instruction in near-real-time for each student based on individual learning preferences, needs, and understanding. Developmentally, these systems have been found to substantially increase engagement and retention, along with improving learning outcomes generally [35, 36]. The contributions of ITS technologies not only occur on the instructional side but will also dramatically enhance higher educational administration, including automating or optimizing workflows, creating analytics dashboards for decision-making by drawing from institutional data, and maximizing efficiency across departments and programs [37].

Although these technologies hold significant promise, the meaningful adoption of ITS necessitates careful incorporation of pedagogical wisdom and curriculum design knowledge, which has often been neglected in favor of technological modification and AI exploration for AI's own sake [38]. The most effective implementations are realized when technology supports educational aims and not the other way around, calling for collaboration between AI developers, researchers, and experienced faculty. AI-enriched smart courses represent the next level in this collaborative process, allowing for sophisticated automated assessment systems, personalized feedback delivery, and support for creative instructional approaches that are impossible to achieve effectively at scale using past methods [Dong and Zhang, 2025; 22]. These systems can suggest to teachers a variety of learning patterns using interaction data, while also tracking learning challenges so that interventions can be proposed in advance of future difficulties.

AI-powered interfaces have been very successful, increasing student engagement far more than traditional systems through dynamic, responsive feedback and support throughout the learning tasks, enhancing interactivity and providing a more satisfying learning experience [39]. Organizations establishing smart campuses are integrating ITS and other learning technologies into larger AI environments, including intelligent classrooms, real-time technical and academic support technologies, and advanced optimization solutions that consider many factors, including the changing needs of educational institutions (Mohanachandran et al., 2021). A wide range of new technologies and functions are emerging for ITS, such as emotional-awareness technologies capable of detecting students' emotions, conversational AI features that allow natural language interactions, and predictive models capable of addressing needs before they are expressly indicated. Yet, many challenges remain regarding scaling them across diverse institutional contexts, being mindful of data privacy and data protection, ethical issues related to algorithmic decision-making in education, and ensuring equitable access to advanced technology [40]. In summary, ITS and AI curricula have the potential to revolutionize higher education, as long as implementation is carried out with interdisciplinary teams, ethical oversight, and an appreciation of the human elements involved in effective education.

AI is transforming higher education by enabling more sophisticated personalized learning pathways and smart curricula that can be tailored to the unique needs of each student, their preferred styles of learning, and their career aspirations. Advanced AI systems, such as Summit Learning and Pounce, have demonstrated the efficacy of providing additional feedback, adaptive learning content, and personal assessment systems (Zhang, 2024). The impact of these technologies can be measured; for example, deep learning-based educational systems in use today demonstrate improvements in student performance, including one study of 250 undergraduate students that reported a 25% improvement in grades and student engagement compared to traditional instruction [14]. These systems are also able to evolve beyond learning personalization, with the ability to dynamically align to new, emerging industry changes through predictive analytics and intelligent design to determine future skills formation and educational offering adjustments. (**Figure 1**)

Adaptive learning technologies, such as Knewton and DreamBox, provide especially innovative ways to personalize learning, offering immediate feedback and personalized learning materials for many different learning modalities, all in an effort to create equitable learning experiences so that all students (regardless of skill level or background) can learn in a supportive, appropriately-challenging learning environment [41]. Research confirms that learning contexts that integrate AI into their systems increase learning efficiency, with students completing tasks at a considerably faster pace while exhibiting higher levels of engagement compared to more traditional educational experiences, and retaining more of the knowledge and skills learned (Abrar et al., 2025). Smart course development based on AI technologies facilitates more flexible, effective, and truly student-centered education methods through the automation of feedback systems and intelligent tutor capabilities, which have been shown to decrease dropout rates, increase knowledge retention, and enhance student satisfaction with their educational experiences [Dong and Zhang, 2025; 35]. When combined, these advances will usher in a transformational change in how universities think about curriculum development, deliver personalized learning experiences, and prepare students for the

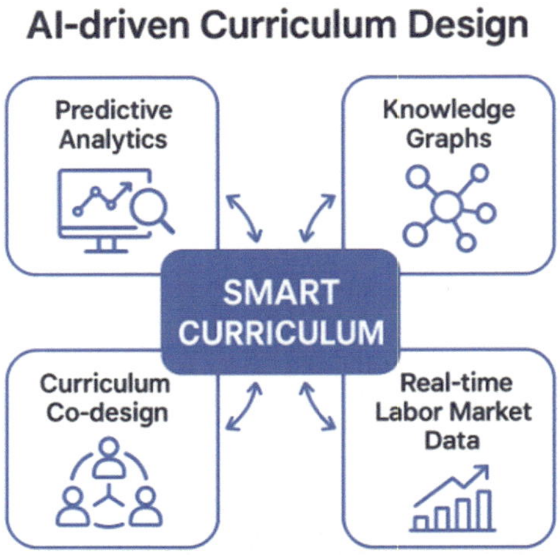

Figure 1.
AI-driven smart curriculum design.

complexities and opportunities of the digital economy. This will ultimately contribute to educational environments that are much more responsive, effective, and reflective of individual student outcomes, needs, and societal context.

3. AI-based meta-universities and the smart curriculum from YouTube to Second Life to Genie 3

AI-based meta-universities are emerging as a continuum that stretches from mass, open platforms toward fully immersive, AI-orchestrated learning worlds – think of the arc "from YouTube to Second Life to Genie 3." At one end, YouTube functions as a primitive meta-university layer: open, flexible, and globally accessible, it scaffolds self-directed learning with on-demand, multimedia-rich content that complements formal instruction [42, 43]. Its efficacy is most visible when learners engage actively with curated materials, boosting writing fluency and content retention [44, 45]. In smart-university ecosystems, YouTube also advances universal access and inclusive models, especially when aligned with data-driven pedagogy [43, 46]. As smart universities push toward adaptive, analytics-infused pathways that personalize trajectories and optimize retention [47], YouTube illustrates the foundational qualities – openness, scalability, and continuous evolution – while still confronting the thorny problem of curriculum alignment [48].

The next milestone in this evolution arrived when higher education began experimenting with Second Life, long before "metaverse" entered common parlance. Universities deployed immersive campuses for distance learning, simulations, and collaborative work, documenting positive student perceptions of usefulness and ease of use that predicted willingness to adopt [49a, 2013b]. Institutions such as the Open University leveraged blended synchronous–asynchronous affordances for postgraduate research supervision and collaboration [50]. In medicine and health, Second Life hosted clinical and informatics simulations that reproduced realistic settings for training [51, 52]. Creative programs built galleries and performance spaces to extend critique and expression [53]. Not every build endured – James

Madison University's campus ultimately closed – offering cautionary lessons on sustainability and institutional support. Even so, faculty development initiatives found Second Life engaging and worth adopting for future teaching [54]. Together, these cases laid crucial groundwork for today's "metaversities."

With maturing hardware and algorithms, virtual reality (VR) and AI have fused into smart curricula that heighten immersion, personalization, and engagement – especially in healthcare and STEM. In nursing and medical education, voice-controlled, AI-enhanced patient simulations improve critical thinking and holistic assessment [55–57]. Smart classrooms that blend VR, augmented reality (AR), and adaptive AI pathways consistently outperform traditional formats on test scores and assignment completion [58, 59]. At the same time, automated VR training for behavioral skills and communication shows promise, yet underscores the need for human-in-the-loop oversight to align automated assessments with human judgment [60]. AI functions across roles – as instructor, tutor, and collaborator – delivering real-time feedback and custom trajectories that especially benefit technical domains [61, 62]. Universities are also building metaverse-style platforms to support interprofessional collaboration [63]. Students tend to respond positively to VR, but persistent challenges – infrastructure, usability, and technical support – must be addressed for sustained impact [64, 65].

AR deepens this shift when paired with AI. Their integration produces adaptive, interactive environments that enhance engagement and retention through real-time content adjustments and simulations [66]. AI-driven smart course design incorporates gamification and AR to foster critical thinking and workforce-ready skills through personalized feedback [67]. In the smart classroom, AR enhances interactivity and fine-grained feedback loops between learners and instructors [68]. More broadly, AI is a cornerstone of the smart-university vision, permeating infrastructure, pedagogy, and administration to elevate instructional quality and streamline processes (Mohanachandran et al., 2021).

Alongside these classroom transformations are collaborative virtual workplaces, which are changing how universities configure teamwork, assessment, and creativity. Collaborative platforms, like Jamboard, can increase engagement and openness in language learning [69]. Contextualized smart classrooms, enhanced by AI, can include virtual assistants that help shape the personalized instruction of learners further while enhancing collaboration and collaborative achievement [70, 71]. VR is also being employed in developing "university hospitals," enabling the creation of authentic basic levels of simulated interprofessional communication (e.g., Prasolova-Førland [72]). Moreover, the whole notion of utilizing cloud suites provides standardized collaboration (or assessment) at scale [73], while globally networked project-based courses develop distributed teamwork, intercultural competence, and narrative imagination [74]. Apparently, even creative writing as collaboration has changed; using AI-supported collaboration can also enhance motivation and orientations to work together [75]. Although a little complex and sometimes oppositional, collective pedagogic collaborative clouds or simulation labs expand the possibilities gained here, helping sustain lifelong learning and increasing the potential for curricular innovation [76, 77].

The metaverse, when tightly integrated with AI-driven smart curricula, pushes further toward personalized, interactive learning ecologies. Evidence shows substantial gains in language and cognitive outcomes relative to conventional classes [78]. Digital twins and intelligent avatars anchor dynamic, problem-centered spaces that elevate motivation, communication, and active engagement [79]. Personalized paths, automated assessment, and real-time feedback support both solo and collaborative modes [80]. Frameworks such as Meta-MILE blend gamification, immersive infrastructure, and AI to raise engagement and competency development [81], while AI chatbots enhance authenticity and interactivity in lessons [82]. Still, systematic reviews flag ethical issues, inequities in access, and a STEM tilt that risks marginalizing the humanities [83]. Posthybrid "tribrid" models – mixing face-to-face, online, and virtual environments under AI orchestration – are emerging to mitigate these gaps and deepen personalization [84].

Beyond classrooms, digital twins, linked with AI, IoT, and 5 G, are transforming campuses into responsive, sustainable organisms. Real-time monitoring and predictive analytics drive down energy use and emissions [85, 86], while sensor networks and analytics optimize building operations, occupancy, and resource allocation [87, 88]. These twins inform security, planning, and decision-making, aligning infrastructure with mission and risk [16, 89]. In learning spaces, twin-driven frameworks personalize experiences and enhance engagement [90, 91]. As living testbeds for smart cities, twin-enabled campuses spearhead urban innovation and policy experimentation [92]. The convergence with big data and 5 G further streamlines services and underpins future-ready education.

All of this coheres within the broader smart-university paradigm – a synthesis of AI, IoT, big data, and cloud technologies that reimagines teaching, learning, and administration as integrated, adaptive services [19, 93]. Data-driven decision-making improves outcomes and efficiency [94, 95], while alignment with national digital transformation policies and overhauled academic information systems enables institutional-scale change [96–100]. The North Star is not only smarter infrastructure but also a smarter academic community – agile, collaborative, and future-ready [Mbombo and Cavus, 2021; 101, 102].

At the culmination of this trajectory sit AI-based meta-universities and smart curricula: AI-native learning systems that orchestrate immersive, multimodal, and autonomous experiences tailored to each learner [79]. Curricula are being restructured around meta-AI literacies – prompt engineering, collaborative AI use, and human–AI teaming – to prepare graduates for an augmented workplace [103]. Smart classrooms equipped with AI and IoT deliver real-time data and personalized instruction at scale [104]. Even evaluation and program design are being optimized with meta-heuristic algorithms [105]. Consistent with broader evidence from AI-driven metaverse education, these designs outperform traditional models academically [78], while intelligent-assisted teaching, automated feedback, and personalized course construction expand capacity in higher education (Dong and Zhang, 2025). To ensure equity and trust, ethical design, active learning, and community engagement must be embedded from the start [106].

Seen through the title's lens – from YouTube's open scaffolding, through Second Life's proto-metaversities, to a "Genie 3" horizon – the direction is clear. We are moving toward generative, agentic learning worlds that can materialize curricula on demand, simulate authentic contexts, and adapt continuously to each learner's goals and community needs. In that destination, the meta-university is not just a place or a platform; it is an AI-orchestrated ecosystem where content, assessment, collaboration, and campus operations coevolve in real time – open like YouTube, immersive like Second Life, and dynamically generative like Genie 3.

4. Conclusion

The hybrid pipeline, stretching from YouTube's open educational scaffolding through Second Life's inflexible proto-metaversities, has taken a significant turn with the advent of generative world models (e.g., Genie 3). This evolution is more than another developmental leap in technology; it is the beginning of truly generative AI-driven learning ecosystems that can generate educational events on demand, adapt to learner needs in real time, and engineer pedagogical experiences not feasible before.

The progression assembled throughout this paper has taken us from primitive adaptive learning systems to sophisticated AI tutoring systems, to immersive virtual environments, to somewhat psychedelic open educational ecosystems where the distinctions between content generation, delivery, and assessment collude to form intelligent learning experiences. AI-based meta-universities are no longer confined to accessible content libraries, static virtual worlds, and programmed behaviors that respond improperly to previously identified educational objectives and detailed learner profiles.

4.1 Genie 3's Transformative implications for smart curriculum design

Firstly, Genie 3's ability to generate interactive 3D worlds from simple text prompts changes the way we design and deliver smart curricula. Now, instead of choosing from an existing lesson or creating simulations that already exist, AI-based "meta-universities" can simply generate immersive learning environments based specifically on curriculum objectives. For example, a professor teaching a history course could ask Genie 3 to create ancient Rome for a historical immersive experience. A professor teaching chemistry could ask Genie 3 to generate molecular-level environments in which students could experiment with atomic structures.

In this way, we expand the concept of the smart curriculum, as implemented through AI, to a process of "adaptive" world generation (learning environments can now be a variable in learning), rather than just "adaptive" content sequencing. The distinction between curriculum design, content generation, and environmental generation disappears, and educational practice can become an automated and rapid AI-engaged experience, adapting to learning demands.

Secondly, the "world memory" capability in the Genie 3 addresses one of the biggest issues in virtual learning environments, which is continuity and consequence across learning sessions. Students can now engage in longer-term projects, believing that their decisions and actions extend beyond a single session, ultimately maximizing their opportunities to engage with a rich set of learning objectives across multiple sessions. This persistence invites new forms of collaborative learning, as students contribute to and build upon one another's work across the constraints of time and space, transforming a mere collaborative learning team into a process of collaborative knowledge construction.

For smart curricula, it means learning pathways can now include cumulative, world-building experiences where students' prior achievements and creations inform their subsequent engagement opportunities. For example, engineering students could design and test structures over several sessions, with a reasonable expectation that these structures will persist in the space, allowing students to pursue iterative design processes that reflect the behaviors of professional practice.

Thirdly, the introduction of promptable world events offers new possibilities for responsive, scenario-based learning. Educators can introduce points of challenge, change the environmental conditions, and create teachable moments based on the levels of performance and engagement demonstrated by the students. This capability transforms smart curricula from predetermined adaptive pathways to truly responsive learning ecosystems that can pivot and adapt based on immediate pedagogical needs.

For instance, an environmental science curriculum could illustrate how an ecosystem might change due to two midsimulation challenges and demonstrate the cause-and-effect relationship within the same real-time framework. The degree of responsiveness allows for pedagogical approaches never before experienced and truly authentic learning experiences.

4.2 Future directions and emerging paradigms

4.2.1 Toward infinite educational possibilities

The use of Genie's 3-level generative capabilities within AI-driven meta-universities indicates a time in education when the scarcity of educational content is a concern of the past. By moving beyond an education program limited to resources and available learning experiences, Keys (now Genie) opens up the potential for institutions to develop and generate an infinite number of learning experience versions and adaptations for different learners' learning styles, cultures, and interests. Whenever learners need high-quality content (real quality), wherever they are situated, they will be able to access updated, authentic, immersive learning experiences based on their aspirations to learn.

Smart curricula will develop from systems that currently adapt existing content to what they generate based on learners' needs. This shift from adaptation to generation will radically change the way we think about curriculum development, transitioning from a resource allocation approach to a resource generation approach that is inherent in education.

4.2.2 The emergence of collaborative AI-human learning partnerships

As AI systems are able to generate more complex learning environments, educators will increasingly have to engage in higher-level orchestration and mentorship roles. Faculty will work with AI systems as cocreators, marrying human pedagogical expertise with AI generative capabilities to develop impactful educational experiences that neither implementation alone could provide.

This collaboration will also extend to students, as they will increasingly work with AI as learning partners, not just passive receivers of content delivered by AI. When students can prompt simulated worlds to generate content, they will be able to develop into cocreators of their own educational experience rather than passive consumers.

4.2.3 Meta-literacies for an AI-generated world

The curriculum of the future, a smart curriculum, needs to prepare students to work not only with AI but also for interaction in AI-generated environments. The criteria will need to establish new forms of meta-literacy to enable students to develop the skills required to communicate with AI systems, fostering meaningful learning experiences and forms of AI collaboration. Other aspects of meta-literacy will be explored in terms of learning to express and evaluate AI-generated concepts, content, and experiences, as well as understanding how to interact in generative virtual environments created by AI. These meta-literacies are key components of a twenty-first-century educational responsibility, as growing numbers of graduates in the future will join organizations whose workplace practices and development are informed by AI-generated content and virtual collaboration.

4.2.4 Challenges and considerations for implementation

The ability to create immersive worlds for educational contexts raises serious ethical issues with respect to representation, bias, and reality. The future of education includes AI. In ensuring the future of AI-based meta-universities, institutions should develop thoughtful ethical guidelines that promote inclusive, accurate, and education-focused experiences in created environments and worlds. Models generated through these worlds must be conscientious of biases, and AI-created content must align with the values and educational interests of the institution.

Genie 3's capabilities are impressive, but their deployment is resource and hardware-heavy. The future of AI-based meta-universities will need to be interrogated through questions of digital equity. The goal should be to avoid propagating existing educational inequities, where increased access to generative educational technologies could now threaten spatial (and digital) equity. It may be that new models of resource sharing, new methods of cloud-based implementation, and new approaches to democratizing high-end AI capabilities across multiple institutional contexts must be developed.

With educational content being more AI-generated, institutions need to develop new modalities for ensuring educational quality and pedagogical efficacy. This will entail determining what needs to be in place to validate learning experiences that are generated by AI, how to maintain quality assurance of educational standards across dynamically generated content, and how to ensure that AI's generative capabilities enhance a human's pedagogical capacities, as opposed to supplanting them.

4.3 The path forward: Recommendations for institutional transformation

4.3.1 Phased implementation strategies

For organizations to realize the value of offering generative AI capabilities, an incremental implementation approach using pilots of discrete disciplines (i.e., academic disciplines or functional divisions) is strongly recommended before embarking on transformational institutional practices. This approach allows room to learn and grow, with lower levels of risk and sustainable uptake of the newly introduced technologies and practices. The viability of AI-enabled meta-universities hinges fundamentally on faculty readiness and commitment. Institutions must dedicate resources to meaningful professional development so that educators become aware of and understand the benefits of generative AI in education while still retaining their designation as pedagogical leaders and mentors. The nature of AI technology development in the future of education is complex and expensive; therefore, it is likely that institutions willing to embrace innovation will benefit from consortium-like opportunities related to innovation (e.g., technology development consortiums, information sharing of best practices regarding implementation, and networks for ongoing research and development with respect to AI as it relates to education).

The introduction of Genie 3 and other generative AI technologies signifies the beginning of a new way of thinking about education in higher education: the extent to which previously considered priorities (e.g., limited physical spaces and resources, static content, and fixed learning spaces) can be replaced with expansive, immediate, and tailored educational experiences. Educational programs formed on the basis of AI-enabled meta-universities with generative world models would allow for globally and locally accessible and individually based learning experiences, and open with them endless possibilities for learning and human development. The smart curriculum of the future will not merely adapt to learners' needs but will generate new learning realities in response to those needs. This transformation requires careful planning, ethical consideration, and sustained investment in human capacity building, but the potential rewards – more effective, engaging, and equitable education for all – justify the effort required. As we stand at the threshold of this generative educational revolution, institutions must embrace both the tremendous opportunities and the significant responsibilities that come with the power to create infinite learning worlds. The future of higher education lies not in choosing between human and AI but in creating synergistic partnerships that leverage the unique strengths of both to create educational experiences that surpass what either could achieve alone.

The journey from YouTube to Second Life to Genie 3 represents more than technological evolution – it represents the transformation of education itself from a resource-constrained activity to a generative, unlimited exploration of human potential. In this future, the only limits on educational possibilities will be our imagination and our commitment to creating learning experiences that serve the full diversity of human learners and aspirations.

Author details

Volkan Duran[1*] and Ferdi Çelik[2]

1 Iğdır University, Iğdır, Türkiye

2 Ondokuz Mayıs University, Samsun, Türkiye

*Address all correspondence to: volkan.duran8@gmail.com

References

[1] Aggarwal D. Integration of innovative technological developments and AI with education for an adaptive learning pedagogy. China Petroleum Processing and Petrochemical Technology. 2023;**23**(2):709–714

[2] Rahardjo S, Marmoah S, Saddhono K, Sri A, Nugraheni C, Nurhasanah F (2024). Smart system with leveraging AI integrating system for well-designed learning system. In: *Proceedings of the 2024 4th International Conference on Advance Computing and Innovative Technologies in Engineering (ICACITE)*. (pp. 901–906).

[3] Krishnan R, Jenefa L, Kandasamy L, Thangarasu G, Vel R (2023). Impact of AI powered resources on students' performance. In: *Proceedings of the 2023 Second International Conference on Smart Technologies for Smart Nation (SmartTechCon)*. (pp. 720–724).

[4] Sarshartehrani F, Mohammadrezaei E, Behravan M, Gračanin D. Enhancing e-learning experience through embodied AI tutors in immersive virtual environments: A multifaceted approach for personalized educational adaptation. Lecture Notes in Computer Science. 2024;272–287

[5] Melnyk YB, Pypenko IS. Implementing artificial intelligence in a higher educational ecosystem. International Journal of Science Annals. 2025;**8**(1). DOI: 10.26697/ijsa

[6] Pakkam Isaac CPX. Cloud-powered higher education: AI-driven student success and digital learning transformation. Open Access Research Journal of Engineering and Technology. 2025;**8**(2):56–72. DOI: 10.53022/oarjet.2025.8.2.0049

[7] Kaur S. Smart learning ecosystems: Crafting a blueprint for AI and IoT in education. Journal of Information Systems Engineering & Management. 2025;**10**(21s):480–493. DOI: 10.52783/jisem.v10i21s.3373

[8] Rötkönen E, Winschiers-Theophilus H, Winschiers-Goagoses N, Zaman T, Itenge H, Tan DYW, Sutinen E. Creating smart connected learning ecosystems: A hybrid model for design-based learning. Interaction Design and Architecture(s). 2022;**52**:81–100

[9] Anon M. Towards smart open education ecosystems through generative AI, blockchain, DAO, MMLA and NFT. SSRN Electronic Journal. 2023. DOI: 10.2139/ssrn.4515129

[10] Zhou Z. Building a smart ecological education in the AI era. Frontiers in Computing and Intelligent Systems. 2024;**8**(1):119–121. DOI: 10.54097/ag0dxn58

[11] Luo Z, Wang Y. Innovative teacher leadership in curriculum construction. Journal of Organizational and End User Computing. 2024;**36**(1):1–22. DOI: 10.4018/JOEUC.348333

[12] Merdian I, Tullius G, Hertkorn P, Burgert O (2018). Interactive learning in smart learning ecosystems. In: *Proceedings of the Reutlingen University Digital Learning Initiative* (pp. 15–22)

[13] Giovannella C, Manca S. Smart learning ecosystems - Design as cornerstone of smart educational

processes and places. Interaction Design and Architecture(s). 2019;**43**:5–7

[14] Naseer F, Khan MN, Addas A, Awais Q, Ayub N. Game mechanics and artificial intelligence personalization: A framework for adaptive learning systems. Education Sciences. 2025;**15**(3):301. DOI: 10.3390/educsci15030301

[15] Sari HE, Tumanggor B, Efron D. Improving educational outcomes through adaptive learning systems using AI. International Transactions on Artificial Intelligence. 2024;**3**(1):21–31. DOI: 10.33050/italic.v3i1.647

[16] Wang H, Cai Y, Yue F, Luo H, Abdipoor S, Goh SL. Digital twin system for smart campuses. *2024 IEEE International Conference on Control Science and Systems Engineering (ICCSSE)*, 2024. pp. 75–80

[17] Ayeni AO, Ovbiye RE, Onayemi AS, Ojedele KE. AI-driven adaptive learning platforms: Enhancing educational outcomes for students with special needs through user-centric, tailored digital tools. World Journal of Advanced Research and Reviews. 2024;**22**(3):2253–2265

[18] Mohanachandran DK, Yap CT, Ismaili Z, Govindarajo NS. Smart university and artificial intelligence. In: The Fourth Industrial Revolution: Implementation of Artificial Intelligence for Growing Business Success Springer. 2021. DOI: 10.1007/978-3-030-62796-6_15

[19] Akhrif O, Benfares C, El Bouzekri El Idrissi Y, Hmina N. Collaborative learning services in the smart university environment. In: *Proceedings of the 4th International Conference*. ACM; 2019. DOI: 10.1145/3368756.3369020

[20] Ralhan P. Artificial intelligence in higher studies: Use of AI-based tools by university students and its challenges. International Journal of Advanced Research. 2024;**12**(09):1282–1285. DOI: 10.21474/IJAR01/19563

[21] Dutta S, Ranjan S, Mishra S, Iwendi C, et al. Enhancing educational adaptability: A review and analysis of AI-driven adaptive learning platforms. In: *2024 4th International Conference on Innovative Practices in Technology and Management (ICIPTM)*. IEEE; February 2024. DOI: 10.1109/ICIPTM59628.2024.10563448

[22] Kazimova D, Tazhigulova G, Shraimanova G, Zatyneyko A, Sharzadin A. Transforming university education with AI: A systematic review of technologies, applications, and implications. International Journal of Engineering Pedagogy (IJEP). 2025;**15**(1):4–24. DOI: 10.3991/ijep.v15i1.50773

[23] Abrar F, Mehmood S, ul Emman SK, Kandhro AN. Cognitive development and AI: A longitudinal study of children and adults navigating problem-solving with AI tools. The Critical Review of Social Sciences Studies. 2025;**3**(1):1888–904. DOI: 10.59075/rw8zd496

[24] Vadisetty R, Polamarasetti A. AI-augmented skill development roadmaps: Tailoring 12-month learning paths for future-ready careers in Education 4.0 and Industry 4.0. In: *2024 13th International Conference on System Modeling & Advancement in Research Trends (SMART)*. 2024

[25] Soomro AA, Khan MH, Umar M, Ali O, et al. AI-driven academic advising in higher education: Leveraging intelligent systems to personalize

student support, improve retention, and optimize career pathways. The Critical Review of Social Sciences Studies. 2025; DOI: 10.59075/vy3v7k17

[26] Jabbour J, Kleinbard K, Miller O, Haussman R, Reddi VJ. SocratiQ: A generative AI-powered learning companion for personalized education and broader accessibility. arXiv. 2025. DOI: 10.48550/arXiv.2502.00341

[27] Lau PN, Ng SCK, Tan LF. An AI-enabled learning system with personalized learning pathways: A pilot study of its impact on learning of statistics. In *The Asian Conference on Education 2023*. January 2024. DOI: 10.22492/issn.2186-5892.2024.104

[28] Pusporini W, Nurdiyanto H. Utilization of artificial intelligence in outcome-based curriculum evaluation and development. Journal of Research in Social Science and Humanities. 2024;**4**(1):132–134.

[29] Iskandarova S, Yusif-Zada K, Mukhtarova S. Integrating AI into higher education curriculum in developing countries. In: *2024 IEEE Frontiers in Education Conference (FIE)*. 2024. pp. 1–9

[30] Schallert-Vallaster S, Nüesch C, Papageorgiou K, Buchner J, et al. Enhancing AI literacy of educators in higher education. Zeitschrift Für Hochschulentwicklung. 2025;**20**(SH-KI-1):147–166. DOI: 10.21240/zfhe/SH-KI-1/09

[31] Gardner-McCune C, Touretzky D, Cox B, Jones A, et al.. Co-designing an AI curriculum with university researchers and middle school teachers. In: *Proceedings of the 54th ACM Technical Symposium on Computer Science Education (SIGCSE 2023)*. ACM; 2023. (pp. xx–xx). DOI: 10.1145/3545947.3576253

[32] Touretzky D, Gardner-McCune C, Martin F, Seehorn D. Envisioning AI for K-12: What should every child know about AI? Proceedings of the AAAI Conference on Artificial Intelligence. 2019;**33**(01):9795-9799. DOI: 10.1609/aaai.v33i01.33019795

[33] Heo J. Exploring research trends for proposing AI-based curriculum development models. Educational Research Institute. 2025;**44**(3):837

[34] Southworth JR, Migliaccio K, Glover J, Glover JM, Reed D, McCarty C, Brendemuhl J, Thomas AO. Developing a model for AI across the curriculum: Transforming the higher education landscape via innovation in AI literacy. Computers and Education: Artificial Intelligence. 2023;**4**:100127

[35] Cairo Rodríguez D, Ramírez Echavarría Y. Smart tutors: Improving the quality of higher education through AI. LatIA. 2023;**1**:8. DOI: 10.62486/latia20238

[36] Ratniece D, Said HM, Salem AM. A study on the smart tutoring systems. International Journal of Education. 2018;**3**:78–83

[37] Thuy PB, Tien PD. AI-powered administration: The role of intelligent tutoring systems in education. International Journal of Religion. 2024;**5**:4560–4569

[38] Yaratan H. Intelligent tutoring system: A tool for testing the research curiosities of Artificial Intelligence researchers. Turkish Online Journal of Educational Technology. 2003;**2**:41–47

[39] Kim B, Suh H, Heo J, Choi Y. AI-driven interface design for intelligent tutoring system improves student engagement. *arXiv*, 2020. abs/2009.08976

[40] Sarfaraj GK. Intelligent tutoring system enhancing learning with conversational AI: A review. International Journal of Scientific Research in Engineering and Management. 2025;**09**:1–9

[41] Akintola AS, Akintayo M, Kadri T, Nwanna M, Oforgu CM. Adaptive AI systems in education: Real-time personalised learning pathways for skill development. Journal of Artificial Intelligence Machine Learning and Data Science. 2024;**3**(1). DOI: 10.51219/JAIMLD/Akinyemi-Sadeeq-Akintola/534

[42] Burhanlı S, Bangir Alpan G. Why do university students prefer YouTube to learn and study? Educational Policy Analysis and Strategic Research. 2021;**16**(4):164–177. DOI: 10.29329/epasr.2021.383.9

[43] Jain R, Srinivasan R. Impact of YouTube on academic enhancement and educational writing. TIJ's Research Journal of Social Science & Management - RJSSM. 2019;**9**:1–8

[44] Alobaid A. Smart multimedia learning of ICT: Role and impact on language learners' writing fluency—YouTube online English learning resources as an example. Smart Learning Environments. 2020;**7**(1). DOI: 10.1186/s40561-020-00134-7

[45] Singh K, Maurya A, Solanki D, Maurya A. SmartBlend: Smart video recommendations on YouTube. In: *Proceedings of the 2024 3rd International Conference on Applied Artificial Intelligence and Computing (ICAAIC)*. IEEE; 2024. DOI: 10.1109/ICAAIC60222.2024.10575509

[46] Mbombo AB, Cavus N. Smart university: A university in the technological age. TEM Journal. 2021;**10**(1):13–17. DOI: 10.18421/TEM101-02

[47] Mitrofanova YS, Glukhova L, Tukshumskaya AV, Popova T. Modeling of residual knowledge estimation in smart university. Smart Education and e-Learning 2020. 2020;375–385

[48] Grimaldi D, Fernandez V. The alignment of university curricula with the building of a smart city: A case study from Barcelona. Technological Forecasting and Social Change. 2017;**123**:298–306

[49] Ali H, Ahmed AA, Tariq TG, Safdar H. Exploring intentions to use Second Life for education at University of Bahrain. In: *Proceedings of the 2013 Fourth International Conference on e-Learning: Best Practices in Management, Design and Development of e-Courses: Standards of Excellence and Creativity*. IEEE; 2013. DOI: 10.1109/ECONF.2013.52

[50] Rapanotti L, Barroca L, Vargas-Vera M, Reeves AJ. Deepthink: A Second Life environment for part-time research students at a distance. In: *2010 10th IEEE International Conference on Advanced Learning Technologies*. IEEE; 2010. (pp. 200–201). DOI: 10.1109/ICALT.2010.61

[51] Sendra-Portero F, Lorenzo-Álvarez R, Rudolphi-Solero T, Ruiz-Gómez MJ. The second life metaverse and its usefulness in medical education after a quarter of a century. Journal of

Medical Internet Research. 2024;**26**: e59005. DOI: 10.2196/59005

[52] Warren JJ, Brixey JJ. Second life: Not your conventional simulation. Studies in Health Technology and Informatics. 2009;**146**:843

[53] Mitchell MC, Bown O. (2013). Towards a creativity support tool in processing: Understanding the needs of creative coders. In Proceedings of the 25th Australian Computer-Human Interaction Conference: Augmentation, Application, Innovation, Collaboration. 2013. DOI: 10.1145/2541016.2541096

[54] Rudolphi-Solero T, Lorenzo-Álvarez R, Ruiz-Gómez MJ, Sendra Portero F. Impact of compulsory participation of medical students in a multiuser online game to learn radiological anatomy and radiological signs within the virtual world Second Life. Anatomical Sciences Education, 2021;**15**(5). DOI: 10.1002/ase.2134

[55] Teixeira L, Mitchell A, Martinez NC, Salim BJ. Virtual reality with artificial intelligence-led scenarios in nursing education: A project evaluation. British Journal of Nursing. 2024;**33**(17):812–820

[56] Casler K, Gawlik KS, Messinger J. Virtual reality to aid in competency-based online nurse practitioner curriculum (VR-NP). Journal of Professional Nursing. 2024;**55**:125–132

[57] Schleicher M. SC2: Incorporating virtual reality simulations into undergraduate nursing curriculum. BMJ Simulation and Technology Enhanced Learning. 2019;**5**:A22

[58] Long Y, Li Z. Scenario construction of smart education in universities: Teaching practice based on management courses. In: *Proceedings of the 2024 14th International Conference on Information Technology in Medicine and Education (ITME)*; 2024; p. 363–367

[59] Zhai C, Wang H, Xu H, Zhou L, et al. On the application of virtual reality technology in smart education. In: *Proceedings of the 2023 the 5th International Conference on Video, Signal and Image Processing (VSIP 2023)*. Association for Computing Machinery; May 2024. DOI: 10.1145/3638682.3638711

[60] King S, Feng L, Glazek C, Bell T, et al. Developing smart virtual reality to teach functional communication training. Journal of Behavioral Education. 2024; Advance online publication. DOI: 10.1007/s10864-024-09569-1

[61] Naqvi WM, Sundus H, Mishra G, Muthukrishnan R, Kandakurti P. AI in medical education curriculum: The future of healthcare learning. European Journal of Therapeutics. 2024;**30**(2): e23–e25. DOI: 10.58600/ejtherapeutics30241

[62] Hunvik SRB, Lindseth F. Making use of virtual reality for artificial intelligence education. In: Lecture Notes in Computer Science. Vol. **1344**. Cham: Springer; 2020. p. 56–70. DOI: 10.1007/978-3-030-67435-9_5

[63] Harder R, Workum D (2024). Shaping the future of healthcare: The University of Manitoba's Virtual Reality Interprofessional Education (VR-IPE) Program. In: *Practitioner Proceedings of the 10th International Conference of the Immersive Learning Research Network (iLRN2024)*

[64] Häkkilä J, Colley A, Väyrynen J, Yliharju A-J. Introducing virtual reality

technologies to design education. Seminar.net. 2018;**14**(1):1–12. DOI: 10.7577/seminar.2584

[65] Rim D, Shin H. Effective instructional design template for virtual simulations in nursing education. Nurse Education Today. 2020;**96**:104624

[66] Tursunova F, Oripova N, Muhammadiyeva M, Nurullayeva S, Hamroyev S, Tishabaeva I. Augmented reality and AI in higher education: Creating immersive learning experiences. In: *2024 International Conference on Knowledge Engineering and Communication Systems (ICKECS)*. Vol. **1**; 2024. p. 1–5

[67] Song J. Integrating artificial intelligence in smart course design: Innovative teaching methods for talent cultivation in higher education. Education Insights. 2024;**1**(1):10–16. DOI: 10.70088/63t0zj06

[68] Ristić J, Barać D, Bojović Ž, Bogdanović Z, Radenković B. Designing augmented reality application for interaction with smart environment. In: *Proceedings of the 10th International Conference on Virtual Learning*. 2015. pp. 273–278. DOI: 10.1016/j.pmcj.2011.02.007

[69] Castillo-Cuesta L, Ochoa-Cueva C, Cabrera-Solano P. Virtual workspaces for enhancing collaborative work in EFL learning: A case study in higher education. International Journal of Emerging Technologies in Learning (IJET). 2022;**17**(2):4–18

[70] Abbood K, Faleih WA, Hodood MN. Integrating artificial intelligence into collaborative teaching strategies: A case study in smart classrooms. Salud, Ciencia Y Tecnología - Serie de Conferencias. 2025;**4**(1506). DOI: 10.56294/sctconf20251506

[71] Nagy A, Tumiwa JR, Arie FV, Erdey L. An exploratory study of artificial intelligence adoption in higher education. Cogent Education, 2024;**11**(1). DOI: 10.1080/2331186X.2024.2386892

[72] Prasolova-Førland E, Steinsbekk A, Fominykh M, Lindseth F. Practicing interprofessional team communication and collaboration in a smart virtual university hospital. In: Uskov V, Bakken J, Howlett R, Jain L. Smart Universities. Cham: Springer; 2017. p. 191–224. DOI: 10.1007/978-3-319-59454-5_770

[73] Hernawan AH, Emilzoli M, Rullyana G, Priandani AP, Saputra Y. Enhancing student collaboration and participation through Google Workspace in higher education. IJOEM Indonesian Journal of E-learning and Multimedia. 2025;**4**(1):30–42

[74] Marutschke DM, Kryssanov V, Chaminda HT, Brockmann P. Smart education in an interconnected world: Virtual, collaborative, project-based courses to teach global software engineering. In: Uskov V, Howlett R, Jain L. Smart Education and e-Learning 2019. Singapore: Springer; 2019. **144**. p. 33–45. DOI: 10.1007/978-981-13-8260-4_4

[75] Emerson N. AI-enhanced collaborative story writing in Japanese university EFL classes. Technology in Language Teaching & Learning. 2024;**6**(3)1–26. DOI: 10.29140/tltl.v6n3.1764

[76] Aker M, Pentón Herrera LJ. Smart literacy learning in the twenty-first century: Facilitating PBSL pedagogic

collaborative clouds. In: Yu S, Ally M, Tsinakos A. Smart Pedagogy of Digital Literacy. Singapore: Springer; 2020. p. 429–445. DOI: 10.1007/978-981-15-0618-5_25

[77] Liu Y, Yu C, Li Y, Wang S. Exploring the establishment of virtual simulation teaching and research rooms for big data technology specialty in the context of "Smart+" perspective: A research study. Integration of Industry and Education. 2024;**6**(2). DOI: 10.6938/iie.060208

[78] Shu X, Gu X. An empirical study of a smart education model enabled by the Edu-Metaverse to enhance better learning outcomes for students. Systems. 2023;**11**(2):75

[79] Chen Y, Chen Y, Zheng Y, Xue T, Lin W, Wen J, Chen G. Harnessing the synergy of real teacher, digital twin, and AI in blended metaverse learning environment: A catalyst for medical education reforms. SSRN Electronic Journal. 2024. DOI: 10.2139/ssrn.4745941

[80] Chen Y, Fan N, Wu H. AI-enabled metaverse for education: Challenges and opportunities. In: Xing C, Lai J, Zhang LJ. Metaverse – METAVERSE 2024. Cham: Springer; 2024. p. 135–150. DOI: 10.1007/978-3-031-76977-1_8

[81] Nouraei Yeganeh L, Fenty NS, Chen Y, Simpson A, Hatami M. The future of education: A multi-layered metaverse classroom model for immersive and inclusive learning. Future Internet. 2025;**17**(2):63. DOI: 10.3390/fi17020063

[82] Hwang Y, Lee S, Jeon J. Integrating AI chatbots into the metaverse: Pre-service English teachers' design works and perceptions. Education and Information Technologies. 2024;**30**(4):4099–4130. DOI: 10.1007/s10639-024-12924-4

[83] González Torres VH, Bracho-Fuenmayor PL, Lucero Baldevenites EV, Santander Erazo RD. Immersive learning in the metaverse: A review of evidence on pedagogical effectiveness and implementation gaps in higher education. Metaverse Basic and Applied Research. 2024;**3**. DOI: 10.56294/mr2024.97

[84] Osadchyi V, Osadcha K. The concept of a metaverse-based tribrid model of learning: Examples of successful use in higher education. Educological Discourse. 2025;**48**(1). DOI: 10.28925/2312-5829/2025.1.1

[85] Li Y. AI-enhanced digital twins for energy efficiency and carbon footprint reduction in smart city infrastructure. Applied and Computational Engineering. 2025;**118**(1):42–47. DOI: 10.54254/2755-2721/2025.20569

[86] Pexyean T, Saraubon K, Nilsook P. AI simulation, IoT, and digital twin for smart campus. Research, Invention, and Innovation Congress: Innovative Electricals and Electronics (RI2C). 2024;176–182. DOI: 10.1109/RI2C64012.2024.10784437

[87] Kim JB, Wang F, Khanna S, Balakrishnan B, Uddin M, Aman J, Thipparthi VVR. Digital twin framework for smart campus to reduce greenhouse gas emission. In: *2023 IEEE Smart World Congress (SWC)*; 2023. p. 1–8

[88] Roda-Sanchez L, Cirillo F, Solmaz G, Jacobs T, Garrido-Hidalgo C, Olivares T, Kovacs E. Building a smart campus digital twin: System, analytics, and lessons learned from a real-world

project. IEEE Internet of Things Journal. 2024;**11**:4614–4627

[89] Fernandez JB, Dhingra M, Mandal S, O'Connor NE, Kerr A, McGuinness K, Intizar A, Cudden J, Mahon K. Smart DCU digital twin: Towards smarter universities. In: *2023 IEEE Smart World Congress (SWC)*. 2023. p. 1–6

[90] She X, Xiao S. Technological implication of the digital twin approach on the intelligent education system. International Journal of Humanoid Robotics. 2022;**20**(1–2250005):23

[91] Song L, Lu Z, Petsangsri S. Reconstruction of smart learning space based on digital twin (DT) technology. In: *2020 7th International Conference on Dependable Systems and Their Applications (DSA)*. 2020. p. 398–406

[92] Mohammadi M, Hajrasouliha A. The smart campus as a testing ground for smart cities. In: *2021 ASEE Virtual Annual Conference Content Access Proceedings*. 2024.

[93] Akhrif O, Benfares C, El Bouzekri El Idrissi Y, Hmina N. (2020). Collaborative approaches in smart learning environment: A case study. Procedia Computer Science. **175**;710–715. DOI: 10.1016/j.procs.2020.07.105

[94] ElRashidy H, Elsabry E. A comparative study of different smart university frameworks. In: *2024 International Mobile, Intelligent, and Ubiquitous Computing Conference (MIUCC)*. IEEE; 2024. p. 8–12

[95] Rico-Bautista D, Guerrero CD, Collazos C, Maestre Gongora GP, Alegría J, Medina-Cárdenas Y, Swaminathan J. Smart university: A vision of technology adoption. Revista Colombiana de Computación. 2021;**22**:44–55

[96] Duc NH, Ha QT, Son PB, Cuong TQ. Conceptual and rating model of the V-SMARTH smart university. VNU Journal of Science: Education Research. 2020;**36**(2):1–13. DOI: 10.25073/2588-1159/vnuer.4400

[97] Hu H. Study on the system of smart education in universities. In: *Proceedings of the International Conference on Modern Educational Technology and Application* 2018. p. 107–111

[98] Pornphol P, Tongkeo T. Transformation from a traditional university into a smart university. In *Proceedings of the 6th International Conference*. Association for Computing Machinery; January 2018. p. 1–5. DOI: 10.1145/3178158.3178167

[99] Sen AA, Aljohani YM, Hakami AAH, Bahbouh N, Alkhodre A, Alghamdi MI. A framework for moving from traditional to smart university. In: *2023 10th International Conference on Computing for Sustainable Global Development (INDIACom)*. 2023. p. 562–569

[100] Van LN. Smart university: From the educational and technological view. Journal of Science: Educational Science. 2023;**68**(1):72–80. DOI: 10.18173/2354-1075.2023-0007

[101] Adamkó A. Building smart university using innovative technology and architecture. In: Uskov V, Bakken J, Howlett R, Jain L. Future Internet. Cham: Springer; 2017; **70**. p. 161–188 DOI: 10.1007/978-3-319-59454-5_6

[102] AlAjmi A. Artificial intelligence and smart universities. In: Studies in Computational Intelligence. Vol. **935**. Springer; 2021. p. 295–310

[103] Sidorkin AM. AI Integration Blueprint: Transforming Higher Education for the Age of Intelligence. *AI-EDU Arxiv. Briefs*. 2025. DOI: 10.36851/ai-edu.vi.5126

[104] Bhosale S, Tejas A, Gaurav G, Akshay S. AI and IoT based smart classroom. International Journal of Advanced Research in Science, Communication and Technology. 2023;**3**(1):626–632. DOI: 10.48175/IJARSCT-13698

[105] Duran V, Ekici G. Designing a draft for a metaheuristic curriculum evaluation model (MCEM) based on the examination of various metaheuristic artificial intelligence optimization applications. International Journal of Turkish Education Sciences. 2024;**12**(2):989–1055. DOI: 10.46778/goputeb.1463058

[106] McBride E, Peters ES, Judd S. Design considerations for inclusive AI curriculum materials. In: *Proceedings of the 52nd ACM Technical Symposium on Computer Science Education*. Association for Computing Machinery; March 5, 2021. p. 1370. DOI: 10.1145/3408877.3439552

Chapter 2

Empowering Higher Education through Virtual Worlds: Competency-Based and Experiential Learning in the Metaverse

Javier Vaca Cabrero, Nicoletta González-Cancelas and Alberto Camarero-Orive

Abstract

The rapid evolution of immersive technologies is reshaping the future of higher education. The metaverse, understood as an interconnected and persistent virtual environment, offers universities the opportunity to create learning experiences that go beyond traditional classrooms and digital platforms. This chapter explores the potential of virtual worlds to support competency-based and experiential learning, positioning students as active participants in dynamic, collaborative, and creative environments. By integrating simulation, experimentation, and social interaction, the metaverse enables the development of both technical and transversal skills, bridging the gap between theory and practice. Practical examples from disciplines such as health sciences, engineering, and social sciences demonstrate the value of immersive learning for fostering motivation, innovation, and intercultural communication. At the same time, critical challenges remain, including digital inequality, infrastructure costs, teacher training, cognitive overload, and ethical concerns around privacy and sustainability. The chapter argues that the true potential of the metaverse in higher education lies not in its technological novelty but in its pedagogical intentionality, inclusiveness, and strategic design. Looking ahead, the integration of the metaverse with artificial intelligence, learning analytics, and sustainable practices could consolidate its role as a transformative catalyst, preparing future professionals for the demands of an interconnected and rapidly changing world.

Keywords: metaverse, higher education, experiential learning, digital pedagogy, inclusive education

1. Introduction

Higher education is in a moment of unprecedented transformation. Driven by technological accelerations, societal changes, and the increasing globalization of knowledge, universities face challenges in preparing students not only with disciplinary content but also with digital competencies, critical thinking, collaborative work, adaptability, and a deep understanding of emerging tools. In this context, the Metaverse and virtual worlds offer new avenues to redefine what it means to learn, teach, and experience in higher education.

Recent research indicates that immersive technologies – virtual reality (VR), augmented reality (AR), and metaverse environments – can support more active, student-centered learning. A systematic study on metaverse pedagogical models found that these technologies have a positive impact on formal educational contexts, although little attention is still paid to the design of balanced immersive experiences focused on meaningful participation [1]. Another study highlights the perception of university students regarding their willingness to use metaverse technologies, showing that previous experiences and digital literacy strongly influence their attitudes and dispositions [2].

The metaverse not only brings technical innovations but also becomes a space to develop transversal digital skills. For example, a study in Mexico reported significant improvements in communication and collaboration skills after educational interventions that integrated immersive environments under the "Education 5.0" paradigms [3]. Another project in Thailand evaluated how a metaverse-based digital learning ecosystem improved digital entrepreneurs' competencies, such as innovative thinking, problem-solving, and creativity, finding an effect of great statistical magnitude [4].

In addition, the experiential dimension of learning becomes central: students not only receive information but also interact in simulated scenarios, virtual laboratories, or collaborative spaces that allow them to practice, make mistakes, reflect, and repeat. A recent study on the educational potential of the metaverse highlights that although much research has focused on the technical aspects (hardware, platforms), there is a lack of robust pedagogical models that integrate reflection, collaboration, and formative assessment in immersive environments [5].

However, the adoption of the metaverse in higher education faces significant challenges. Technological infrastructure, equitable access, teacher training, costs, and curricular integration are obstacles that many recent studies have pointed out. A study by professionals in the university field reveals these barriers as well as opportunities, emphasizing that strategic institutional support and pedagogical alignment are key to fully taking advantage of metaverse environments[6].

In the face of these possibilities and challenges, this chapter proposes that the metaverse represents more than just a technological innovation: it is a strategic opportunity to reconfigure higher education toward models focused on skills and experiences. It is proposed that virtual worlds, if designed with pedagogical intentionality, can serve to close the gap between theory and practice, increase student engagement, foster relevant learning for a digitalized world, and promote sustainable and inclusive education goals.

With this objective, this chapter is structured as follows: first, the key concepts such as metaverse, immersive reality, experiential learning, and digital skills will be defined; then, it will review how these concepts have been applied in higher education through recent studies; next, we will explore how to design effective virtual learning spaces, including accessibility and sustainability considerations; then, real case studies with lessons learned will be presented; finally, the challenges will be discussed, and future perspectives will be raised, especially linking the metaverse and artificial intelligence, for higher education that trains citizens and professionals prepared for the challenges of the twenty-first century.

2. Conceptual framework

2.1 The metaverse in the educational context

In recent years, the term "metaverse" has established itself as one of the most debated notions in the field of educational innovation. Although there is no single definition, most research agrees in describing it as a three-dimensional, immersive, and persistent virtual environment in which users, represented by avatars, can interact, build shared experiences, and develop activities in real time. Unlike traditional online teaching, which relies mainly on content management platforms, the metaverse offers a space that seeks to replicate and, at the same time, expand the experience of face-to-face learning, creating scenarios where social interaction, exploration, and collaboration take on a central role [7].

Recent literature suggests that the educational metaverse cannot be understood in isolation but in relation to other technologies that constitute or complement it, such as virtual reality, augmented reality, mixed reality, and, in general, the umbrella concept of extended reality (XR). Virtual reality is characterized by offering completely digital environments that replace physical perception, while augmented reality combines the real world with superimposed virtual elements, and mixed reality seeks to integrate both interactively. The metaverse thrives on these modalities but transcends them by proposing interconnected, persistent virtual universes with a strong social component, in which the user experience is oriented not only toward the consumption of content but also toward creation and active participation [8].

In this sense, the value of the metaverse for higher education lies in its potential to generate learning environments that combine presence, interaction, and continuity [6]. They point out that university teachers perceive these spaces as catalysts for experiential learning, although they insist that their integration must be supported by a clear pedagogical intention and adequate infrastructure. The sense of presence offered by avatars and the digital representation of students not only increases motivation and a sense of belonging but also favors the construction of academic and professional identities in simulated contexts. Similarly, the possibility of interacting in real time with other participants, manipulating virtual objects, or exploring custom-designed scenarios allows for active learning that is difficult to replicate in other digital environments.

The pedagogical benefits of this proposal are especially linked to competency-based learning. The immersive and collaborative nature of the metaverse makes it a laboratory where students can practice technical and transversal skills in realistic situations: from problem-solving in a virtual engineering lab to decision-making in a business simulation or clinical practice in a digital medical environment. In each case, metaverse environments offer the opportunity to experiment, reflect, make mistakes, and try again, following the principles of experiential learning described by Kolb [9] and embraced by much of contemporary pedagogy.

However, the literature also warns of the challenges of transferring the concept of the metaverse to the educational field. One of the recurring problems is the lack of standardization: while some studies include any immersive experience with virtual reality glasses within the metaverse, others understand it as a much broader ecosystem, with components of interoperability, persistence, and social construction [7]. This ambiguity makes it difficult to compare research and formulate consistent pedagogical frameworks. In addition, most of the documented experiences remain small-scale pilots, with few longitudinal studies to assess the real impact on the acquisition of complex skills and long-term academic performance.

The technical and social obstacles are not minor either. Unequal access to virtual reality devices, implementation costs, the need for teacher training, privacy and security issues, and even the risks of exclusion for those who do not have the necessary digital skills are factors that condition the adoption of the metaverse in universities [6]. Despite these limitations, the emerging consensus is that the metaverse represents a unique opportunity to rethink higher education beyond simply digitizing content. Its value lies not only in technological novelty but also in the possibility of articulating new forms of teaching and learning based on experience, collaboration, and the construction of knowledge in community.

In short, the educational metaverse can be understood as a hybrid space that combines the best of face-to-face and digital learning, with the ability to overcome physical restrictions and open up new possibilities for pedagogical interaction. Its integration into higher education will depend on the conceptual clarity, pedagogical intent, and inclusive design with which the experiences are implemented. As they put it [7, 8], the metaverse is not an end in itself but a means that, if harnessed strategically, can contribute to redefining university practices in an increasingly digital, interconnected, and skills-oriented world of the twenty-first century.

2.2 Relevant pedagogical approaches

The value of the metaverse in higher education lies not only in its technological sophistication but also in its ability to embody and enhance pedagogical frameworks that have guided university teaching for decades. For immersive environments to become meaningful experiences, it is essential to situate them within established educational theories such as experiential learning, constructivism, active pedagogies, and competency-based learning. In this way, the metaverse is understood not as an end in itself but as a means to implement student-centered approaches.

One of the most solid references is the experiential learning proposed by [9], which suggests a continuous cycle of experimenting, reflecting, conceptualizing, and applying. In an immersive environment, this cycle materializes with ease: students can engage in a laboratory simulation, collectively reflect on the results, conceptualize the theoretical principles involved, and reapply their knowledge under new conditions. Recent research indicates that metaverse platforms favor precisely this dynamic by allowing safe and repeatable scenarios where students can "learn by doing" [6].

The metaverse also dialogs with constructivism, particularly with the perspectives of [10, 11]. From this vision, knowledge is built in an active and social way through interaction with others and with the environment. Virtual worlds provide collaborative scenarios in which students can build joint projects, manipulate digital objects, and solve problems as a team. According to [7], this collaborative dimension is one of the most cited in the literature on the metaverse in higher education, as it encourages participation and a sense of academic community, even in remote environments.

Related to constructivism is student-centered learning, which shifts the focus from the teacher as transmitter to the student as the protagonist of his or her own training process. In this context, the metaverse is configured as a space in which students can explore, make decisions, and assume responsibilities in the construction of knowledge. Nguyen et al. [8] emphasize that immersive experiences offer unique opportunities to develop autonomy and self-regulation, fundamental competencies for education in the twenty-first century.

Another relevant approach is that of active pedagogies, such as problem-based learning (PBL), project-based learning, or the flipped classroom model. These methodologies find fertile ground in the metaverse, as they allow for the design of environments that simulate real-world problems, encourage collaboration between peers, and offer a flexible space for co-creation. Recent studies show that metaverse experiences aligned with PBL manage to increase student engagement and improve knowledge transfer to practical contexts [12].

In turn, gamification has become especially important in the design of immersive experiences. Virtual worlds allow you to incorporate game-specific dynamics – challenges, levels, symbolic rewards – that increase motivation and a sense of achievement. When these dynamics are integrated with a competency-based learning approach, students not only acquire knowledge but also develop transversal skills such as communication, creativity, and problem-solving. This connects directly with international frameworks such as the European Commission's DigCompEdu [13], which establishes the digital teaching competences necessary to guide students in active and meaningful learning in digital environments.

Finally, inclusive digital pedagogy emerges as an essential element. The metaverse opens up possibilities for designing accessible experiences that overcome physical and geographical barriers, but it also poses risks of exclusion for those who lack resources or digital literacy. As they point out [6], the responsible adoption of virtual worlds in universities requires institutional strategies that guarantee equity and sustainability, in line with the United Nations' Sustainable Development Goal 4 (SDG4) on inclusive and quality education.

In summary, the relevant pedagogical approaches show that the metaverse is not a substitute for traditional educational theories, but a catalyst that can make them more tangible and effective. From cyclical experimentation to active, student-centered pedagogies, immersive environments make it possible to put ideas that previously depended on limited face-to-face contexts into practice.

2.3 Relevant pedagogical approaches

The transformative potential of the metaverse in higher education is closely linked to the development of digital skills and its ability to foster inclusive and sustainable learning environments. Beyond technological innovation, the key lies in how these immersive spaces can prepare students to navigate an interconnected, equitable, and globally challenged world.

Digital skills have been recognized as fundamental for the twenty-first century. In the context of the metaverse, they are not limited to the technical handling of devices but include effective communication, collaboration in virtual environments, creative problem-solving, and adaptability. A recent study in Mexico showed that integrating Education *5.0-based* educational experiences with virtual worlds significantly improved engineering students' ability to communicate and collaborate digitally [3]. These results show that the metaverse can act as a catalyst for transversal skills that are critical in employability and contemporary professional practice.

The notion of *metaverse literacy* adds another layer to this discussion [8]. It states that it is not enough to teach how to use immersive platforms; students must also develop cognitive, ethical, emotional, and attitudinal skills that allow them to function critically and responsibly in these environments. In this sense, the metaverse is not just a technical laboratory but a space to learn how to interact in digital communities in a conscious and sustainable way, considering aspects of identity, privacy, and ethics.

The inclusive dimension of virtual worlds is another crucial aspect. Although often presented as democratizing environments, unequal access to devices, connectivity, and infrastructure can widen the existing digital divide. A recent systematic review on virtual reality in higher education stresses that these technologies can improve social inclusion and offer new learning opportunities to students in remote contexts but also warns that institutions must ensure resources and training to avoid exclusion [14]. This double-edged sword forces the design of policies that ensure the metaverse is accessible to everyone, including students with disabilities or economic limitations.

In addition, the degree of immersion and the pedagogical design of the experiences condition their effects [15]. It was shown that deep learning and motivation are highly dependent on how social and collaborative interactions are structured within the metaverse. This means that inclusion is not only technological but also pedagogical: a poorly designed immersive environment can generate symbolic exclusion or demotivation, even if technical access is guaranteed.

Sustainability represents a third, inseparable axis. The metaverse can contribute to reducing physical infrastructure and travel costs, thereby lowering the carbon footprint associated with certain academic activities. However, it also raises questions about the power consumption of virtual reality servers and devices [16]. Stresses that while these technologies offer opportunities to promote education for sustainable development and align with the Sustainable Development Goals (especially SDG 4 on inclusive and quality education), they must be accompanied by institutional strategies that minimize their environmental impact. This includes everything from energy efficiency in technological infrastructures to raising awareness among students themselves about sustainable digital practices.

The metaverse in higher education articulates three inseparable dimensions: digital skills, inclusion, and sustainability. It is not enough for students to learn how to use immersive technologies; it is necessary for them to develop a critical literacy that contemplates the ethical, the emotional, and the social. It is also not enough to create attractive scenarios; it is essential to guarantee accessibility and equity in their implementation. And finally, sustainability, both social and environmental, must be considered as an integral part of any educational strategy based on virtual worlds. Only from this broad vision can the metaverse become a transformative tool that contributes not only to academic excellence but also to the construction of a fairer, more inclusive, and responsible higher education for the future.

3. Metaverse and digital skills in higher education: Practical applications

The potential of the metaverse in higher education is most clearly manifested when you look at its concrete application in university settings. Different disciplines have begun to explore how virtual worlds can become scenarios where students develop technical and transversal skills through immersive and collaborative experiences. This section examines how these applications are being deployed, what lessons are learned from recent experiences, and what challenges accompany practice.

One of the areas where the metaverse has shown a more visible impact is in the health sciences. The teaching of medicine, nursing, and dentistry has experimented with virtual environments that simulate clinical and surgical procedures, offering students the possibility of practicing without the risks associated with real interventions. A study by [17] in Taiwan looked at a virtual surgery program in a metaverse environment and found that students not only improved in technical accuracy but also reported higher levels of confidence and emotional readiness before facing real patients. Similarly, research at universities in Europe and Latin America has shown that immersive simulators in dentistry and nursing favor knowledge retention and the acquisition of motor skills, while allowing procedures to be repeated as many times as necessary without the limits of physical resources or ethical risks [18].

Engineering and experimental sciences are another fertile ground for metaverse applications. Virtual labs that replicate expensive or dangerous physical environments have proven to be effective tools to complement face-to-face practices. In chemistry teaching, for example, immersive virtual reality experiences have been documented, allowing students to manipulate molecules in 3D, observe reactions at the molecular scale, and understand complex processes more intuitively. A study by [19] showed that these types of environments improve conceptual understanding and foster more meaningful learning by placing students in interactive scenarios that are difficult to replicate in traditional physical labs. For their part [20], they highlight that teaching chemistry in the metaverse opens up opportunities for collaboration between students and the reduction of barriers to access expensive laboratory practices, while posing challenges in terms of pedagogical design and technological equity.

In the social sciences and humanities, metaverse environments have also begun to be successfully explored. In training in law, economics, or international relations, virtual worlds allow you to recreate mock trials, trade negotiations, or scenarios of multilateral organizations where students must adopt specific roles and argue in collaborative environments. A recent study by [21] looked at how virtual reality can work as a public diplomacy tool, showing that immersive environments influence the perception of foreign audiences and generate a higher level of engagement in negotiation and international relations. Although their focus is on public diplomacy, their findings are transferable to higher education, as they suggest that simulations in virtual worlds can help students of political science and international relations develop cross-cultural competencies and negotiation skills in realistic scenarios. These experiences, in addition to facilitating theoretical understanding, offer a space for authentic practice where participants must manage conflicts, make decisions as a team, and communicate in multicultural contexts – skills that are increasingly valued in university education.

The impact of the metaverse is not limited to specific technical skills but encompasses a broad set of transversal skills. Recent research identified that learning experiences in virtual worlds especially strengthen collaboration, creative problem-solving, and communication in multicultural teams. For example, Sharma et al. [22] documented how university students, when using avatars in collaborative metaverse environments, perceive greater equity in participation, better mutual understanding, and a reduction of social barriers typical of physical classrooms.

In addition, the metaverse opens up new ways to assess competencies in immersive environments. Studies such as [23] show that not only does knowledge retention increase but also collaboration in group tasks, demonstrating that competencies such as decision-making, creativity, and leadership can be valued within virtual simulations.

However, assessment remains one of the least developed yet most critical aspects of metaverse-based education. To ensure validity and comparability, competency assessment in immersive environments should combine automated analytics with human evaluation. Learning analytics and AI-driven observation tools can capture behavioral evidence (collaboration patterns, decision-making processes, and problem-solving pathways), while rubrics and reflective journals preserve the qualitative dimension of assessment. A future challenge for universities and accreditation agencies will be to align these new assessment models with formal competency frameworks, such as EQF or ABET standards, enabling recognition of learning outcomes achieved in virtual worlds.

International case studies reinforce that the metaverse is already being used with real impact. For example, the review points to multiple projects in higher education where virtual worlds have been used for collaborative practices, simulations, and intercultural interactions, integrating sustainability principles [24]. There are also works that investigate the role of avatars [25], exploring how avatars can reduce some social biases and facilitate more egalitarian interactions between students.

However, these experiences also indicate practical challenges. Cost, infrastructure, teacher training, and the need for sound pedagogical design continue to appear as recurring barriers. Studies, such as, point out these limitations in their literature reviews.

Another major challenge is cognitive overload and sensory fatigue. Although I have not found a specific study that calls it a "positive disinhibiting effect" with Jung and Dieck, there is research on cognitive limits when immersive environments are not well-structured [26]. It analyzes cognitive, affective, and psychomotor effects of immersive environments and highlights the need for guides and structures to prevent the experience from backfiring.

Despite these challenges, practice shows that the metaverse is not a fad. Students report greater motivation, engagement, and meaning in their learning when immersive experiences are well-designed.

4. Challenges and limitations of the metaverse in higher education

The incorporation of the metaverse into higher education has sparked considerable enthusiasm, but its practical implementation faces a number of challenges and limitations that cannot be overlooked. These challenges encompass technological, pedagogical, social, economic, and ethical issues and constitute a critical terrain for understanding what conditions must be in place for the metaverse to consolidate itself as a transformative educational tool.

One of the main obstacles is the digital divide. Although the costs of virtual reality devices have decreased, they are still prohibitive for many students and institutions, especially in developing countries. The necessary technological infrastructure – bandwidth, powerful servers, compatible management systems – also limits the expansion of large-scale pilot projects [14]. In their review of virtual reality in higher education, they point out that inequality of access to devices and connectivity is one of the factors that most conditions equity in immersive experiences. Thus, far from democratizing education, a poorly implemented metaverse can widen the existing gaps between those who have access to technological resources and those who do not.

Another crucial challenge is teacher training. The adoption of the metaverse cannot be understood as a mere incorporation of tools but requires changes in pedagogical practices [27]. It is stressed that, without a solid didactic foundation, immersive experiences risk becoming anecdotal activities with no real educational value. For the metaverse to impact learning, teachers must develop both technical and pedagogical skills, which implies investment in training and institutional support. In addition, cultural resistance persists on the part of the teaching staff and universities themselves, who see these innovations as fads or as additional workloads.

From a technical point of view, the metaverse faces interoperability and scalability issues. There are multiple platforms with different standards, which make it difficult to create shared and persistent environments. This technological fragmentation limits the possibility of integrating pilot projects into comprehensive and sustainable educational programs [22]. In their review of collaborative learning in the metaverse, they highlight that the lack of common standards generates difficulties for replicability and comparison of results between studies. Added to this is the complexity of managing classes with dozens or hundreds of students simultaneously in immersive environments, something that still has technical performance limitations.

Another aspect that worries the academic community is cognitive overload and the well-being of students. Prolonged immersion in virtual reality environments can lead to eye strain, spatial disorientation, and reduced performance [26]. They point out that immersive environments, if not carefully designed, can increase cognitive load to levels that make it difficult to assimilate knowledge. Therefore, they recommend balancing sensory richness with a clear pedagogical design that guides interactions. In addition, there are risks of digital fatigue, especially when students must combine activities in the metaverse with other e-learning modalities and face-to-face classes.

Ethical and privacy aspects represent another major challenge. Unlike other digital platforms, virtual worlds generate highly detailed data about users, from their social interactions to their physical movements, facial expressions, or voice patterns [28]. It warns that this level of data collection poses serious risks of surveillance, algorithmic bias, and misuse by technology providers. In educational settings, where students are a particularly vulnerable group, these concerns become even more relevant. Hence, the need to establish clear regulatory frameworks that guarantee the data protection and digital security of participants.

The legal and regulatory dimensions of immersive education are still evolving. Universities operating in the metaverse face new questions regarding intellectual property (such as ownership of digital assets or student-generated content), as well as accreditation and quality assurance in virtual courses. Accreditation agencies are beginning to explore frameworks for validating competencies demonstrated in virtual environments, but the absence of standardized procedures remains a barrier. Moreover, data governance in the metaverse extends beyond traditional privacy concerns: it involves defining who owns, manages, and can reuse biometric and behavioral data collected during immersive sessions. Establishing transparent governance models, aligned with GDPR and UNESCO recommendations on digital ethics, will be crucial for ensuring trust and accountability in virtual learning ecosystems.

Emerging risks are linked to the increasing use of AI-driven analytics and biometric tracking within immersive environments. Eye movements, gestures, voice tone, and physiological responses can be captured to adapt learning experiences, but they also create new layers of surveillance. Algorithmic bias (embedded in facial recognition or behavioral scoring systems) can unintentionally reproduce inequalities or penalize neurodiverse learners. Therefore, ethical frameworks for metaverse education must address algorithmic transparency, informed consent, and students' right to opt out of data-intensive monitoring systems. Universities should develop internal protocols for auditing AI systems used in virtual education to prevent discriminatory outcomes.

Economic and environmental sustainability is another key aspect. Implementing immersive experiences requires not only an initial investment in hardware and software but also constant maintenance, which can be costly for universities. In addition, the operation of powerful servers and virtual reality devices involves significant energy consumption [24]. It posits that while the metaverse may reduce the need for physical infrastructure or academic travel, its environmental footprint should not be underestimated. Sustainable adoption involves institutional strategies to optimize resources and reduce the ecological impact of digitalization.

Added to these structural limitations is the lack of long-term empirical evidence. Many of the experiences reported in the literature correspond to pilot projects of short duration, with small samples, and without longitudinal follow-up.

An additional challenge is linked to social and cultural inclusion. While the metaverse can create spaces for cross-cultural interaction, it can also reproduce inequalities of gender, language, or cultural capital [25]. In their review of avatars in metaverse education, they point out that students with less digital literacy tend to participate less actively and remain in peripheral positions within virtual groups. Likewise, the personalization of avatars can lead to dynamics of exclusion or stigmatization if diverse and inclusive options are not designed.

Finally, the risk of commercial instrumentalization must be considered. Several metaverse platforms are powered by large tech corporations, raising questions about reliance on private providers in an area as sensitive as education [27]. He warns that there is a danger that universities may adopt these technologies more due to market pressure than a true pedagogical intention, which could lead to superficial uses that do not respond to real educational needs.

Taken together, these challenges and limitations do not mean that the metaverse has no future in higher education, but rather that its implementation requires strategic planning, clear institutional policies, and an ethical and sustainable commitment. For the metaverse to fulfill its transformative promise, it is essential to address the digital divide, invest in teacher training, design accessible and sustainable environments, and ensure student privacy and security. Only in this way will it be able to go from being an emerging innovation to consolidating itself as a true catalyst for university education in the twenty-first century.

Beyond individual resistance, the integration of the metaverse requires comprehensive institutional strategies. Successful initiatives often rely on structured capacity-building programs that combine technical training, pedagogical mentoring, and interdisciplinary collaboration. Universities can foster adoption through incentive systems (such as innovation grants, workload recognition, or teaching excellence awards) that acknowledge the extra effort required to design immersive experiences. Equally important are leadership and organizational culture: appointing "digital learning champions" and establishing innovation hubs within faculties can facilitate peer learning and long-term institutional transformation. In this sense, capacity-building must be conceived not as an isolated course but as a continuous process of professional development that aligns technological innovation with the academic mission of the institution.

5. Conclusions

The journey made throughout this chapter has shown that the metaverse is one of the most disruptive and promising innovations for contemporary higher education. Its potential lies in the possibility of offering immersive and participatory experiences that transcend the limits of the physical classroom and conventional digital learning. Beyond the technological fascination, the metaverse opens the door to a profound change in the way we conceive teaching and learning, placing the student at the center of meaningful, competency-oriented experiences.

The experiences analyzed show that the metaverse is not limited to reproducing content in a three-dimensional format but also introduces dynamics that favor experimentation, reflection, and collaboration. From clinical simulations and virtual labs to historical reenactments or negotiation environments, these worlds allow theory and practice to be connected in the same space. The result is more active, engaging, and relevant learning, capable of fostering transversal competencies such as creativity, teamwork, intercultural communication, and decision-making in complex contexts.

However, the metaverse is not an end in itself. Its true educational value unfolds when it is integrated into pedagogical projects with clear objectives, active methodologies, and criteria of inclusion and sustainability. Technology, by itself, does not guarantee meaningful learning; it is the pedagogical design that turns virtual environments into high-impact training experiences. This observation forces universities and teachers to assume a leading role in the definition of strategies for use, preventing technological enthusiasm from leading to superficial implementations or implementations that are detached from the real needs of students.

At the same time, the analysis has highlighted the many challenges that accompany this innovation. The digital divide, infrastructure costs, insufficient teacher training, and ethical doubts about privacy and data use represent serious limitations. Added to these are the risks of cognitive overload, digital fatigue, and the need to establish standards that allow scalability and accessibility. These challenges should not be interpreted as insurmountable brakes but as reminders that the implementation of the metaverse requires strategic planning, institutional accompaniment, and an explicit commitment to equity and educational quality.

The dimension of sustainability also emerges as a decisive aspect. The metaverse offers the possibility of reducing travel and optimizing physical infrastructures, but at the same time, it demands an intensive use of energy and technological resources. Universities will have to find a balance between innovation and environmental responsibility, aligning the development of immersive environments with the objectives of sustainability and social well-being.

Looking ahead, it is possible to identify several lines of evolution that will mark the future of the metaverse in higher education. The first will be pedagogical consolidation, that is, moving from pilot experiences to comprehensive programs in which the metaverse is not an occasional resource but a structural piece of the educational strategy. The second line will be equity and accessibility, with the need to design environments that do not exclude those with fewer resources or fewer digital skills but act as catalysts for inclusion. And the third line will be technological integration, in which the metaverse is combined with artificial intelligence, learning analytics, and emerging technologies to generate more personalized, secure, and scalable experiences.

In this horizon, the role of universities will be decisive. These institutions will have to decide whether to conceive of the metaverse as a passing fad or as a strategic tool to rethink their educational mission in a digital, interconnected, and globalized world. The difference will not be made by technology itself, but by the ability of universities to place the student at the center, to design experiences that truly develop useful skills, and to ensure that technological innovation contributes to the values of equity, inclusion, and sustainability that define higher education in the twenty-first century.

In conclusion, the metaverse should not be understood as a simple extension of digital education but as a catalyst for new ways of learning and teaching. Its success will depend less on the spectacularity of virtual environments and more on the pedagogical vision with which it is built and applied. If harnessed strategically, the metaverse can become a true engine of transformation, capable of redefining the university experience and preparing new generations to face the challenges of an ever-changing world.

Conflict of Interest

The authors declare no conflict of interest.

Author details

Javier Vaca Cabrero[1,2*], Nicoletta González-Cancelas[1,2] and Alberto Camarero-Orive[1,2]

1 Department of Transport, Territorial and Urban Planning Engineering, Universidad Politécnica de Madrid, Madrid, Spain

2 R&D&I Centre for Smart and Sustainable Civil Infrastructure (CIVILis), Universidad Politécnica de Madrid, Madrid, Spain

*Address all correspondence to: j.vaca@upm.es

References

[1] Zunic M, Dlab MH, Hoic-Bozic N, Pribičević Z. Educational Potential of the Metaverse. International Journal of Distance Education Technologies. 2025;**23**:1–50. DOI: 10.4018/IJDET.382480

[2] Misirlis N, Nikolaidis Y, Sabidussi A. Should I use metaverse or not? An investigation of university students behavioral intention to use MetaEducation technology. arXiv. 2023; **arXiv**:2311.15251. DOI: 10.48550/arXiv.2311.15251

[3] Peláez-Sánchez C, Andrade S, Glasserman-Morales L. Digital Competencies in Communication and Collaboration: Assessing metaverses in Education 5.0. Tokyo: ICEEL; 2024. DOI: 10.1145/3719487.3719510

[4] Meepung T. A Digital Learning Ecosystem through Metaverse Experiences to Develop Modern Digital Entrepreneurs Competencies. Journal of Education and Learning. 2024;**17**:68–87. DOI: 10.5539/jel.v14n1p94

[5] Zunic M, Dlab MH, Hoic-Bozic N, Pribičević Z. Educational Potential of the Metaverse. International Journal of Distance Education Technologies. 2025;**23**(1). DOI: 10.4018/IJDET.382480

[6] Bakk ÁK, Bényei J, Ballack P, Parente F. Current possibilities and challenges of using metaverse-like environments and technologies in education. Frontiers in Virtual Reality. 2025;**6**. DOI: 10.3389/frvir.2025.1521334

[7] Woick A, Rinn H, Grogorick L, Mühleisen T, Markgraf D. Metaverse in Higher Education – A Systematic Literature Review. 37th Bled eConference Resilience Through Digital Innovation: Enabling the Twin Transition. 2024. p. 57–76. DOI: 10.18690/um.fov.4.2024.4

[8] Nguyen T, Nguyen H, Gia TN. Exploring the integration of edge computing and blockchain IoT: Principles, architectures, security, and applications. Journal of Network and Computer Applications. 2024;**226**:103884

[9] Kolb D. Experiential Learning: Experience as the source of Learning and Development Second Edition. 2015

[10] Vygotskiĭ LS. The Collected Works of L.S. Vygotsky: The History of the Development of Higher Mental Functions. **Vol. 4**. Springer Science & Business Media; 1997

[11] Piaget J, 'Psychology and epistemology: Towards a theory of knowledge', 1972. [Online]. Available from: https://philpapers.org/rec/PIAPAE-3 [Accessed: 2025-September-18]

[12] Deng G, Zhang J. Technological pedagogical content ethical knowledge (TPCEK): The development of an assessment instrument for pre-service teachers. Computers & Education. 2023;**197**:104740. DOI: 10.1016/j.compedu.2023.104740

[13] Redecker C, Punie Y, European framework for the digital competence of educators: DigCompEdu. Publications Office of the European Union, 2017. [Online]. Available from: https://data.europa.eu/doi/10.2760/159770 [Accessed: 2025-September-18]

[14] Llanos-Ruiz D, Abella-García V, Ausín-Villaverde V. Virtual Reality in

Higher Education: A Systematic Review Aligned with the Sustainable Development Goals. Societies. 2025;**15**(9):251. DOI: 10.3390/soc15090251

[15] Aziz F, Li C, Khan AU. Immersive learning in virtual worlds: A two-step analysis SEM and NCA for assessing the impact of Metaverse education on knowledge retention and student collaboration. Technology in Society. 2025;**81**(C):102871. Available from: https://ideas.repec.org//a/eee/teinso/v81y2025ics0160791x25000612.html

[16] Roy R, Rao A, Pal D, Anuradha S, Mukherjee S. Metaverse-based education for sustainable development and improving the performance: Discussing the future research agenda. Sustainability Futures. 2025;**10**. DOI: 10.1016/j.sftr.2025.101091

[17] Li Q, Duan H, Zhou X, Sun X, Tao L, Lu X. The use of metaverse in medical education: A systematic review. Clinical Medicine. 2025;**25**(3):100315. DOI: 10.1016/j.clinme.2025.100315

[18] Ryan GV, Callaghan S, Rafferty A, Higgins MF, Mangina E, McAuliffe F. Learning outcomes of immersive technologies in health care student education: systematic review of the literature. Journal of Medical Internet Research. 2022;**24**(2):e30082

[19] van Dinther R, de Putter L, Pepin B. Features of Immersive Virtual Reality to Support Meaningful Chemistry Education |. Journal of Chemical Education. 2025;**100**(4):1537–1546. DOI: 10.1021/acs.jchemed.2c01069

[20] Amirbekova E, Shertayeva N, Mironova E. Teaching chemistry in the metaverse: the effectiveness of using virtual and augmented reality for visualization. Frontiers in Education. 2024;**8**. DOI: 10.3389/feduc.2023.1184768

[21] Ertem-Eray T, Ki E-J. Examining Virtual Reality as a New Opportunity for Public Diplomacy Efforts. Rochester, NY: Social Science Research Network; 2024. 5027929 p. DOI: 10.2139/ssrn.5027929

[22] Sharma A, Sharma L, Krezel J. Exploring the Use of Metaverse for Collaborative Learning in Higher Education: A Scoping Review. In International Conference on Human-Computer InteractionScoping Review. Cham: Springer Nature Switzerland. 2023. p. 240–251. DOI: 10.1007/978-3-031-48060-7_19

[23] Aziz F, Li C, Khan AU. Immersive Learning in Virtual Worlds: A Two-step Analysis SEM and NCA for Assessing the Impact of Metaverse Education on Knowledge Retention and Student Collaboration. Technology in Society. 2025;**81**:102871. DOI: 10.1016/j.techsoc.2025.102871

[24] Roy R, Rao GA, Pal D, Anuradha S, Mukherjee S. Metaverse-based education for sustainable development and improving the performance: Discussing the future research agenda. Sustainability Futures. 2025;**10**:101091. DOI: 10.1016/j.sftr.2025.101091

[25] Islam MZ, Wang G. Avatars in the educational metaverse. Visual Computing for Industry, Biomedicine, and Art. 2025;**8**(1):15. DOI: 10.1186/s42492-025-00196-9

[26] Pata K, Väljataga T, 'The Learning Effects in Immersive Technologies', In: Integrating Emerging Technologies into Education and Training: Proceedings of the 2nd ETELT 2024 Workshop,

Kim TE, Milrad M, Remolar I, Eds. Cham: Springer Nature Switzerland; 2025. p. 98–108. DOI: 10.1007/978-3-031-84170-5_9

[27] Gourlay L. Postdigital/More-Than-Digital: Ephemerality, Seclusion, and Copresence in the University. In: Jandrić P, MacKenzie A, Knox J, editors. Postdigital Research. Postdigital Science and Education. Cham: Springer Nature Switzerland; 2023. p. 51–68. DOI: 10.1007/978-3-031-31299-1_4

[28] Srivastava A, Vaidya V, Murthy S, Dasgupta C. GeoSolvAR: Scaffolding spatial perspective-taking ability of middle-school students using AR-enhanced inquiry learning environment. British Journal of Educational Technology. 2024;**55** (6):2617–2638. DOI: 10.1111/bjet.13456

Chapter 3

Immersive Worlds for Metalearning: Revolutionizing Scientific Understanding in the Metaverse

Sana Jamshaid

Abstract

This chapter explores the transformative potential of incorporating the metaverse, artificial intelligence (AI), and metaintelligence into science education. Traditional educational approaches, such as textbooks, lectures, and static visual aids, do not always adequately explain complex concepts such as atomic structure, quantum physics, and space–time theory. Animation and film have piqued people's interest, but new technology allows us to experience things firsthand rather than just explain them. The immersive, interactive, and adaptive virtual environments in the metaverse allow students to experience scientific phenomena very closely, as students can walk through atomic structures, observe quantum interactions, and manipulate dynamic simulations. The AI-powered personalization and metaintelligence tailor lesson content to the learning style of the student, improving comprehension and retention of material. This chapter also explores case studies, theoretical foundations, practical frameworks, and ethical issues related to the implementation of metaverse education, emphasizing the possible use of immersive technologies to bridge the gap between conceptual scientific ideas and concrete interpretations.

Keywords: virtual reality (VR) in classrooms, metaintelligence, future of science education, cognitive learning, metaversal revolution

1. Introduction

I remember staring at diagrams of atoms in my textbooks as a student. Little circles, arrows, and labels showed the movement of particles. But honestly, most of the time, it just looked like a bunch of lines on a page. And this has been a long-standing challenge in science education: How do we make something visible that we cannot see?

We are living in an era of unprecedented technological change, and with every advancement, our learning tools and educational expectations continue to change. Instead of reading about cells, the metaverse can immerse us in science, allowing us to walk through cells instead of imagining them. Instead of simply memorizing diagrams of atoms, we can stand on the edge of an unimaginable black hole in real time and watch atoms spin. Therefore, I believe science learning will move from memorization and listening to actual real-time experiences with the help of the metaverse, AI, and metaintelligence. This chapter explores how science learning is moving from passive listening to active discovery, from memorizing diagrams to experiencing phenomena. These technologies are not only improving the quality of education but are also fundamentally reshaping what it means to truly experience science.

2. Theoretical foundations

For decades, educational researchers and cognitive scientists have developed important theories that explain how knowledge is acquired, processed, and retained (**Figure 1**). Three foundational theories, such as constructivist learning theory, cognitive load theory, and embodied cognition, provide a roadmap for building learning environments that enable active and meaningful engagement rather than passive reception. Each of these theories offers a different perspective on how humans truly absorb and retain knowledge [1–3].

The constructivist perspective, developed through the work of Jean Piaget (1970) and Lev Vygotsky (1978), asserts that knowledge is not passively received but actively constructed through interaction and collaboration [4]. In a traditional classroom, students might read about ecosystems with pictures or watch documentaries, but the metaverse can provide an opportunity for students to immerse themselves in the ecosystems, measure water pH in a simulated rainforest stream, observe predator–prey interactions, and discuss intervention strategies with their peers in real time. Dalgarno and Lee (2010) found that 3D virtual environments significantly improve spatial knowledge, engagement, and conceptual understanding by enabling authentic and interactive tasks [5]. However, a challenge explained by cognitive load theory (Sweller, 1988) is that enriching interactions alone are not enough if they overly drain our cognitive resources [6]. Sweller distinguishes between three types of mental load:

Intrinsic load: The inherent complexity of the material [7].

Extraneous load: Mental effort wasted on poor instructional design [8].

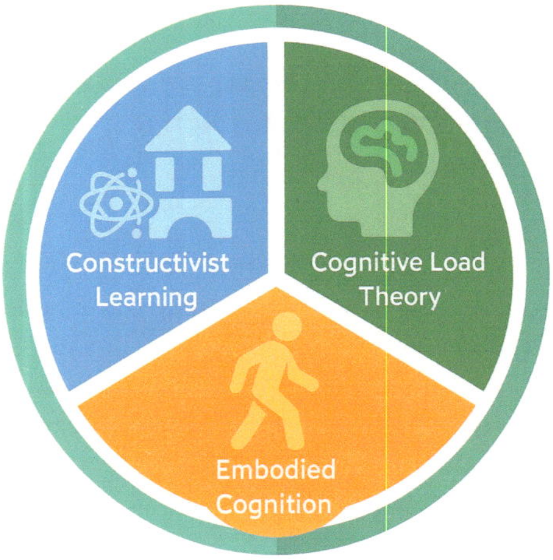

Figure 1.
Theoretical foundations of learning.

Germane load: Effort invested in building and refining mental models [9].

Traditional methods often overburden students with irrelevant demands, such as interpreting static diagrams of quantum entanglement [10]. In contrast, the metaverse directly visualizes these phenomena, allowing learners to see entangled particles react instantaneously across space [11]. By reducing extraneous load and increasing relevant load, immersive 3D models help learners focus on meaning-making rather than decoding, which is consistent with Makransky and Petersen's [12] findings that VR-based science simulations improve learning efficiency and motivation [12].

Finally, embodied cognition [13] emphasizes that thinking is deeply connected to physical movement and sensory experience [13]. In immersive environments, students can walk through a DNA double helix, bend the grid lines of a simulated space–time structure, or assemble molecular chains with their virtual hands. These kinesthetic interactions anchor abstract scientific concepts in physical experience. This connection is supported by research by Lindgren and Johnson-Glenberg [14], who showed that physical interaction in learning environments improves conceptual understanding and recall [14].

Constructivism, cognitive load theory, and embodied cognition theory collectively help to explain why immersive technologies such as the metaverse are not only visually striking but also educationally transformative [15–17]. These technologies shift science education from observing space to inhabiting it, making learning not only more engaging but also more deeply rooted in the way humans naturally construct knowledge (see **Figure 2**).

3. Challenges in traditional science education

We learn basic science concepts that form the foundation of science, such as the fact that matter is made up of tiny particles called atoms and that energy, like light and sound, travels in waves, simply by thinking about them every day. But when we move beyond these foundations and delve into topics such as atomic structure, quantum physics, and space–time, things become much more complex, and this is where many students begin to struggle. In many traditional classrooms, these difficult topics are often taught in ways that make understanding even more challenging. Here are a few examples to illustrate the challenges we face in traditional science teaching.

3.1 Atomic structure

It is often introduced using the Bohr model, in which electrons orbit the nucleus in perfect circles, like planets orbiting the sun. However, electrons are not fixed particles and behave more like waves in a natural cloud. Therefore, it is difficult to distinguish between the apparent orbital model and the actual behavior of electrons for many students.

3.2 Quantum physics

It introduces phenomena that challenge what we think we know about how the world works. Particles at the atomic nucleus level exhibit behaviors that oppose conventional thinking, such as the ability to pass through boundaries (quantum tunneling) and exist in multiple states simultaneously (superposition). These concepts are typically taught in

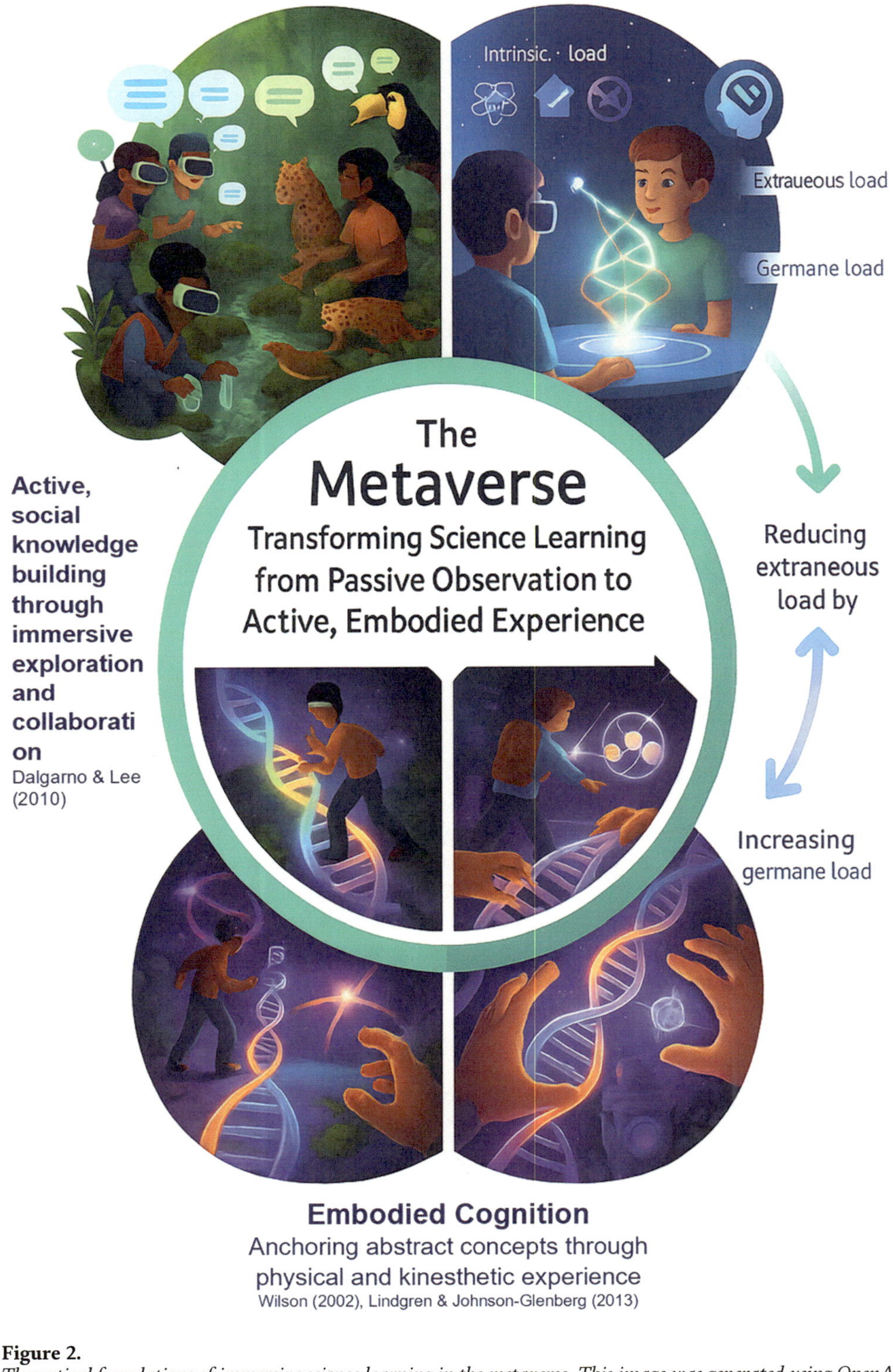

Figure 2.
Theoretical foundations of immersive science learning in the metaverse. This image was generated using OpenAI (2025, ChatGPT (DALL·E) (image generated on 11 August 2025), using the prompt "The metaverse: Transforming science learning from passive observation to active, embodied experience."

schools using complex theories and theoretical algebra, which confuses students and leaves them disconnected from the phenomena.

3.3 Space–time

It is a concept that blends the three dimensions of space (length, width, and height) with time to create a fourth-dimensional "fabric" that can be bent, stretched, and distorted. This concept is fundamental to understanding gravity and the structure of the universe in Einstein's theory of relativity. These concepts are typically taught in schools using complex theories and theoretical algebra, which confuse students and leave them disconnected from the phenomena.

In these fields, a noticeable trend arises: Conventional pedagogical approaches excessively depend on static representations, imposing a significant cognitive load on students while failing to provide experience-based foundational knowledge. This typically leads to shallow memorization instead of deep understanding, which makes people less curious and causes science to seem like a collection of random data rather than a cohesive investigation of the cosmos.

4. Metaverse: Unlocking a new dimension for scientific discovery and learning

The metaverse represents a revolutionary shift in how science is taught and experienced: Instead of passively reading textbooks and watching videos, students can enter immersive, interactive, three-dimensional worlds and actively explore complex scientific phenomena (**Figure 3**) [18–21]. Through these hands-on interactions, complex concepts are transformed into vivid, concrete experiences, making difficult concepts easier to understand and learning more enjoyable.

Here is how the metaverse directly tackles the challenges that traditional science education struggles with:

4.1 Exploring the invisible subatomic world

Suno and Ohno [22] presented "Virtual Hydrogen," a virtual reality (VR) learning tool designed to promote understanding of atomic and quantum phenomena in physical chemistry education. Their study demonstrates that VR allows learners to immerse themselves in a three-dimensional representation of the hydrogen atom, going beyond the two-dimensional illustrations of traditional textbooks. In a virtual environment, students can visualize and explore the spatial distribution of electron clouds and observe quantum mechanical effects, such as tunneling, in an interactive and intuitive manner. By translating complex theoretical concepts into experiential, manipulable phenomena, Virtual Hydrogen provides an educational bridge between formal quantum theory and student understanding, highlighting the value of VR as a tool for deepening conceptual understanding in science education [22].

4.2 Performing simulated experiments beyond the classroom

According to Saphira et al. [23], the metaverse represents a paradigm shift in STEM education by enabling science learning experiences in an immersive

Figure 3.
Traditional teaching often relies on static images and passive learning, while the metaverse enables immersive, interactive experiences that bring abstract scientific concepts to life. This image was generated using OpenAI (2025, ChatGPT (DALL·E)) (image generated on 11 August 2025), using the prompt "Traditional vs. metaverse science learning: Passive reading vs. immersive exploration."

virtual environment, where learners can safely engage in molecular- and atomic-level experiments, such as manipulating particles and combining elements, and receive instant feedback from the system. Additionally, the metaverse enables the visualization of complex scientific principles that are inaccessible in physical environments. For example, the theory of relativity phenomena, such as time dilation and space contraction, can be experienced by simulating travel at near the speed of light in an immersive environment. In this way, complex mathematical concepts can be transformed into visual, interactive experiences for deeper conceptual understanding and increased learner engagement in science education [23].

4.3 Experiencing time dilation and relativity

The visualization study by Creagh et al. (2009) and the virtual relativity studies by Boffi et al. [24] demonstrated that VR environments can simulate relativistic distortions of space–time, allowing learners to directly perceive phenomena such as time dilation and length contraction. In this interactive environment, students observe how clocks slow down and distances shrink as they approach relativistic speeds, helping them intuitively understand principles that are usually conveyed through complex mathematical formulas [24].

Furthermore, VR-based modules can extend to quantum phenomena; the modification of one particle instantaneously influences its entangled partner across virtual space (**Figure 4**), referred to by Einstein as "spooky action at a distance." Such immersive demonstrations transform theoretical abstractions into observable and manipulable experiences, fostering both conceptual comprehension and critical inquiry.

Figure 4.
Quantum entanglement: Entangled particles instantly mirror each other changes. This image was generated using OpenAI (2025, ChatGPT (DALL·E)) (image generated on 11 August 2025), using the prompt "Quantum entanglement conceptual illustration."

5. AI and metaintelligence: Personalized learning

Education has long followed a "one-size-fits-all" model: Students sit in the same classrooms, read the same textbooks, and take the same tests. But the reality is that not all students learn the same way. Some understand quickly; others take longer. Some prefer visual cues, others respond to stories, and still others learn best through hands-on experience. However, our traditional education systems are largely unable to adapt to these differences, which is where artificial intelligence (AI) and metaintelligence come in. The metaverse provides the stage for immersive learning, and AI and metaintelligence are the brains and heart that bring this stage to life [25].

Artificial intelligence acts as your personal tutor, observing your learning pace, weaknesses, and interests, and adapting the material to help you understand it better. For example, if you are faced with a problem that requires you to select a concept, AI will become your assistant and explain everything to you at your level of understanding. If it is deemed too easy, it will increase the difficulty level to maintain your interest. AI gives precise, personalized feedback tailored to your strengths and weaknesses. It even adapts to your learning style, providing visuals if you understand better with pictures, narration if you understand better with audio, and simulations if you prefer an interactive learning style [26, 27]. Numerous AI platforms we are already familiar with, such as ChatGPT and Google Socratic (which provide instant explanations in different styles based on user questions), Grammarly (which provides personalized writing improvement suggestions), Duolingo (which adapts language lessons based on user mistakes), and Consensus (which instantly extracts insights from thousands of scientific papers), demonstrate how AI can personalize both learning and innovation.

Metaintelligence is a revolutionary approach that goes beyond traditional teaching methods. It considers student mood, interaction, and motivation to detect when learners are struggling, losing attention, making more mistakes, or becoming frustrated. This system creates a more engaging learning environment for challenging subjects by slowing down lessons, changing the way material is presented, and providing supportive feedback rather than continuing unadjusted. It also enhances collaboration by pairing students and turning group activities into opportunities for joint discovery. Platforms such as Classcraft and Minecraft can turn lessons into challenges for students and reward them for attentiveness and persistence, which keeps them engaged. Research shows that AI-driven platforms such as DreamBox, Smart Sparrow, Classcraft, Minecraft, and CogBooks effectively adapt learning, improving student performance and engagement [28–31].

Artificial intelligence and metaintelligence are working together to make learning dynamic and personalized, evolving from rote learning to an experience that is tailored to each student's cognitive style, learning pace, and emotional state. The future of education may favor guided learning experiences over traditional classroom learning, allowing each student to pursue their own unique learning journey. AI provides smart adaptation, while metaintelligence provides emotional connection, and together they transform learning into an experience of discovery.

6. Case studies from the frontlines of the metaverse classroom

Case studies provide insightful information about how customized AI tools and immersive learning environments are transforming the way education is taught. **Table 1** details the problems, solutions, findings, and limitations of each study and demonstrates improved learning outcomes while highlighting the remaining challenges and gaps. Comparing these innovations side by side helps us understand their potential and the conditions for success (or failure).

6.1 ATOM: VR for learning atomic structure

In [32], Bhowmick et al. developed ATOM, a head-mounted VR learning interface designed to teach ninth-grade students about atomic structure, chemical bonding, and important historical experiments in atomic theory. In preliminary testing with 10 students, ATOM significantly increased students' interest, motivation, and playfulness. However, students also noted some usability issues with the interface [32].

Theme	Cross-case insights	Gaps/limitations	Future directions
Engagement vs. mastery	All studies reported increased curiosity, motivation, and short-term retention.	Not long-term mastery or transfer.	Conduct longitudinal studies to track sustained knowledge and real-world application.
Integration with practice	Virtual laboratories and simulations reduce risk and allow repetition.	May displace essential hands-on skills, narrowing authentic laboratory experiences.	Use blended models that combine immersive tools with physical experiments.
Assessment and curriculum fit	Tools encourage responsibility, systems thinking, and creativity.	Outcomes are often attitudinal, with weak alignment to standardized assessments or curricular goals.	Align immersive learning with curricula and formal testing frameworks.

Table 1.
Comparative synthesis of case studies.

6.2 Virtual environments in high school biology

Páez-Andrade et al. [33] conducted a case study in an Ecuadorian secondary school to evaluate the impact of a virtual environment on high school biology learning. Using a quantitative and descriptive approach with two different measurement instruments, they found that educators perceived technology-assisted learning positively. Furthermore, their findings suggest that the virtual environment supported improved academic performance and increased students' interest, attention, and motivation in biology classes [33].

6.3 Gamified virtual chemistry laboratories

In [34], Tauber et al. created two gamified virtual chemistry experiments in 2022, using interactive videos and 360-degree virtual tours. These served as a complete replacement for distance learning students and as an additional learning resource for in-person students. These virtual experiments allowed students to learn theory at their own pace while engaging in an immersive environment. When asked about this method, both groups of students were positive about it. All stated that the virtual laboratory was a great way to learn and that they valued understanding concepts over rushing to get things done. There was clear potential for this delivery method to allow educators to adapt to the Open University and distance learning paradigm [34].

6.4 Robotics and physics

Hornung et al. developed three immersive and interactive robotic learning platforms in 2023: TOURINGS, RoLe4D, and Robot Hub Academy. These platforms are aimed at manufacturing professionals, remote university students, and school-age boys and girls. Students benefit from interactive video lessons and XR environments, operate collaborative robots in virtual training, gain more hands-on experience in remote laboratories, and engage with STEM education. These projects demonstrate that robotics education is becoming more accessible and widespread, that the classroom is becoming more closely connected to the real world of work, and that people of all ages and learning levels are becoming increasingly interested in and actively participating in robotics [35].

6.5 Space exploration

In [36], Lee et al. designed an immersive virtual reality system (IVRS) that allowed students to "fly around" a scientifically accurate solar system constructed from NASA photographs. By changing perspectives, calculating distances, and dynamically moving through space, students explored planetary orbits, Earth–Moon interactions, seasonal variations, and more. Over 80% of the 22 undergraduate science education students who took the test said that IVRS significantly deepened their understanding of astronomy and increased their immersion in learning, proving that immersive virtual reality (VR) can transform abstract space science into an accessible and engaging experience [36].

6.6 Challenges in marine biology

The Marine Biology VR Learning Support System, developed by Akaike et al. in [37], immerses students in a virtual underwater world, allowing them to observe and experience realistic simulations of fish swimming. This technology aims to deepen students' understanding of the field of marine biology by providing a fun and interactive experience. VR systems allow students to explore aquatic ecosystems, observe fish behavior, and learn about marine life dynamics in a safe virtual environment. The immersive learning resource has been proven to increase understanding and engagement with complex scientific topics [37].

These studies, conducted at various levels of science education, demonstrate how emerging technologies such as the metaverse, AI, and metaintelligence are transforming traditional teaching and learning. However, their true value will depend on how well they are integrated into more equitable and inclusive educational institutions that balance innovation, rigor, accessibility, and long-term impact (**Table 1**).

7. Implementation framework: Building the future of science learning

To realize the vision of incorporating metalearning into science education, educational institutions need more than just enthusiasm; they need a clear, strategic roadmap for transforming traditional classrooms into metaverse classrooms, where students can gain hands-on experience with theoretical scientific concepts in an immersive environment. Here is how this journey unfolds:

7.1 Laying the groundwork

To provide students with an immersive experience, classrooms need to be equipped with a strong network that transports learners into immersive worlds, a stable Internet that ensures a smooth, real-time experience, haptic controllers that allow them to "feel" molecules, and spatial audio systems that create realistic soundscapes.

7.2 Crafting the experience

Developing effective metaverse technology requires collaboration between educators who understand curriculum objectives, designers who create engaging virtual worlds, and AI experts who personalize learning paths. This collaboration enables the creation of modular lessons that fit into existing science curricula for both teachers and learners and are accessible across a variety of devices, from sophisticated VR equipment to everyday smartphones.

7.3 Empowering the teachers

To navigate this new educational landscape, educators need training on how to leverage technology and new teaching methods to harness the unique possibilities of the metaverse and confidently engage students in immersive learning. Workshops on implementing immersive pedagogies and building vibrant communities of practice allow educators to share tips, solve challenges, and continue to hone their skills together.

7.4 Ethical considerations

Before, immersive technologies raised complex ethical considerations that are fundamental to educational effectiveness and learning outcomes. Case studies have shown that immersive technologies can improve engagement and short-term retention, but the impact varies depending on inclusivity, cognitive load, governance, and equitable access. Motivational tools that are effective in one setting may have limited effectiveness in another, where structural supports are weaker or underlying inequalities inhibit meaningful engagement. These characteristics, outlined in **Table 2**, overlap with the realities of the educational setting. Therefore, to create lasting and meaningful learning outcomes, ethical application must be incorporated as a fundamental element.

The success of immersive learning depends on developing strategies that align technological innovation with teacher development, organizational support, and curriculum design. Cross-disciplinary collaboration can proactively address potential gaps, from unequal access to unintended cognitive and social consequences. Immersive technologies implemented with ethical foresight can create classrooms that are engaging, inclusive, and foster deep conceptual understanding. Conversely, neglecting these considerations risks undermining both educational effectiveness and equity.

By synthesizing evidence from case studies and ethical analysis, a core principle emerges: The transformative potential of immersive science education relies not only on innovative tools but also on ethical and systemic integration. Future research, policy, and practice must focus on sustainable, accountable, and equitable approaches that support sustained learning, foster trust, and expand access.

By combining robust infrastructure, engaging content, well-prepared educators, and ethical guardrails, our institutions can successfully take metaverse science education from a futuristic concept to an everyday classroom reality, connecting students with the wonder of science.

Dimension	Critical issue	Implications	Proposed solutions
Equity and access	Expensive VR/AI tools; lack of teacher support.	Risk of wider achievement gaps and dual-level education.	Public–private collaborations, small-scale designs, grants, and teacher preparation.
Data governance and privacy	Collection of biometric, behavioral, and performance data.	Potential surveillance, misuse, and lack of informed consent.	Transparency, voluntary agreement, privacy, and unbiased supervision.
Bias and inclusivity	Narrow datasets reinforcing stereotypes.	Minority students are excluded, and adaptive feedback is unfair.	Inclusive data collection, algorithmic transparency, participatory design.
Well-being and cognitive load	Overstimulation, VR-induced discomfort, cognitive overload.	Frustration, mental fatigue, developmental risks.	Developmental boundaries, structured experiences, and hybrid learning models.
Ethical integration	Lack of systemic frameworks.	Inconsistent hiring: Ethical risks remain.	Cross-sector collaboration, standards, policy guidance, teacher ethical literacy.

Table 2.
Ethical considerations.

Figure 5.
Global learners united through AI-powered immersive education. This image was generated using OpenAI (2025, ChatGPT (DALL·E)) (image generated on 11 August 2025), using the prompt "AI-assisted global digital learning environment."

The fusion of AI, metaintelligence, and the metaverse promises to dramatically transform science education. By incorporating these cutting-edge tools, we can unlock the full potential of science education, fostering curiosity, expanding knowledge, and nurturing the success of the next generation. Imagine a future where classrooms are connected not by walls or borders but by continents, and students from all over the world come together in the same virtual environment (**Figure 5**). This distributed learning environment removes geographical limitations, making high-quality science education accessible to everyone, anywhere, and anytime.

8. Conclusion

The combination of AI, metaintelligence, and the metaverse represents a paradigm shift in science education, where using these tools can transform theoretical concepts into immersive, interactive experiences, moving from memorization to true conceptual understanding. In a metaverse classroom, students can actively explore scientific reality by observing electron orbitals, walking through atoms, and interacting directly with the dynamics of physical and quantum systems. This shift from explanation to experience creates new possibilities for customizable, flexible learning paths that meet the needs of diverse learners. However, careful assessment of infrastructure, accessibility, and ethical implications is essential for successful implementation. The ability to reimagine the teaching and learning of complex scientific concepts through immersive education holds the potential to ultimately improve understanding, retention, and impact for future generations.

Acknowledgments

The author is thankful to Jeonbuk National University, Jeonju, South Korea, for facilitating the completion of this chapter.

Conflict of interest

The author declares no conflict of interest.

Author details

Sana Jamshaid
Department of Chemistry, Jeonbuk National University, Jeonju, South Korea

*Address all correspondence to: sanajamshaid41@gmail.com; sanajamshaid@jbnu.ac.kr

References

[1] Ausubel DP. The Acquisition and Retention of Knowledge: A Cognitive View. Springer Science & Business Media Dordrecht, Originally published by Kluwer Academic Publishers 2000, eBook Published in 2012; DOI: 10.1007/978-94-015-9454-7

[2] Ausubel DP. Preview of basic concepts of meaningful reception learning and retention. In: The Acquisition and Retention of Knowledge: A Cognitive View. Dordrecht: Springer, Netherlands; 2000: 38–66. DOI: 10.1007/978-94-015-9454-7_3

[3] Kim JW, Ritter FE, Koubek RJ. An integrated theory for improved skill acquisition and retention in the three stages of learning. Theoretical Issues in Ergonomics Science. 2013;**14**(1):22–37. DOI: 10.1080/1464536X.2011.573008

[4] Oeberst A, Halatchliyski I, Kimmerle J, Cress U. Knowledge construction in Wikipedia: A systemic-constructivist analysis. Journal of the Learning Sciences. 2014;**23** (2):149–176. DOI: 10.1080/10508406.2014.888352

[5] Lee MJ, Dalgarno B. Scaffolding discovery learning in 3D virtual environments: Challenges and considerations for instructional design. In: Virtual Immersive and 3D Learning Spaces: Emerging Technologies and Trends Edited by Shalin Hai-Jew . Hershey, PA: IGI Global Scientific Publishing; 2011. p. 138–169. DOI: 10.4018/978-1-61692-825-4.ch008

[6] Абдукаххорова М, Хазраткулова Э. Cognitive load theory and its application for learning. Инновации В Современной Лингвистике И Преподавании Языков. 2025;**1**(1):143–145. DOI: 10.47689/ZTTCTOI-vol1-iss1-pp143-145

[7] Sweller J. Cognitive load theory, learning difficulty, and instructional design. Learning and Instruction. 1994;**4**(4):295–312. DOI: 10.1016/0959-4752(94)90003-5

[8] Van Merriënboer JJG, Ayres P. Research on cognitive load theory and its design implications for e-learning. Educational Technology Research and Development. 2005;**53**(3):5–13. DOI: 10.1007/BF02504793

[9] Leppink J, van Gog T, Paas F, Sweller J. Cognitive load theory: Researching and planning teaching to maximise learning. In: Cleland, Jennifer, J. Durning, Steven. Researching Medical Education. Wiley-Blackwell; 2015. p. 207–218. DOI: 10.1002/9781118838983.ch18.

[10] Ruan S, Yuan R, Guan Q, Lin Y, Mao Y, Jiang W, et al. Venus: A geometrical representation for quantum state visualization. Computer Graphics Forum. 2023;**42**(3):247–258. DOI: 10.1111/cgf.14827

[11] Fickler R, Krenn M, Lapkiewicz R, Ramelow S, Zeilinger A. Real-time imaging of quantum entanglement. Scientific Reports. 2013;**3**(1):1914. DOI: 10.1038/srep01914

[12] Makransky G, Petersen GB. The cognitive affective model of immersive learning (CAMIL): A theoretical research-based model of learning in immersive virtual reality. Educational Psychology Review. 2021;**33**(3):937–958. DOI: 10.1007/s10648-020-09586-2

[13] Wilson M. Six views of embodied cognition. Psychonomic Bulletin & Review. 2002;**9**(4):625–636. DOI: 10.3758/BF03196322

[14] Lindgren R, Johnson-Glenberg M. Emboldened by embodiment: Six precepts for research on embodied learning and mixed reality. Educational Researcher. 2013;**42**(8):445–452. DOI: 10.3102/0013189X13511661

[15] Kye B, Han N, Kim E, Park Y, Jo S. Educational applications of metaverse: Possibilities and limitations. Journal of Educational Evaluation for Health Professions. 2021;**18**:32. DOI: 10.3352/jeehp.2021.18.32

[16] Onu P, Pradhan A, Mbohwa C. Potential to use metaverse for future teaching and learning. Education and Information Technologies. 2024;**29**(7):8893–8924. DOI: 10.1007/s10639-023-12167-9

[17] Chamola V, Peelam MS, Mittal U, Hassija V, Singh A, Pareek R, et al. Metaverse for education: Developments, challenges, and future direction. Computer Applications in Engineering Education. 2025;**33**(3):e70018. DOI: 10.1002/cae.70018

[18] Matovu H, Ungu DAK, Won M, Tsai CC, Treagust DF, Mocerino M, Tasker R. Immersive virtual reality for science learning: Design, implementation, and evaluation. Studies in Science Education. 2023;**59**(2):205–244. DOI: 10.1080/03057267.2022.2082680

[19] Cooper G, Thong LP, Tang KS. Transforming science education with virtual reality: An immersive representations model. Educational Media International. 2024;**61**(3):229–251. DOI: 10.1080/09523987.2024.2389348

[20] Kuhail MA, ElSayary A, Farooq S, Alghamdi A. Exploring immersive learning experiences: A survey. Informatics. 2022;**9**(4):75. DOI: 10.3390/informatics9040075

[21] Tene T, Guevara M, Moreano G, Vera J, Vacacela Gomez C. The role of immersive virtual realities: Enhancing science learning in higher education. Emerging Science Journal. 2024;**8**:88–102. DOI: 10.28991/ESJ-2024-SIED1-06

[22] Suno H, Ohno N. Virtual Hydrogen, a virtual reality education tool in physics and chemistry. Procedia Computer Science. 2023;**25**:2283–2291. DOI: 10.1016/j.procs.2023.10.219

[23] Saphira HV, Prahani BK, Hariyono E, Marianus M. Metaverse: A paradigm shift in STEM education for science learning beyond the review. E3S Web of Conferences. 2024;**482**:04004. DOI: 10.1051/e3sconf/202448204004

[24] Boffi A, Puppin E, Contran M. 20 July. Virtual relativity: An interactive simulation of the special theory of relativity in virtual reality. arXiv. 2024. DOI: 10.48550/arXiv.2408.01442

[25] Almeman K, EL Ayeb F, Berrima M, Issaoui B, Morsy H. The integration of AI and metaverse in education: A systematic literature review. Applied Sciences. 2025;**15**(2):863. DOI: 10.3390/app15020863

[26] Chen L, Chen P, Lin Z. Artificial intelligence in education: A review. IEEE Access. 2020;**8**:75264–75278. DOI. 10.1109/ACCESS.2020.2988510

[27] Holmes W, Tuomi I. State of the art and practice in AI in education. European Journal of Education. 2022; **57**(4):542–570. DOI: 10.1111/ejed.12530

[28] Putra A, Gram D, Stefanou C, Santoro D. The use of adaptive learning technology to enhance learning in clinical veterinary dermatology. Journal of Veterinary Medical Education. 2022;**9**(1):118–125. DOI: 10.3138/jvme-2020-0069

[29] Foster ME. Evaluating the impact of supplemental computer-assisted math instruction in elementary school: A conceptual replication. Journal of Research on Educational Effectiveness. 2024;**17**(1):94–118. DOI: 10.1080/19345747.2023.2174919

[30] Barbieri CA, Rodrigues J, Dyson N, Jordan NC. Improving fraction understanding in sixth graders with mathematics difficulties: Effects of a number line approach combined with cognitive learning strategies. Journal of Educational Psychology. 2020;**112**(3):628–643. DOI: 10.1037/edu0000383

[31] Slattery EJ, Butler D, O'Leary M, Marshall K. Teachers' experiences of using Minecraft Education in primary school: An Irish perspective. Irish Educational Studies. 2023;**43**(4):965–984. DOI: 10.1080/03323315.2023.2185276

[32] Bhowmick S, Kaushik A, Bhatia R, Sorathia K. ATOM: HMD-VR interface to learn atomic structure, bonding and historical research experiments. Proceedings of the 26th ACM Symposium on Virtual Reality Software and Technology. 2020;pp1–2. DOI: 10.1145/3385956.3422120

[33] Páez-Andrade M, Pazos-Espinoza K, Pérez-Silva P, Galarza CR. Virtual environments in learning the biology of high school students. intelligent human systems integration (IHSI 2022). Integrating People and Intelligent Systems. 2022;**22**(22). DOI: 10.54941/ahfe100977

[34] Tauber AL, Levonis SM, Schweiker SS. Gamified virtual laboratory experience for in-person and distance students. Journal of Chemical Education. 2022;**99**(3):1183–1189. DOI: 10.1021/acs.jchemed.1c00642

[35] Hornung L, Puljiz D, Augenstein P, Gonzalez C, Wurll C, Bellalouna F. Fostering robotics education through immersive and interactive learning content. in edulearn23 proceedings. IATED. 2023:6425–6433. DOI: 10.21125/edulearn.2023.1708

[36] Lee H, Park ST, Kim HS, Lee H Students' understanding of astronomical concepts enhanced by an immersive Virtual Reality system (IVRS). In: 3rd International Conference on Multimedia and Information and Communication Technologies in Education. Available from: https://citeseerx.ist.psu.edu/document?repid=rep1&type=pdf&doi=666be0141d6df58d8b7de56729fa27eefe3f3125 [Accessed: 2005-June]

[37] Akaike M, Takishita Y, Wenjun L, Hoshino J. Nicograph International (NICOInt), Tokyo, Japan, 2021; 2021:86–89. DOI: 10.1109/NICOINT52941.2021.00023

Chapter 4

Integrating Extended Reality and Artificial Intelligence in Education: Training, Challenges, and Reflections from Pre- and In-Service Teachers

Stavros Pitsikalis and Ilona-Elefteryja Lasica

Abstract

This paper presents the design, implementation, and evaluation of a professional development programme conducted in Greece (Rhodes Island) during 2024–2025, focusing on the integration of extended reality (XR) and artificial intelligence (AI) in education. A total of 101 teachers (53 pre-service, 48 in-service) participated in five training sessions that combined theoretical input, hands-on exploration, and scenario-based instructional design. Grounded in Digital Competence of Educators (DigCompEdu), Technological Pedagogical Content Knowledge (TPACK), and the Cognitive Affective Model of Immersive Learning (CAMIL), the programme positioned teachers as designers of immersive and AI-enhanced learning activities rather than passive tool users. Mixed-methods evaluation, including questionnaires, focus groups, artefact analysis, and observation, revealed strong intentions to integrate XR/AI, heightened self-efficacy, and recognition of motivational gains for students. Key supports identified included access to ready-to-use lesson scenarios, mentoring, device availability, IT assistance, and leadership backing. Barriers centred on time constraints, infrastructure, and curricular rigidity. The findings underscore the importance of extending existing competence frameworks to address immersive pedagogy and ethical AI use, while situating XR/AI integration within the realities of institutional and national contexts. The paper concludes with recommendations for sustainable adoption, emphasising infrastructure investment, leadership engagement, ethical safeguards, and continuous communities of practice.

Keywords: adult education, teacher professional development, extended reality, artificial intelligence, virtual reality, augmented reality

1. Introduction

The educational landscape is changing fast. Technologies like extended reality (XR) – including virtual reality (VR), augmented reality (AR), and mixed reality (MR) – and artificial intelligence (AI) are no longer just experimental; they have become standard classroom tools [1]. XR often stands out for its set of affordances that matter for learning: presence, interactivity, adaptability, and scalability. Together, these elements create learning experiences that go beyond what traditional classrooms can typically offer [2]. Within the broader rise of metaverse-style learning spaces, XR and AI can be combined to create persistent, shared environments where teachers and students work together, practice difficult tasks, and create resources from different locations, all related to curriculum goals. Typical examples include the safe practice of high-risk procedures, virtual field trips, embodied exploration of abstract ideas, and spatial problem-solving with peers who are not in the same room [1–6]. In parallel, AI supports personalised practice, instruction that adapts to the learner, and content generation, which can improve daily teaching if used wisely [7, 8]. In short, XR and AI can be combined to design inquiry-based, hands-on, context-rich activities across different subjects, which can lead to better knowledge, motivation, and performance [9]. In teacher training, XR also provides a safe space to practice managing a classroom or having difficult conversations, while AI can give clear prompts and analyses that encourage reflection [10]. Government policies at the national and European levels include both areas in their plans for digital and media skills; the EU's Digital Education Action Plan mentions that they are important for both initial and continuing teacher education [11, 12].

In reality, practice lags behind what is possible. Tools arrive before teachers have enough time or structured support to integrate them [13]. Established frameworks, such as Digital Competence of Educators (DigCompEdu) [11], have improved confidence with general digital tools, but they have not been revised to fully include the details of immersive, multi-sensory settings or the practical issues of AI-driven data analysis and customized teaching [4]. Studies also point out a group of needs that arise when schools try to use XR/AI: spatial instructional approaches, immersive assessment, presence management, ethics and privacy concerns in avatar-mediated spaces, and ways to manage a classroom and student well-being [5, 6, 13]. Many teachers feel comfortable with mainstream technology but report limited familiarity when the context shifts to immersive media or AI-supported teaching [10]. This is more visible where device access, support from school leaders, and clear policy guidance vary across regions.

Given this situation, this chapter discusses a systematic evaluation of a teacher professional development (TPD) programme delivered in 2024–2025. The programme ran across five sessions with 101 participants (53 pre-service; 48 in-service) and focused on activities using XR and AI. Instead of focusing on basic technical skills, the program emphasised scenario-based, practice-centred design, drawing on DigCompEdu [11], the Technological Pedagogical Content Knowledge (TPACK) model [14], and the Cognitive Affective Model of Immersive Learning (CAMIL) [15]. Hands-on exploration, reflection, and collaborative design were key components, intended to reveal both the benefits and limitations as perceived by different groups of teachers.

This chapter has two main contributions. First, it gives a roadmap for using XR/AI in teacher education in a way that is sustainable and inclusive, based on data. It shows how a structured XR/AI TPD affects intentions and confidence and identifies the teacher skills that are most affected: professional engagement, immersive scenario design, assessment, and learner empowerment. Second, it identifies the pedagogical, technical, and institutional supports that teachers say they need to keep using XR and AI regularly in the Greek context, translating those insights into practical plans for teacher preparation, institutional policy, and technology design. The chapter uses a mixed-methods design – questionnaires, focus groups, participants' artefacts, and reflective observation – to address two research questions:

(RQ1) How does taking part in a structured XR/AI professional development program affect teachers' intentions and confidence in using these technologies in their teaching?

(RQ2) What pedagogical, technical, and institutional supports do teachers identify as necessary for implementing XR and AI in a sustained way?

2. Theoretical framework

This section reviews how XR and AI are used across school, vocational, and higher education, and what tends to help or hinder adoption. It describes key ideas, typical applications in teacher education, and TPD models that move beyond 'tools training' to effective instruction. It then talks about core competence frameworks – DigCompEdu, TPACK, and CAMIL – and notes how these are being extended for immersive contexts. It ends with a framework that guided the training design and later analysis.

2.1 XR and AI in education and TPD: Current state and potential

XR is now used across all educational levels. Three mechanisms appear repeatedly in evaluations [1, 3]. First, presence and agency: learners act within a coherent 3D scene rather than watching from the outside. This can support attention and motivation when cognitive load is managed. Second, embodiment and spatiality: abstract structures (like anatomical, architectural, and geographic) become manipulable in space, helping learners connect multiple representations. Third, safe rehearsal: procedures and teaching methods can be practised without real-world risk and then reviewed in debrief [15, 16]. Reviews and project syntheses report steady gains in involvement and conceptual understanding when experiences are purposefully designed and paired with activities before and after the experience [16–19]. In teacher education, common uses include classroom-management simulations, 360° video cases for practicing sensitive conversations, role-playing parent–teacher meetings, micro-teaching and observation in simulated classrooms, practicing accommodations in special education, and socio-emotional awareness scenarios. Each of these is usually paired with a structured introduction and guided review so that ideas can be transferred back to classroom practice [13, 16–18].

AI is used with XR and in standalone ways. In immersive activities, AI can offer prompts that adapt to the learner, perform data analysis, convert speech to text, and provide translation to increase access, as well as enable easy content creation [8, 10]. Separately, AI supports lesson and assessment design (drafting objectives, rubrics, and question banks), conversational tutoring, automated feedback on writing or code, and analytics integrated with learning platforms [7, 8]. Most guidance recommends using AI where it supports activities and feedback while keeping pedagogy and curriculum in mind [8].

At the policy level, EU and national initiatives increasingly recognise XR and AI in teacher-development agendas and are taking practical steps to integrate them into training [16]. The Council of the EU has urged member countries to embed 'digital pedagogy' – including immersive XR and AI – within initial teacher education and to support in-service upskilling [20]. European strategy documents similarly note that AI, VR/AR, and related technologies are reshaping educators' roles and expect teachers to co-design effective learning experiences [21]. Projects across Europe reflect this. In Greece, the Erasmus + PAX project proposed a pedagogical model for XR in teacher education with modules on literacies, immersive scenario design, and assessment [18, 22]. MetaCivicEdu implemented immersive civic education scenarios supported by AI-driven design tools such as CADMOS and ChatGPT, offering blended training for future instructional designers [9, 10, 23]. The shared aim is to align initial and continuing preparation with technological innovation so teachers can adopt XR/AI with confidence and purpose.

TPD programmes for XR and AI tend to have more impact when they frame educators as designers of learning, not only as tool users [10, 13]. Research on teachers as designers shows that professional growth increases when educators iteratively plan, enact, and reflect on technology-enhanced activities with authentic curriculum goals in mind, supported by design representations that make pedagogical intent visible [24–26]. Short conceptual inputs combined with hands-on design and experimentation – e.g., micro-teaching in simulations or rapid prototyping of immersive scenarios – help build confidence and practical judgment [27]. These programs commonly have the same structure: a short introduction to explain goals and roles, a guided experience with XR/AI (often in pairs or small groups, rotating through teacher, learner, and observer roles), and a debrief using artefacts (screenshots, short clips, notes) to link experience to assessment, accessibility, and classroom management [9, 10, 13, 18]. This structure enables participants to connect interaction patterns – like taking turns in spaces with many users or giving prompts in an AI tutor – to inclusion and curriculum goals, while developing a common language for feedback.

Working together between developers and educators is also important. A recent European project [17] uses a stepwise Capture → Plan → Realise → Apply process to move curriculum needs to implementations that are ready for the classroom. Capture explains the learning problem and context; Plan specifies didactic flow, roles, assessment evidence, and accessibility checkpoints; Realise selects or builds the XR/AI experience; and Apply focuses on classroom trials and changes. Following this has led developer teams to add features teachers ask for (pause/resume, timers within the experience, data analysis that can be exported), which improves usability and integration [19]. Instructional design guidance specific to immersive media – such as task size, navigation hints, and review examples – supports creating designs that are scalable and useful for teaching [2, 28].

Within TPD, AI is increasingly applied beyond its role in classroom scenarios. Teacher-design teams mainly use AI to draft learning objectives, create rubrics, generate question banks and scenario descriptions, or synthesise peer feedback into concrete next steps [7, 8]. In our view, this accelerates the process without displacing pedagogical judgment: teachers still set intent, verify accuracy, and adapt outputs to learner profiles and equity aims [29]. For collaborative XR tasks, emerging theory suggests that clear role scripts, shared task views, and reflection prompts make a difference – elements that can be rehearsed in TPD and later reused in classroom practice [15].

Finally, practical support tools help enactment. Scenario cards mapped to DigCompEdu domains, setup and safety checklists for different devices, and ready-to-use reflection protocols for both teachers and students create continuity across groups and contexts [9, 18]. New XR-specific competence descriptions give quick prompts – what to explain, observe, and document for assessment – that are useful to novices and experienced educators alike [2, 4].

2.2 Digital competence frameworks

The European Framework for the DigCompEdu sets out 22 educator competences across six areas: professional engagement, digital resources, teaching and learning, assessment, empowering learners, and facilitating learners' digital competence. It also describes progression across six proficiency levels (A1–C2). In practice, it helps with goal-setting, self-assessment, and programme planning and evaluation [11]. Immersive, multi-user environments add requirements beyond the original descriptors. Teacher groups working with XR report common needs, such as managing synchronous 3D activities (clear roles, turn-taking routines, and virtual safety zones), managing presence and agency while pacing cognitive load, gathering evidence from interaction data (e.g., logs, screenshots) for assessment, and planning review examples that support reflection. Accessibility, physical safety, and data protection also need explicit attention in shared virtual spaces [16–18]. In response, recent initiatives suggest XR-oriented extensions to the DigCompEdu – often in the form of card sets and planning aids that align each domain with real classroom practices and prompts for briefing, enactment, and debrief – so teachers can work within a familiar framework while addressing XR-specific decisions [2, 4, 16–18].

TPACK adds to DigCompEdu by asking how content, pedagogy, and technology come together in a particular lesson design, rather than treating these domains separately. In XR/AI contexts, this is often enriched with constructs from immersive-learning research, especially the CAMIL, which explains how presence, agency, and cognitive/affective load shape learning and offers practical guidance on giving signals, managing speed, and reviewing [14, 15]. A growing stream of work translates this into 'enriched TPACK' ideas for immersive lessons: align XR tasks with explicit outcomes and qualification frameworks, specify navigational hints and interaction granularity, and plan for assessment examples that can be captured during or after the experience [2, 28]. Where AI is also part of the design process, complementary guidance helps teams decide where AI supports planning (e.g., drafting objectives, creating rubrics), feedback, and analytics while maintaining educators' autonomy [29].

Used together, DigCompEdu (and its XR-focused extensions), TPACK, CAMIL, and related design guidance provide a solid basis for listing competence goals, making principled design choices, and preparing assessment and reflection processes that fit XR/AI-enhanced teaching [2, 4, 11, 14–16, 18, 28, 29].

2.3 Challenges and considerations

Findings from reviews and fieldwork tend to agree on a small set of conditions that shape adoption and continued use. **Figure 1** summarises these conditions.

Practically, programmes pay attention to device availability and sharing, classroom space and safety (clear play areas, cable management, supervision), network reliability, and routines for setup and maintenance (checklists, charging, updates). Institutions that specify who prepares the equipment, how long the setup takes, and where the devices are stored tend to move from pilots to regular use more smoothly [5, 16–19]. Pedagogically, effective implementations start from clear learning outcomes and bring XR/AI into a lesson only where it adds value compared to existing methods. Design work specifies brief–experience–debrief sequences, scaffolds, and evidence of learning to be captured during or after the activity. Provision for accessible alternatives is made – desktop views, captions, narration, or alternative inputs – so all learners can participate [2, 6, 24–26].

At an organisational level, there is a need for clarity around permission, privacy, and data flows in multi-user platforms, timetabling that fits device logistics, and

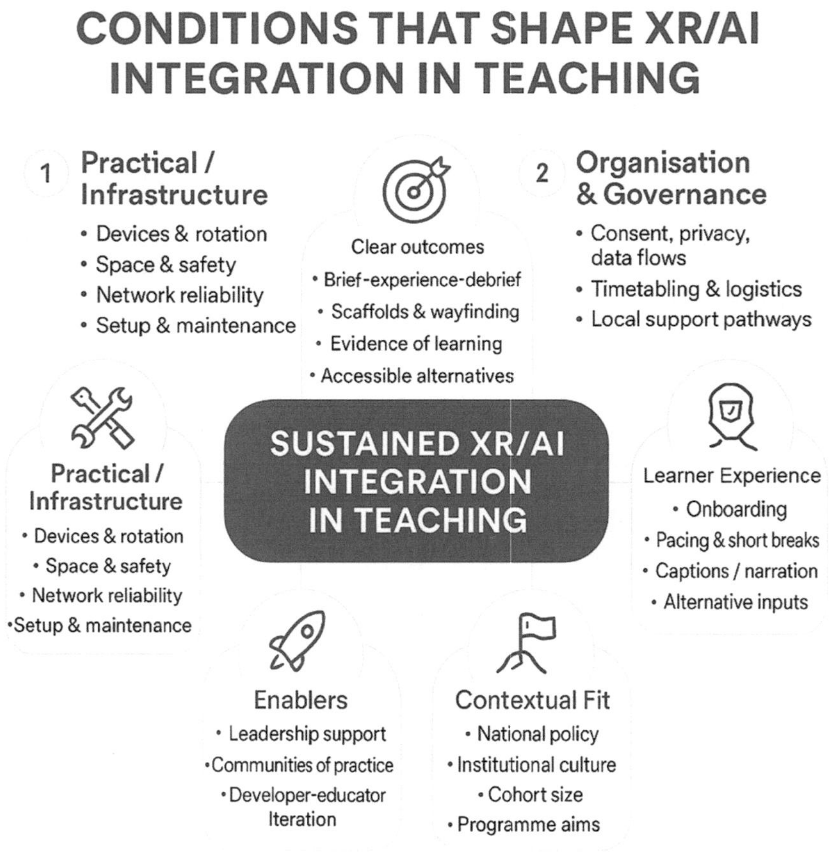

Figure 1.
Conditions that shape XR/AI integration in teaching (partially created with AI tools ChatGPT/DALL-E).

local support pathways (who to contact when something fails). These concerns align with European guidance on digital education and the integration of emerging technologies in teacher preparation and continuing professional development [12, 19–21].

Paying attention to the learner experience is also important. Short onboarding sequences help first-time users; sessions are paced with brief breaks to reduce motion sickness; captions and narration support understanding; and alternative inputs are available where needed. These measures are associated with stronger engagement and more equitable participation in evaluations of immersive activities [2, 5, 6, 16]. Finally, several enablers recur: leadership support (time allocations, device pools, micro-credentials), communities of practice (peer mentoring, co-teaching, scenario sharing), and switching between developers and educators to improve features based on classroom feedback. Ready-to-use reflection tools – for instance, structured focus-group prompts – offer reliable ways to review experience, learning, and transfer to everyday teaching [16–19, 24–26, 30]. Context still matters – policy, school culture, group size, programme aims. Approaches that adapt to local conditions while keeping a consistent pedagogical structure (brief–experience–debrief) tend to be more sustainable [16–18].

3. Methodology

This study examined the outcomes of a structured TPD programme using a mixed-methods design. The approach integrated a post-training questionnaire, researchers' observation notes, examples of participants' artefacts, and short semi-structured focus group discussions. The goal was to understand not only whether the programme changed self-reported competence and intentions, but also how teachers understood the pedagogical, technical, and institutional conditions for sustained use. Quantitative items provided breadth; qualitative materials added depth.

A total of 101 teachers, both pre-service and in-service, took part across five independent sessions (October 2024–April 2025). The design was intended to create evidence about individual skill/confidence and about the contextual factors that help or hinder the integration of immersive and AI-enhanced pedagogies.

3.1 Research design

In this research, we adopted a convergent parallel mixed-methods design [31, 32]. Quantitative and qualitative data were collected in parallel, analysed separately, and then brought together for interpretation. The focus was on three outcomes:

- self-assessed competences,
- intentions to integrate XR/AI, and
- perceived enablers and barriers across pedagogical, technical, and institutional dimensions.

The main data source was a post-session questionnaire. This was complemented by (a) structured observation notes recorded by the researchers (who also served as trainers), (b) thematic analysis of indicative participant artefacts (lesson plans, immersive scenarios, AI-generated resources), and (c) short semi-structured focus groups at the end of selected sessions. The combination allowed triangulation and aligns with recommendations for evaluating TPD enhanced with technology [4, 11, 14–16, 31, 32].

While the mixed-methods approach provided a detailed and multi-layered account of participants' experiences, the study is constrained by several factors. Data were limited to immediate post-training measures and reflections, which are informative but time-bound; they do not capture longer-term transfer into classroom practice. The sample was geographically concentrated (Rhodes) and composed of a specific mix of in-service and pre-service teachers with strong academic backgrounds. The findings should be read as showing trends within this context rather than being broadly representative.

3.2 Participants

In total, 101 teachers (74 female and 27 male) participated across five training sessions held between October 2024 and April 2025 on the island of Rhodes, Greece. Ages ranged from 20 to 54 years; pre-service teachers were mainly between 20 and 24, while in-service teachers covered a wider range. Recruitment utilised institutional mailing lists, partner networks, and invitations during dissemination events. Participation was voluntary and not compensated.

The in-service teachers (*n* = 48) came from different fields – mathematics, science, IT, social studies, languages, religious education, and history. All held at least a Master's degree, while some were current students or graduates of the MSc in New Forms of Education and Learning (NFEL) at the University of the Aegean. Their professional experience ranged from early-career (<5 years) to highly experienced teachers (>20 years). The pre-service teachers (*n* = 53) were bachelor-level students enrolled in the Department of Preschool Education Sciences & Educational Design (TEPAES) at the University of the Aegean. Most were in their final or second-to-last year of study. They knew the basics of educational technology but had limited hands-on experience with XR/AI in teaching. **Table 1** presents the distribution of participants by session and demographic composition.

Training session	Total participants	In-service teachers	Pre-service teachers	Female	Male	Average age
1	10	**10**	**0**	7	3	42,3
2	9	**9**	**0**	6	3	41,7
3	34	**16**	**18**	25	9	33,6
4	23	**13**	**10**	16	7	31,7
5	25	**0**	**25**	20	5	21,2
Total	**101**	**48**	**53**			

Table 1.
Participants' distribution by training session.

The study population was geographically similar (Rhodes) but different in career stages, subject backgrounds, and qualifications – which was helpful for comparing perspectives between in-service and pre-service teachers.

3.3 Professional development programme structure

The XR/AI TPD programme was delivered as five independent sessions, each lasting about three hours, structured around a brief–experience–debrief cycle common in immersive learning contexts [15, 18, 27]. Short inputs were blended with hands-on exploration, collaborative design, and guided reflection. Core thematic areas included: (a) basics of XR/AI in education (benefits, limits, ethics), (b) immersive scenario design through rapid prototyping, (c) AI-supported planning and assessment (objectives, rubrics, reflective prompts), (d) managing a classroom in XR environments with many users, and (e) assessment methods appropriate for immersive learning.

The curriculum was based on DigCompEdu [11], TPACK [14], and the CAMIL [15]. **Table 2** maps frameworks to XR-specific competences and example activities. Teachers were positioned not simply as technology users but as designers of learning experiences [24–26]. DigCompEdu informed the competence targets (e.g., digital content creation, pedagogical use, learner empowerment). Following the XR-specific extensions proposed by PAX [4], we

Framework/ Dimension	XR-enriched competences	Example training activities
DigCompEdu – digital content creation	Design immersive resources with spatial presence and embodied interaction aligned to objectives.	Group design of 360° science field trips; AI-assisted 3D objects for history.
DigCompEdu – pedagogical use	Adapt immersive tools to curricular goals; manage XR for many users; add accessibility.	Accessible XR language modules with translation and adjustable interaction modes.
DigCompEdu – learner empowerment	Foster agency using roles, exploratory tasks, and adaptive feedback in XR.	Peer-led immersive debates with AI-generated reflection prompts.
TPACK – technological knowledge	Select/use XR/AI tools with attention to specific benefits.	Headset setup; XR app choice; AI resource generation.
TPACK – pedagogical knowledge	Blend active learning strategies with XR/AI benefits.	Project-based XR tasks in math and social studies.
TPACK – content knowledge	Ensure subject accuracy and connection within XR-enhanced content.	XR history tours with accurate timelines, AI narration, and contextual artefacts.
CAMIL – cognitive processing	Manage cognitive load with short, scaffolded tasks, and debrief.	Short VR lab simulations; guided debrief on results.
CAMIL – emotional engagement	Build emotional connection through story and perspective.	VR role-plays on cultural empathy and inclusion.
CAMIL – motivational alignment	Balance challenge and skill; connect to inner goals.	Gamified XR challenges connected to the curriculum with personalised feedback.

Table 2.
Mapping frameworks to XR-specific competences and example activities.

included competences for spatial presence, embodied interaction, multi-user classroom management, and accessibility. TPACK required participants to connect what they were teaching, how they were teaching it, and XR/AI choices explicitly. The CAMIL informed sequencing to manage cognitive load and support emotion/motivation: short immersive activities, clear introductions, and structured reflections to combine learning.

Participants worked with standalone VR headsets, 360° video platforms, and collaborative virtual environments to explore immersive simulations, heritage tours, and civic debates. For AI, they used tools such as ChatGPT to co-create learning objectives, rubrics, and write prompts [8, 29]. Tools were chosen for school-friendly adoption and educational licensing. Previous involvement in European projects (PAX, MetaCivicEdu) provided access to tested pedagogical frameworks and XR/AI tools validated in real settings [9, 10, 18, 23].

Throughout the programme, participants rotated between the roles of designer, learner, and peer reviewer. As designers, participants created immersive scenarios or AI-enhanced lesson plans aligned with curriculum goals. As learners, they experienced their peers' scenarios. As peer reviewers, they used checklists derived from DigCompEdu and CAMIL to comment on accessibility, engagement, and pedagogical structure. Seeing a design from multiple angles helped participants anticipate challenges with classroom management and adapt scenarios to different learner needs [4, 11, 14, 15].

Assessment was part of the learning process instead of being a separate component. Peers and researchers offered feedback during presentations, and reflection protocols prompted links to classroom practice [24–26, 33]. Each participant left with a tangible artefact (scenario or lesson plan) and a plan for applying it soon.

3.4 Data collection tools

Data were collected through four sources to support triangulation (**Table 3**): (a) a post-training questionnaire, (b) researchers' observation notes, (c) participant-created artefacts, and (d) short focus group discussions.

Tool	Purpose	Example outputs
Post-training questionnaire	Capture self-assessed competence gains, intentions, perceived enablers/barriers, and feedback on design.	Likert ratings, written suggestions, and examples of planned XR/AI lessons.
Researchers' observation notes	Document interactions, role-rotation, and responses to technical/pedagogical challenges.	Time-stamped notes; short quotes; setup observations.
Participant-generated artefacts	Assess alignment with objectives, XR/AI integration, and accessibility.	360° field trips, virtual history walks, and language dialogues with comfort settings.
Focus group discussions	Find out shared reflections and priorities; compare pre-service and in-service perspectives.	Transcripts with points of agreement, differences, and practical suggestions.

Table 3.
Overview of data collection tools.

3.4.1 Post-training questionnaire

A structured questionnaire was provided immediately after each session, with thematic sections that captured:

- Competence perceptions aligned with DigCompEdu and its XR enrichment (e.g., 'I can design immersive resources that align with curricular goals'/'I can manage multi-user XR activities with equitable participation') [4, 11, 16–18].
- Intention to integrate XR/AI within the next school period (e.g., I intend to use XR/AI in at least one lesson within the next three months').
- Perceived enablers/barriers at pedagogical, technical, and institutional levels (e.g., 'Lack of time for classroom setup limits XR use'; 'School network capacity is sufficient for XR/AI activities').
- Training design feedback (clarity, pacing, usefulness of role rotation, adequacy of safety/accessibility guidance).

The questionnaire combined five-point Likert items with open-ended questions/statements (e.g., "Name one scenario you would implement next and what support you would need") and a short demographic section. Competence items were based on DigCompEdu and PAX XR-specific descriptors (digital content creation; pedagogical use; learner empowerment; presence/embodiment; multi-user classroom management; accessibility), while intention and barrier items adapted formulations from recent XR/AI TPD evaluations [4, 11, 16–18, 24–27, 29].

3.4.2 Researchers' observation notes

In their dual role as trainers and observers, researchers used a structured field-note template to document enactments with time-stamped entries. The protocol included:

- Context/activity: session, activity, role rotation phase.
- CAMIL cues: cognitive load indicators (task confusion, help-seeking), emotional engagement markers (verbal/non-verbal enthusiasm, frustration), and motivational alignment (persistence, voluntary exploration) [15].
- DigCompEdu/TPACK focus: evidence of XR-aware content–pedagogy–technology integration; accessibility moves (font/contrast, locomotion options, comfort settings) [4, 11, 14].
- Classroom management and technical: set-up time, device issues, mitigation strategies.
- Illustrative evidence: brief quotes or example references.

Before each session, focus was checked using a short alignment checklist. After each session, note-pairs were combined into a memo, noting agreements and differences [31, 32].

3.4.3 Participants' artefacts

Outputs produced and collected during the training included immersive scenarios, AI-supported lesson plans, assessment tools, and safety or ethics briefings. Each randomly selected artefact was reviewed for its alignment with the stated learning objectives, the effective integration of XR/AI benefits, and the incorporation of measures to ensure accessibility and cater to diverse learners. Examples included a 360° "field trip" for science with AI-generated prompts for inquiry, a virtual history walk with time-lined hotspots, and a language-learning dialogue featuring comfort motion options and peer-review checkpoints.

3.4.4 Focus group discussions

To complement individual self-reports, short semi-structured focus groups were conducted at the end of some sessions, following good-practice guidance for discussion design and facilitation [30]. Each group comprised a small, mixed set of participants to discover different ideas (~6–8 participants; ~20–30 minutes). The protocol covered five thematic areas:

- Enablers/barriers ('What would make XR/AI feasible next term?').
- Classroom management ('What would you adjust to support different learners?').
- Assessment and evidence ('What counts as convincing evidence in your subject?')
- Safety, ethics, accessibility ('Which comfort or inclusion features mattered?').
- Support needs ('Which aids or policies would help you sustain use?').

Moderation used turn-taking triggers, brief summaries, and invitations to quieter participants to talk. With consent, discussions were recorded, transcribed, anonymised, and analysed alongside open-ended questionnaire responses and field notes. This multiple data collection tools strategy enabled alignment checks across frameworks and strengthened the credibility of findings through methodological triangulation [31, 32].

3.5 Data analysis

The analysis followed a convergent parallel mixed-methods approach, in line with the study's overall research design [31, 32]. Quantitative and qualitative datasets were analysed separately and then brought together to address the research questions. This allowed numerical trends to be cross-checked and enriched with observations, artefacts, and group reflections.

For the questionnaire (quantitative analysis), Likert scale items were coded numerically (from 1 = strongly disagree to 5 = strongly agree) and analysed using descriptive statistics (means, standard deviations, and frequency distributions) to identify patterns in perceived competence, intentions to integrate XR/AI, and perceived enablers/barriers. Where relevant, comparisons were made to explore variation. Open-ended responses were not analysed statistically but were included in the qualitative synthesis. Data processing was carried out using Microsoft Excel and IBM SPSS (v.29) for transparent, repeatable reporting.

For the qualitative data, thematic coding was used with both deductive and inductive strategies [33]. Deductive codes came from the theoretical framework (DigCompEdu with XR descriptors, TPACK, CAMIL), covering immersive content creation, classroom management, accessibility, presence management, and AI-assisted design. Inductive codes captured patterns that emerged, for example, 'creative AI integration', where teachers adapted AI feedback for culturally responsive tasks. Concretely:

- Observation notes were reviewed to extract situations that showed cognitive, affective, or motivational patterns, such as moments where learners kept trying through headset setup difficulties or spontaneously extended an XR role-play beyond the allocated time.

- Participants' artefacts were analysed for structural and pedagogical coherence, alignment with learning objectives, and integration of XR/AI affordances.

- Focus group transcripts and open-ended questionnaire responses were coded thematically to identify shared priorities (e.g., 'access to mobile VR headsets' as a top technical enabler) and differences between in-service and pre-service perspectives (e.g., pre-service teachers emphasising curriculum fit, while in-service teachers stressed time constraints for setup).

To support trustworthiness, both researchers separately coded a subset of data (e.g., focus-group excerpts on assessment), discussed differences, and agreed on final labels, thereby reducing individual bias. Data triangulation was implemented with cross-comparison of findings across tools to confirm similar trends (e.g., both survey and groups highlighting the need for accessible options). Finally, coding memos, statistical output logs, and data management records have been kept by the researchers to support transparency and repeatability.

4. Results

This section presents the study's results, organised by research question. For each, we present questionnaire findings first, followed by qualitative insights from observation notes, artefacts, and focus groups.

4.1 Teachers' intentions and self-efficacy for using XR and AI technologies

Following participation, the intention to integrate XR/AI in the near term was generally high. Across sessions, 82% selected '*agree*' or '*strongly agree*' for '*I intend to use XR/AI in at least one lesson in the next three months*' (M = 4.2, SD = 0.6). Among pre-service teachers (n = 53), 85% reported an increased intention to integrate XR/AI in their future teaching, but only 68% felt skilled enough to design and manage such activities. In contrast, in-service teachers (n = 48) showed more moderate intention levels (72%) but stronger perceptions of competence (77%). These trends are visualised in **Figure 2**. There was no statistical evidence that higher perceived competence was directly connected to higher intention. In-service teachers tended to score higher on curriculum alignment (M = 4.2) but lower on classroom management confidence (M = 3.7) than their pre-service peers (M = 4.0 and 4.1, respectively) – suggesting that experienced teachers saw clearer curricular links but were more cautious about practical management.

Qualitative materials help explain these patterns. Participants connected XR/AI scenarios to real teaching practices. For example, a pre-service teacher who designed a virtual science field trip commented: '*This is exactly how I would introduce ecosystems in my real classroom.*' An in-service language teacher noted that AI-assisted lesson plans '*cut hours off preparation time.*' Teachers repeatedly expected motivational gains. One history teacher commented during a focus group: '*If students can walk inside a virtual city, they will remember much more than from pictures.*' Observation notes documented excitement during role-rotation, with some groups working beyond the allocated time. Many teachers framed XR/AI as a way of improving teaching practice. One pre-service participant stated: '*This makes me feel I am teaching in the 21st century, not stuck in the past.*' Several artefacts showed AI being used beyond simple prompts – for example, to create reflective journal questions designed for immersive debates. However, intention was sometimes limited. One in-service teacher summarised: '*I want to use it, but unless my school gives me the time and devices, it will remain an idea, not a reality.*'

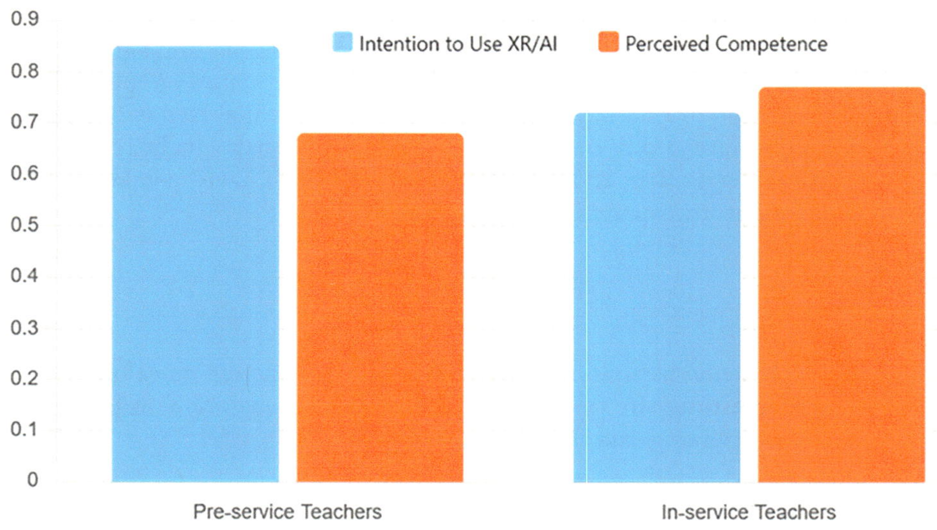

Figure 2.
Comparison of intention to use XR/AI and perceived competence between pre-service and in-service teachers.

4.2 Pedagogical, technical, and institutional supports needed for sustained use

Questionnaire items targeted three domains. Pedagogically, 76% of the respondents agreed that *'Access to ready-to-use XR/AI lesson scenarios would help me integrate these tools.'* Similarly, 71% agreed with the statement *'Peer support and mentoring would increase my confidence to use XR/AI in class.'* Technically, 84% of teachers said that *'Access to devices is a limiting factor'*, while 69% chose *'agree'* or *'strongly agree'* for *'IT support is necessary for XR/AI use in schools.'* Institutionally, 73% of respondents agreed that *'Time constraints are a barrier to XR/AI implementation'*, 68% agreed with the need for curriculum alignment, and 62% indicated that leadership support was essential.

Qualitative data contextualised these numeric trends. Focusing on the pedagogical dimension, teachers asked for adaptable, curriculum-linked repositories – *'lesson banks,' 'ready-made modules'* – and emphasised peer mentoring: *'If I had someone in my school to show me how to troubleshoot or adapt a scenario, I'd be much more confident.'* Micro-credentials also came up, especially among pre-service participants, as evidence of XR/AI skills for future employment. For technical support, device access was the most frequently mentioned issue. During one focus group, a participant noted: *'We had one headset to share among 25 students – it's inspiring here, but not realistic in my school.'* Observation notes captured setup problems and similar interruptions, while teachers argued for quick troubleshooting pathways and short guides with pictures or videos. Referring to institutional support, the strongest concerns were about time and curricular fit. In-service teachers highlighted time pressures: *'Even five minutes to set up is a problem when lessons are forty-five minutes long'*. Several argued that official curriculum links would make it easier to get principal support (e.g., *'If XR is part of the official curriculum, principals will support it; otherwise, it feels optional.'*). Leadership support was linked to long-term sustainability, as one teacher noted: *'Without our principal's support, this will not last once the initial enthusiasm fades.'*

5. Discussion

The findings of this study carry important pedagogical implications for integrating XR and AI into TPD. In particular, the results show the importance of working within existing competency frameworks while also extending them to cover immersive and AI-related skills and practices. As recent work suggests, general digital frameworks often fall short of specifying XR-specific competencies [2, 4]. Our observations support calls to update such models and frameworks to address immersive teaching practices and ethical AI use. This will ensure that teachers are prepared for XR/AI tools. The PAX initiative's XR pedagogical framework aligns with this priority by focusing on co-design and hands-on training for teachers in virtual and augmented environments. Similarly, elements of the CAMIL are reflected in our data. For example, teachers described strong initial motivation among students but also pointed out concerns about cognitive overload and the risk that novelty effects would fade. These insights align with the CAMIL's focus on balancing engagement and cognitive demand in immersive learning experiences [15, 34]. To sum up, our study suggests that effective XR/AI integration in TPD should be grounded in established frameworks but also push their boundaries to incorporate immersive, AI-driven pedagogies and protect students' well-being (e.g., managing cognitive load and privacy considerations).

Comparing our findings with the broader literature reveals several similar trends. Consistent with prior studies [15–18], we found that teachers recognize the potential of XR/AI for enriching instruction but remain cautious in adoption. Many teachers in our program saw the benefit of these technologies to engage students, which aligns with evidence that XR can boost motivation and participation [25, 26]. However, some participants remain hesitant to use XR/AI without substantial support [15, 17]. Key barriers mentioned – such as a lack of confidence in using new tools, limited time for lesson redesign, and lack of ready-made digital content – have been widely observed in the literature [15–17]. A further pattern, also seen in prior work [15], was the gap between expectations and reality: enthusiasm sometimes turned to frustration when devices did not work or sessions were disrupted. Such comparative insights highlight that the diffusion of XR in education remains gradual [24, 25] and highly dependent on teacher readiness and context. At the same time, our results add to the growing evidence of positive outcomes when integration does occur. Teachers reported that students were more curious and involved during XR lessons, reflecting the motivational benefits found in recent studies [25, 26]. Thus, our study both supports and extends existing knowledge. It points out known facilitators and obstacles but also shows how these dynamics play out in a specific national system.

This context is particularly crucial in the case of Greece, where systemic and ethical considerations strongly affect the space for innovation. The Greek education system features a centralized curriculum and strict regulations that shape how and whether XR/AI tools can be used in schools. Our teachers noted that inflexible syllabi and high-stakes exams leave little room for trying new things, a challenge in line with prior studies of educational innovation [13, 16]. Moreover, infrastructural constraints in Greek schools emerged as a significant theme. Many schools (especially public ones) lack reliable broadband or Wi–Fi, and policies often restrict mobile devices in class (unless special permission is given), creating a paradox where teachers trained in XR have limited means to implement it [13]. This highlights how disparities in access and restrictive regulations can limit the impact of even well-designed TPD initiatives – a challenge also noted in other research on digital innovation in schools [13, 24]. Ethical and equity implications also come up. Teachers focused on the importance of equal opportunities: if only some schools with support can deploy XR/AI, it could widen disparities. They also expressed concern about ensuring student safety and privacy when using AI-driven educational software, reflecting the broader ethical debates around AI in education (e.g., avoiding bias in algorithms and protecting student data). In Greece, as in other EU contexts, any adoption of AI in classrooms must follow emerging ethical guidelines and GDPR regulations, adding another layer of consideration for TPD programs. Our discussion highlights that successful integration of XR/AI is not just a technical or pedagogical issue, but a contextual one. It needs to follow local policy, infrastructural support, and robust ethical rules.

Finally, it is important to acknowledge the limitations of this study. The study was relatively small in both scale and duration, which limits the generalisability of the findings [24]. Similar pilot studies integrating AR/VR in teacher training have cautioned that results may not easily transfer to all settings or scales without further validation [24, 25]. The group of participating teachers was self-selected and motivated, which may have introduced a positive bias, also observed in similar TPD studies [15, 18]. Additionally, the evaluation of impact was short-term, focusing on immediate changes in teacher practice and student engagement following the TPD. Our results provide an initial snapshot – for example, teachers did implement XR/AI activities and observed enthusiastic student responses – but we cannot confirm if these changes last over time. Prior research has emphasized the need for longitudinal studies to determine whether initial gains are sustained once the novelty of technology fades [13, 25]. Technical and institutional constraints also shaped the implementation: device shortages, software issues, and school policies limiting mobile AR all affected the work, as seen in other resource-constrained contexts [26]. Recognising these limitations positions our study within the wider landscape of exploratory research. Future work should therefore extend the approach to larger groups, over longer periods, and across more varied school settings to assess transferability [24–26]. Despite the limitations, the findings provide practical insight into what is needed – from policy support to technical infrastructure – to effectively bring XR and AI into the TPD.

6. Conclusion

This research began to explore two key questions regarding the integration of XR and AI in TPD. Addressing RQ1, the results show several factors affecting teachers' willingness to adopt XR/AI. The most significant were external supports and internal readiness; adoption was more likely when technologies aligned with curricular aims, leadership-offered support, and infrastructure, such as devices and connectivity, was reliable. Equally important were personal factors such as the teachers' own digital confidence and motivation to innovate. The study points out that XR/AI integration is facilitated by a supportive environment and by training that builds teachers' self-efficacy in using these tools.

In response to RQ2, the study provides concrete insights and strategies. We noticed that successful integration goes beyond introducing new tools; it involves merging XR/AI into pedagogically meaningful activities. Teachers in our program learned to design immersive lesson plans that were tightly linked to their curriculum goals. They reported that these approaches not only engaged students through interactivity and rich visualization but also encouraged student-centered learning, as shown by increased student curiosity and participation during the XR/AI-supported lessons. However, the integration worked best when teachers adapted the technology to their context: starting with small, manageable implementations (such as a single AR-enhanced project), aligning them with existing lesson objectives, and gradually scaling up as confidence grew. This points to XR/AI adoption as an iterative process: try, reflect, and refine. Moreover, our results emphasize that TPD programs should model these strategies, providing teachers with hands-on experience in XR/AI, opportunities to collaborate and share experiences, and guidance on troubleshooting technical or classroom management challenges. By doing so, TPD can translate the promise of XR/AI into actual classroom practice.

Overall, the study demonstrates that, with the right support and preparation, teachers can integrate XR and AI in ways that enrich learning experiences, addressing both research questions. The challenge and the opportunity lie in building the ecosystems – pedagogical, technical, and institutional – that enable that integration to take root and grow. Below, we translate these insights into actionable recommendations for stakeholders looking to build on this work and advance XR/AI integration in education:

- Align teacher training with digital competence frameworks: Design and implement TPD programs that map onto known frameworks like DigCompEdu, extending them to include XR/AI-specific skills. This alignment will ensure that professional development not only builds practical classroom techniques but also meets broader educational standards for teachers' digital competencies.

- Invest in infrastructure and technical support: Prioritise funding and resources to equip schools with the necessary technology (high-speed internet, AR/VR devices, and updated software) and on-site technical support. Reliable infrastructure is foundational for teachers to confidently integrate XR/AI tools, and such investment reflects a broader educational commitment to digital innovation and equity.

- Foster a supportive school culture and leadership engagement: Encourage school leaders to actively support experimentation with XR and AI in teaching. This can include providing teachers with dedicated time for collaborative planning, reducing the fear of failure by celebrating innovative attempts, and integrating XR/AI goals into the school's development plans. Strong administrative backing creates an environment where teachers feel safe and valued when adopting new methodologies, in line with wider calls for transformative school leadership in digital education.

- Integrate ethics and data privacy into XR/AI initiatives: Ensure that any introduction of AI-driven tools or data-intensive XR applications in education comes with clear guidelines and training on ethical use. Teachers should be prepared to address issues such as student data privacy, informed consent for using AI recommendations, and recognizing potential biases in AI content. By embedding these discussions in TPD, educational authorities can align the micro-level implementation with macro-level priorities, like the EU's ethical guidelines for AI in education, thus promoting responsible innovation.

- Provide continuous mentorship and communities of practice: Move beyond one-off workshops by establishing ongoing support mechanisms – such as mentoring by experienced XR/AI educators or professional learning communities (PLCs) – where teachers can share experiences, troubleshoot challenges, and collectively develop best practices. This sustained support mirrors effective PD models in other domains and helps maintain momentum, ensuring that initial gains in teacher capacity lead to long-term changes in practice.

- Plan for long-term and scalable evaluation: Incorporate evaluation plans that monitor the impact of XR/AI integration over extended periods and across multiple schools. By collecting data on both short-term successes and longer-term outcomes (e.g., how teaching strategies and student performance evolve after one year), stakeholders can make informed decisions about scaling up the initiatives. Such a commitment to evidence-based scaling resonates with broader educational priorities of accountability and continuous improvement in innovation adoption.

Acknowledgements

This work was partially supported by the European Commission under the project PAX—Pedagogical Alliance for XR-Technology in (Teacher) Education—ERASMUS-EDU-2023-PI-ALL-INNO, Project No. 101139827. We also extend our thanks to all collaborators and partners involved.

Author details

Stavros Pitsikalis[1] and Ilona-Elefteryja Lasica[2*]

1 University of the Aegean, Department of Preschool Education Sciences & Educational Design, Rhodes, Greece

2 University of the Aegean, Rhodes, Greece

*Address all correspondence to: e_ilona@aegean.gr

References

[1] Alnagrat A, Ismail RC, Idrus SZ, Alfaqi RM. A review of extended reality (XR) technologies in the future of human education: Current trend and future opportunity. Journal of Human Centered Technology. 2022;**1**(2):81–96. DOI: 10.11113/humentech.v1n2.27

[2] Pitsikalis S, Lasica IE, Kostas A, Vitsilaki C. Educational design guidelines for teaching with immersive technologies—updating learning outcomes of the European qualification framework. Trends in Higher Education. 2024;**3**(4):1091–1108. DOI: 10.3390/higheredu3040064

[3] Burke D, Crompton H, Nickel C. The use of extended reality (XR) in higher education: A systematic review. TechTrends. 2025;**17**:1–4. 10.1007/s11528-025-01092-y

[4] Rutten N, Brouwer-Truijen K. Defining XR-specific teacher competencies: Extending the DigCompEdu framework for immersive education. Trends in Higher Education. 2025;**4**(1):11. DOI: 10.3390/higheredu4010011

[5] Thomason J. Metahealth-how will the metaverse change health care?. Journal of Metaverse. 2021;**1**(1):13–16.

[6] Garzón J, Pavón J, Baldiris S. Systematic review and meta-analysis of augmented reality in educational settings. Virtual Reality. 2019;**23**(4):447–459. DOI: 10.1007/s10055-019-00379-9

[7] Chiu TK, Xia Q, Zhou X, Chai CS, Cheng M. Systematic literature review on opportunities, challenges, and future research recommendations of artificial intelligence in education. Computers and Education: Artificial Intelligence. 2023;**4**. DOI: 10.1016/j.caeai.2022.100118

[8] Ouyang F, Jiao P. Artificial intelligence in education: The three paradigms. Computers and Education: Artificial Intelligence. 2021;**2**. DOI: 10.1016/j.caeai.2021.100020

[9] Tsaramirsis K, Lasica I, Lampropoulos G, Tsinakos A, Kazanidis I, Terzopoulos G, Bafes K, Hazboun S, Mangina E Empowering civic education through Metaverse-enriched teaching scenarios. In: Proceedings of the 2025 Annual Conference of the European Association for Extended Reality (EuroXR 2025). 2025

[10] Retalis S, Lasica IE, Lampropoulos G, Pana I, Aretou G Designing immersive educational scenarios for civic education: Training future instructional scenario designers (in Greek). In: Proceedings of the 14th Conference "ICT in Education" (ETPE 2025). 2025

[11] Redecker C, Punie Y, editor. European Framework for the Digital Competence of Educators: DigCompEdu. Luxembourg: Publications Office of the European Union; 2017. DOI: 10.2760/159770

[12] European Commission. Directorate-general for education, youth, sport and culture. In: Digital Education Action Plan 2021-2027: Improving the Provision of Digital Skills in Education and Training. Luxembourg: Publications Office of the European Union online ; 2023. 10.2766/149764

[13] Pitsikalis S, Lasica IE, Kostas A, Vitsilaki C Integrating augmented reality into education and training: Remarks and insights from a five-year experience in the field. In: EDULEARN22 Proceedings 2022 (pp. 1565–1571). IATED. DOI: 10.21125/edulearn.2022.0414

[14] Alemán-Saravia AC, Technology D-A-A, Pedagogy and Content (TPACK framework): Systematic literature review. In: 2021 XVI Latin American Conference on Learning Technologies (LACLO) 2021 Oct 19. (pp. 104–111). IEEE. DOI: 10.11 09/LACLO54177.2021.00069

[15] Makransky G, Petersen GB. 2021. The cognitive affective model of immersive learning (CAMIL): A theoretical research-based model of learning in immersive virtual reality. Educational Psychology Review. **33** (3):937–958. DOI: 10.1007/s10648-020-0 9586-2

[16] Verdegaal S, Morssink-Santing VE, Brouwer-Truijen K, Rutten N. Examining the Educational Effectiveness of VR and AR: Insights from Recent Literature (V1.0). PAX Project, Work Package 2, Deliverable 2.2. Enschede: Saxion University of Applied Sciences; 2024

[17] Rutten N, Brouwer-Truijen K. An Analysis of Diverse Perspectives on Teaching with XR Resulting in Concrete Building Blocks for XR-based Educator Professionalization. PAX Project, Work Package 2, Task 2.1. Enschede: Saxion University of Applied Sciences; 2024

[18] Albert S, Burian R, Purgaj J, Khongklad C, Matz F, Wirbatz K, et al. PAX Framework for Teachers (1st Draft). PAX Project, Deliverable D3.1. Vienna: University of Teacher Education Vienna; 2024

[19] Khongklad C, Krüger M, Winters S, Smets J, Sagir N, Zachariadis A. PAX Guideline for Developers (1st Draft). PAX Project, Work Package 4, Deliverable D4.1. Münster: FH Münster University of Applied Sciences; 2024

[20] Council of the European Union. Council recommendation of 23 November 2023 on the key enabling factors for successful digital education and training (C/2024/1115) [Internet]. *Official Journal of the European Union*, C 2024/1115, 2024. Available from: https://eur-lex.europa.eu/legal-content/EN/TXT/PDF/?uri=OJ/:C_202401115 [Accessed: 2025-August-12]

[21] European Commission. Digital education action plan 2021–2027: Resetting education and training for the digital age [Internet]. Luxembourg: Publications Office of the European Union; 2020. Available from: https://education.ec./eu/ropa./eu/focus-topics/digital/education/-action-plan [Accessed: 2025-August-12]

[22] PAX Project. The PAX framework: Pedagogical model for integrating XR in teacher education [Internet]. Erasmus+ Programme; 2024. Available from: https://pax-project./eu// [Accessed: 2025-August-12]

[23] Project M. Designing immersive civic education scenarios with XR and AI tools [Internet]. Erasmus+ Programme; 2024. Available from: https://metacivic.eu// [Accessed: 2025-August-12]

[24] Asensio-Pérez JI, Dimitriadis Y, Pozzi F, Hernández-Leo D, Prieto LP, Persico D, Villagrá-Sobrino SL. Towards teaching as design: Exploring the interplay between full-lifecycle learning design tooling and teacher professional development. Computers & Education.

2017;**114**:92–116. 10.1016/j.compedu.2017.06.011

[25] Laurillard D, Kennedy E, Charlton P, Wild J, Dimakopoulos D. 2018. Using technology to develop teachers as designers of TEL: Evaluating the learning designer. British Journal of Educational Technology. **49** (6):1044–1058. DOI: 10.1111/bjet.12697

[26] Pozzi F, Asensio-Perez JI, Ceregini A, Dagnino FM, Dimitriadis Y, Earp J. Supporting and representing learning design with digital tools: In between guidance and flexibility. Technology, Pedagogy and Education. 2020;**29**(1):109–128. DOI: 10.1080/1475939X.2020.1714708

[27] Boloudakis M, Retalis S, Psaromiligkos Y. Training novice teachers to design moodle-based units of learning using a CADMOS-enabled learning design sprint. British Journal of Educational Technology. 2018;**49** (6):1059–1076. DOI: 10.1111/bjet.12678

[28] Castelhano M, Morgado L, Pedrosa D. Instructional design models for immersive virtual reality: A systematic literature review. SIIE23. XXV Simpósio Internacional de Informática Educativa. 2023;272–278

[29] Carvalho L, Martinez-Maldonado R, Tsai YS, Markauskaite L, De Laat M. How can we design for learning in an AI world?. Computers and Education: Artificial Intelligence. 2022;**3**. DOI: 10.1016/j.caeai.2022.100053

[30] O. Nyumba T, Wilson K, Derrick CJ, Mukherjee N. 2018. The use of focus group discussion methodology: Insights from two decades of application in conservation. Methods in Ecology and Evolution. **9**(1):20–32. DOI: 10.1111/2041-210X.12860

[31] Plano Clark VL. Mixed methods research. The Journal of Positive Psychology. 2017;**12**(3):305-6. DOI: 10.1080/17439760.2016.1262619

[32] Johnson RB, Onwuegbuzie AJ. Mixed methods research: A research paradigm whose time has come. Educational Researcher. 2004;**33** (7):14–26. DOI: 10.3102/0013189X033007014

[33] Peel KL. A beginner's guide to applied educational research using thematic analysis. Practical Assessment Research and Evaluation. 2020;**25**(1). DOI: 10.7275/ryr5-k983

[34] Zhi Y, Wu L. Extended reality in language learning: A cognitive affective model of immersive learning perspective. Frontiers in Psychology. 2023;**14**. DOI: 10.3389/fpsyg.2023.1109025

Chapter 5

Perspective Chapter: Transforming Education Through Gamification Supported by Metaintelligence Frameworks

Nevenka Popović Šević and Aleksandar Šević

Abstract

Following an initial discussion of conceptual complexities inherent in defining intelligence, this paper proposes a comprehensive theoretical framework for intelligence, with a particular emphasis on the notion of metaintelligence. Metaintelligence involves developing AI that adapts efficiently across diverse systems in response to change. Following Sternberg et al.'s view, it integrates analytical and practical activities to creatively solve problems. Subsequently, the concept of gamification is systematically examined, highlighting its implementation within educational contexts. This examination is grounded in empirical findings, analyses of relevant software tools, and illustrative case studies. Additionally, the paper critically evaluates the integration of artificial intelligence within metaintelligence frameworks, elucidating both beneficial outcomes and potential adverse effects. Combining gamification with AI offers benefits such as personalization, enhanced engagement, data-driven design, and scalability, but also raises concerns over privacy, complexity, manipulation, and addiction. When applied ethically and transparently, AI-based gamification can substantially boost user engagement while safeguarding user welfare.

Keywords: gamification, education, metaintelligence framework, artificial intelligence, case study

1. Introduction

The term "intelligence" has been a point of interest, but also a challenging phenomenon to observe and measure. It spans across all living creatures, but for humans, especially with the advancement of AI, there is an intent to gauge it as accurately and meaningfully as possible. We may be the current masters of this planet, but with the advancement of artificial intelligence (AI), this place is far from secure, even in the near future. If intelligence allows for solving hard problems efficiently [1, 2], then it is rather limited to the performative aspect. If control and coordination of rational agents are added, then a variety of steps in the decision-making process become clearer and not too difficult to explain. In this complex problem-solving environment, we refer to the concepts of metaintelligence outlined by Sternberg et al. [3] and gamification to explore recent advancements in the educational process. Gamification uses game design elements, ways of thinking, and mechanics for nongame activities [4]. In education, it primarily seeks to enhance students' motivation and concentration [5] and to increase the efficiency of the learning process [6, 7]. Given the consistently positive impact of gamification on students' performance, the careful design of gamified tasks and projects is crucial [8]. To achieve maximum effectiveness, such design should consider the educational level (primary, secondary, or higher education), respect individual differences among students [9], and incorporate their preferences, learning styles, and the intended structure of knowledge acquisition [10].

The advancement of the Internet was supposed to be a great breakthrough in human development, which it certainly proved to be. However, there are some limited indications that IQ, especially among younger people, may have dropped since the 1980s in some developed countries, but these results were primarily examined in light of the nutrition hypothesis [11, 12]. Even if it is the result of a change in digital prowess and, perhaps, old IQ tests no longer reflect this shift, it is evident that PISA education test results have recently declined across all categories and many countries [13]. Was it just a result of a one-off COVID-19 anomaly?! Most likely not, because the pandemic has had a profound impact on how we work and, most likely, study. Students have access to numerous online sources and AI assistants, which, from a logical perspective, means that the learning process can be as smooth and joyful as practically possible. The concept of gamification is not new, but the term itself has gained prevalence in the last decade. The offer of digital platforms is also quite ample because AI systems are as effective as the labeled data used in training them. If the population is large and inputs are scarce to cut costs, then biases will be quite noticeable. The bottom line is that every AI product is rarely the top selection for the largest cohort of users, largely due to this imperfection.

Gamification allows instructors and students to facilitate the learning process, rendering it joyful and interesting. Since students receive rewards or points upon the completion of tasks, there is an apparent drive to excel, but if the focus is mainly on the prize, the main goal of internal motivation will be affected. Deep learning will be replaced by a cryptic learning process.

In this paper, we shall define gamification and apply it in the educational context. Then, the discussion on metaintelligence and AI integration will be provided, followed by empirical evidence and relevant case studies. Following the challenges and limitations, we provide concluding remarks.

2. Gamification and educational context

In the last decades, the educational sector has become ever more inclined to apply innovative methods to enhance motivation, engagement, and learning outcomes for students. One such method is gamification, which relies on the application of game elements in an educational context. However, to achieve its optimal performance, it is necessary to introduce advanced cognitive and metacognitive strategies, which can be accomplished through the development and application of metaintelligence.

The term "gamification" was first mentioned in 2010 by Rajat Paharia, the founder of the Bunchball firm, specializing in the commercial application of game theories [14]. It managed to survive and thrive among many other competing constructs, such as productivity games, funware, and applied gaming. What is important is that the term refers to the game industry trend that has been around at least since the early 1980s. The quest for observing game users' experiences and boosting funology and playfulness as part of human–computer interaction paved the way for the widespread use of gaming in business and academia [15]. Accordingly, gamification uses game designs in nongame frameworks [15], or more broadly represents the practice of using game design elements, mechanics, and thinking in nongame activities [4]. A gamified application could include any or all the levels of game design elements: interface design patterns, game design patterns and mechanics, models, methods, and game design principles and heuristics [15]. However, the most popular for academic use are points, badges, levels, and leaderboards, followed to a much lesser extent by virtual goods and avatars, which implies that elements grouped as game interface design patterns occupy a dominating place [16].

Gamification relates to two similar concepts: game-based learning and serious games. Game-based learning allows learners to acquire knowledge via game achievements. Learning outcomes are revealed in the game, but it is necessary to go through the problem-solving steps to enhance knowledge [17]. Unlike gamification, which applies selected game components, serious games are complete games used in academia, industries, training, or simulations. Ultimately, it remains common for all these categories that users have enjoyable experiences in achieving specific goals [18].

Game-based learning involves students in the learning process by rendering the experience more fun-filled. In theory, cognitive development should be promoted, as difficult, boring, complex, or overly sophisticated subjects are made more accessible to audiences that are otherwise disinterested. Computer games are primarily associated with immediate gratification and enjoyment, and when this is applied to acquiring new knowledge, reviewing, and reinforcement, the students' attitude is, a priori, positive. However, the caveat is that young people also believe that mathematics, statistics, and other challenging topics could be made more approachable if gamified, which means that almost anything could be mastered if converted into a game [4].

This simplification of the learning process, promoted by gamification, can be juxtaposed with its impact on deep learning processes. Deep learning techniques have demonstrated substantial improvements over traditional learning methods, particularly in fields such as image processing and natural language classification [19]. Their key advantage lies in delivering effective solutions that address the limitations of conventional approaches, offering greater accuracy and scalability [20].

However, motivation for deep learning in educational contexts can diminish when various AI-based tools are integrated into the teaching process. For instance, gamification can replicate the cognitive processes students use to analyze and solve tasks, potentially reducing the need for deeper, independent engagement. Fundamentally, deep learning operates through a hierarchical computation of task features, presenting information progressively from lower to higher levels of abstraction [21].

Computer technology that finds widespread use in educational gamification is virtual reality (VR). Wearing VR helmets, users are immersed in a virtual world and monitored thanks to installed sensors. The sensation of being transported to another environment augments the student's joy and motivation to learn. In turn, educators can easily analyze the points viewed by users, the gaze length, or their movements in the constrained space. From the student's perspective, the benefits include experiential learning, an effective learning process, knowledge applicability, and a simulation that closely resembles real-life experiences [22]. In [23], the authors evaluate the relevance of VR in education by comparing all papers published in this area. While the top three positions are assigned to prolific colleagues in Spain, the UK, and Germany, the results are more striking when individual papers are compared in tabular form. The development goals for almost all studies were cognitive, with the exception of several applications that promoted dancing routines or developed transversal skills. The participants in studies are almost always at a higher educational level, with the rest being secondary or K-12 attendees. Moreover, the areas of research are multifaceted and mainly dominated by architecture, medicine, mathematics, and natural sciences, where virtual 3D models significantly facilitate the learning process [23]. As a concluding observation, we can agree that gamified applications boost students' intrinsic motivation to enjoy the learning process and extrinsic motivation to participate in the game, collect points, and reap awards. Nevertheless, it is essential to strike a balance between these two categories to avoid the loss of intrinsic drive. Finally, both processes will diminish the occurrence of amotivation, whereby the participants are indifferent to the learning approach [24, 25].

3. Metaintelligence and AI integration

It is challenging to define intelligence because it implies varying aspects for different observers. In addition, it may be observed and measured not only in humans but also in animals, and, what is pertinent for this study, in AI [26]. Claiming that numerical and linguistic abilities are the most important areas is problematic because machines are increasingly demonstrating the ability to deal with them. Alternatively, the focus could shift toward resolving hard problems in difficult environments, that is, performance [1, 2], and ultimately on efficiency that is achieved in changing environments and with evolving goals and requests, while also facing limitations in resources, speed, complexity, and computational abilities [27, 28]. General intelligence is associated with individuals' cognitive abilities, but without the adaptive intelligence originating in coexistence with the environment, it is highly probable that either an individual or a species would cease to exist [29].

Since definitions cannot provide a single all-encompassing solution, it is not surprising that the current notion of metaintelligence is quite complex. Sternberg et al. [3] discuss it from the perspective that explores control and coordination in creative, analytical, practical, and wisdom-based steps in solving problems. *Creativity* offers novel solutions, while *analytical skills* select the rationally sound alternatives. The practicality of selected options allows for their implementation under individual and external constraints, and, ultimately, the *wisdom-based skills* uphold the interests of the wider community. Each one of these skills is conditioned by the remaining three, but these constraints are not only individual. A change in Zeitgeist would render previously dominant attitudes antiquated. Behavioral patterns differ across cultures, religions, or continents, which ultimately changes the decision-making processes [3].

Metaintelligence refers to the ability to recognize, understand, and regulate one's own cognitive processes, which enables students to use gamified elements more effectively for the improvement of their educational results. Metaintelligence is credited with integrating different forms of intelligence (cognitive, emotional, social), and, thanks to this integration, adaptive and personalized educational experiences are created. In the context of gamification, AI can analyze learning data, recognize behavior patterns, and adapt educational content in real time, thereby increasing student engagement and motivation [30].

There is also a term, metalearning, referring to the study of "learning to learn." More precisely, it is a scientific field that systematically examines different aspects of machine learning across a wide range of tasks, with the goal of making the learning process more effective in education [31]. In other words, just as traditional methods and strategies are adopted in cognitive learning, similar principles of learning are also applied by machine learning algorithms. Through metalearning techniques, a predictive model acquires the ability to learn independently, skillfully bypassing trial-and-error processes. This, in turn, shapes the neural network more effectively and enhances the model's autonomy in its operations [32].

With the advancement of AI, a wide range of course- and study-support products have been offered on the market. Some of them offer services to identify and inform students. A majority of them are used for teaching courses, studying languages, offering assessment items, and training. Ultimately, the adaptive systems aimed at evaluating and improving student performance, as well as assisting in boosting knowledge about programming languages, are becoming quite powerful with the advancement of AI [33]. There are many competing platforms, as it is challenging to find a single model that consistently outperforms others at the user level. In improving models, metalearning is used to acquire knowledge about new tasks, particularly in environments where labeled data are scarce, and previous knowledge is leveraged to address the so-called data sparsity issue. If the previous knowledge is from a limited, more homogeneous area, then it is possible to address user-specific issues originating in a similar area more accurately, and vice versa [34]. Data scarcity issues are caused by the inability to collect data due to data protection laws or if costs are prohibitively high in annotating relevant details. As a phenomenon, it is reflected in user sparsity, when users interact with a limited number of items and it is difficult to draw general conclusions; item sparsity, when some items are used by only a handful of users; interaction sparsity, caused by missing data that impedes the provision of meaningful interaction between items and users; and, finally, feature sparsity, when specific features in recommendation systems are used but are inadequately implemented due to the lack of data [35].

4. Empirical evidence and case studies

Integration of AI into educational processes, especially through gamification, represents an innovative approach that can significantly enhance the learning experience [36]. In this section, we investigate how AI-powered gamification strategies, within the conceptual framework of metaintelligence, can contribute to creating immersive educational experiences by analyzing empirical studies and specific examples from practice.

Gamification in education, in a broader sense, refers to the application of elements from educational games to learning processes with the goal of enhancing student engagement and motivation. However, for gamification to be truly effective, it is necessary to integrate metaintelligence – the ability to recognize, understand, and regulate one's own cognitive processes [37].

Artificial Intelligence today is closely associated with various assistive technologies in gaming, primarily due to their inherent functionality, which includes player modeling and often the presence of nonplayer characters [38]. In *gamification applied to education*, the Internet of Things (IoT) is being increasingly utilized, offering significant scientific potential. Thanks to powerful hardware support and intermediary software integrated within the IoT ecosystem, educational processes are evolving into virtual activity environments based on game principles [39].

Experientially and developmentally, *gaming in education* today has introduced unprecedented interactivity, showcasing the full potential of VR, augmented reality (AR), and mixed reality (MR). Furthermore, with the integration of the metaverse, the role of gaming in education has gained significant prominence. It is assumed that the metaverse will introduce revolutionary changes in game-based education, as it allows students to experience learning environments that are personalized, interactive, and highly user-friendly [40].

Numerous case studies and documented applications highlight the use of gamification in education, supported by metaintelligence tools. One prominent example is Duolingo and its *gamified approach to language learning*. Duolingo is a notable application that successfully integrates gamification with AI. By using elements such as points, badges, and leaderboards, the application enhances user engagement. Although there is an ongoing challenge to balance entertainment and learning efficiency, Duolingo has achieved notable success in motivating students [41]. According to a metaanalysis conducted by Li et al. [42], gamification demonstrated a significant positive effect on learning outcomes, with an average effect size of $g = 0.822$, indicating substantial improvement in the performance of students who participated in gamified educational activities.

Gamification in foreign language learning can play an important educational role by fostering an engaging and enjoyable atmosphere that supports the acquisition of new vocabulary and expressions. Some scholars argue that when gamification is integrated into the learning process through motivational games, language learning becomes more interactive, stimulating, and rewarding for students [43]. More specifically, gamification can enhance independent learning, build self-confidence, promote learner autonomy, and encourage more effective collaboration in virtual teamwork settings [44].

In this context, gamification also emphasizes both student competence and social connectedness, thereby making peer interaction more dynamic [45]. Research in this area has primarily focused on core language skills such as reading, vocabulary, pronunciation, writing, grammar, listening, teamwork, and overall performance in foreign language acquisition.

Nevertheless, several studies highlight challenges in applying gamification to language learning. From a pedagogical perspective, grammar–translation exercises often lack meaningful context and communicative tasks [46], while issues such as relatively low accuracy in translation tasks have also been noted [47]. In addition, technological barriers may arise, particularly when students have limited access to mobile devices or stable Internet connections [48].

If teachers lack relevant experience or sufficient training in nonteaching roles, such as classroom management, gamification enables the introduction of software products that facilitate the process. Class Dojo is a tool for generating a Behavior Management Chart, which can be accessed via tablets, phones, and computers. Students select an avatar for communication and receive a positive point for good behavior. Points are deducted individually or for the entire class if the teacher believes that there are valid reasons for the decision. Concerns, mainly voiced by parents, were related to privacy issues, not knowing how long the data will be stored and used by the platform, and claims that the vivid graphics of monsters may not be conducive to learning. Finally, there was a concern that points should not be made public to all class attendees but only to specific children and their respective parents [49]. Class Dojo is essential in developing transversal competencies among primary and secondary students, relevant for meeting employers' requirements in modern economies. Latorre-Cosculluela et al. [50] find that this platform, at the university level, improves competencies related to class attendance, creativity, and interest in the subject, in addition to the betterment of social relationships and cooperation. There is also some evidence that it contributes to enhanced motivation to learn. ClassCraft includes an adventure game in the course infrastructure, where students, as team players, collect points. If they assist others and are successful in producing good papers, rewards are provided. By contrast, inappropriate behavior is penalized [4].

In research conducted at UniDistance Suisse, students used an AI tutor app that generated micro-learning based on existing course materials. The results showed that students who actively used the AI tutor achieved significantly better outcomes, with an average improvement of 15 percentile points compared to a parallel course without the AI tutor [51]. Research in engineering education has demonstrated that combining gamification with an intelligent tutoring system within a serious game setting can significantly enhance student engagement. The system adaptively provided support based on data collected from students' in-game actions and assessed their emotional states via a camera, which increased engagement by up to 25%. The study demonstrated that gamification in teaching AI literacy has a positive impact on both the affective and cognitive engagement of students. Through the use of elements such as leaderboards and points, students were more motivated and engaged in learning AI concepts.

Meta intelligence includes abilities such as metacognition, emotional intelligence, and self-regulation, which enable students to better understand and control their own cognitive processes. A study conducted by Redondo-Rodríguez et al. [52] showed that developing emotional intelligence through gamified activities can improve academic performance and strengthen social connections among students. The use of Minecraft Education Edition for gamified, *AI-powered math assessments demonstrated a significant improvement in learning*, with students showing increased engagement and enjoyment during gamified sessions, which resulted in better learning outcomes [53].

Ben Bertoli, a sixth-grade teacher in Indianapolis, developed ClassRealm, a platform that gamifies the classroom environment. Students earn points and achievement badges for activities such as completing tests, helping peers, and reading additional books. Parents can track the progress of their children, and teachers can set individual goals and tasks. ClassRealm enables personalized assignments and incorporates gaming elements to make learning more enjoyable and engaging [54].

At Stellenbosch University, the use of *gamification in the educational process* has shown a positive impact on the development of students' metacognitive skills. Students have demonstrated an increased ability to reflect on their own learning strategies and progress, which has contributed to better academic performance. This study highlights the importance of integrating metacognition into gamified educational activities [55].

Although gamification can have positive effects, there are also potential negative consequences. A study conducted by Almeida and colleagues [56] identified 87 papers reporting undesirable effects of gamification, including reduced motivation, poorer performance, and ethical issues such as cheating.

A study involving 80 higher education students showed that digital gamification can enhance both cognitive and emotional aspects of learning. Students demonstrated increased activity and improvements in self-esteem and emotional well-being after using gamified resources. This study indicates the effectiveness of gamification in higher education when applied with an optimal level of cognitive load [57].

5. Challenges and limitations

The integration of gamification in education through the lens of the metaintelligence framework presents both opportunities and challenges. This framework emphasizes the fusion of knowledge, context, and self-awareness in learning. When applied to gamification, it deepens the analysis of how games shape educational environments. We specifically refer to the technical, ethical, pedagogical, and psychological challenges that arise within this framework.

From a metaintelligence perspective, the technical dimension is not limited to infrastructure but concerns how technology supports integrated and reflective learning. Access to gamification tools and reliable Internet is not equally available to all students. Difficulties also occur with system integration, particularly in aligning gamified platforms with existing curricula. Moreover, gamification generates extensive datasets, whose interpretation can be complex [58]. The central technical challenge lies in the continuous updating of gamified educational systems, which demands both professional expertise and financial support from school administrations.

For the successful implementation of gamification and metaintelligence in education, a robust technological infrastructure is necessary. This includes a reliable Internet connection, access to appropriate devices (such as computers and tablets), and compatibility with learning platforms. The lack of these resources can lead to digital divides and hinder access to high-quality education. For example, research has shown that schools in rural areas often do not have adequate Internet access, which limits the possibility of implementing advanced educational technologies [59].

When we talk about latency and challenges in real-time use, gamified educational applications often require processing real-time data to ensure interactivity and student engagement. However, network latency can significantly influence the performance of these applications. For example, in the context of cloud gaming, latency can reduce the quality of the user experience, which is especially challenging when applied to educational platforms that use AR or VR [60].

The ethical dimension raises significant concerns. Issues of fairness and the responsible use of data collected during gameplay must be addressed. In addition, such systems risk marginalizing students who are less inclined toward this mode of learning, particularly those who are noncompetitive or who require more time to master course material.

Pedagogical challenges include the prioritization of short-term student engagement over sustained, deeper learning. Equally important is the fact that many educators lack adequate training in implementing gamification effectively [61]. Furthermore, gamified activities do not always capture the depth of students' comprehension, especially when evaluated against broader subject mastery [62].

Gamification in education, the integration of game elements into the classroom process, aims to increase student engagement and motivation. However, its application can also cause *psychological challenges*, especially in the context of addiction and the interaction between intrinsic and extrinsic motivation.

Evaluating metaintelligence in the digital context presents several challenges. Being addicted to the Internet increases the risk of contracting ADHD [63], while spending much time on social networks reduces the amount of time that would otherwise be dedicated to interacting with other relatives or acquaintances. Spending a significant amount of time in front of the screen disrupts sleep patterns, which, in the younger generation, affects brain development. However, in the older population, it increases the risk of Alzheimer's disease [64]. As socioeconomic progress reaches developed country levels, IQ peaks and then starts to decline [65], but this decline could be more severe for younger cohorts of the population, as Flynn confirmed that, from 1979 until 2008, the IQ dropped by more than two points for 14-year-olds in the UK [11, 12]. With the advancement of chatbots, another anomaly, known as AI-Chatbot-Induced Cognitive Atrophy, has emerged, which is the deterioration of human cognitive abilities resulting from excessive AI use. In the context of cognitive offloading, AI chatbots help us become more efficient; however, if too many functions are relegated to AI, basic cognitive processes, especially among young people, will be severely disrupted [66]. When comparing users who use either large language models (LLMs), search engines, or the brain only in completing assignments, it has been found that the highest level of neural activity and the ability to recall what has been written is associated with the brain-only category. LLM users were persistently at the bottom of the comparison scale over the four-month period [67]. This lack of cognitive effort prevents the creation of the long-term procedural memory essential in acquiring routines at an intuitive level. Even in the declarative memory realm preceding procedural memory creation, the heavy reliance on external assistance forces users to frequently recall basic processes because they are not being internalized effectively [68].

Excessive use of gamification can lead to system dependence, where students become too focused on achieving virtual rewards, ignoring actual educational content. A study on the Duolingo app showed that users can become overly focused on gamified elements, which interferes with efficient language learning [69]. Addiction to gamified systems can lead to several negative psychological effects: reduction of intrinsic motivation, as excessive use of rewards can reduce the internal desire to learn; increase in stress and anxiety, as competitive elements can create pressure and stress among students; and neglect of real learning, as focusing on virtual rewards can deter attention from real educational content [70].

Gamification in education, the integration of game elements into the classroom process, has the potential to increase student engagement and motivation. However, to achieve the long-term sustainability of these approaches, it is necessary to consider different aspects, including design, ethical guidelines, and integration with broader educational goals. For example, the literature has developed different design frameworks for sustainable gamification. One such framework, 7GOALS, integrates elements such as personalization of experiences, use of narrative, allowance for errors, social engagement, and the provision of feedback in order to achieve a balance between play and education [71].

The implementation of gamification in education faces ethical challenges, including the manipulation of student behavior, social comparison, and privacy protection. The development of guidelines is recommended, emphasizing transparency, user autonomy, and data protection in order to minimize negative effects [72].

6. Concluding remarks

Integrating AI into gamification in education, through access to metaintelligence, shows significant potential for improving student engagement and motivation. Empirical research and case studies have confirmed the effectiveness of these strategies in various educational contexts. However, for optimal performance, it is essential to address implementation challenges and continuously monitor the long-term effects on educational outcomes. We have examined metaintelligence and gamification in the educational context, focusing not only on advantages but also on challenges faced by users in the AI era.

Case studies suggest that gamification can positively influence educational outcomes – provided it is thoughtfully designed and implemented. Successful integration hinges on aligning gamification with principles of metaintelligence, enabling the development of both cognitive and emotional competencies. Without this alignment, gamification risks promoting superficial engagement, where competition overshadows genuine learning.

The implementation of gamification and metaintelligence in education faces numerous technical challenges, including infrastructural obstacles, network latency, and limitations of edge computing. Overcoming these challenges requires investment in technological infrastructure, development of efficient network protocols, and optimization of applications for devices with limited resources. Key issues include the need for ongoing professional development for educators, resolving technical difficulties, and aligning the curriculum with emerging technologies. Moreover, conducting longitudinal research is essential to evaluate the long-term impact of AI-based gamification on learning outcomes.

Although gamification can increase student engagement, it is necessary to carefully design systems to avoid psychological challenges, such as addiction and negative effects on motivation. Balancing intrinsic and extrinsic motivators, with careful planning of rewards, is a key to achieving positive educational outcomes. At the same time, its long-term sustainability requires thoughtful design, ethical approaches, and alignment with broader educational goals. Considering the rapid pace of technological progress, continuous evaluation and adaptation of strategies are essential for achieving sustainable educational results.

Incorporating metaintelligence into gamified learning activities can enhance the effectiveness of gamification, mitigate potential drawbacks, and improve educational results. Developing students' metacognitive skills plays a central role in this process, as it helps them better understand their learning strategies, thereby boosting motivation and engagement. However, for gamification to be truly effective, its design must be carefully considered to avoid pitfalls such as excessive competition or an overemphasis on extrinsic rewards at the expense of meaningful learning.

Conflict of interest

The authors declare no conflicts of interest.

Author details

Nevenka Popović Šević[1] and Aleksandar Šević[2]*

1 Faculty of Contemporary Arts, University Business Academy in Novi Sad, Belgrade, Serbia

2 Trinity College Dublin, Trinity Business School, Dublin, Ireland, and Information Technology School, Belgrade, Serbia

*Address all correspondence to: a.sevic@tcd.ie

References

[1] Minsky M. The Society of Mind. New York: Simon and Schuster; 1988

[2] Goertzel B. The Hidden Pattern: A Patternist Philosophy of Mind. Boca Raton, Florida: Brown Walker Press; 2006

[3] Sternberg RJ, Glaveanu V, Karami S, Kaufman JC, Phillipson SN, Preiss DD. Meta-Intelligence: Understanding, control, and interactivity between creative, analytical, practical and wisdom-based approaches in problem solving. Journal of Intelligence. 2021;**9**(2):19. DOI: 10.3390/jintelligence9020019

[4] Al-Azawi R, Al-Faliti F, Al-Blushi M. Educational gamification vs. game based learning: Comparative study. International Journal of Innovation, Management and Technology. 2016;7(4):132–136. DOI: 10.18178/ijimt.2016.7.4.659

[5] Hallifax S, Lavoué E, Serna A. To tailor or not to tailor gamification? An analysis of the impact of tailored game elements on learners' behaviours and motivation. In: Bittencourt I, Cukurova M, Muldner K, Luckin R, Millán E, editors. Artificial Intelligence in Education. AIED 2020. Lecture Notes in Computer Science. Vol. **12163**, Cham: Springer; 2020:216–227. DOI: 10.1007/978-3-030-52237-7_18

[6] Metwally AHS, Yousef AMF, Yining W. Micro design approach for gamifying students' assignments. In: 2020 IEEE 20th International Conference on Advanced Learning Technologies (ICALT). Tartu, Estonia: IEEE; 2020. p. 349–351. DOI: 10.1109/ICALT49669.2020.00112

[7] Zainuddin Z, Shujahat M, Haruna H, Chu SKW. The role of gamified e-quizzes on student learning and engagement: An interactive gamification solution for a formative assessment system. Computers and Education. 2020;**145**:103729. DOI: 10.1016/j.compedu.2019.103729

[8] Rapp A, Hopfgartner F, Hamari J, Linehan C, Cena F. Strengthening gamification studies: Current trends and future opportunities of gamification research. International Journal of Human-Computer Studies. 2019;127,1–6. DOI: 10.1016/j.ijhcs.2018.11.007

[9] Mustafa A. The personalization of e-learning systems with the contrast of strategic knowledge and learner's learning preferences: An investigatory analysis. Applied Computing and Informatics. 2020;**17**(1):153–167. DOI: 10.1016/j.aci.2018.08.001

[10] Lo CK, Hew KF. A comparison of flipped learning with gamification, traditional learning, and online independent study: The effects on students' mathematics achievement and cognitive engagement. Interactive Learning Environments. 2020;**28**(4):464–481

[11] Thomson H. 'Don't ask what AI can do for us, ask what it is doing to us', are ChatGPT and co harming human intelligence? The Guardian. 2025

[12] Flynn JR. Requiem for nutrition as the cause of IQ gains: Raven's gains in Britain 1938 – 2008. Economics and Human Biology. 2009;**7**(1):18–27. DOI: 10.1016/j.ehb.2009.01.009

[13] OECD. PISA 2022 results (Volume I): The state of learning and equity in education. Paris: PISA, OECD Publishing; 2023. DOI: 10.1787/53f23881-en

[14] Owen P. How Gamification Can Help Your Business Engage in Sustainability. London and New York: Routledge; 2017

[15] Deterding S, Dixon D, Khaled R, Lennart N. From game design elements to gamefulness: Defining "Gamification". In: MindTrek '11: Proceedings of the 15th International Academic MindTrek Conference: Envisioning Future Media Environments. 2011; pp. 9–15. DOI: 10.1145/2181037.2181040

[16] Dicheva D, Dichev C, Agre G, Angelova G. Gamification in education: A systematic mapping study. Journal of Educational Technology and Society. 2015;**18**(3):75–88. http://www.jstor.org/stable/jeductechsoci.18.3.75

[17] Qian M, Clark KR. Game-based learning and 21st century skills: A review of recent research. Computers in Human Behavior. 2016;**63**:50–58. DOI: 10.1016/j.chb.2016.05.023

[18] Krath J, Schurmann L, von Korflesch HFO. Revealing the theoretical basis of gamification: A systematic review and analysis of theory in research on gamification, serious games and game-based learning. Computers in Human Behavior. 2021;**125**:106963. DOI: 10.1016/j.chb.2021.106963

[19] Goodfellow I, Bengio Y, Courville A, Bengio Y. Deep Learning. Vol. **1**. Cambridge, MA, USA: MIT Press; 2016

[20] Shafqat W, Byun YC. Incorporating similarity measures to optimize graph convolutional neural networks for product recommendation. Applied Sciences. 2021;**11**(1):1366. DOI: 10.3390/app11041366

[21] Hassan E, Khalil Y, Ahmad I. Learning feature fusion in deep learning-based object detector. Journal of Engineering. 2020;**11**:7286187. DOI: 10.1155/2020/7286187

[22] Kwemoi KC. The Integration of virtual reality and gamification in education. Research Output Journal of Biological and Applied Science. 2024;**3**(1):7–12

[23] Lampropoulos G, Kinshuk. Virtual reality and gamification in education: A systemic review. Educational Technology Research and Development. 2024;**72**:1691–1785. DOI: 10.1007/s11423-024-10351-3

[24] Deci EL, Ryan RM. editors. Handbook of Self-determination Research. Rochester: University Rochester Press; 2004:141–161

[25] Cheung SY, Ng KY. Application of the educational game to enhance student learning. Frontiers in Education. 2011;**6**:623793. DOI: 10.3389/feduc.2021.623793

[26] Legg S, Hutter E. Universal intelligence: A definition of machine Intelligence. Minds & Machines. 2007;**17**(4):391–444. DOI: 10.48550/arXiv.0712.3329

[27] Poole D, Mackworth A, Goebel R. Computational Intelligence: A logical approach. New York, NY: Oxford University Press; 1998

[28] Newell A, Simon HA. Computer science as empirical enquiry: Symbols and search. Communications of the Association for Computing Machinery. 1976;**19**(3):113–126. DOI: 10.1145/360018.360022

[29] Sternberg RJ. A Theory of Adaptive Intelligence and its relation to general Intelligence. Journal of Intelligence. 2019;7(4):23. DOI: 10.3390/jintelligence7040023

[30] Mohammed SY, Aljanabi M, Gadekallu TR. Navigating the Nexus: A systematic review of the symbiotic relationship between the metaverse and gaming. International Journal of Cognitive Computer and Engineering. 2024;**5**:88–103. DOI: 10.1016/j.ijcce.2024.02.001

[31] Vanschoren JM-L. Hutter F, Kotthoff L, Vanschoren J, editors. Automated Machine Learning. The Springer Series on Challenges in Machine Learning. Cham: Springer; 2021. pp. 35–62. DOI: 10.1007/978-3-030-05318-5

[32] Zoph B, Vasudevan V, Shlens J, Le Q. Learning transferable architectures for scalable image recognition. In: Proceedings of the IEEE computer society conference on computer vision and pattern recognition. 2018. pp. 8697–8710. DOI: 10.1109/CVPR.2018.00907

[33] Kabudi T, Pappas I, Hakon D. AI-enabled adaptive learning systems. A systematic mapping of the literature, Computers and Education. Artificial Intelligence. 2021;**2**(100017). DOI: 10.1016/j.caeai.2021.100017

[34] Wang L, Jin B, Huang Z, Zhao H, Lian D, Liu Q, Chen E. Preference-adaptive meta-learning for cold-start recommendation. In: Proceedings of the Thirtieth International Joint Conference on Artificial Intelligence (IJCAI-21), 2021; pp. 1607–1614

[35] Chen Z, Gan W, Wu J, Hu K, Lin H. Data scarcity in recommendation systems: A survey. ACM Transactions on Recommender Systems. 2025;**3**(3): 1–31. DOI: 10.48550/arXiv.2312.10073

[36] Mitsea E, Drigas A, Skianis C. A systematic review of serious games in the era of Artificial Intelligence, immersive technologies, metaverse and neuro-technologies: Transformation through meta-skills training. OSF. January 7, 2025. Available online: https://osf.io/2ukfm [Accessed: 2025-April-17]

[37] Pérez-Manzano A, Almela-Baeza J. Gamification and transmedia for scientific promotion and for encouraging scientific careers in adolescents. Media Education Research Journal. 2018;**26**(55):93–103. https://eric.ed.gov/?id=EJ1174603

[38] Westera W, Prada R, Mascarenhas S, Santos PA, Dias J, Guimarães M, Georgiadis K, Nyamsuren E, Bahreini K, Yumak Z. Artificial Intelligence moving serious gaming: Presenting reusable game AI components. Education and Information Technologies. 2019;**25**:351–380. DOI: 10.1007/s10639-019-09968-2

[39] Henry J, Tang S, Mukhopadhyay S, Yap MH. A randomized control trial for measuring student engagement through the internet of things and serious games. Internet of Things. 2021;**13**:100332. DOI: 10.1016/j.iot.2020.100332

[40] Getchell K, Oliver I, Miller A, Allison C. Metaverses as a platform for

game-based learning. In: Proceedings of the 2010 24th IEEE International Conference on Advanced Information Networking and Applications. Perth, Australia: April 20–23, 2010

[41] Arce N, Valdivia A. Adapting competitiveness and gamification to a digital platform for foreign language learning. International Journal of Emerging Technologies in Learning. 2020;**15**(20):194–209. DOI: 10.3991/ijet.v15i20.16135

[42] Li M, Ma S, Shi Y. Examining the effectiveness of gamification as a tool promoting teaching and learning in educational settings: A meta-analysis. Frontiers in Psychology. 2023. Available at: https://www.frontiersin.org/articles/10.3389/fpsyg.2023.1253549/full [Accessed: 2025-May-10]

[43] Purgina M, Mozgovoy M, Blake J. WordBricks: Mobile technology and visual grammar formalism for gamification of natural language grammar acquisition. Journal of Educational Computing Research. 2019;**58**(1). DOI: 10.1177/073563311983301

[44] Cruaud C. The playful frame: Gamification in a French-as-a-foreign language class. Innovation in Language Learning and Teaching. 2018;**12**(4):330–343. DOI: 10.1080/17501229.2016.1213268

[45] Landers RN, Bauer KN, Callan RC, Armstrong MB. Psychological theory and the gamification of learning. In: Reiners, Torsten, Wood, Lincoln C. Gamification in Education and Business. Cham: Springer; 2015. pp. 165–186. DOI: 10.1007/978-3-319-10208-5_9

[46] Loewen S, Crowther D, Isbell DR, Kim KM, Maloney J, Miller ZF, Rawal H. Mobile-assisted language learning: A Duolingo case study. ReCALL. 2019;**31**(3):293–311. DOI: 10.1017/S0958344019000065

[47] Munday P. The case for using DUOLINGO as part of the language classroom experience. RIED: Revista Iberoamericana de Educacion a Distancia. 2016;**19**(1):83–101

[48] Medina EGL, Kahoot! HCPR. A digital tool for learning vocabulary in a language classroom. Revista Publicando. 2017;**4**(12 (1)):441–449. https://revistapublicando.org/revista/index.php/crv/article/view/673

[49] Krach SK, McCreery MP, Rimel H. Examining teachers behavioral management charts: A comparison of class dojo and paper-pencil methods. Contemporary School Psychology. 2017;**21**(3):267–275. DOI: 10.1007/s40688-016-0111-0

[50] Lattore-Cosculluela C, Sierra-Sanchez V, Vazquez-Toledo S. Gamification, collaborative learning and transversal competences: Analysis of academic performance and students' perceptions. Smart Learning Environments. 2025;**12**(2). DOI: 10.1186/s40561-024-00361-2

[51] Robinson MM, Steyvers M. Linking computational models of two core tasks of cognitive control. Psychological Review. 2023;**130**(1):71–101. DOI: 10.1037/rev0000395

[52] Redondo-Rodríguez C, Becerra-Mejías JA, Gil-Fernández G, Rodríguez-Velasco FJ. Influence of gamification and cooperative work in peer, mixed and interdisciplinary teams on emotional intelligence, learning strategies and life goals that motivate

university students to study. International Journal of Environmental Research and Public Health. 2023;**20**(1):547. DOI: 10.3390/ijerph20010547

[53] Bar-El D, Ringland KE. Crafting game-based learning: An analysis of lessons for minecraft education edition. In: Proceedings of the 15th International Conference on the Foundations of Digital Games. 2020. pp. 1–4. DOI: 10.1145/3402942.3409788

[54] Bertoli B. Ben Bertoli's ClassRealm is gamifying the classroom. Wired. 2012. Available at: https://www.wired.com/2012/05/ben-bertolis-classrealm [Accessed: 2025-June-8]

[55] Henning M, Hagedorn-Hansen D, Leipzig K. Metacognitive learning: Skills development through gamification at the Stellenbosch learning factory as a case study. South African Journal of Industrial Engineering. 2017;**28**. DOI: 10.7166/28-3-1845

[56] Almeida C, Kalinowski M, Uchoa A, Feijo B (2023). Negative effects of gamification in education software: Systematic mapping and practitioner perceptions. arXiv https://arxiv.org/abs/2305.08346

[57] Bencsik A, Mezeiová A, Samu B. Gamification in higher education (case study on a management subject). International Journal of Learning, Teaching and Educational Research. 2021;**20**:211–231. DOI: 10.26803/ijlter.20.5.12

[58] Kaufman JC. Beghetto RA. In praise of Clark Kent: Creative metacognition and the importance of teaching kids when (not) to be creative. Roeper Review. 2013;**35**(3):155–165. DOI: 10.1080/02783193.2013.799413

[59] Zakarya M, Gillam L, Ali H, Rahman I, Salah K, Khan R, Rana O, Buyya R. epcAware: A game-based, energy, performance and cost-efficient resource management technique for multi-access edge computing. IEEE Transactions on Services Computing. 2022;**15**(3):1634–1648. DOI: 10.1109/TSC.2020.3005347

[60] Al-Ansi A, Al-Ansi A, Muthanna A, Elgendy I, Koucheryavy A. Survey on intelligence edge computing in 6G: Characteristics, challenges, potential use cases, and market drivers. Future Internet. 2021;**13**:118. DOI: 10.3390/fi13050118

[61] Ackerman PL, Kanfer R. Work in the 21st century: New directions for aging and adult development. American Psychologist. 2020;**75**(4):486–498. DOI: 10.1037/amp0000615

[62] Preiss DD, Cosmelli D, Grau V, Ortiz D. Examining the influence of mind wandering and metacognition on creativity in university and vocational students. Learning and Individual Differences. 2016;**51**:417–426. DOI: 10.1016/j.lindif.2016.07.010

[63] Ko CH, Yen JY, Yen CF, Chen CS, Chen CC. The association between Internet addiction and psychiatric disorder: A review of the literature. European Psychiatry. 2012;**27**(1):1–8. DOI: 10.1016/j.eurpsy.2010.04.011

[64] Small GW, Lee J, Kaufman A, Jalil J, Siddarth P, Gaddipati H, Moody TD, Bookheimer SY. Brain health consequences of digital technology use. Dialogues in Clinical Neuroscience. 2020;**22**(2):179–187. DOI: 10.31887/DCNS.2020.22.2/gsmall

[65] Trahan L, Stuebing KK, Hiscock MK, Fletcher JM. The Flynn effect: A meta-analysis. Psychological Bulletin. 2014;**140**(5):1332–1360. DOI: 10.1037/a0037173

[66] Dergaa I, Ben Saad H, Glenn JM, Amamou B, Ben Aissa M, Guelmami N, Fekih-Romdhane F, Chamari K. From tools to threats: A reflection on the impact of artificial-intelligence chatbots on cognitive health. Frontiers in Psychology. 2024;**15**:1259845. DOI: 10.3389/fpsyg.2024.1259845

[67] Kosmyna N, Hauptmann E, Yuan YT, Situ J, Liao XH, Beresnitzky AV, Braunstein I, Maes P. Your brain on ChatGPT: Accumulation of cognitive debt when using an AI assistant for essay writing task. Computer Science, Artificial Intelligence. 2025. DOI: 10.48550/arXiv.2506.08872

[68] Oakley B, Johnston M, Chen KZ, Jung E, Sejnowski T. The memory paradox: Why our brains need knowledge in an age of AI. In: The Artificial Intelligence Revolution: Challenges and Opportunities, 2025. Springer Nature; forthcoming.50. DOI: 10.48550/arXiv.2506.11015

[69] Hadi Mogavi R, Guo B, Zhang Y, Ul Haq E, Hui P, Ma X. When gamification spoils your learning: A qualitative case study of gamification misuse in a language-learning app. In: Proceedings of the Ninth ACM Conference on Learning @ Scale (L@S '22). 2022, Association for Computing Machinery. New York, NY, USA: pp. 175–188. DOI: 10.1145/3491140.3528274

[70] Denny P, McDonald F, Empson R, Kelly P, Petersen A. Empirical support for a causal relationship between gamification and learning outcomes. In: Proceedings of the 2018 CHI Conference on Human Factors in Computing Systems. Association for Computing Machinery. New York, NY, USA: 2018. pp. 1–13. DOI: 10.1145/3173574.3173885

[71] Oliveira RP, CGd S. Reis AdC, Souza WMd. Gamification in e-learning and sustainability: A Theoretical Framework. Sustainability. 2021;**13**(21):11945. DOI: 10.3390/su132111945

[72] Kyewski E, Krämer NC. To gamify or not to gamify? An experimental field study of the influence of badges on motivation, activity, and performance in an online learning course. Computers and Education. 2018;**118**:25–37. DOI: 10.1016/j.compedu.2017.11.006

Chapter 6

Supercharging Teaching and Learning Practical Skills within AI-Enabled Interactive Technologies

Fabio Oliveira

Abstract

This chapter examines the integration of AI-enabled interactive technologies into higher education, focusing on their potential to develop practical skills required for contemporary work environments. Drawing upon qualitative methods and illustrative examples from immersive virtual reality, conversational AI systems, and digital human avatars, the chapter explores how these tools support simulation-based learning, iterative practice, and personalised feedback. While the findings offer valuable insights into design considerations, pedagogical frameworks, and implementation strategies, they are not intended to be generalised due to the study's methodological approach, sample size, and the specific institutional context in which the data were collected. Limitations of the study are primarily contextual and include the absence of longitudinal data, which restricts the ability to assess long-term impacts. Nonetheless, the chapter contributes to ongoing debates on the evolving role of universities in preparing graduates for the workplace and provides evidence-informed guidance for educators seeking to adopt these technologies in a sustainable and scalable manner.

Keywords: Generative AI, AI, immersive technologies, practical skills, higher education, learning, teaching, lifelong learning

1. Introduction

Higher education is undergoing a period of significant transformation, shaped by economic, political, social, and technological developments. Over the past decade, these shifts have become increasingly visible, affecting how universities operate, how students engage with learning, and how institutions prepare graduates for employment [1]. Among these influences, interactive artificial intelligence (AI) technologies, particularly generative systems, virtual environments, and large language models, are beginning to exert a strong and immediate impact on student expectations, behaviour and learning experiences [1, 2].

This chapter discusses how such technologies are being introduced into learning environments to support the development of practical, work-relevant skills [1]. It is informed by academic literature as well as my own experience designing and delivering immersive learning sessions using immersive technologies. These include the use of immersive virtual reality (VR) environments populated by digital human avatars and the pilot of a conversational Generative AI (GenAI) tool designed to help students practice interpersonal skills through dialogues using a voice-only interface.

The wider relevance of this discussion lies in the continuing debate within academia and the public sphere regarding the role of universities in preparing graduates for the workplace. Employers increasingly expect graduates to contribute from the outset, applying both technical knowledge and a set of interpersonal and behavioural skills [3]. These practical abilities, such as communication, adaptability, empathy, and leadership, are now seen as essential complements to disciplinary knowledge [1, 2]. For instance, a business graduate beginning a career in sales must not only understand pricing models and closing techniques but also manage client expectations, listen actively, and adapt their style under pressure. These are not easily acquired through lectures or exams alone.

Traditional university environments, whether in-person or online, often struggle to deliver these forms of learning at scale [1, 2]. Role-plays and scenario-based activities can be effective, but they require time, preparation, and often the involvement of trained facilitators or actors. They can also be emotionally demanding for learners and difficult to deliver consistently across large groups [4]. As a result, while universities recognise the importance of practical skills, many students only develop them later in the workplace [1–3].

Recent advances in GenAI now offer tools that can help bridge this gap. These technologies allow educators to facilitate experiences that are realistic, adaptable, and scalable [5]. GenAI can create interactive scenarios, provide immediate feedback, and adjust its responses to individual users. These systems are powered by large language models, which generate spoken or written content based on patterns learned from vast datasets. Though they do not possess understanding in a human sense, they are capable of producing natural, context-aware responses in real time. When used thoughtfully, they can support personalised learning in a way that is flexible and responsive to individual needs.

These applications typically run on cloud infrastructure, which enables them to operate at scale and remain accessible to users without the need for specialised hardware. AI–as–a-Service allows institutions to deploy sophisticated systems without building them from scratch. A further development, known as retrieval-augmented generation (RAG), allows AI tools to incorporate external sources of information, making the learning experience more relevant and grounded in the subject matter being taught.

This chapter offers a reflective account of how these technologies are being used to support teaching and learning [6, 7]. The first part focuses on immersive VR. Between 2023 and 2025, I facilitated more than 700 VR training sessions involving learners from a wide range of contexts. These included sixth-form students in schools across Berkshire in England, undergraduate and postgraduate students, academic staff, civil servants, and professionals from the private sector. Each session focused on developing practical communication skills, including interview preparation, negotiation, conflict management, and leadership communication.

The VR experiences were delivered using a commercially available platform (www.bodyswaps./co) that combines digital human avatars with structured scenarios built around conceptual frameworks.

Qualitative data were gathered to capture participants' perceptions and reflections about their experiences training soft skills in VR. Out of more than 700 participants who completed a VR experience, a total of 123 participants completed an online survey; 35 of them then voluntarily provided written reflections in response to an open-ended prompt: 'Describe your experience of training a soft skill in a Virtual World with Digital Human Avatars'.

The sample profile of respondents primarily consisted of young people and students across various academic levels. Out of 123 active responses, the majority were young people (53), followed by undergraduate students (39), master's students (21), PhD students (4), and academic/faculty members (6). This diverse mix indicates a strong representation of learners at different stages of their educational journey, with a predominant focus on early-career individuals. The demographic composition suggests that the feedback reflects the perspectives of those actively engaged in academic development and likely to benefit from innovative learning tools, such as VR-based soft skills training.

For this chapter, only the qualitative accounts were analysed. All responses were anonymous to ensure participants' privacy and confidentiality in line with ethical research practices [8]. The textual data were subjected to a thematic analysis following six-phase approach, which supports the identification of recurring patterns in participants' subjective experiences [9].

This inductive analysis allowed themes to emerge directly from the data without applying a pre-defined coding frame, which is suitable when exploring experiential or interpretative questions [10]. Codes were grouped into higher-order themes, including the value of self-directed learning, the role of feedback and reflection, the challenge of emotional presence, the importance of realism in practice, the motivational effects of gamification, barriers to learning in digital contexts, and learners' expectations of personalised experiences. Each of these themes is discussed in turn in the following section. Thematic analysis was selected as it offers a flexible yet rigorous framework for interpreting qualitative data in educational settings [9].

The second part of the chapter presents findings from a study with second-year undergraduate students enrolled in a business and management module at a British university. Students were invited to take part in an optional activity in which they practised a simulated sales call using a GenAI companion. The AI acted both as a potential customer interested in purchasing a product and as a virtual mentor, offering guidance and feedback after each interaction.

The inductive data analysis [10] draws on interviews with twelve students and transcripts of interactions from thirty sessions between the students and the GenAI companion, carried out between February and May 2025. Only insights were extracted from the data to report students' perceptions of practicing a sales call with a GenAI system. Among other insights discussed in this chapter, I discuss the student's perceptions that the simulation helped them reflect on their communication style and build confidence before engaging in a real-world similar situation. They were often surprised by the AI's ability to vary its responses and introduce unexpected challenges. These findings are explored in detail later in the chapter.

The author reduced internal bias by cross-checking outputs with educators during seminars and workshops promoted at one international conference and two workshops delivered by the author to academics in two British universities. These sessions with academics were recorded, transcribed, and used by the researcher to support data analysis and interpretation. The data collected were stored securely in a private institutional cloud repository, and all data were anonymised.

Only the researcher has access to this data. The data collection was reviewed by the ethics committee of the leading university and granted ethical approval. The questionnaires for the VR project were answered voluntarily, and participants provided consent in doing so by scanning a QR code provided just after the experiences, in which only respondents who consented to participate answered. All participants were informed that the data collected would be anonymised and used only for academic writing. Access to the data can be requested from the corresponding author.

The remainder of this chapter is organised into four parts. First, it presents findings from immersive VR sessions using digital human avatars. Second, it discusses the use of conversational GenAI to support interpersonal skill development. Third, it explores adaptive learning approaches enabled by AI and their role in lifelong learning. Fourth, it considers the ethical challenges raised by these technologies, focusing on issues of bias, privacy, and accessibility, before concluding with reflections on their implications for higher education.

2. Learning with digital human avatars: Student voices and data-driven insights

Imagine entering a virtual setting that closely replicates the physical world with remarkable detail. This immersive, three-dimensional environment is inhabited by AI-driven digital avatars designed to communicate in a natural and emotionally expressive way. These avatars are capable of maintaining eye contact, actively listening, and engaging in meaningful dialogue that reflects contextual awareness and emotional intelligence. Within this space, learners can interact with avatars in scenarios that demand critical thinking and empathy, whether negotiating agreements, resolving disputes, or participating in simulated job interviews. The overall experience is crafted to feel both realistic and emotionally resonant, enhancing the sense of presence and engagement.

This immersive environment illustrates the principles of active learning pedagogy [7], in which learners are directly engaged in activities that require analysis, problem-solving, and decision-making rather than passively receiving information. By engaging in realistic role-play and scenario-based activities, learners actively build their understanding, experiment with various approaches, and reflect on the consequences of their decisions. The interactive nature of these simulations promotes deeper cognitive engagement and the development of transferable skills, as participants must navigate evolving situations and respond to subtle emotional and contextual cues. The safe virtual environment encourages exploration, the seeking of feedback, and repeated practice, enabling learners to hone both interpersonal and cognitive competencies that are vital for tackling complex, real-world challenges.

VR headsets significantly enhance the realism of virtual learning environments by tracking learners' eye movements, vocal tone, speech pace, and head motion. These features are vital for creating a genuine sense of presence and embodiment, both of which are essential for meaningful interaction within virtual settings [11, 12]. At the end of each session, learners receive personalised feedback through an AI-generated performance dashboard. This typically includes whether they maintained eye contact, the clarity of their speech, their use of filler words, and how their body language may have been perceived. These insights play a central role in the learning process by highlighting specific areas for improvement and prompting immediate reflection.

The transition from traditional face-to-face learning to learning with digital human avatars can be understood by examining key dimensions of the learning experience. **Table 1** presents a side-by-side comparison of these two approaches, highlighting how the shift in interaction mode, emotional engagement, feedback mechanisms, scalability, and adaptability alters the nature of active skill development. This comparison illustrates how immersive, AI-powered environments extend the possibilities of active learning by combining realistic, context-rich scenarios with the benefits of automation, scalability, and personalised feedback.

Such analytical feedback supports the learner's ability to assess and develop practical skills, such as communication, presentation, and negotiation. These personalised data points contribute to increased self-awareness and allow learners to monitor their progress more effectively [13]. In particular, GenAI avatars embedded within high-fidelity three-dimensional (3D) environments have been

Dimension	From: Active learning (face-to-face)	To: Learning with digital human avatars
Interaction mode	Physical presence with human actors or peers	Virtual presence with AI-powered digital human avatars
Emotional engagement	Generated through in-person cues, such as body language and tone	Generated through realistic avatar behaviour, voice synthesis, and emotional AI
Feedback	Provided by facilitators or peers, variable in immediacy and detail	Immediate, consistent, data-driven AI feedback on communication and non-verbal cues
Scalability	Limited by time, space, and the availability of skilled facilitators	Scalable for large groups, accessible from anywhere with internet and hardware (mobile, desktop, or VR headsets)
Cost & resources	Requires trained facilitators, physical venues, and scheduling	Requires VR/AR equipment and platform licences, lower marginal cost per learner
Psychological safety	May involve social pressure or performance anxiety	Reduced social judgement, allowing safe experimentation and failure
Adaptability	Adjustments depend on the facilitator's awareness and skill	AI can adapt scenarios in real-time based on learner responses
Repetition	Limited by time and resource availability	Unlimited practice opportunities with scenario resets
Data capture	Mostly observational, subject to facilitator bias	Automated collection of interaction metrics for detailed progress tracking

Source: Compiled by the author.

Table 1.
From face-to-face active learning to digital human-avatar learning.

shown to support realistic, context-sensitive conversations that mirror real-world interactions [14, 15]. These systems respond to learner input in natural language, allowing for a more lifelike learning experience.

The value of such immersive simulations is especially evident when learners must navigate complex social situations [16]. Previous research suggests that learners prefer avatar-based simulations over traditional video, citing fewer distractions and greater focus on the learning message [15–17]. Unlike video, avatar-led experiences reduce the intimidation that learners may feel when faced with human actors, while still encouraging emotional engagement and concentration. This enables learners to build communication skills in a psychologically safe environment [15, 16].

The visual appearance of avatars also influences learner engagement. Consistency in avatar behaviour, coupled with realistic gestures, facial expressions, and voice tone, contributes to a stronger sense of connection [18, 19]. Participants in virtual learning sessions reported feeling a stronger presence of avatars, which contributed to reduced feelings of isolation and increased willingness to engage in tasks. These findings are consistent with earlier studies on the role of presence and embodiment in digital learning environments [11, 12, 14].

Nevertheless, limitations persist. Some learners experience physical discomfort, such as motion sickness and fatigue, particularly during longer sessions. The technology also raises concerns about privacy, as VR systems collect extensive personal data, including movement, gaze, and voice patterns [20]. Additionally, not all learners are comfortable using VR hardware, especially those less familiar with immersive technologies. These factors highlight the importance of inclusive design, clear guidance, and technical support during implementation.

Despite these constraints, immersive environments supported by AI show significant potential for enhancing educational outcomes. VR can facilitate all stages of active learning [7], not only offering hands-on experience but also supporting action and reflection [7]. This is particularly valuable in developing skills such as leadership, negotiation, and communication, which require learners to practise in dynamic, context-rich environments that feel emotionally and socially authentic [15, 21].

Learners consistently emphasised how VR encouraged active, self-directed learning. Rather than passively absorbing content, participants navigated evolving scenarios based on their responses, reinforcing their sense of control and agency [22, 23]. Several participants stated they felt 'more in control' of their learning, particularly when they were able to rehearse presentations or interviews in a low-risk environment. One student remarked that the experience was 'a very unique experience', while another stated, 'It reminded me of a lot of qualities that I forget are important'. Such reflections reinforce the cognitive and reflective elements supported by active learning pedagogy [7]. Moreover, feedback emerged as a key driver of improvement. Participants highlighted that AI-driven feedback, focused on tone, clarity, and delivery, was more consistent and immediate than that offered by human facilitators, enhancing both self-awareness and performance [21, 22].

Feedback emerged as a powerful learning mechanism. Participants noted that, unlike human facilitators who may hesitate to provide honest criticism, the system delivered direct and consistent feedback. This included metrics on speech speed, tone, clarity, and posture. One participant noted, 'The feedback was immediate and really helped me understand what to improve', while another shared, 'I want to improve and try again after seeing how I sounded'. These comments reinforce the role of the AI system in supporting a feedback loop that fosters reflection and active experimentation [7].

Emotional engagement also featured prominently. While some expressed nervousness before their first session, many acknowledged that the realistic digital human avatars and immersive setting prompted genuine emotional responses. Learners described moments of hesitation, empathy, and self-reflection, particularly when discussing sensitive topics with avatars trained to simulate distress or disagreement. A student commented, 'I was nervous at first but felt more confident by the end', while another described the scenario as 'engaging and very realistic'. These insights accentuate the emotional realism and sense of presence evoked by embodied VR interactions [15, 24, 25].

Realism and embodiment were also linked to the effectiveness of feedback. Learners appreciated how avatars responded to subtle changes in tone and body language, and how these nuances were included in their performance feedback. A participant captured this perspective when stating, 'It was like seeing yourself from the other side of the table'. Such comments highlight how embodiment and perspective-taking function as integral parts of the learning process, enhancing the learner's ability to reflect on their behaviour and performance in realistic social settings [25, 26].

In comparing these findings with global research, similar studies highlight consistent themes. For instance, Dubiel et al. [26] emphasised how VR-based soft skills training in professional education improved communication and teamwork, echoing the experiences observed here. Other international studies [15, 22] noted both opportunities and constraints, reinforcing that, while VR promotes engagement, challenges around accessibility and inclusivity remain globally relevant [15, 22]

Finally, several learners explicitly likened the training to gameplay, indicating that gamification positively influenced motivation. Some described it as 'enjoyable and immersive', while others said it made them 'want to improve and try again'. These reactions suggest that the training's game-like structure, with performance indicators and repeated trials, encouraged persistence and a desire for improvement, particularly among younger participants. The motivational effect of this structure supports existing assumptions about the efficacy of gamification in skill development [27].

Gamified virtual environments were seen as promoting self-directed learning, as students explored, repeated tasks, and interacted with non-player characters (NPCs) at their own pace [27]. Similar to our study participants, younger students in prior research reported that the rewards and immediate feedback loops helped them 'want to improve and try again', validating the motivational power of gamification [27]. Moreover, authors found that students immersed in gamified metaverse experiences displayed higher levels of engagement and intrinsic motivation compared to traditional approaches, reinforcing the relevance of these elements in education beyond entertainment [28].

Finally, learners demonstrated a clear desire for personalisation. Many wished for the system to provide adaptive tips, learning pathways, or suggested practice routines tailored to individual weaknesses. This was particularly relevant for those with prior experience in communication or public speaking, who felt that more advanced challenges would maintain their engagement.

These VR training experiences, drawn from a range of contexts and analysed through participants' voices, reflect the growing potential of immersive technology to enhance practical learning. They also highlight several implementation challenges – technical, pedagogical, and organisational – that educators must consider. The analysis suggests that when VR is well-designed and carefully facilitated, it supports meaningful learning and equips learners with critical social and communication skills for increasingly complex and dynamic professional settings.

3. Conversational GenAI: Practicing skills, companionship, and personalised constructive feedback

Early chatbot systems in education were based on rule-driven conversational structures. These relied on predefined dialogue paths and could only respond when the user's input matched a programmed utterance. An utterance referred to the exact words or phrases entered, while the intent described what the user was trying to achieve, such as asking for a deadline or clarification. These systems, although innovative at the time, lacked flexibility and often failed to manage variations in language or unexpected user queries. For example, while a chatbot might respond correctly to 'When is my essay due?', it might not recognise 'What's the hand-in date for the paper?', unless specifically programmed. As a result, the exchanges often felt mechanical, superficial, and limiting in terms of user engagement.

Despite their limitations, rule-based chatbots initially supported administrative tasks such as routine queries and reminders. However, their rigidity and maintenance demands made them unsuited for developing interpersonal or reflective skills. Conversational chatbot systems have evolved significantly from their early, rule-based forms to the advanced GenAI and digital human agents available today. While early models supported basic administrative functions such as routine queries and reminders, their limited adaptability and reliance on pre-programmed responses made them unsuitable for developing complex interpersonal or reflective skills.

Over time, advances in natural language processing, sentiment analysis, and intent recognition have enabled systems to interact with greater context awareness, realism, and coherence. These capabilities are now applied across diverse domains, including municipal services. **Table 2** outlines this progression, showing the timeline of key systems, their core capabilities, and their limitations.

GenAI has brought forward more sophisticated solutions. For instance, the City of Amarillo introduced Emma, a digital human assistant able to converse in over 60 languages, designed and deployed with Dell's infrastructure and AI Factory framework [29, 30]. In aviation, Qatar Airways partnered with UneeQ to create Sama 2.0, a digital human flight attendant who engages customers with empathetic, real-time conversations via apps, kiosks, and immersive platforms [31, 32]. These implementations illustrate how GenAI has evolved systems from functional chatbots to adaptive, emotionally attuned digital human agents offering richer learning and service experiences.

These systems now respond with context awareness, realism, and coherence, enabling more authentic and flexible interaction. They are being integrated into teaching and learning processes as tools for developing practical competencies through simulation, feedback, and repeated practice. For example, Alelo provides cloud-based GenAI sessions in which professionals engage in challenging

Year	Example	Capabilities	Limitations
1966	ELIZA (MIT)	Basic pattern matching simulates conversation by recognising keywords	No understanding of context; limited to pre-programmed scripts
2001	SmarterChild (AOL/ MSN Messenger)	Interactive Q&A, entertainment, basic info retrieval	Limited adaptability; fixed responses; no emotional intelligence
2014	Microsoft XiaoIce	Emotionally aware conversation; context retention across sessions	Cultural/linguistic constraints; limited domain knowledge
2023	City of Amarillo 'Emma' (Dell AI Factory)	Converses in 60 + languages; supports city services	Domain-limited to municipal services; dependent on accurate data
2024	Qatar Airways Sama 2.0 (UneeQ)	Digital human flight attendant: empathetic, real-time conversation via multiple channels	Primarily customer service-focused; not a full training platform
2025	Alelo AI training	Cloud-based professional simulations; real-time personalised feedback; practice anytime	Requires internet access; dependent on the quality of AI feedback
2025	Retorio AI coaching	Simulates sales conversations; analyses verbal and non-verbal communication	Requires camera and microphone; accuracy varies with the environment
2025	Mursion	Blends immersive simulation with live coaching for workplace skills	High setup cost; limited scalability without automation.
2025	Promova Practice with AI	Language learning with idioms and vocabulary, real-time corrections, and context-rich practice	Focused on language learning; limited professional application.

Source: Compiled by the author.

Table 2.
Timeline evolution of conversational chatbot systems.

conversations with socially intelligent avatars, receiving immediate, personalised feedback and practicing as often as needed, resulting in significantly faster skill acquisition than with traditional methods [33].

Similarly, Retorio offers AI coaching software that simulates sales conversations and delivers tailored feedback on both verbal and non-verbal communication, helping staff refine their approach in a secure environment [34]. Mursion blends immersive simulations with expert coaching to support upskilling in workplace interactions, such as giving feedback or managing difficult dialogues, with evidence of strong learner engagement and transfer to real-world practice [35].

In the domain of language learning, several mobile applications support users in practising idioms through context-rich, bite-sized lessons. For instance, Promova's Practice With AI feature enables students to engage in dynamic vocabulary exercises, prompting them to use new words in sentence form, receive real-time corrections and guidance, and gradually build speaking confidence as they practise at their own pace [36].

The use of conversational AI companions in simulation-based training supports not only technical proficiency but also the development of critical thinking and communication strategies. These tools enable learners to exercise both individual judgement and social reasoning, reflecting recent calls to strengthen both dimensions of critical thinking in management education [37].

This study contributes to this agenda by examining how students cognitively and emotionally engage with AI companions when practising tasks that require persuasion, adaptability and reflection. Through structured role-play, reflective feedback, and user interactions, the study offers insight into how students engage cognitively and affectively with AI companions as part of their learning journey [37]. To support these aims, I have developed and implemented a voice-enabled AI tool for undergraduate business students to practise sales dialogues.

The AI plays two roles: first, as a customer interested in purchasing a VR headset, and second, as a sales mentor providing personalised feedback. Students access the system through a web interface and initiate voice interactions. The system introduces the simulation, explains its purpose, and invites the student to begin. The student is expected to identify the customer's needs, link these to the product's value and features, and manage any objections that arise. If the customer agrees to purchase, the student concludes the session by simulating payment collection. After the call, the AI delivers feedback linked to assessment criteria and provides an example of a model script. All interactions are stored securely and can be reviewed by educators to track progress and identify learning needs.

The tool provides a structured environment in which learners can repeatedly practise and refine professional behaviours. These learning opportunities reflect the principles of active learning pedagogies described by Scheuring and Thompson [38], whose research demonstrated that simulation-based experiences significantly support learners' self-assessed development of essential life skills, including adaptability, emotional intelligence, and decision-making. Their findings emphasise that simulations offer a safe space for experimentation, facilitate the application of theoretical knowledge in practice, and help build confidence in managing complex, real-world challenges.

These insights are directly relevant to the AI-powered sales simulation employed in this study, where learners are required to respond to diverse and often unpredictable scenarios in real time. This is particularly significant given previous research indicating that learners increasingly perceive such systems as supportive learning companions. These AI tools help extend understanding and encourage contextual application of knowledge, offering consistent and non-judgemental responses [39]. Similarly, Moundridou et al. [40] observed that GenAI systems enhanced the design and implementation of inquiry-based learning activities. Their ability to support task development, content adaptation, and guided questioning contributed to a more active and learner-centred approach.

Although their focus was on lesson planning, the implications for skill development are significant. The adaptability of these systems enables learners to move through stages of a task with real-time support, which is particularly relevant for practising skills such as negotiation, decision-making, and customer communication. This was reinforced by Maurya [41], who used ChatGPT as a simulated client in counselling training. Students practised responses, received immediate feedback, and repeated sessions until they felt confident. This iterative engagement helped to solidify learning, reinforcing the idea that AI companions can act as safe, private rehearsal spaces for developing interpersonal skills. These parallels emphasise the relevance of conversational AI not just in business education but also in emotionally complex domains such as counselling.

The benefits of early exposure to such simulations were explored by observing that first-year university students showed greater skill development than their final-year counterparts [38]. This supports the case for embedding AI-supported simulations early in degree programmes, particularly in modules that introduce professional communication and interpersonal skill-building. Furthermore, their extension of the life skills framework to include adaptability and resilience is especially relevant in AI-mediated simulations, where students are required to adjust to the AI's dynamic responses, manage uncertainty, and reflect on their performance.

From an educator's perspective, these technologies introduce opportunities for designing scalable, accessible, and personalised simulations [42]. By using cloud-based tools and natural language prompting, educators can create role-play experiences that adjust to each learner's level of performance. The strength of GenAI lies in its ability to simulate human-like engagement while remaining consistent and available at all times [43]. This opens new possibilities for offering continuous practice without increasing the teaching workload.

Students involved in the AI simulation research described the system as both useful and engaging. They were surprised by the variety and unpredictability of the AI's responses and felt encouraged to improve their product knowledge in preparation for subsequent attempts. These reactions are consistent with previous research, where it was found that business simulations not only improve subject-specific knowledge but also enhance self-assessed skills such as adaptability and resilience [38, 42]. Additionally, the findings of this study are consistent with those observed in studies of business simulations, which have been shown to strengthen both technical understanding and transferable skills [38]. In both cases, learners value the realism of the task, the safety of the environment, and the chance to fail without consequence.

The students' feedback also pointed to increased motivation and confidence. They valued the ability to practise multiple times in a private, low-pressure environment, at their own pace. Many preferred practising with the AI rather than with peers or tutors, citing the absence of social judgement and the system's consistent performance. Similar findings documented that students described AI voicebots as supportive, fair, and helpful [44]. Their presence filled a gap where human guidance was not available, particularly in formative stages of learning. Previous studies suggest that students practising counselling scenarios with ChatGPT not only improved their technical skills but also formed a sense of connection with the system [42].

This emotional engagement nurtured motivation to repeat and refine the interaction, an outcome echoed in my own study. Students reported feeling 'glad and happy' to use the sales companion, recognising the benefit of a non-judgemental partner that allowed for failure, experimentation, and growth. Students' willingness to engage repeatedly with the AI system indicates not only their desire to improve task performance but also an emerging disposition to revisit their assumptions and reframe their strategy. This affective dimension of critical thinking, curiosity, openness, and tolerance for ambiguity is crucial in preparing learners for AI-mediated work environments [37].

Despite these positive outcomes, several limitations must be noted. Students expressed a need for improved voice recognition, particularly for accents and varied phrasings. There were also occasional concerns about response consistency and the accuracy of information. These are valid observations, substantiated by other authors [39], who found that while learners appreciated the support of GenAI, they questioned the reliability of content and expressed concern about over-reliance on automated systems.

While learners valued the 24/7 availability and non-judgemental tone of the AI companion, there is a pedagogical risk that they may come to view its feedback as definitive. Authors caution that GenAI systems, due to their confident and coherent communication style, may lead students to adopt their outputs uncritically [37]. To mitigate this, we encourage educators to integrate reflection checkpoints that prompt learners to compare AI feedback with other sources or to explore what the AI might be omitting.

This discussion reinforces the need for careful oversight and integration by educators to ensure that AI tools complement rather than replace critical human judgement and feedback. This can be achieved with post-simulation debriefs, where students can be invited to reflect not only on their individual performance but also on the ethical and social dimensions of the simulated exchange. This reflects calls to develop students' social critical thinking and their capacity to question the broader societal assumptions embedded in AI-generated dialogues [37].

These findings align with global evidence. For example, Maurya [41] found that ChatGPT-based counselling simulations enhanced reflective practice among students, while Nyaaba et al. [39] described genAI as a 'learning buddy' valued for non-judgemental support. This comparative evidence suggests that the affective dimension of AI learning companions – motivation, confidence, and reflection – is consistently reported across diverse disciplines.

In summary, the integration of conversational genAI into higher education offers a valuable means of supporting the development of practical and transferable skills. These systems, when designed and deployed with pedagogical care, allow learners to practise, receive feedback, and grow in ways that reflect both industry expectations and academic standards. As Scheuring and Thompson [38] demonstrate, simulation-based learning can make a meaningful contribution to graduate employability. When combined with the flexibility and scalability of genAI, such tools represent a promising direction for enhancing life skills and learner agency in complex, technology-rich environments.

4. AI-enabled adaptive learning for lifelong learning

Adaptive learning refers to the use of technology, particularly AI, to personalise educational content and pace according to an individual learner's needs, abilities, and progress. Rather than following a fixed curriculum, adaptive systems analyse real-time data on learner performance, such as correct responses, time spent on tasks, and patterns of engagement, to adjust the level of difficulty, sequence of topics, and type of instructional resources provided [**45**]. This approach draws on AI algorithms for natural language processing, predictive analytics, and recommendation systems to ensure that the learner receives content that is both challenging and achievable, facilitating mastery before progression [46].

By providing personalised pathways and timely feedback, adaptive learning can nurture the motivation and confidence required for individuals to engage in learning as an ongoing practice rather than a one-off activity. When integrated into traditional teaching design, AI-enabled adaptive systems can complement existing curricula by offering targeted interventions, self-paced progression, and context-relevant challenges. This integration not only supports immediate mastery of subject matter but also cultivates the habits, self-regulation, and adaptability that underpin lifelong learning, equipping individuals to continuously update their knowledge and skills in response to evolving demands.

In this context, lifelong learning has become essential for career resilience, employability, and active participation in society [47]. It supports professional agility by ensuring that workers can update and expand their skills in response to emerging technologies and shifting market needs. In the age of AI, lifelong learning is particularly critical for professionals whose roles are being reshaped by automation and intelligent systems. The World Economic Forum [47] highlights that technological change is increasing the demand for cognitive skills such as analytical thinking, problem-solving, and creativity, alongside interpersonal abilities such as communication, emotional intelligence, curiosity, and collaboration. Without structured opportunities for continuous skill development, professionals risk skill obsolescence and reduced competitiveness in the labour market.

AI-enabled adaptive learning systems offer a scalable solution for fostering lifelong learning. By tailoring content and learning trajectories to individual needs, these systems become a cognitive partner that can support diverse learners, from undergraduates to senior professionals, in acquiring new competencies efficiently. They enable self-paced, personalised experiences, allowing learners to revisit challenging topics or accelerate through familiar material without relying on one-size-fits-all instruction [48]. Moreover, adaptive learning environments can integrate real-world simulations, scenario-based tasks, and AI-driven feedback loops to promote both technical and soft skills.

The benefits of AI-enabled adaptive learning systems are well-documented. Meta-analytic evidence indicates that these systems have a medium-to-large positive effect on cognitive learning outcomes compared with non-adaptive approaches [46]. They can enhance learner motivation, reduce dropout rates, and improve mastery by providing timely interventions and customised feedback [45]. Additionally, adaptive learning contributes to inclusivity by accommodating diverse learning styles, linguistic backgrounds, and levels of prior knowledge. Therefore, AI-enabled adaptive learning can be the catalyst for real symbiotic human–machine collaboration, fostering the development of unique human capabilities that distinguish themselves from AI capabilities. These are the skills and abilities previously cited in the World Economic Forum Report [47].

Practical applications demonstrate the versatility of these systems. Alelo's AI-driven avatars allow professionals to practise communication in high-stakes scenarios, offering immediate personalised feedback that accelerates skill acquisition. Similarly, Mursion blends AI simulations with live coaching to support skill development in leadership and customer service contexts. In language learning, platforms such as Promova integrate AI conversation partners for practising idioms and vocabulary, providing real-time corrections that improve fluency and confidence. Evidence from these implementations shows improvements in learner engagement, knowledge retention, and application of skills to real-world contexts [46, 48].

Findings from this study resonate with broader global research. Strielkowski et al. [45] argue that adaptive AI systems can transform educational delivery by supporting equity and inclusivity, while Wang et al. [46] provide meta-analytic evidence of medium-to-large positive effects on learning outcomes. Demartini et al. [48] further demonstrate how adaptive platforms in higher education foster targeted skill acquisition, consistent with the personalised pathways observed in this chapter.

Recent global work by UNESCO [49] also points to the transformative potential of genAI in reshaping assessment and pedagogy. The authors of this report argue that legacy assessment systems, particularly standardised testing, often constrain authentic learning and create systemic inequities. GenAI, when integrated into carefully designed educational environments, can enable continuous formative feedback, support multimodal knowledge creation, and reduce reliance on summative tests [49]. These perspectives align with the findings reported here, where adaptive AI tools fostered personalised and reflective learning pathways, and they underline the importance of designing AI use around principles of equity, inclusion, and epistemic justice.

However, several challenges remain. Ethical concerns include data privacy, algorithmic bias, and transparency in decision-making [45]. The successful adoption of AI-enabled adaptive systems also depends on educators' digital literacy, institutional readiness, and the availability of infrastructure. Over-reliance on AI tools risks reducing opportunities for human-to-human interaction, which remains essential for social learning and the development of empathy.

AI-enabled adaptive learning holds significant potential to transform lifelong learning by offering personalised, flexible, and effective educational experiences. By integrating these systems into both formal and informal learning pathways, education providers can equip learners with the skills necessary for professional resilience in an AI-driven world. However, realising these benefits requires addressing challenges around ethics, equity, and implementation to ensure that adaptive learning remains a tool for empowerment rather than exclusion.

5. Challenges and ethical assumptions in learning with AI-enabled interactive technologies

Despite the potential benefits of AI-immersive tools in education, several challenges and ethical considerations were raised. Many participants described their experiences with VR headsets as positive, while others highlighted barriers to effective learning. Some found online and independent learning demotivating without external structure, while a few reported motion sickness or discomfort when using the headset. Others expressed a preference for group activities or human feedback, noting the limitations of interacting solely with avatars. These perspectives underscore the importance of integrating VR into blended learning environments rather than offering it as a standalone solution.

The use of voice-over genAI simulations also presents challenges, particularly for international students whose first language is not English. Although the technology supports multi-language delivery, educators must consider whether it is appropriate for students to engage with content in their native language, even when enrolled in English-speaking programmes. Furthermore, when designing these applications, it is essential to ensure they are inclusive and accessible to learners with disabilities that may limit their ability to use such tools effectively.

Another critical issue is bias in AI models. Since these systems are trained on historical data, they may inadvertently replicate or amplify existing cultural, social, or linguistic biases, potentially affecting learners' experiences in unintended ways. Privacy and data security are also paramount concerns, as these tools often collect sensitive information, such as voice recordings, performance metrics, and behavioural patterns.

Additionally, there is a risk of over-reliance on automated systems, which could diminish opportunities for human interaction and peer learning if not carefully balanced. Finally, ensuring cultural appropriateness and inclusivity in avatar design, dialogue structures, and feedback mechanisms is vital to creating AI-enhanced learning environments that effectively serve diverse learner populations.

6. Conclusion

AI-enabled interactive technologies, such as conversational agents and digital human avatars, are reshaping how learners acquire and practise skills in both professional and educational contexts. Their ability to deliver personalised, context-aware, and realistic simulations offers clear benefits for developing practical competencies, critical thinking, and adaptability. However, these opportunities are accompanied by challenges related to ethics, bias, privacy, and cultural alignment. The effective integration of these tools requires a balanced approach that leverages their strengths while mitigating potential risks. This chapter has outlined their evolution, current applications, and implications for teaching and learning, highlighting the need for continued research into their impact and responsible use.

Acknowledgments

The author gratefully acknowledges the voluntary support provided by Gabriel Rodrigues de Oliveira during the facilitation of VR sessions conducted for data collection. In addition to assisting with the sessions, Gabriel also developed the Generative AI-based web application used by the students. The VR data collection was partially funded by the University of Reading's internal grant scheme, which the author received in 2022.

The author declares that there are no known financial or personal conflicts of interest that could have appeared to influence the work reported in this chapter.

Author details

Fabio Oliveira
Henley Business School, Reading, Henley, England.

*Address all correspondence to: f.deoliveira@henley.ac.uk

References

[1] Turnitin, Research Report. Crossroads: Navigating the intersection of AI in education. 2025. Available from: https://media.licdn.com/dms/document/media/v2/D4E10AQEohFRH1wP3kw/ads-document-pdf-analyzed/B4EZb8okkVHIAY-/0/1747995218312/TII_GL_AI_Research_EduFocussedSurvey_Ebook_US_0425pdf?e=1750323600&v=beta&t=TEqaezvxN9IyRmRiWW9jtuWtj-j654ant7_RaS-UTqo [Accessed: 2025-August-03]

[2] European Commission. European Skills, Competences, Qualifications and Occupations. 2025. Available from: https://esco.ec.europa.eu/en/classification/skill_main#overlayspin [Accessed: 2025-February-24]

[3] Fortune. Managers' latest complaints about Gen Z: They lack soft skills and have unrealistic workplace expectations. 2024. Available from: https://fortune.com/2024/01/23/gen-z-lacks-soft-skills-unrealistic-workplace-expectations/ [Accessed: 2025-February-24]

[4] Bradford DL. Ethical issues in experiential learning. Journal of Management Education. 2019;**43**(1):89–98. DOI: 10.1177/1052562918807500

[5] Oliveira FGD, Belitski M, Kakabadse N, Theodorakopoulos N. Unveiling the potential of digital human avatars in modern marketing strategies. International Marketing Review. 2024; DOI: 10.1108/IMR-12-2023-0339

[6] Coker JS, Heiser E, Taylor LA. Impacts of experiential learning depth and breadth on marketable skill development. Journal of Experiential Education. 2016;**40**(1):5–23. DOI: 10.1177/1053825916678265

[7] Prince M. Does active learning work? A review of the research. Journal of Engineering Education. 2004;**93**(3):223–231. DOI: 10.1002/j.2168-9830.2004.tb00809.x

[8] Brown R. Ethical dilemmas in education research: Tick boxes and trials. In: Iphofen R, editors. Handbook of Research Ethics and Scientific Integrity. Cham: Springer International Publishing; 2020. pp. 851–871. DOI: 10.1007/978-3-030-16759-2_47

[9] Braun V, Clarke V. Using thematic analysis in psychology. Qualitative Research in Psychology. 2006;**3**(2):77–101. DOI: 10.1191/1478088706qp063oa

[10] Nowell LS, Norris JM, White DE, Moules NJ. Thematic analysis: Striving to meet the trustworthiness criteria. International Journal of Qualitative Methods. 2017;**16**(1):1–13. DOI: 10.1177/1609406917733847

[11] Nowak KL, Biocca F. The effect of the agency and anthropomorphism on users' sense of telepresence, copresence, and social presence in virtual environments. Presence: Teleoperators and Virtual Environments. 2003;**12**(5):481–494. DOI: 10.1162/105474603322761289

[12] Alrehaili EA, Al Osman H. A virtual reality role-playing serious game for experiential learning. Interactive Learning Environments. 2022;**30**(5):922–935. DOI: 10.1080/10494820.2019.1703008

[13] Gao H, Lindquist M, Vergel RS. AI-Driven avatars in immersive 3D environments for education workflow and case study of the Temple of Demeter, Greece. Journal of Digital Landscape Architecture. 2024;640–651. doi:10.14627/537752059

[14] Basmaci F, Bulut AC, Ozcelik E, Zerdali Ekici S, Kilicarslan MA, Cagiltay NE. Evaluation of the effects of avatar on learning temporomandibular joint in a metaverse-based training. Journal of Dental Education. 2024; DOI: 10.1002/jdd.13806

[15] Radianti J, Majchrzak TA, Fromm J, Wohlgenannt I. More than experience? On the unique opportunities of virtual reality to afford a holistic experiential learning cycle. The Internet and Higher Education. 2021;**50**:100804. DOI: 10.1016/j.iheduc.2021.100804

[16] Chae RL, Lee H, Kim E. The Effects of Avatar Human-Likeness on Psychological Closeness in Virtual-Reality. Psychology & Marketing. 2025;**42**(4):1132–1145. DOI: 10.1002/mar.22168

[17] Donovan P. Actors and avatars: Why learners prefer digital agents. European Journal of Training and Development. 2015;**39**(9):738–768. DOI: 10.1108/EJTD-06-2015-0041

[18] Yuan Q, Gao Q. Being there and being together: Avatar appearance and peer interaction in VR classrooms for video-based learning. International Journal of Human–Computer Interaction. 2023;**40**(13):3313–3333. DOI: 10.1080/10447318.2023.2189818

[19] Miao F, Kozlenkova IV, Wang H, Xie T, Palmatier RW. An emerging theory of avatar marketing. Journal of Marketing. 2022;**86**(1):67–90. DOI: 10.1177/0022242921996646

[20] Cho M, Park J, Hong SW. Virtual vs. actual body: Applicability of anthropomorphic avatars to enhance exploratory creativity in architectural design education. Architectural Science Review. 2019;**62**(6):520–527. DOI: 10.1080/00038628.2019.1669526

[21] Chen Y, Chen Y, Lin W, Zheng Y, Xue T, Chen C, Chen G. Application of active learning strategies in metaverse to improve student engagement: An immersive blended pedagogy bridging patient care and scientific inquiry in pandemic. Available from: SSRN 4098179. 2022; DOI: 10.2139/ssrn.4098179

[22] Mayer RE, Makransky G, Parong J. The promise and pitfalls of learning in immersive virtual reality. International Journal of Human–Computer Interaction. 2023;**39**(11):2229–2238. DOI: 10.1080/10447318.2022.2108563

[23] Jones R, Bursens P. The effects of active learning environments: How simulations trigger affective learning. European Political Science. 2015;**14**(3):254–265. DOI: 10.1057/eps.2015.22

[24] Parmar D, Makransky G, Mayer RE. How immersion and self-avatars in VR affect learning programming and computational thinking in middle school education. Computers & Education. 2023;**191**:104640. DOI: 10.1109/TVCG.2022.3169426

[25] Saksvik-Lehouillier I. Experiencing the sense of presence within an educational desktop virtual reality. Heliyon. 2023;**9**:e17196. DOI: 10.1016/j.heliyon.2023.e17196

[26] Dubiel A, Kamińska D, Zwoliński G, Ramić-Brkić B, Agostini D, Zancanaro M. Virtual reality for the training of soft skills for professional education: Trends and opportunities. Interactive Learning Environments. 2025;1–21. DOI: 10.1080/10494820.2025.2450634

[27] Chen -C-C, Lin -Y-Y, Lo F-Y, Chang C-H, Lin H-M. From readers to players: Exploring student engagement in a gamified metaverse and its effect on reading interest. Education and Information Technologies. 2025;**30**:421–447. DOI: 10.1007/s10639-024-13068-1

[28] Ali M.Fostering engagement and motivation: evaluating gamified learning in the metaverse for architectural history education. International Journal of Interactive Mobile Technologies. 2025;**19**(6). DOI: 10.3991/ijim.v19i06.53841

[29] Dell Technologies. Digital Assistant Solutions update with Dell and NVIDIA. 2024. Available from: https://www.dell.com/en-us/blog/digital-assistant-solutions-update-with-dell-and-nvidia/ [Accessed: 2025-August-11]

[30] Konkel F. Meet Emma, Amarillo's AI assistant and 'digital human'. Route Fifty Available from: https://www.route-fifty.com/digital-government/2024/05/meet-emma-amarillos-ai-assistant-and-digital-human/396884/. 2024 Accessed 31 October 2025

[31] UneeQ. Media release: UneeQ and Qatar Airways elevate passenger experiences with Sama 2.0, the first digital human in aviation. 2024. Available from: https://www.digitalhumans.com/blog/uneeq-and-qatar-airways-elevate-passenger-experiences-with-sama-the-first-digital-human-in-aviation. [Accessed: 2025-August-11]

[32] Qatar Airways. Qatar Airways showcases new features of world's first AI virtual digital human cabin crew. March. Qatar Airways Newsroom. [Accessed: 2025-August-11]

[33] Alelo. Simulation training with artificial intelligence avatars. 2025. Available from: https://www.alelo.com/. [Accessed: 2025-August-11]

[34] Retorio. The pioneer in AI sales coaching. 2025. Available from: https://www.retorio.com/ . [Accessed: 2025-August-11]

[35] Mursion. Upskilling platform with immersive simulations. 2025. Available from: https://www.mursion.com/ . [Accessed: 2025-August-11]

[36] Promova. Learn English idioms through bite-sized lessons and real-life scenarios. 2025. Available from: https://promova.com/page/practice-with-ai [Accessed: 2025-August-11]

[37] Larson BZ, Moser C, Caza A, Muehlfeld K, Colombo LA. Critical thinking in the age of generative AI. Academy of Management Learning & Education. 2024;**23**(3):373–378. DOI: 10.5465/amle.2024.0338

[38] Scheuring F, Thompson J. Enhancing graduate employability: Exploring the influence of experiential simulation learning on life skill development. Studies in Higher Education. 2025;**50**(2):256–270. DOI: 10.1080/03075079.2024.2334837

[39] Nyaaba M, Shi L, Nabang M, Zhai X, Kyeremeh P, Ayoberd SA, Akanzire BN (2024) 'Generative AI as

a learning buddy and teaching assistant: Pre-service teachers' uses and attitudes', arXiv preprint, arXiv:2407.11983. DOI: 10.48550/arXiv.2407.11983

[40] Moundridou M, Matzakos N, Doukakis S. Generative AI tools as educators' assistants: Designing and implementing inquiry-based lesson plans. Computers and Education: Artificial Intelligence. 2024;7:100277. DOI: 10.1016/j.caeai.2024.100277

[41] Maurya RK. Using AI based chatbot ChatGPT for practicing counseling skills through role-play. Journal of Creativity in Mental Health. 2024;**19**(4):513–528. DOI: 10.1080/15401383.2023.2297857

[42] Akpan IJ, Kobara Y, Wolabi J, Bomicrsca I. Generative Artificial Intelligence and human–Chatbot interaction in education and research. International Transactions in Operational Research. 2025;**32**(3):1251–1281. DOI: 10.1111/itor.13522/

[43] Mittal U, Wang Y, Abdelghani R, Zhu M, Alasadi EA. A comprehensive review on generative AI for education. IEEE Access. 2024;**12**:142725–142751. DOI: 10.1109/ACCESS.2024.3468368

[44] Essel HB, Vlachopoulos D, Loglo MY, Zawacki-Richter O, McKie L. Exploring the impact of VoiceBots on student learning experiences. British Journal of Educational Technology. 2025;**56**(1):277–291. DOI: 10.1111/bjet.13504

[45] Strielkowski W, Grebennikova V, Lisovskiy A, Rakhimova G, Vasileva T. 'AI -driven adaptive learning for sustainable educational transformation'. Sustainable Development. 2025;**33**(2):1921–1947. DOI: 10.1002/sd.3221

[46] Wang X, Huang RT, Sommer M, Pei B, Shidfar P, Rehman MS, Ritzhaupt AD, Martin F. The efficacy of artificial intelligence-enabled adaptive learning systems from 2010 to 2022 on learner outcomes: A meta-analysis. Journal of Educational Computing Research. 2024;**62**(6):1348–1383. DOI: 10.1177/07356331241240459

[47] World Economic Forum. The Future of Jobs Report 2025. 2025. Geneva: World Economic Forum. Available from: https://www.weforum.org/publications/the-future-of-jobs-report-2025/digest/. [Accessed: 2025-August-13]

[48] Demartini CG, Sciascia L, Bosso A, Manuri F. Artificial intelligence bringing improvements to adaptive learning in education: A case study. Sustainability. 2024;**16**(3):1347. DOI: 10.3390/su16031347

[49] UNESCO. AI and the Future of Education: Disruptions, Dilemmas and Directions. 2025. Paris: United Nations Educational, Scientific and Cultural Organization. Available from: https://www.unesco.org/en/articles/ai-and-future-education-disruptions-dilemmas-and-directions [Accessed: 2025-September-10]

Section 2

Metaverse Medicine: Immersive Health, Ethics, and the Future of Care

Chapter 7

Healthcare and the Metaverse: Reimagined or Refragmentation of Care?

Pranavsingh Dhunnoo

Abstract

From virtual waiting rooms to AI-driven digital twins that predict adverse conditions, the metaverse promises to reimagine the very concept of healthcare. However, the new types of seamless digital experiences that it enables also necessitate prerequisites that can further fragment an already scattered system. This chapter narratively reviews the emergence of healthcare in the metaverse to: 1) map current metaversal healthcare activity and 2) identify systemic challenges that could devolve healthcare in the metaverse into 'multi-verse' fragments. It synthesises these findings to propose a translational framework – the metaversal healthcare framework. By adopting innovative medical futures techniques, the framework aims to guide implementation, converting speculative hype into evidence-based roadmaps and ensuring that infinite virtual worlds augment, rather than compromise, real-world well-being.

Keywords: healthcare metaverse, digital health, medicine, healthcare, future, medical futures, metaversal healthcare framework

1. Introduction

Since being coined in 1992 by author Neal Stephenson [1], the term 'metaverse' has captivated the imagination of subsequent generations and the broader tech industry. This immersive, virtual universe was meant to herald the successor to the Internet, and numerous attempts have been made to realise this concept. The most prominent push was in 2021 when Facebook, Inc. rebranded itself as Meta Platforms to indicate its dedication to bringing the metaverse from concept to reality [2]. Even Neal Stephenson has cofounded Lamina1 with the mission of building an open metaverse [3].

This has driven significant momentum to apply the metaverse across domains, from entertainment to education [4], with varying degrees of success. Some have even contemplated its application in healthcare, a field that has traditionally lagged behind in adopting new technology [5]. Bernstein et al. identified five constants – namely budget, supportive leadership, project management, implementation, and end-user involvement – that influence the adoption of information technology in the healthcare domain [6]. Each of these constants might have been positively influenced by the recent interest in the metaverse and the paradigm shift that ensued from the COVID-19 pandemic, which encouraged the adoption of virtual care modalities [7].

Extant literature identifies true potential in having a healthcare experience in the metaverse. Bansal et al.'s comprehensive survey recognises metaverse applications for healthcare that range from remote care and drug development to medical education and mental well-being [8]. By the end of the decade, Wang et al. expect further developments in the application of the metaverse for healthcare purposes that will enhance care delivery, improve patient outcomes, and advance medical research [9].

However, a metaversal healthcare experience raises critical concerns. Taking into consideration current popular 'proto-metaverses' such as Roblox and Fortnite, which are considered to provide adequate insights into the functioning of a fully realised metaverse [10], their content and experiences are not interoperable and lack standardisation. Content that has been bought or created in Fortnite is not carried over to Roblox and vice versa. In a healthcare setting, a similar situation might unfold. If left to individual entities, multiple individual metaverses, or 'multi-verses', could arise that are not interoperable. This would worsen the very interoperability, privacy, and equity issues that plague today's digital health systems [11]. In addition, the metaverse, being subject to much hype, risks being an overused term to benefit for-profit companies and attract investors, rather than patients and the healthcare ecosystem.

This chapter contemplates the emergence of the healthcare metaverse, outlining the key opportunities and challenges that the nexus of corresponding technologies entails. It also proposes a translational framework, which draws from empirical studies and medical futures techniques, to translate hype into safe, evidence-based practice.

2. Accessing the healthcare metaverse: Current and future enablers and enabler supports

Accessing healthcare in the metaverse will require specific platforms or even devices. However, despite the decades-long existence of the term and equally lengthy attempts to realise it, there is no definitive and universally accepted description of the 'metaverse' [12]. This represents challenges and confusion over the prerequisites if one were to access the metaverse.

Etymologically, 'metaverse' is a conjoining of the terms 'meta', which refers to 'after' or 'beyond' in Greek, and 'verse', which is adopted from the English word 'universe'. From this etymological description, the metaverse conveys the concept of transcending the universe or, more likely – based on the origins of the term [1] – what comes after the virtual universe or Internet.

If we were to go by its description by Stephenson in Snow Crash [1], the metaverse, as the successor to the Internet, would be a computer-generated universe accessed by the user's digital avatar through a setup that comprises a computer, goggles, and earphones, where the computer generates the audiovisual components, which are then relayed to the goggles and earphones for the user to experience. Such a description closely aligns with current virtual reality (VR) equipment, and the metaverse, in a strict sense, could be described as a VR-based embodiment of the Internet that users interact with via digital avatars.

While the level of interaction and immersiveness that VR enables closely aligns with the metaverse as described in Snow Crash, it is not the only contemporary technology that facilitates such levels of virtual communication. It is generally accepted that the 'core enablers' of the metaverse include immersive extended reality (XR) technologies, which comprise VR, augmented reality (AR), and mixed reality (MR) [13]. At the same time, supportive technologies, or 'enabler supports', are considered essential to the metaverse in order to foster a persistent, immersive virtual world with its own economy. These include digital twins, artificial intelligence (AI), high-speed and stable broadband, and blockchain [12]. Digital twins would serve as the user's avatar, representing a digital rendering of the physical body from which health-related insights can be drawn for assessing and forecasting the user's healthcare status. AI would assist in various tasks, such as analysing health insights or enabling human-like interactions with nonuser avatars. High-speed and stable broadband would be essential to support a reliable and interconnected virtual experience. Blockchain technology would enable the secure handling of sensitive health data in a decentralised fashion. As such, proto-metaverses such as Roblox and Fortnite, being experienced mostly through flat screens and non-XR devices without the extensive network of enabler supports, are working towards the ideal metaversal experience, as they do not offer the same level of interactivity and immersion of the 'embodied Internet' that the metaverse is expected to be.

However, in the future, other technologies could offer similar levels of immersiveness in virtual environments that XR technologies currently provide. Therefore, it would be advisable not to limit the metaverse to current technologies but also to consider future ones that might not yet be mature or even exist. For such reasons, core enablers of the metaverse could be considered as any technology – current or future – that adds a layer of virtual elements to the human senses and the real environment, and provides access to the 'virtuality continuum' beyond the real environment (**Figure 1**). Milgram and Kishino define this continuum as one where real environments with only real elements are located at one end and virtual environments with only virtual elements are located at the opposite end, with MR being a superset of the components between the two extremes [14].

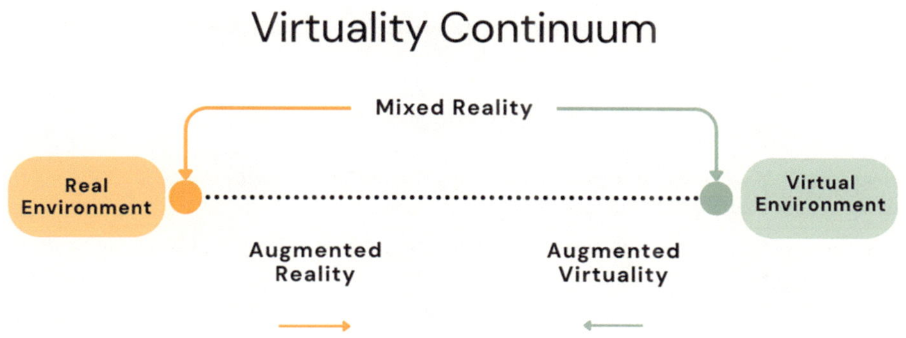

Figure 1.
The 'virtuality continuum'. Adapted and redrawn from Milgram and Kishino [14] under Creative Commons license.

Considering the different levels of maturity of metaverse enablers within the virtuality continuum, to provide better perspectives on their roles in healthcare, we can consider them as current core enablers and future core enablers. Current core enablers are technologies that are currently used or are available as products for use in healthcare practice within the metaverse. These include XR technologies such as VR, AR, and MR, which have matured over the decades and are offered as commercial products for healthcare use [8]. Future core enablers are those that are at a conceptual stage, with no publicly available products for healthcare metaverse purposes. These include technologies such as retinal prostheses, brain–computer interfaces (BCI), and other neural implants. Such technologies have been considered potential metaverse enablers [15, 16], but are not currently available as readily usable products and remain within research and theoretical realms, even if they have been used for other purposes such as prosthesis control or vision assistance. However, their availability, as well as that of other immersive audiovisual technologies, is likely to change in the future, and they could provide access to the metaverse just as XR technologies currently do. Considering enabler supports, they are likely to evolve alongside the core enablers and occupy a more flexible and experimental area. For example, blockchain technology was introduced in a whitepaper in 2008 [17], but is now considered an essential enabler support for the metaverse [8, 12]. Such supportive technologies might become related to or even lose association with the metaverse as they mature. **Table 1** summarises the current core enablers, future core enablers, and enabler supports of healthcare in the metaverse, along with their corresponding, nonexhaustive examples.

3. Glimpses of the healthcare metaverse: Current proto-precursor metaversal activities

While the potential of the healthcare metaverse has been acknowledged by researchers [8, 12, 18], the prospect can generally be considered at a conceptual stage. Extant literature identifies individual, potential metaverse-like applications in healthcare [8, 12, 18], while a truly immersive, all-encompassing healthcare metaverse resides within conceptual and theoretical realms. Even proto-metaverse experiences akin to Roblox and Fortnite for healthcare do not exist at the time of writing this chapter in 2025 [13]. As such, it could be suggested that healthcare currently consists of proto-precursors to the metaverse, which provide very early glimpses of what healthcare metaverse experiences might look like.

	Description	Examples
Current core enablers	Technologies that are currently used or are available as products to be used in practice in the healthcare metaverse.	XR technologies
Future core enablers	Technologies that are at a conceptual stage, with no publicly available product for healthcare metaverse purposes.	BCI, retinal prosthesis
Enabler supports	Supportive technologies that are considered essential to the metaverse in order to foster a persistent, immersive virtual world.	AI, digital twin, blockchain

Table 1.
Summary of metaverse core enablers and enabler supports in healthcare.

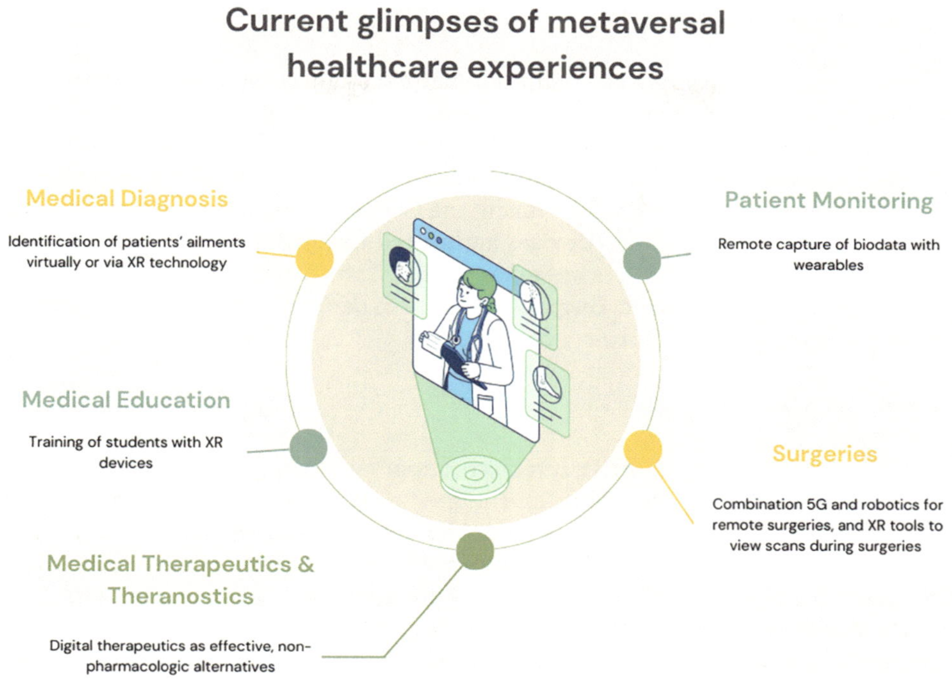

Figure 2.
A summary of the categories of metaverse healthcare applications. Adapted and redrawn from Chengoden et al. [18], under Creative Commons license.

Nevertheless, the current proto-precursor healthcare metaverse state can potentially provide an adequate peek at how the metaverse could enable a reimagined healthcare experience. Reviews have indicated that these glimpses are present across disciplines and areas of healthcare [8, 12, 18]. Chengoden et al. group healthcare metaverse applications into five general categories, namely medical diagnosis, patient monitoring, medical education, surgeries, and medical therapeutics and theranostics [18]. For clarity and to help better visualise potential metaversal healthcare experiences, we can consider the current applications of proto-precursors to the healthcare metaverse along those categories. **Figure 2** provides a visual summary, adapted from Chengoden et al.'s categorisation, and the categories are expanded upon below.

3.1 Medical diagnosis

In a metaverse environment, identifying a patient's ailment would not be unlike a virtual consultation, which has been on the rise, but it would involve a three-dimensional space along with remote or even digital diagnostic tools. An example of such tools is from NeuroSync. The company has developed several VR-based solutions to assess brain health and diagnose conditions such as concussions [19]. Over time, most medical disciplines could potentially have diagnoses in a virtual world.

3.2 Patient monitoring

The recent rise in remote care adoption has led to an increase in remote patient monitoring, which has been found to be beneficial, especially for patients with chronic conditions who necessitate regular checkups [20]. The biodata is typically collected by wearables and remote monitors at the patient's location and is shared with the healthcare team digitally. During the COVID-19 pandemic, the US FDA issued a list of such monitoring devices authorised for use during the public health emergency [21]; however, there are many more on the market. The same approach can potentially extend to a metaversal healthcare experience, with insights from data collected remotely shared during a consultation.

3.3 Medical education

The metaverse promises more interactive approaches to medical education and training, enabling medical students and trainees to practice their skills in their own time. For example, Case Western Reserve University has developed the HoloAnatomy Software Suite to teach anatomy lessons through MR headsets [22]. In 2020, all of the first-year students from the university's School of Medicine used this method due to physical restrictions imposed by the pandemic [23]. For medical professionals, Zimmer Biomet's OptiVu Mixed Reality uses MR to enable care teams to learn about complex procedures, collaborate remotely with specialists, and visualise procedures [24]. This approach could also potentially extend to patient education, informing them of upcoming treatment procedures or about medication side effects while they are undertaking a consultation in a metaverse environment.

3.4 Surgeries

Metaverse-based surgeries could potentially increase access to surgical expertise while also enhancing the experience for the surgical team. In 2020, Johns Hopkins neurosurgeons performed the institution's first AR surgeries [25]. With the aid of an AR headset that provided images of the patient's internal anatomy, they were able to perform spinal surgeries. This enabled the surgeons to visualise the patients' scans in a natural way, instead of referring to separate screens. As a virtual-first experience, the healthcare metaverse would also enable remote surgeries to be conducted. Such interventions have been conducted with the combination of robotic surgery systems and 5 G technology in domains such as urology, orthopaedics, and gastroenterology [26–28]. This approach could possibly extend into the metaverse by supplementing surgeons with XR goggles while operating surgical robots remotely for a more immersive experience.

3.5 Medical therapeutics and theranostics

Medical therapeutics refers to the treatment of medical conditions, while theranostics combines therapeutics and diagnostics. With the advent of digital therapeutics (DTx), medical therapeutics has already taken a digital spin that indicates the possibility of being integrated in the healthcare metaverse. For example, the FDA-approved EndeavorRx software from Akili Interactive Labs is a video game-based DTx that has been shown to be effective in treating ADHD among children in clinical trials [29]. XR-based therapies have also been shown to be effective, nonpharmacologic alternatives to treating anxiety disorders with minimal side effects [30]. Section 3.1 already discussed how VR technology can be used for medical diagnoses, and it could potentially be combined with DTx for theranostic purposes in the healthcare metaverse. As metaverse enablers mature, there is the possibility that they converge to provide personalised care by forecasting ailments and adverse conditions from new treatments. In particular, through simulations on a patient's digital twin and insights drawn from AI-based analyses, the healthcare team could determine the optimal pathway for individual patients.

4. From healthcare metaverse to healthcare multi-verse: The risks of further fragmentation

While the individual glimpses of metaversal healthcare experiences highlighted in Section 3 of this chapter provide a promising, virtual-first future for healthcare that could potentially represent the next stage of the digital health era, they also indicate the possibility of a scattered, nonstandardised future. These raise critical concerns over the resulting fragmented, siloed healthcare metaverses or 'multi-verses' that go against the very concept of the metaverse as an open, interactive version of the whole Internet. Academics have elaborated on the challenges that the healthcare metaverse will face [8, 12, 18], and these can generally be grouped into the four core categories below for clarity on how they could further fragment the healthcare experience.

4.1 Interoperability

Digital health systems have a notorious legacy of interoperability issues [11], which could potentially worsen with the metaverse. The current proto-precursor healthcare metaverse experiences are almost exclusively standalone experiences. Using the examples from Section 3 of this chapter, a patient cannot currently use analyses from NeuroSync and, in the same virtual space, bring them to Johns Hopkins neurosurgeons to derive insights for an upcoming intervention. The latter, in turn, cannot use NeuroSync in their virtual space with OptiVu Mixed Reality to collaborate with specialists. Being proprietary, each of the examples requires different devices and platforms, which produce different data that cannot be easily transferred, even if they relate to the same patient.

4.2 Equity and access

The digital divide is a growing concern in digital health implementation. As novel healthcare tools and approaches increasingly rely on digital enablers and the corresponding resources, their equitable access becomes a pressing challenge [31]. There is a possibility for the metaverse to widen this divide due to the need for core enablers and enabler supports by both the healthcare workforce and patients. The up-front cost of these resources necessary to access the metaverse provides an indication that virtual, embodied healthcare might possibly be available only to resource-rich areas and populations, aggravating the digital divide.

4.3 Data privacy, security, and regulatory oversight

By shifting healthcare into a virtual world, the metaverse will handle unprecedented amounts of personal data, ranging from biometrics to individual behaviour in digital formats [8, 12, 18]. Ensuring patient privacy while enabling data sharing will be significantly challenging [32], and the amount of sensitive health information in the healthcare metaverse is likely to become an attractive target for malicious third parties. The security standards and regulatory oversight for such data have not been established, making the current individual proto-precursor metaverse experiences likely to remain siloed beyond their current nascent status until new regulations can ensure patient safety across metaversal experiences.

4.4 Evidence and hype

The healthcare metaverse is still very much speculative [8, 12, 18], with only glimpses of what the experience could be being hinted at. However, the interest in the metaverse has attracted investment, and there is the possibility that software developers might claim that their services are metaverse ones without actually implementing such features or aiming to connect them to a broader virtual healthcare system. Ideally, evidence-based solutions should be adopted, but consumer-facing products that might not be subject to regulatory oversight could potentially bypass such compliance and perpetuate a fragmented ecosystem.

5. A reliable healthcare metaverse: The metaversal healthcare framework

While theoretical, the challenges highlighted in Section 4 of this chapter indicate a very plausible, although unfavourable, future for the healthcare metaverse. However, this future is only possible if adequate measures are not taken to regulate and standardise this emerging sector to ensure safe and equitable access from its proto-precursor state. This state comes with a silver lining. Although it currently indicates a potential fragmentation in the long run, this very early stage holds opportunities to 'correct course' with adequate measures and prevent a fragmented 'multi-verse' of virtual healthcare experiences from manifesting in favour of a truly open, unified metaverse for reimagined healthcare.

With novel technologies and approaches increasingly being implemented in healthcare, researchers have stressed the need to adopt medical futures studies techniques to better anticipate trends and challenges, as well as for their effective implementation [33]. These techniques draw from interdisciplinary academic futures studies to contemplate possible futures with the aim of building an anticipatory mindset. Techniques within this field, such as the Futures Wheel, scenario analysis, Delphi studies, and policy analysis, have been successfully used in healthcare planning and policy formulation [33]. Considering the relative novelty and nascent stage of the healthcare metaverse, medical futures studies could be considered a recommended approach to address potential shortcomings of a future healthcare metaverse with a view to the successful implementation of relevant virtual services.

Drawing from these techniques and the core challenges identified in Section 4 of this chapter, I propose the following 'metaversal healthcare framework' for assisting

Framework component	Description	Relevant medical futures technique(s)
Governance model	Implement new and updated policies to ensure data privacy, accountability, and user safety.	Policy analysis
Standardisation, privacy, and security	Account for interoperability, privacy, and security concerns with cross-industry collaboration to establish compliance standards and regulatory oversight.	Policy analysis, Futures Wheel
Collaborative ideation and development	Engage multidisciplinary teams from the outset to address real-world needs and foresee equity challenges.	Trend analysis, technology assessment
Phased evidence roadmap and key performance indicator (KPIs)	Follow a phased evidence roadmap with measurable KPIs to build on the evidence base ahead of implementing tools in the healthcare metaverse.	Scenario analysis, technology assessment

Table 2.
Summary of the metaversal healthcare framework.

the translation of healthcare metaverse development and innovation into practice while avoiding further fragmentation of care. Through such a framework, stakeholders can translate metaversal projects into concrete, future-ready improvements to the healthcare experience. The sequential components of the framework are summarised in **Table 2** and are further discussed below, including operational details on how to enact the respective component.

5.1 Governance model

To enable the regulation and implementation of the healthcare metaverse and foster collaboration among stakeholders, a 'metaverse governance model', as Uzun proposes [34], would be recommended for policymakers to enforce. This would require, as a primary focus, updated laws to ensure the protection of personal data and the privacy of such information in relation to the metaverse. Another area of focus would relate to the transparency and accountability of metaverse developers and service providers to ensure the security of the infrastructure with which users interact. There is also the role of ethical governance in the metaverse to prevent, for example, the spread of false information or the abuse of intellectual property. In addition, governance of the metaverse would account for undesired and illegal behaviours within the virtual spaces to ensure user safety.

To enact this component, policymakers can employ the futures method of policy analysis [35]. By examining issues pertinent to healthcare in the metaverse and assessing potential policy measures, they gain a better understanding of future scenarios and are better informed to shape new resilient and future-proof policies.

5.2 Standardisation, privacy, and security

To account for interoperability, as well as concerns over data privacy, security, and regulatory oversight, there needs to be cross-industry collaboration while advocating for secure and interoperable standards within the healthcare metaverse.

While there are existing metaverse-related standards [36], healthcare-specific ones appear to be lacking. Existing metaverse-related standards and healthcare-related standards could be coupled and adopted in view of establishing a standards map for the deployment of metaversal healthcare services.

For digital data sharing, the Fast Health Interoperability Resources (FHIR) standard could be adopted, as it is suited for such exchanges in a trustworthy manner and has been recommended to address interoperability issues [37]. This can be coupled with the ISO/IEEE 11073 Personal Health Device (X73) standards, which have been established to facilitate health data exchange from personal health monitors and have been recommended in the context of digital twins for health and well-being [38]. The OpenXR standard is acknowledged as an adequate way for the multi-platform development and deployment of XR products [39], and service developers could comply with this standard to potentially account for interoperability across core enablers. For the management of privacy risk in the metaverse, compliance with the NIST Privacy Framework could be recommended, as it can minimise privacy harm and build user trust in a proactive manner [40].

Enacting this framework component would require software developers and policymakers to collectively consider such standards and collaborate to establish those required by healthcare tools prior to their deployment in the metaverse going forward. To facilitate this process, futures techniques of policy analysis could aid in determining an adequate policy response [35], and the Futures Wheel could help map the direct and indirect impacts of specific events [41].

5.3 Collaborative ideation and development

When devising metaverse projects or services, multidisciplinary teams involving the whole spectrum of stakeholders should be engaged from the outset. The aim would be to assist in identifying real-world challenges and collaboratively formulate solutions in an inclusive manner, as recommended by Zallio and Clarkson in relation to designing the metaverse [42]. This could, in turn, address equity and access challenges from the ideation stages and incorporate solutions into the development process. For example, a tiered development strategy could be adopted to account for resource-poor areas, focusing on low bandwidth for basic and necessary healthcare metaverse experiences, with the option to progressively scale up and integrate new experiences as the infrastructure and resources improve.

In this framework component, stakeholders can be engaged in participatory design approaches, such as codesign workshops [43], and adopt futures techniques such as trend analysis [44] and technology assessment [45] to help align commercial innovation through metaversal technologies with real-world user needs, while following the governance model and standards map in place (Sections 5.1–5.2).

5.4 Phased evidence roadmap and KPIs

Akin to clinical trials, healthcare metaverse tools could follow an 'evidence roadmap'. By moving through successive and iterative stages of development and implementation, the tools progress through a predefined pathway to implementation.

After conforming to established standards (Section 5.2), they would obtain corresponding certifications, such as 'FHIR-conformant' and 'OpenXR-conformant', allowing them to move to the pilot stage to assess feasibility. If acceptable usability and no serious safety signals are identified, they can progress to larger trials measuring clinical outcomes and key performance indicators (KPIs). For healthcare metaverse, the latter could potentially relate to patient outcomes, clinical efficiency, user engagement, and operational efficiency, although new robust and validated metrics, such as the measurement of avatar performance, might need to be developed [46]. At this stage, KPIs could also factor in equity considerations, such as the penetration across socioeconomic strata and usability scores across user demographics. Such KPIs should also be continuously reported at this stage to enable future optimisation as tools that are proven to be safe and beneficial progress to the implementation stage. Subsequently, the findings across each stage of the roadmap could be shared in peer-reviewed academic journals to build on the evidence base with factual results and KPI metrics and move away from hype, further supporting real-world implementation. The research findings could be further disseminated to the wider public to encourage patient and healthcare workforce education on the safe and sensible use of metaversal tools.

Methods such as technology assessment [45] and scenario analysis [47] are relevant to enacting this component of the framework. These could help better visualise and understand the impacts of plausible future scenarios with the new tools.

6. Conclusion

From the glimpses that proto-precursor examples provide, the healthcare metaverse could truly reimagine the healthcare experience, providing personalised, accessible care and global, interdisciplinary collaboration. However, realising this potential requires careful consideration of a number of challenges that threaten to cause further fragmentation in an already scattered field, risking siloed 'multi-verses' instead of a unified metaverse. This chapter proposes a novel metaversal healthcare framework that could help navigate these challenges and shape the next stage of healthcare. Through interdisciplinary collaboration and evidence-based implementation, the metaverse could augment human well-being rather than undermine it with a fragmented fantasy.

Conflict of interest

The author declares no conflict of interest.

Notes/thanks/other declarations

The author would like to thank IntechOpen for the opportunity to contribute to this book and Neal Stephenson for the metaversal inspirations.

Author details

Pranavsingh Dhunnoo[1,2*]

1 Atlantic Technological University, Letterkenny, Ireland

2 Prans Lab, Creve Coeur, Mauritius

*Address all correspondence to: pranavsingh.dhunnoo@research.atu.ie, lab.prans@gmail.com

IntechOpen

References

[1] Stephenson N. Snow Crash. New York: Bantam Books; 1992

[2] The Facebook Company is now Meta. [Internet]. 2021. Available from: https://about.fb.com/news/2021/10/facebook-company-is-now-meta/ [Accessed: 2025-August-19]

[3] “Lamina1 whitepaper.”. [Internet]. Available from: https://www.lamina1.com [Accessed: 2025-August-19]

[4] Bhattacharya P, Saraswat D, Savaliya D, Sanghavi S, Verma A, Sakariya V, Tanwar S, Sharma R, Raboaca MS, Manea DL. Towards future internet: The metaverse perspective for diverse industrial applications. Mathematics. 2023;**11**(4):941

[5] Steiner P. Investment in health technologies calls for lessons to be learned. International Journal of Healthcare Management. 2014;**7**(1):3–4

[6] Bernstein ML, McCreless T, Cote MJ. Five constants of information technology adoption in healthcare. Hospital Topics. 2007;**85**(1):17–25

[7] Jiménez-Rodríguez D, Santillán García A, Montoro Robles J, Rodríguez Salvador MD, Muñoz Ronda FJ, Arrogante O. Increase in video consultations during the COVID-19 pandemic: Healthcare professionals’ perceptions about their implementation and adequate management. International Journal of Environmental Research and Public Health. 2020;**17**(14):5112

[8] Bansal G, Rajgopal K, Chamola V, Xiong Z, Niyato D. Healthcare in metaverse: A survey on current metaverse applications in healthcare. IEEE Access. 2022;**10**:119914–119946

[9] Wang Y, Zhu M, Chen X, Liu R, Ge J, Song Y, Yu G. The application of metaverse in healthcare. Frontiers in Public Health. 2024;**12**:1420367

[10] Dwivedi YK, Hughes L, Baabdullah AM, Ribeiro-Navarrete S, Giannakis M, Al-Debei MM, Dennehy D, Metri B, Buhalis D, Cheung CM, Conboy K. Metaverse beyond the hype: Multidisciplinary perspectives on emerging challenges, opportunities, and agenda for research, practice and policy. International Journal of Information Management. 2022;**66**:102542

[11] Iroju O, Soriyan A, Gambo I, Olaleke J. Interoperability in healthcare: Benefits, challenges and resolutions. International Journal of Innovation and Applied Studies. 2013;**3**(1):262–270

[12] Ullah H, Manickam S, Obaidat M, Laghari SU, Uddin M. Exploring the potential of metaverse technology in healthcare: Applications, challenges, and future directions. IEEE Access. 2023;**11**:69686–69707

[13] Park SM, Kim YG. A metaverse: Taxonomy, components, applications, and open challenges. IEEE Access. 2022;**10**:4209–4251

[14] Milgram P, Kishino F.A taxonomy of mixed reality visual displays. IEICE TRANSACTIONS on Information and Systems. 1994;**77**(12):1321–1329

[15] Xi N, Ye J, Chen CP, Chu Q, Hu H, Zou SP. Implantable metaverse with retinal prostheses and bionic vision

processing. Optics Express. 2023;**31**(2):1079–1091

[16] Zhu HY, Hieu NQ, Hoang DT, Nguyen DN, Lin CT.A human-centric metaverse enabled by brain-computer interface: A survey. IEEE Communications Surveys and Tutorials. 2024;**26**(3):2120–2145

[17] Nakamoto S Bitcoin: A peer-to-peer electronic cash system

[18] Chengoden R, Victor N, Huynh-The T, Yenduri G, Jhaveri RH, Alazab M, Bhattacharya S, Hegde P, Maddikunta PK, Gadekallu TR. Metaverse for healthcare: A survey on potential applications, challenges and future directions. IEEE Access. 2023;**11**:12765–12795

[19] NeuroSync website. [Internet]. Available from: https://www.neurosync.health/ [Accessed: 2025-August-19]

[20] Dhunnoo P, Kemp B, McGuigan K, Meskó B, O'Rourke V, McCann M Evaluation of telemedicine consultations using health outcomes and user attitudes and experiences: Scoping review. Journal of Medical Internet Research. 2024;**26**: e53266

[21] Center for Devices and Radiological Health. Remote or wearable patient monitoring devices EUAs, U.S. Food and Drug Administration. n d. Available at: https://www.fda.gov/medical-devices/covid-19-emergency-use-authorizations-medical-devices/remote-or-wearable-patient-monitoring-devices-euas [Accessed: 2025-August-19]

[22] Case Western Reserve University. HoloAnatomy® Software Suite. 2024. Available at: https://case.edu/holoanatomy/ [Accessed: 2025-August-19]

[23] Holoanatomy goes remote, learning goes on during pandemic. [Internet]. 2020. Available from: https://www.newswise.com/articles/holoanatomy-goes-remote-learning-goes-on-during-pandemic [Accessed: 2025-August-19]

[24] OptiVu Mixed Reality. [Internet]. Available from: https://www.zimmerbiomet.com/en/products-and-solutions/zb-edge/optivu.html [Accessed: 2025-August-19]

[25] Johns Hopkins performs its first augmented reality surgeries in patients, Johns Hopkins Medicine. [Internet]. 2021. Available from: https://www.hopkinsmedicine.org/news/articles/2021/02/johns-hopkins-performs-its-first-augmented-reality-surgeries-in-patients [Accessed: 2025-August-19]

[26] Li J, Yang X, Chu G, Feng W, Ding X, Yin X, Zhang L, Lv W, Ma L, Sun L, Feng R. Application of improved robot-assisted laparoscopic telesurgery with 5G technology in urology. European Urology. 2023;**83**(1):41–44

[27] Tian W, Fan M, Zeng C, Liu Y, He D, Zhang Q. Telerobotic spinal surgery based on 5G network: The first 12 cases. Neurospine. 2020;**17**(1):114

[28] Guo H, Tian Y, Shi J, Yang P, Yang J, Ding P, Zhao X, Zhang Z, Zhao Q. Pioneering case: Robot-assisted remote radical distal gastrectomy for gastric cancer based on 5G communication technology. Intelligent Surgery. 2024;**7**:22–26

[29] Kollins SH, Childress A, Heusser AC, Lutz J. Effectiveness of a digital therapeutic as adjunct to treatment with medication in pediatric ADHD. NPJ Digital Medicine. 2021;**4**(1):58

[30] Dhunnoo P, Wetzlmair LC, O'Carroll V. Extended reality therapies for anxiety disorders: A systematic review of patients' and healthcare professionals' perspectives. Science. 2024;**6**(2):19

[31] Saeed SA, Masters RM. Disparities in health care and the digital divide. Current Psychiatry Reports. 2021;**23**(9):61

[32] Turab M, Jamil S.A comprehensive survey of digital twins in healthcare in the era of metaverse. BioMedInformatics. 2023;**3**(3):563–584

[33] Meskó B, Kristóf T, Dhunnoo P, Árvai N, Katonai G. Exploring the need for medical futures studies: Insights from a scoping review of health care foresight. Journal of Medical Internet Research. 2024;**26**:e57148

[34] Uzun MM. Metaverse governance. In Metaverse: Esen, FS, Tinmaz, H, Singh, M. Technologies, Opportunities and Threats. Singapore: Springer Nature Singapore; 2023. pp. 231–244

[35] Wright D, Stahl B, Hatzakis T. Policy scenarios as an instrument for policymakers. Technological Forecasting and Social Change. 2020;**154**:119972

[36] Wang Y, Su Z, Zhang N, Xing R, Liu D, Luan TH, Shen X.A survey on metaverse: Fundamentals, security, and privacy. IEEE Communications Surveys and Tutorials. 2022;**25**(1):319–352

[37] Ayaz M, Pasha MF, Alzahrani MY, Budiarto R, and Stiawan D. The Fast Health Interoperability Resources (FHIR) standard: Systematic literature review of implementations, applications, challenges and opportunities. JMIR Medical Informatics. 2021;**9**(7):e21929

[38] Laamarti F, Badawi HF, Ding Y, Arafsha F, Hafidh B, El Saddik A. An ISO/IEEE 11073 standardized digital twin framework for health and well-being in smart cities. IEEE Access. 2020;**8**:105950–105961

[39] Taylor S, Soneji S. Bioinformatics and the metaverse: Are we ready? Frontiers in Bioinformatics. 2022;**2**:863676

[40] Hiller JS, Russell RS. Privacy in crises: The NIST privacy framework. Journal of Contingencies and Crisis Management. 2017;**25**(1):31–38

[41] Glenn JC. The futures wheel. Futures Research Methodology—version. 2009;**3**:19

[42] Zallio M, Clarkson PJ. Designing the metaverse: A study on inclusion, diversity, equity, accessibility and safety for digital immersive environments. Telematics and Informatics. 2022;**75**:101909

[43] Donetto S, Pierri P, Tsianakas V, Robert G. Experience-based co-design and healthcare improvement: Realizing participatory design in the public sector. The Design Journal. 2015;**18**(2):227–248

[44] Agami NM, Omran AM, Saleh MM, El-Shishiny HE. An enhanced approach for trend impact analysis. Technological Forecasting and Social Change. 2008;**75**(9):1439–1450

[45] Bechtold U, Fuchs D, Gudowsky N. Imagining socio-technical futures–challenges and opportunities for technology assessment. Journal of Responsible Innovation. 2017;**4**(2):85–99

[46] Tsappi E, Papageorgiou G. Towards deriving organizational key performance indicators in a metaverse workplace: A systematic literature review. In: Proceedings of the 16th international conference on pervasive technologies related to assistive environments July 5, 2023. (pp. 374–383)

[47] Spaniol MJ, Rowland NJ. The scenario planning paradox. Futures. 2018;**95**:33–43

Chapter 8

Perspective Chapter: Medical Jurisprudence Considerations for Therapeutic Metaverse Immersion

Sarah Katz

Abstract

While metaverse technology has seen increasing use in various healthcare settings, the issues of user data privacy violations and bodily harm due to these devices still pose significant risks. This chapter reviews the existing laws surrounding patient data privacy, as well as details how metaverse technologies, such as augmented and virtual reality applications, could harm users due to neurological disturbances. The chapter weighs the benefits versus the costs of implementing artificial intelligence (AI) to enhance these technologies for more secure handling of user data and bodily welfare. The chapter concludes with a set of Python code for a proposed algorithm, allowing an integrated AI functionality to assess and securely store biometric feedback in metaverse immersive environments for a safer and more customized experience.

Keywords: artificial intelligence, augmented reality, virtual reality, metaverse, healthcare, privacy law

1. Introduction

The rising use of metaverse technology, such as augmented reality (AR) and virtual reality (VR), in both healthcare and medical education has led to increased investigations into the potential security and safety ramifications for users [1]. Furthermore, the use of artificial intelligence (AI) to enhance these technologies adds an extra layer of nuance to consider – namely, how AI can be leveraged to protect versus harm user safety and data security.

Thus far, vertigo has emerged as a common risk for users of metaverse technologies in a healthcare context. Vertigo is a common and often debilitating condition that can be caused by both underlying neurological conditions, such as migraine and traumatic brain injury, or environmental factors, such as positional disorientation [2]. While AI can be used to help diagnose the root cause of vertigo, AI-enhancing features in metaverse technologies for medical purposes could also pose a vertigo risk due to a more intensive audiovisual immersion experience. Such immersive experiences could arise from the use of VR headsets and other healthcare wearable technologies [3].

Alongside the risk of bodily harm to the user arises the potential for privacy infringement, particularly in the case of AR – in-app advertisements or even surveillance by the application developers. For healthcare wearable technology specifically, the implementation of transnational laws like the General Data Protection Regulation (GDPR) demonstrates an increased cohesive effort to address these risks across borders. Notwithstanding, while advertisements might be easier to control by regulating what kind of user data developers are permitted to collect, wearable medical devices, such as those used for fitness monitoring, often collect user data as a primary function for wellness tracking [4]. This monitoring could include data on both physical and psychological states, such as insulin levels and stress levels. Thus, the line between patient data security and health can grow more ambiguous in this area [5]. Moreover, the sophistication of AI capabilities, such as machine learning (ML), could entail even greater use of both historical and current user data.

2. Risk of user privacy violation and bodily harm during metaverse immersion

Existing privacy measures tend to center on the Health Insurance Portability and Accountability Act (HIPAA) of 1996, which has been recently expanded to include healthcare technology such as the metaverse and wearable devices used for medical purposes. HIPAA covers three overall categories of individuals or organizations within its scope: 1) health plans, 2) healthcare clearinghouses, and 3) healthcare providers. The first entails medical insurance plans such as Cigna, the second pertains to entities that manage community health records or billing, and the third constitutes clinical providers such as individual physicians and psychologists [6].

Unfortunately, wearable healthcare technology can sometimes fly under the radar, especially if the manufacturing organizations of these technologies are not considered covered entities. This potential gap in oversight could result in the recording of protected health information (PHI), which could then be transmitted from a wearable medical device in an unencrypted manner.

Nonetheless, some legal scholars argue that laws such as GDPR and HIPAA could actually limit the development and dissemination of wearable and other metaverse technologies for healthcare [7]. Therefore, a balance is needed between user privacy and the relevant device's data monitoring and tracking functionality. Such a balance could allow for AI-equipped metaverse technologies that safeguard user information privacy while continually tracking said data through sophisticated measures like biometric tracking [8]. Device developers could achieve this middle ground by developing an algorithm to ensure that patient data is never transferred to the cloud without explicit user permission.

The second risk of metaverse healthcare technologies involves bodily harm, such as neurological disorientation during immersion with wearable VR headsets [9]. In contrast to the aforementioned privacy risk with therapeutic metaverse devices, biometric tracking could actually be used to help record individual user limits for a safer, customized, and more productive experience.

On the whole, however, the metaverse's expansion beyond extended reality (XR), such as AR and VR, to include less immersive digital experiences, such as chat platform avatars, means a smart wearable medical device often poses different risks from, for example, an unencrypted connection between a patient and a healthcare provider communicating over the Internet [10]. This means that although an XR device might be regulated by certain data or physical security policies, these laws might differ from those governing general chat-based communication.

3. Metaverse-induced bodily harm as a tort

For metaverse-related incidents resulting in physical harm to a user, tort law – or law pertaining to injury to a person – could apply. To that effect, bodily harm such as VR-induced balance issues, as well as threats made in a virtual space, could both be governed by tort law. While a VR device that ends up damaging the user's vision due to faulty manufacturing would qualify as negligence, bullying or threats made over a virtual communication session present a grayer area, as psychological harm from such interactions can be difficult to prove [11]. This means that the precise nature of the encounter must be taken into account on a case-by-case basis, and a final verdict determined by a judge, which tends to involve subjectivity.

That said, physical bodily harm tends to be more provable when stemming directly from the use of a device, such as vision loss correlated with VR headset usage. Still, the exact source of liability can be murkier, especially when uncertainty arises regarding whether the human manufacturers or any AI features caused the actual harm [12]. In cases where the point of user injury must be determined for appropriate accountability and liability purposes, an integrated algorithm could further assist in identifying the timing of injury, with biometric tracking – such as irregular eye movement – serving as a control. In this scenario, the algorithm would monitor the amount of time passed between device startup and the initiation of biometric irregularity.

4. Proposed algorithm for preventing privacy infringement and bodily harm during metaverse immersion

Thus, an algorithm to safeguard both user data and physical security would need to be capable of defending against attacks such as evasion and irregular queries during inference, poisoning attacks, Byzantine attacks (nodes intentionally and maliciously sending misinformation to other nodes in the network), and irregular distribution during training [13]. In particular, user privacy protection would have to be implemented during the initial distributed learning stage and model inference at deployment, as well as continuously upheld by an appropriate quality of AI fair governance.

The algorithm would also have to prioritize local, encrypted storage of PHI for safe, reliable tracking of user data. This data could include metrics like heart rate in response to immersion, to customize a tailored user experience going forward.

The appendix of this chapter provides sections of Python code to illustrate a rudimentary foundation for the proposed algorithm, which encompasses user data privacy as well as bodily well-being for VR and AR technologies, respectively. The code aims to help balance user privacy with bodily safety by supplying mechanisms for both biometric tracking and encryption measures. The algorithm presents a theoretical basis for the intended technology ethics component of this study.

5. Conclusion

5.1. Policy considerations

Prioritization of adapting existing data privacy and physical protection measures for metaverse healthcare technology users will require the combined efforts of governing bodies that craft AI and technology governance alongside those setting forth healthcare security policies. Alongside safeguards against bodily harm, such as taking into account the limitations of individual users, policy should also focus on enforcing the confidentiality of user data gathered by the device, ensuring that device developers cannot monitor user activity or information.

Currently, a sample joint initiative in the context of the United States would entail entities such as the US Department of Health and Human Services (HHS) and the Food and Drug Administration (FDA) consulting with the United Nations' AI Advisory Body and the World Economic Forum for secure metaverse technology development for healthcare.

These governing bodies could use European and US concepts of tort law to help navigate the metaverse security landscape, keeping in mind the need to adapt all behaviors of practitioners and technologies alike to existing healthcare policies for patient protection by HIPAA. These in-place policies could be supplemented by newer regulations set forth by entities like the UN AI Advisory Board to enhance accountability assurance for both human practitioners and manufacturers, as well as best practices for defining such accountability (as with configuring these healthcare devices to track the point of liability that caused harm to the user).

A challenge that could arise when restricting developer visibility into user data during VR device use entails potential overreliance on the user to be capable of interpreting or even remembering to examine the results of their biometric device log reports. Similarly, AR healthcare devices could pose obstacles for users who do not check log reports from their integrated AR application and smart wearable device. These challenges could be overcome with time by healthcare practitioners and metaverse healthcare device manufacturers promoting the importance of patient self-monitoring to track their own limitations and sensitivities during immersion.

Overall, existing law should be applied to, and ideally adapted according to, evolving immersive healthcare technology, which might require a balance of user privacy and biometric data collection for both personal tracking and interpretation by a medical provider for further treatment.

5.2. Future research

Future studies could adopt quantitative methods to investigate whether the majority of extended reality healthcare device users experience issues with data privacy or bodily harm during immersion. Such findings could help guide prioritization for policymaking surrounding both user protection from developer-side surveillance and physical injury. Furthermore, the proposed algorithm presented could be empirically validated to test its integration into immersive healthcare technology. Finally, perhaps as its own study, the many potential psychological effects of cyberbullying in a therapeutic metaverse environment could also be examined.

Appendix

Python code for VR user safety algorithm, focusing on biometric tracking and encryption

```
from cryptography.fernet import Fernet
import time
import random
import json
from datetime import datetime

# Thresholds
HEART_RATE_THRESHOLD = 10
EYE_MOVEMENT_VARIATION = 10

# Baselines
baseline_heart_rate = 70
baseline_eye_movement = 50

# File paths
KEY_FILE = "/mnt/data/encryption.key"
ENCRYPTED_LOG_FILE = "/mnt/data/encrypted_vr_response_log.json"

# Generate and store encryption key
key = Fernet.generate_key()
with open(KEY_FILE, "wb") as key_file:
 key_file.write(key)
fernet = Fernet(key)

# Simulated sensor data functions
def read_heart_rate():
 return baseline_heart_rate + random.randint(-5, 20)

def read_eye_movement():
 return baseline_eye_movement + random.randint(-20, 20)

# Alert function
def alert_user():
 print("ALERT: A notable pattern in physiological response was
detected!")

# Log encrypted event
def log_encrypted_event(heart_rate, eye_movement):
 event = {
 "timestamp": datetime.now().isoformat(),
 "heart_rate": heart_rate,
 "eye_movement": eye_movement
 }
```

```
 encrypted_data = fernet.encrypt(json.dumps(event).encode())
 with open(ENCRYPTED_LOG_FILE, "ab") as file:
 file.write(encrypted_data + b"\n")

# Monitor loop with logic for eye movement decrease then increase
previous_eye = baseline_eye_movement
eye_decreased = False

for _ in range(20): # simulate 20 data points
 heart_rate = read_heart_rate()
 eye_movement = read_eye_movement()

 heart_rate_increased = heart_rate > baseline_heart_rate +
HEART_RATE_THRESHOLD

 if not eye_decreased and eye_movement < previous_eye -
EYE_MOVEMENT_VARIATION:
 eye_decreased = True
 elif eye_decreased and eye_movement > previous_eye +
EYE_MOVEMENT_VARIATION:
 eye_pattern_detected = True
 else:
 eye_pattern_detected = False

 if heart_rate_increased and eye_decreased and eye_pattern_detected:
 alert_user()
 log_encrypted_event(heart_rate, eye_movement)
 eye_decreased = False # reset to catch future patterns

 previous_eye = eye_movement
 time.sleep(1)

 ENCRYPTED_LOG_FILE
```

Heart rate and eye movement were used as the sample biometrics in the sample code shown in the appendix of this chapter, based on the aforementioned identification of these metrics as determinants for patient anxiety levels and vertigo, respectively. Upon successful validation of this code, a functional algorithm should be in place for integration into total-immersion (VR) and partial-immersion (AR) metaverse technologies that help ensure user physical and data security.

Python code for AR user safety algorithm, focusing on keyboard haptic feedback and data privacy

```
from cryptography.fernet import Fernet
import tkinter as tk
from PIL import Image, ImageTk
import time
import random
import json
from datetime import datetime
import threading
```

```
# Constants
BASELINE_HEART_RATE = 70
HEART_RATE_THRESHOLD = 10
KEY_FILE = "gui_hr_encryption.key"
LOG_FILE = "gui_encrypted_hr_log.json"

# Generate and save encryption key
key = Fernet.generate_key()
with open(KEY_FILE, "wb") as kf:
 kf.write(key)
fernet = Fernet(key)

# Simulated haptic feedback
def simulate_haptic_feedback():
 print("Simulated haptic feedback triggered.")

# Simulated heart rate sensor
def read_heart_rate():
 return BASELINE_HEART_RATE + random.randint(-5, 25)

# Log encrypted event
def log_encrypted_event(hr):
 event = {
 "timestamp": datetime.now().isoformat(),
 "heart_rate": hr
 }
 encrypted = fernet.encrypt(json.dumps(event).encode())
 with open(LOG_FILE, "ab") as log_file:
 log_file.write(encrypted + b"\n")

# GUI application
def start_gui_monitor():
 root = tk.Tk()
 root.title("Heart Rate Monitor")
 root.geometry("500x500")

 label = tk.Label(root, text="Monitoring heart rate in response to
image...", font=("Arial", 14))
 label.pack(pady=10)

 # Display placeholder image
 img = Image.new("RGB", (400, 300), color="skyblue")
 photo = ImageTk.PhotoImage(img)
 image_label = tk.Label(root, image=photo)
 image_label.image = photo
 image_label.pack(pady=20)

 alert_text = tk.StringVar()
 alert_label = tk.Label(root, textvariable=alert_text, fg="red",
font=("Arial", 16))
 alert_label.pack(pady=20)

 def monitor():
```

```
 for _ in range(15):
 hr = read_heart_rate()
 print(f"Heart Rate: {hr}")
 if hr > BASELINE_HEART_RATE + HEART_RATE_THRESHOLD:
 alert_text.set("ALERT: Heart rate spike detected!")
 simulate_haptic_feedback()
 log_encrypted_event(hr)
 else:
 alert_text.set("")
 time.sleep(1)

 threading.Thread(target=monitor, daemon=True).start()
 root.mainloop()

start_gui_monitor()
```

The same code, adapted for headless environments – devices without a typical graphical user interface, such as a keyboard for haptic (touch-based) feedback rather than a monitor – is shown below:

```
from cryptography.fernet import Fernet
import tkinter as tk
from PIL import Image, ImageTk
import time
import random
import json
from datetime import datetime
import threading

# Constants
BASELINE_HEART_RATE = 70
HEART_RATE_THRESHOLD = 10
IMAGE_PATH = "/mnt/data/sample_image.jpg" # Simulated image path
KEY_FILE = "/mnt/data/gui_hr_encryption.key"
LOG_FILE = "/mnt/data/gui_encrypted_hr_log.json"

# Generate and save encryption key
key = Fernet.generate_key()
with open(KEY_FILE, "wb") as kf:
 kf.write(key)
fernet = Fernet(key)

# Simulated haptic feedback
def simulate_haptic_feedback():
 print("Simulated haptic feedback triggered.")

# Simulated heart rate sensor
def read_heart_rate():
 return BASELINE_HEART_RATE + random.randint(-5, 25)

# Log encrypted event
def log_encrypted_event(hr):
 event = {
```

```
"timestamp": datetime.now().isoformat(),
"heart_rate": hr
}
encrypted = fernet.encrypt(json.dumps(event).encode())
with open(LOG_FILE, "ab") as log_file:
log_file.write(encrypted + b"\n")

# GUI application with alert display
def start_gui_monitor():
root = tk.Tk()
root.title("Heart Rate Monitor")
root.geometry("500x500")

label = tk.Label(root, text="Monitoring heart rate in response to
image…", font=("Arial", 14))
label.pack(pady=10)

# Load and display image
img = Image.new("RGB", (400, 300), color="skyblue") # Placeholder
image
photo = ImageTk.PhotoImage(img)
image_label = tk.Label(root, image=photo)
image_label.image = photo
image_label.pack(pady=20)

alert_text = tk.StringVar()
alert_label = tk.Label(root, textvariable=alert_text, fg="red",
font=("Arial", 16))
alert_label.pack(pady=20)

def monitor():
for _ in range(15):
hr = read_heart_rate()
print(f"Heart Rate: {hr}")
if hr > BASELINE_HEART_RATE + HEART_RATE_THRESHOLD:
alert_text.set("ALERT: Heart rate spike detected!")
simulate_haptic_feedback()
log_encrypted_event(hr)
else:
alert_text.set("")
time.sleep(1)

# Run monitoring in a separate thread to keep GUI responsive
threading.Thread(target=monitor, daemon=True).start()
root.mainloop()

start_gui_monitor()
```

Python code for a VR user safety algorithm, focusing on the time between immersion initiation and irregular biometric activity

```
import time
import os
```

```
import json
from datetime import datetime
from random import uniform # Mock eye-tracking
import psutil # For monitoring AI processes

# === CONFIGURATION ===
DATA_FILE = os.path.expanduser("~/vr_eye_movement_log.json") #
Saved only to user directory
AI_KEYWORDS = ['ai_module', 'neural', 'deep_learning'] # Keywords to
identify AI software processes

# === MOCKED FUNCTIONS (replace with actual SDK hooks) ===

def get_eye_movement_value():
 """Simulate eye movement value. Replace with actual VR SDK call."""
 return uniform(0.0, 10.0)

def get_active_ai_processes():
 """Check for AI-related processes running on the system."""
 ai_processes = []
 for proc in psutil.process_iter(['pid', 'name', 'cmdline']):
 try:
 if any(keyword in ' '.join(proc.info['cmdline']).lower() for key-
word in AI_KEYWORDS):
 ai_processes.append({
 'pid': proc.info['pid'],
 'name': proc.info['name'],
 'cmdline': proc.info['cmdline']
 })
 except (psutil.NoSuchProcess, psutil.AccessDenied):
 continue
 return ai_processes

# === MAIN SCRIPT ===

def detect_irregular_eye_movement():
 """Detects increase then decrease in eye movement."""
 history = []
 while True:
 value = get_eye_movement_value()
 history.append(value)
 if len(history) > 5:
 history.pop(0)
 if len(history) == 5 and history[0] < history[1] < history[2] and
history[2] > history[3] > history[4]:
 return {
 'timestamp': datetime.now().isoformat(),
 'eye_movement_values': history
 }

def save_log(log):
 """Save findings locally, visible only to the user."""
 with open(DATA_FILE, 'w') as f:
```

```
 json.dump(log, f, indent=4)

def main():
 startup_time = time.time()
 print("VR headset startup time recorded.")

 print("Monitoring eye movement for irregular patterns...")
 detection = detect_irregular_eye_movement()
 detection_time = time.time()

 ai_status = get_active_ai_processes()

  log = {
  'startup_time': datetime.fromtimestamp(startup_time).isoformat
(),
  'irregular_eye_movement_detected_at': detection['timestamp'],
  'elapsed_time_sec': round(detection_time - startup_time, 2),
  'eye_movement_pattern': detection['eye_movement_values'],
  'active_ai_processes': ai_status
  }

  save_log(log)
  print("Irregular eye movement detected. Log saved locally.")

  if __name__ == '__main__':
  main()
```

The secure logging functionality ensures only local visibility by storing results in the user's home directory.

Additionally, the modular design will separate AI detection, logging, and eye-tracking logic.

Finally, the mock inputs in this sample script include placeholders for eye-tracking and AI status detection, which should be replaced with actual APIs in a real VR setup.

Meanwhile, as the OpenVR eye-tracking extension is most configurable for the C++ programming language, the sample code below illustrates the biometric component in C++.

Objective: Monitor the time elapsed between VR headset startup and the onset of irregular eye movements (characterized by an increase followed by a decrease in eye motion), and log the AI software's activity status at that moment.

1. **OpenXR initialization**:

    - Enable the XR_EXT_eye_gaze_interaction extension.
    - Create an OpenXR instance and session.
    - Establish the necessary reference spaces.developer.varjo.comdeveloper-docs.magicleap.cloud

2. **Eye-tracking setup**:

    - Verify the availability of eye-tracking support.
    - Initialize eye-tracking by creating an eye-tracker handle.

- Retrieve eye gaze data using xrLocateEyeGazeEXT. community.khronos.org + 2developer.varjo.com + 2developer.android.com + 2github.com + 6developer.android.com + 6community.khronos.org + 6

3. **Eye movement monitoring**:

   - Continuously poll eye-gaze data at a suitable frequency (e.g., 60 Hz).
   - Calculate the magnitude of gaze direction vectors to quantify eye motion.
   - Detect patterns where the eye motion magnitude increases and then decreases, indicating irregular movement.

4. **AI activity logging**:

   - Upon detecting irregular eye movements, log the current status of the AI software within the VR application.

5. **Data logging**:

   - Record the startup time, the time of irregular eye movement detection, and the AI activity status to a local file accessible only to the user.

Code sample (pre-error handling):

```
#include <openxr/openxr.h>
#include <openxr/openxr_platform.h>
#include <chrono>
#include <fstream>
#include <vector>

// Function to calculate the magnitude of a 3D vector
float CalculateMagnitude(XrVector3f vector) {
 return sqrt(vector.x * vector.x + vector.y * vector.y + vector.z *
vector.z);
}

// Function to detect irregular eye movement
bool DetectIrregularMovement(const std::vector<float>& magnitudes)
{
 if (magnitudes.size() < 5) return false;
 return (magnitudes[magnitudes.size() - 5] < magnitudes[magnitudes.
size() - 4] &&
 magnitudes[magnitudes.size() - 4] < magnitudes[magnitudes.size() -
3] &&
 magnitudes[magnitudes.size() - 3] > magnitudes[magnitudes.size() -
2] &&
 magnitudes[magnitudes.size() - 2] > magnitudes[magnitudes.size() -
1]);
}

int main() {
```

```
// Initialize OpenXR instance and session with eye gaze interaction
extension enabled
// [Initialization code here]

// Record startup time
auto startup_time = std::chrono::steady_clock::now();

std::vector<float> eye_motion_magnitudes;
bool irregular_movement_detected = false;

while (!irregular_movement_detected) {
// Poll eye gaze data
XrEyeGazeSampleTimeEXT eyeGazeSample;
// [Code to retrieve eye gaze data and populate eyeGazeSample]

// Calculate magnitude of gaze direction vector
float magnitude = CalculateMagnitude(eyeGazeSample.
gazeDirection);
eye_motion_magnitudes.push_back(magnitude);

// Check for irregular movement pattern
if (DetectIrregularMovement(eye_motion_magnitudes)) {
irregular_movement_detected = true;
auto detection_time = std::chrono::steady_clock::now();
auto elapsed_time = std::chrono::duration_cast<std::chrono::sec-
onds>(detection_time - startup_time).count();

// Log AI activity status
// [Code to retrieve AI activity status]

// Save findings to a local file
std::ofstream log_file("eye_movement_log.txt");
log_file << "Startup Time: " << /* startup_time */ "\n";
log_file << "Irregular Movement Detected At: " << /* detection_time */
"\n";
log_file << "Elapsed Time (s): " << elapsed_time << "\n";
log_file << "AI Activity Status: " << /* AI status */ "\n";
log_file.close();
}

// Sleep or wait for the next polling interval
std::this_thread::sleep_for(std::chrono::milliseconds(16)); //
Approx. 60 Hz
}

// Cleanup and shutdown
// [Cleanup code here]

return 0;
}
```

Python code for AR user safety algorithm, focusing on the time between immersion initiation and irregular biometric activity (heart rate)

```
import time
import os
import json
import psutil
from datetime import datetime

# === CONFIGURATION ===
DATA_FILE = os.path.expanduser("~/pokemon_go_hr_log.json")
AI_KEYWORDS = ['ai', 'neural', 'ml', 'tensorflow', 'torch']
HEART_RATE_THRESHOLD = 100 # Customize based on resting HR
SAMPLING_INTERVAL = 5 # Seconds

# === MOCK FUNCTION (replace with smartwatch API integration) ===
def get_heart_rate():
 """
 Fetch the current heart rate from a smartwatch.
 Replace this with actual API calls.
 """
 import random
 return random.randint(60, 130) # Simulated HR for testing

def is_pokemon_go_running():
 for proc in psutil.process_iter(['name']):
 try:
 if "pokemon" in proc.info['name'].lower():
 return True
 except (psutil.NoSuchProcess, psutil.AccessDenied):
 continue
 return False

def get_ai_processes():
 ai_procs = []
 for proc in psutil.process_iter(['pid', 'name', 'cmdline']):
 try:
 if any(keyword in ' '.join(proc.info['cmdline']).lower() for key-
word in AI_KEYWORDS):
 ai_procs.append({
 'pid': proc.info['pid'],
 'name': proc.info['name'],
 'cmdline': proc.info['cmdline']
 })
 except (psutil.NoSuchProcess, psutil.AccessDenied):
 continue
 return ai_procs

def save_log(log):
 with open(DATA_FILE, 'w') as f:
 json.dump(log, f, indent=4)

def main():
 print("Waiting for Pokémon GO to start...")
 while not is_pokemon_go_running():
 time.sleep(2)
```

```
 print("Pokémon GO launched. Monitoring heart rate via smartwatch...")
 app_start_time = time.time()

 while True:
 hr = get_heart_rate()
 print(f"Heart Rate: {hr} BPM")
 if hr >= HEART_RATE_THRESHOLD:
 spike_time = time.time()
 ai_status = get_ai_processes()
 elapsed = round(spike_time - app_start_time, 2)

 log = {
 'pokemon_go_start_time': datetime.fromtimestamp(app_start_time).
isoformat(),
 'heart_rate_spike_time': datetime.fromtimestamp(spike_time).iso-
format(),
 'elapsed_time_sec': elapsed,
 'heart_rate': hr,
 'ai_processes': ai_status
 }

 save_log(log)
 print("Heart rate spike detected. Log saved.")
 break

 time.sleep(SAMPLING_INTERVAL)

if __name__ == '__main__':
 main()
```

The above code assumes an AR mobile application (in this case, Pokemon GO) integration with a smart sensor, such as a Fitbit. The code below shows the integration and configuration process for pairing Fitbit with Pokemon GO.

```
pip install fitbit requests cherrypy

import time
import os
import json
import psutil
import fitbit
import cherrypy
from datetime import datetime
from fitbit.api import FitbitOauth2Client

# === CONFIGURATION ===
DATA_FILE = os.path.expanduser("~/pokemon_go_hr_log.json")
AI_KEYWORDS = ['ai', 'neural', 'ml', 'tensorflow', 'torch']
HEART_RATE_THRESHOLD = 100
SAMPLING_INTERVAL = 30 # Fitbit intraday API limits to 1/min
CLIENT_ID = 'YOUR_CLIENT_ID'
CLIENT_SECRET = 'YOUR_CLIENT_SECRET'

# === OAuth2 Token Storage ===
```

```
TOKENS_FILE = 'fitbit_tokens.json'

def save_tokens(token_dict):
 with open(TOKENS_FILE, 'w') as f:
 json.dump(token_dict, f)

def load_tokens():
 if os.path.exists(TOKENS_FILE):
 with open(TOKENS_FILE, 'r') as f:
 return json.load(f)
 return None

def authorize_fitbit():
 server = cherrypy._cpserver.Server()
 server.socket_port = 8080
 server.socket_host = '0.0.0.0'

 class OAuth2CallbackServer:
 @cherrypy.expose
 def index(self, code):
 token = client.fetch_access_token(code)
 save_tokens(token)
 cherrypy.engine.exit()

 tokens = load_tokens()
 if tokens:
  return fitbit.Fitbit(CLIENT_ID, CLIENT_SECRET, access_token=to-
kens['access_token'],
 refresh_token=tokens['refresh_token'], refresh_cb=save_tokens)

 client = FitbitOauth2Client(CLIENT_ID, CLIENT_SECRET)
 url, _ =
client.authorize_token_url(redirect_uri='http://localhost:8080')
 print("Go to the following URL and authorize the app:\n", url)

 cherrypy.quickstart(OAuth2CallbackServer())
 tokens = load_tokens()
  return fitbit.Fitbit(CLIENT_ID, CLIENT_SECRET, access_token=to-
kens['access_token'],
 refresh_token=tokens['refresh_token'], refresh_cb=save_tokens)

def is_pokemon_go_running():
 for proc in psutil.process_iter(['name']):
 try:
 if "pokemon" in proc.info['name'].lower():
 return True
 except (psutil.NoSuchProcess, psutil.AccessDenied):
 continue
 return False

def get_ai_processes():
 ai_procs = []
```

```
for proc in psutil.process_iter(['pid', 'name', 'cmdline']):
try:
if any(keyword in ' '.join(proc.info['cmdline']).lower() for key-
word in AI_KEYWORDS):
ai_procs.append({
'pid': proc.info['pid'],
'name': proc.info['name'],
'cmdline': proc.info['cmdline']
})
except (psutil.NoSuchProcess, psutil.AccessDenied):
continue
return ai_procs

def save_log(log):
with open(DATA_FILE, 'w') as f:
json.dump(log, f, indent=4)

def main():
print("Authorizing with Fitbit...")
fb = authorize_fitbit()

print("Waiting for Pokémon GO to start...")
while not is_pokemon_go_running():
time.sleep(2)

print("Pokémon GO launched. Monitoring heart rate via Fitbit...")
app_start_time = time.time()

while True:
now = datetime.now()
date_str = now.strftime('%Y-%m-%d')
time_str = now.strftime('%H:%M:%S')

hr_data = fb.intraday_time_series('activities/heart', base_date=-
date_str, detail_level='1sec')
try:
hr_points = hr_data['activities-heart-intraday']['dataset']
if hr_points:
latest_hr = hr_points[-1]['value']
print(f"Heart rate: {latest_hr}")
if latest_hr >= HEART_RATE_THRESHOLD:
spike_time = time.time()
ai_status = get_ai_processes()
elapsed = round(spike_time - app_start_time, 2)


log = {
'pokemon_go_start_time': datetime.fromtimestamp(app_start_time).
isoformat(),
'heart_rate_spike_time': datetime.fromtimestamp(spike_time).iso-
format(),
```

```
'elapsed_time_sec': elapsed,
'heart_rate': latest_hr,
'ai_processes': ai_status
}
save_log(log)
print("Heart rate spike detected. Log saved.")
break
except Exception as e:
print("Error retrieving heart rate:", e)
time.sleep(SAMPLING_INTERVAL)
if __name__ == '__main__':
main()
```

Author details

Sarah Katz
Capitol Technology University, Laurel, USA

*Address all correspondence to: morag.katz@gmail.com

References

[1] Diaconu I. Wearable patient monitoring and metaverse-enabled healthcare systems, immersive medical simulation and remote care technologies, and deep learning disease prediction and diagnosis algorithms for Artificial Intelligence-powered individualized. American Journal of Medical Research. 2024;**11**(1):39–54. https://www.ceeol.com/search/article-detail?id=1335015

[2] Alshraideh M, Alkayed Y, Alshraideh A, AlTrabsheh Y, Alshraideh B, Alshraideh H, Alfayoumi B, Alshraideh N. Advancing Vertigo diagnosis with large language models: A multimodal, AI-driven approach to etiology differentiation. Journal of Integrated Science and Technology. 2025;**13**(4):1079. DOI: 10.62110/sciencein.jist.2025.v13.1079.

[3] Sabry F, Eltaras T, Labda W, Alzoubi K, Malluhi Q, Wu Y. Machine learning for healthcare wearable devices: The big picture. Journal of Healthcare Engineering. 2022; **2022**: 1–25. 4653923. DOI: 10.1155/2022/4653923.

[4] Woll S, Birkenmaier D, Biri G, Nissen R, Lutz L, Schroth M, Ebner-Priemer UW, Giurgiu M. Applying AI in the context of the association between device-based assessment of physical activity and mental health: Systematic review. JMIR mHealth and uHealth. 2025;**13**:e59660. DOI: 10.2196/59660.

[5] Sivakumar V, et al. Addressing privacy concerns with wearable health monitoring technology Wiley interdisciplinary reviews. data mining and knowledge Discovery/Wiley Interdisciplinary reviews. Data Mining and Knowledge Discovery. 2024;**14**(3). DOI: 10.1002/widm.1535

[6] Katuska J. Wearing down HIPAA: How wearable technologies Erode privacy protections. The Journal of Corporation Law. 2021;**44**: *University of Iowa School of Law*. jcl.law.uiowa.edu/sites/jcl.law.uiowa.edu/files/2021-08/Katuska_Final_Web.pdf

[7] Preston R. Stifling innovation: How Global data protection regulation trends inhibit the growth of healthcare research and start-ups. Emory Law Scholarly Commons. 2023;**37**1.scholarlycommons.law.emory.edu/eilr/vol37/iss1/4

[8] Balasubramaniam S, et al. AI based advancements in biometrics and its applications. 1st edn. 2024. CRC Press.

[9] Zhou S, Gromala D, Wang L. Ethical challenges of virtual reality technology interventions for the vulnerabilities of patients with Chronic Pain: Exploration of technician responsibility. Journal of Medical Internet Research. 2023;**25**: e49237. DOI: 10.2196/49237.

[10] Pasa B, Bernes A, Gaggioli A, Tuccari E, Zollo F, Vulpiani G, Pignolo L, Scala A, Cerasa A. *LawVerse*: The legal framework for clinical metaverse content. Journal of Medical Extended Reality. 2025;**2**(1):13–19. DOI: 10.1089/jmxr.2024.0028.

[11] Nicholson A, Udofa K, Collins A. Trespass to the 'person' in the metaverse. International Review of Law, Computers & Technology. 2025;1–22. DOI: 10.1080/13600869.2025.2479891

[12] Mrčela M, Vuletić I.Navigating criminal liability in an era of AI-assisted medicine. Medicine, Law & Society. 2025;**18**(1). DOI: 10.18690/mls.18.1.93-108.2025.

[13] Wei W, Liu L. Trustworthy distributed AI systems: Robustness, privacy, and governance. ACM Computing Surveys. 2025;**57**(6):143. 42. DOI: 10.1145/3645102

Section 3

Building Responsible Metaverses: Digital Identity, Safety, and Societal Futures

Chapter 9

Building Responsible Metaverse

Feng Liu

Abstract

The metaverse is emerging as the next major online platform where people can conduct daily activities in three-dimensional (3D), immersive, and intuitive environments. Current development efforts focus on replicating real-world settings and experiences through 3D technologies and artificial intelligence (AI); however, the integration of virtual and physical worlds raises critical challenges. A central concern is how to ensure that the metaverse complements, rather than replaces, real-world human experiences. Equally important is the need to embed moral and ethical principles into virtual environments to promote positive outcomes in real life. This chapter explores both the opportunities and risks of an AI-driven metaverse, with a particular focus on the younger generation, who are most vulnerable to its effects. Using one of the top metaverse platforms, Roblox, as a case study, the chapter begins by examining potential negative impacts of virtual environments with insufficiently rigorous design, then presents key considerations for building a responsible metaverse that encourages connections to the physical world, supports balanced engagement with the virtual world through healthy disconnection, and integrates psychological principles into user experience (UX) design. The chapter concludes with a suggested checklist for integrating psychological principles and AI into metaverse UX design to promote responsible and sustainable virtual worlds in our daily lives.

Keywords: responsible metaverse, metaverse UX design, metaverse design checklist, AI in metaverse, game addiction, metaverse engagement and disconnection, children and metaverse, psychological concerns in metaverse, 3D immersive environments design, metaverse and social responsibilities

1. Introduction

As human activities increasingly migrate to online and mobile platforms, the metaverse is anticipated to become the next major form of digital community. In this immersive environment, people may shop in three-dimensional (3D) online stores, socialize with friends over virtual coffee, purchase virtual real estate, conduct banking transactions, attend school, or even seek medical care virtually, regardless of physical location. Gartner [1] predicted that by 2026, 25% of people will spend at least one hour per day working, shopping, studying, or socializing in the metaverse. Yet, despite such projections, adoption has been slower than expected. For example, only 17% of US adults reported using a virtual reality

 IntechOpen

(VR) headset, according to IT Pro [2]. Many experts now anticipate that augmented reality (AR) and mixed reality (MR), such as smart glasses overlaying digital information, may become more integrated into daily life than full VR immersion in the metaverse.

The long-term outlook remains questionable. According to Pew Research [3], 54% of technology experts expect a refined, immersive metaverse to become a regular part of daily life for over half a billion people by 2040, while 46% remain skeptical. Barriers such as safety concerns, lack of regulation, and insufficient user experience (UX) design continue to slow development. These issues are especially critical for the metaverse designed particularly for younger users, who have not yet formed mature values or life perspectives, and that group of users is more likely to experience a hard time distinguishing between beneficial and harmful virtual experiences.

When we look closely at the demographic data of the metaverse applications, it highlights the urgency of this concern. Market.us [4] reported that 38% of metaverse users are between 10 and 20 years old, making this the largest age group. Another 36% fall between ages 21 and 35, 22% between 36 and 50, and only 4% are over 50. Other sources suggest that younger users dominate even more strongly. For instance, Roblox's 2025 Quarter II report [5] shows there are over 111 million daily active users, with nearly 40% of its players under the age of 13. The Roblox user distribution shows that the Asia-Pacific region has the most users at 35.7%, followed by Europe at 20.9%, and the United States and North America at 19%.

Over the past twenty years, several major technological revolutions have made real-time virtual environments possible. High-performance graphics processing units (GPUs) [6] now enable real-time rendering and ray tracing [7] to produce lifelike visuals, while spatial mapping technologies such as LiDAR and SLAM [8–10] reconstruct physical spaces so that virtual environments can closely mirror the real world. These advances have made the creation of real-time digital twin environments achievable. At the same time, cloud infrastructure provides the backbone for large-scale multiplayer participation and real-time interaction. Together, these technologies form the foundation for the development and sustainability of the metaverse.

Given the trends and user distributions described earlier, and the increasing maturity on the technical side, the next frontier lies in understanding and shaping human behavior within these metaverse environments. To move forward, is it necessary for designers and developers to embed ethical, psychological, and social responsibility considerations into metaverse design? And how can this be achieved? Let's start with a discussion on the potential social impacts of the metaverse, particularly on the younger generation user group.

2. Metaverse's potential negative impacts on the younger generation

One of the long-standing goals in virtual world design has been to maximize immersion. Designers work hard to make these spaces as engaging and believable as the real world. Some positive impacts are reflected in studies on the use of the metaverse in both education and entertainment. For example, research on shared interactive VR [11] found that virtual environments can increase positive emotions when experienced with others. Similarly, studies on video games [12] have shown that they can improve memory, problem-solving, and even comprehension.

But on the flip side, other research has shown more negative impacts. Gottschalk's OECD (Organisation for Economic Co-operation and Development) working paper in 2019 [13] reviewed the literature and found links between heavy use of online games and serious problems such as sleep disruption, anxiety, and depression. Social skills and academic performance may also suffer when children spend less time on homework or face-to-face interaction. Harvard Health has also pointed out risks to physical health, including vision strain, repetitive injuries like "gamer's thumb," and even obesity. Beyond that, the World Health Organization now recognizes "gaming disorder," which involves symptoms such as withdrawal and the loss of healthy daily functioning [14]. A study in Child and Adolescent Psychiatry and Mental Health [15] added that children with higher levels of gaming addiction showed measurable deficits in memory and attention, raising concerns about long-term academic and cognitive outcomes.

Recent data highlight the scale of the issue. According to Qustodio [16], American children using Roblox spent an average of 139 minutes per day in 2023 on the platform. Experts recommend countermeasures such as screen-time limits, encouraging outdoor activities, monitoring game content, and maintaining open family discussions about online life. In a related area, reports on social media [17] show that teenagers also spend excessive amounts of time online, facing similar risks of social media and metaverse addiction.

Some recent reports [18, 19] reach a more balanced position. For example, Metaverse and Mental Health [19] discusses the potential of virtual environments to support growth if designed carefully. Likewise, Emergence of the Metaverse and Psychiatric Concerns in Children and Adolescents [18] warns that poorly designed platforms may aggravate psychiatric risks but also suggests that a carefully designed metaverse could have the opposite effect. The key takeaway is clear: if the metaverse is to become a safe place for younger generations, UX design must integrate not just technical excellence but also psychological insight.

One of the attractions of the metaverse is that it makes some impossible things in real life possible, which makes it fun and exciting. However, nonstop play can bring problems, including social isolation, addiction, and weaker communication skills in the real world [20]. In a family setting, parents often attempt to set rules around online and gaming time. However, when children ignore these rules, conflict arises. Research shows that such conflict can actually worsen addictive behaviors [21, 22]. Over time, this cycle becomes difficult to break and weakens the parent–child relationship. While there are no precise statistics on how many students drop out of school because of game addiction, many real-life examples show that students who once did well academically later became addicted and eventually dropped out of school [23]. To help break this cycle, metaverse systems should include features – such as health warnings or reminders to log off – that encourage more balanced use.

This chapter argues that psychological principles, ethical considerations, and social responsibility should be used as a guide in UX design for the metaverse. In the following case study, we will examine how younger children often spend excessive time on platforms such as Roblox or Minecraft, and what kinds of social problems emerge when there is no UX design that encourages healthy disconnection from virtual worlds. Later, we will discuss how metaverse design could be supported by both psychological principles and artificial intelligence (AI), which might help children disconnect in healthy ways and return to real physical-world activities smoothly. Such features could help create what we call a responsible metaverse.

3. A case study: Children's experiences on Roblox, one of the popular metaverse platforms

To better understand how younger children engage with the metaverse, an interview and observation study was conducted with four parents and their six children, ranging from second grade to seventh grade. The interviews with the parents focused on the amount of time the children spent playing online games, whether they could stop voluntarily, and whether gaming interfered with daily routines. The results were consistent across families: none of the parents reported being able to effectively control their children's gaming time. On average, the children played for about two hours per day, which aligns with the statistical data collected by Roblox. Another finding from the interviews was that Roblox and Minecraft were the most frequently mentioned platforms. Three of the four parents also admitted that they did not know how to use parental controls or set up time limits on their devices.

In this case study, alongside the interviews, the children were observed during a weekend playdate. The observation was conducted during a pre-arranged playdate gathering at one of the participants' houses. The playdate gathering began on a Saturday morning at 10 a.m., and instead of listening to the parents' recommendation to engage in some outdoor activities, the children immediately logged into Roblox and dived into their virtual world play on their iPads and computers. By the afternoon at 3 p.m., five of the six children were still playing, totaling nearly four and a half hours of uninterrupted screen time. One second-grade boy switched from Roblox to Minecraft after about half an hour and stayed there for the rest of the time until the parents intervened with the call of "stop." Across the group, the children explored between five and seven different games in Roblox during that period of time. Although later, several children expressed that they sometimes feel bored with certain older games, they continued to come back to check if there were new releases in virtual spaces within Roblox.

Breaks were minimal. While some children grabbed snacks, their attention never fully left the screen, and none paused for a proper lunch. When asked afterward whether the games offered prompts to take breaks, the answer was unanimous: "Of course not." Their reasons for enjoying the platforms were simple but revealing:

> "I think it is cool."
> "I can create my land or my world and do stuff."
> "I can talk with my friends."
> "I just roam around to see what is happening."
> "Some of the games are educational; I can make a word game."
> "Some of the games are out of date. I am bored with them, but I go there to check if there are any new ones."

The responses call attention to both the appeal and the risks of these platforms. The ability to socialize, explore, and create is central to their attractions, yet the lack of built-in features to encourage breaks or healthy disconnection makes it difficult for children to regulate their usage and easily exceed the time limit without parental control or interference. Even hunger or fatigue did not pull them fully out of the virtual experience.

This case study points to a significant design gap. Roblox and similar platforms currently provide little to no support for time management and balance, leaving the responsibility entirely to parents, many of whom lack the tools or knowledge to enforce limits. If future metaverse environments continue to prioritize continuous engagement without considering the developmental needs of children, they may unintentionally reinforce patterns of overuse and disconnection from real-world activities. For UX designers, the challenge is to rethink these systems not only as entertainment platforms but as environments with real social and psychological consequences.

4. Metaverse UX design with psychological concerns in mind

In this section, we will continue analyzing UX design for the metaverse, using the previous case study as a reference scenario. Responsible metaverse design requires that UX principles be integrated with psychological insights to promote balanced use and healthy engagement, particularly for younger users. How can we make it happen? The following seven design strategies illustrate how real-world principles can be embedded into a virtual environment to promote a responsible metaverse.

4.1 Scheduled break reminders

Users often lose track of time while playing in immersive environments. To counter this problem, platforms should integrate scheduled reminders that encourage players to pause and return to real-world activities. For example, in the middle of the day, a metaverse system could provide an AI-generated message that suggests a lunch break with some visual lunch selections to stimulate hungry feelings; or, around sleep time at night, a system-controlled dimming screen along with a "time to go to bed" message could simulate a real-world parent turning off the lights. These features connect the virtual with the real world, helping children align online behavior with natural routines. Nielsen's well-known usability heuristic, "Match between the system and the real world" [24], supports this idea. The concept is the same as children taking recess in school; so too should virtual environments provide built-in pauses.

4.2 Incentivized breaks

Beyond simple reminders, 3D games and metaverse platforms can create a reward system to encourage users to voluntarily take breaks. For example, a user might earn extra points or unlock a small bonus after stepping away for ten minutes. By turning disconnection into a positive experience, designers can reduce resistance to leaving the game while promoting healthier time management. As we can imagine, the disconnection opportunity may lead to a longer time away from the computer and reduce the possibility of addiction.

4.3 Clear navigation

Theories of cognitive load suggest that when interfaces are too complex, they can overwhelm users, making it harder to disengage. Simplified navigation, clear goals, and thoughtful pacing can help children move more easily between virtual and offline activities. Designing with cognitive limits in mind also reduces fatigue, making breaks feel more natural rather than disruptive. One example is always having an exit sign in the virtual world to allow users to get offline. Think about being in a shopping mall and getting lost; you should be able to find an "exit" to get out. The navigation system should align with reality, which users are already familiar with.

4.4 Leveraging social influence

Children, as one of the major user groups, are strongly affected by peer norms and social expectations. Metaverse environments can incorporate features that encourage teamwork, politeness, and respectful interaction. By embedding these social values, morals, and cues directly into the platform, designers promote a healthier community. For example, in-game prompts could highlight positive behaviors like respect, collaboration, care, and so on, or reward teams for achieving goals together rather than only for individual achievements.

4.5 Goal setting and customization

Allowing users, especially children, to set personal goals for time spent online or to define what they want to achieve in each session can encourage reflection and self-regulation. This function bridges virtual actions with real-world behaviors, such as practicing time management and accountability.

4.6 Tools for parents

Families play a central role, and metaverse platforms can make this role much easier or harder. Built-in tools that let parents set time limits, monitor their child's activity, or receive alerts when usage becomes excessive are essential. Yet, in the Roblox case described earlier, such features were largely absent. Many parents admit they struggle with technical settings or even knowing where to begin. In fact, a kid can create an account without a parent's permission.

For welcoming parents to be part of the metaverse, let's call a function a parental assistant instead of parental control. The parental assistant function has to be simple, clear to use, and accessible. If the parental assistant (parental control) is buried in menus or too complicated to set up, most parents will not use it, and the tools end up meaningless. By contrast, when parental assistant functions are thoughtfully designed, they create a real partnership between families and developers. In that case, virtual platforms do not just keep children engaged; they also help them grow up with healthier digital habits and stronger connections to the world outside the screen.

4.7 Raising awareness of impacts

Finally, platforms can educate users by displaying real-time messages that highlight the immediate benefits of taking breaks or provide health tips for the eyes, neck, and spine. They can reinforce awareness of the negative impacts of game addiction and emphasize the benefits of taking breaks or going offline for a period of time. These educational messages can help children resist the temptation to remain in virtual worlds for extended periods. By receiving this important information from the metaverse system, children may find it easier to stop playing and recognize the value of reconnecting with real-world activities.

5. AI in future metaverse UX design

AI is expected to play a central role in shaping the next generation of metaverse experiences. When combined with psychological principles, AI has the potential to guide healthier patterns of use for metaverse system design.

First of all, personalization is a key area that generative AI and AI agencies can support in the design and development of metaverse applications. AI-driven platforms can adapt reminders and interventions to fit the unique needs of each child player. For example, some children may respond better to playful avatars that remind them to take a break, while others may benefit from more direct feedback about screen time. The AI agency can study reaction patterns from the player's behavior and offer the best approach to reach out to them. This adaptive approach ensures that guidance feels supportive rather than intrusive.

Secondly, AI can provide behavior analysis. AI can monitor patterns of engagement, such as how long children play, which activities keep them online, and identify the moments that tend to lead to natural breaks. By recognizing these patterns, platforms can introduce timely prompts that suggest stepping away when immersion becomes excessive. In effect, AI could predict when a child is at risk of overuse and provide a gentle nudge toward healthier behavior. Currently, parents have to manually monitor and determine when and how to stop a child from gaming. However, in reality, this process often involves conflict. AI can make the metaverse intelligent enough to recommend that the game be paused or disconnected smoothly, keeping parents out of the conflict and protecting the parent–child relationship.

Another contribution of AI is to extend support to parents. Intelligent parental tools could provide insights into a child's activity patterns, recommend healthy limits, and issue alerts when overuse is detected. As discussed in the previous section, these assistant tools need to be clear and user-friendly. By integrating AI recommendations, parental assistants could become smarter and easier to use. In this way, AI becomes a partner in shared goals between developers and families.

Finally, AI-powered virtual assistants may play a role in shaping the social environment of the metaverse. These assistants could act as moderators, coaches, or guides, helping children resolve conflicts, encouraging teamwork, or modeling healthy digital habits. Such features could mimic the presence of a teacher or mentor, blending human-like support with technological scalability.

Overall, the integration of AI into metaverse UX design and application development is invaluable. If applied responsibly, AI can help create environments that are not only immersive but also supportive of balanced use, particularly for younger users who may struggle with self-regulation.

6. Suggested checklist for UX design in metaverse applications

With an understanding of how AI technology can be applied in metaverse development, as well as the psychological and moral roles in UX design for metaverse applications, this section outlines a checklist for designing metaverse environments for younger users. Building on the case study, metaverse companies are encouraged to carefully apply these checkpoints and implement steps to test and address vulnerabilities to better protect young users. While this checklist is intended for younger users, the underlying principles also apply to the majority of metaverse applications.

6.1 Accessibility

The first step of interaction with any digital platform begins at the point of downloading the application. This stage sets the foundation for the entire UX and requires careful consideration of fundamental questions: Who are the intended users of the application? Who should be eligible to download it, and how can this process be made both intuitive and safe? Establishing clear entry points is critical because it not only shapes user expectations but also determines how well the application aligns with the age group, needs, and safety requirements of its target audience.

At the same time, it is equally important to address how non-eligible users can be effectively prevented from downloading and accessing the application. This raises the issue of what kind of supervision or safeguards should be embedded into the design. For example, while platforms like Roblox claim to provide parental controls, test results show that children under 13 can still create accounts with little or no parental supervision. Such gaps between stated policy and actual design practice highlight a critical weakness in current systems. To ensure a safer digital environment, developers must seal these gaps by aligning their security measures with real-world use, enforcing stricter controls, and designing with parental supervision as a built-in access requirement.

6.2 Setting rules for metaverse

Clear rules need to be embedded in applications from the very beginning, especially when addressing users' physical and mental health concerns. In the physical world, social rules and health regulations guide our daily lives – a doctor may warn patients about overeating or overdrinking, and restaurants often limit dining times to ensure fairness. Similar rules should be built into virtual environments, particularly in applications targeted at children, to prevent overstaying in the digital world. Recommendations such as break reminders, total time-use reports, or AI assistants acting as mentors could help monitor usage and support healthy disconnection at the software design level.

Software should also emphasize behavioral standards. To prevent abuse and bullying, platforms need built-in functions for monitoring user behavior and clear procedures for addressing misconduct. Just as a school principal is responsible for handling disciplinary issues, virtual spaces must also have mechanisms in place to respond to harmful behaviors. Establishing these systems ensures that digital environments are not only engaging but also safe and respectful for all users.

6.3 Navigation

To make returning to the real world easier, "logoff" or "pause" signs should be clearly visible in every virtual environment – much like exit signs in shopping malls in the physical world. These indicators provide users with a simple and intuitive way to disengage, reducing the risk of losing track of time or getting trapped in a virtual space.

Applications should also integrate real-world time to help users stay grounded. Features such as displaying clocks, syncing with a personal calendar, or daily reminders and to-do lists can keep users aware of their daily routines. These connections serve as an important bridge between the virtual and physical worlds, reminding users that balance and healthy boundaries are essential for sustained well-being.

6.4 Social responsibilities

Before an application is released, user testing and data analysis should be conducted to assess its social impact. Metaverse companies should be required to submit public reports on active users and their demographics. If as per data, a metaverse is having a significant negative impact on users' physical or mental well-being, UX design should be reevaluated and adjusted. For example, maximum daily time-use thresholds may need to be enforced.

Finally, we would like to say that the points on the above checklist are not meant to serve as rigid rules but as guiding principles for responsible metaverse design. They highlight the importance of aligning virtual experiences with real-world expectations, from accessibility and supervision to health safeguards and navigation. If companies take these measures seriously, the metaverse can evolve into an environment that supports creativity, learning, and connection without sacrificing children's well-being. Ignoring them, however, risks creating virtual spaces that intensify the very problems – addiction, isolation, and harm – that designers should be working to prevent.

As technology advances, laws and regulations for virtual spaces must evolve as well. Unlawful behavior in virtual environments should carry consequences, just as it does in the physical world. Furthermore, companies that deliberately encourage overuse in ways that harm children's development should be held accountable. The future of the metaverse will depend not only on technical innovation but also on the willingness of its creators to place responsibility at the heart of its design.

7. Conclusion and future work

As the metaverse becomes a new platform for our human community, it will increasingly blur the difference between real and virtual, merging immersive virtual worlds and real-world activities together. The challenge of designing a responsible metaverse grows more urgent. This chapter has highlighted how psychological principles and AI could be used to support healthier patterns of engagement for metaverse users. The discussion began by outlining the risks of poorly designed environments, continued with a case study of children's experiences on one of the popular metaverses used mostly by kids under 16, Roblox, and then proposed design strategies that emphasize balance, breaks, and parental involvement. Finally, it explored how AI can potentially extend these principles by predicting patterns of use, personalizing interventions, and supporting families. The main lesson is that the metaverse should not be designed only to maximize time on the metaverse platform. Instead, it must be developed to foster balanced engagement, encouraging immersion when appropriate but also promoting healthy disconnection. This shift requires metaverse companies to invest in UX designers and developers to integrate insights from psychology, education, human–computer interaction, and social responsibilities alongside the most advanced technical innovation.

The target users in the above case study were children. This case study is exploratory in nature and is intended to provide preliminary insights. The findings highlight key issues and UX considerations in building metaverse applications, including those designed for adult users. Future studies should be conducted, particularly to examine the design of metaverse applications for adult user groups or for different age groups targeted by metaverse applications. In addition to the case study scenario mentioned in Section 3 of the chapter, continued study with a larger sample size is necessary to evaluate how scheduled breaks provide an incentive to disconnect and how AI-driven parental tools work across diverse groups of children. Furthermore, prototypes of metaverse environments that integrate these features could provide valuable data on usability and effectiveness.

For developing a responsible metaverse application, collaboration among metaverse UX designers, psychologists, educators, and legal experts, along with greater technological maturity and awareness of user impacts through iterative testing, will be essential to ensure that the metaverse develops in ways that benefit society as a whole. In short, the future of the metaverse is not only a technical question but also a human one. By implementing responsibility into its design, the metaverse can grow into a space that supports creativity and connection and improves human beings' lives.

Acknowledgments

First of all, I would like to thank parents who shared their children's struggles with gaming addiction. Those life stories were a wake-up call for me as a researcher specializing in user experience study and 3D virtual reality environment design and development. I never imagined that the exciting possibilities of the metaverse could also bring such serious negative social impacts.

Special thanks go to the families and children who participated in the interviews and observations and offered their candid opinions. The data they provided were eye-opening and pushed me to study these issues more deeply.

I am especially grateful to my daughter, who brought her friends' stories to my attention. These stories that parents might never hear otherwise. Her support throughout my research, along with her willingness to share her own honest views, gave this work a personal meaning that I could not have gained from academic sources alone.

Ethical statement

To ensure accurate data collection, the observational study was conducted without the children being aware that they were under observation. Following the study, they were informed and consented to the collected data being used anonymously for research purposes.

Author details

Feng Liu
Mercer University, Atlanta GA, USA

*Address all correspondence to: LIU_F@Mercer.edu

References

[1] Gartner. Gartner Predicts 25% of People Will Spend at Least One Hour Per Day in the Metaverse by 2026 [Internet]. Gartner Press Release; 2022. Available from: https://www.gartner.com/en/newsroom/press-releases/2022-02-07-gartner-predicts-25-percent-of-people-will-spend-at-least-one-hour-per-day-in-the-metaverse-by-2026 [Accessed: 2025-November-26]

[2] IT Pro. Only 17% of US adults used VR headsets in 2023 [Internet]. IT Pro; 2023. Available from: https://www.itpro.com/business/business-strategy/why-is-meta-still-funding-the-metaverse?utm_source=chatgpt.com [Accessed: 2025-November-26]

[3] Pew Research Center. The metaverse in 2040 [Internet]. Pew Research; 2022. Available from: https://www.pewresearch.org/internet/2022/06/30/the-metaverse-in-2040 [Accessed: 2025-August-22]

[4] Market.us. Metaverse market size, share, and age demographics report [Internet]. Market.us; 2024. Available from: https://market.us/report/metaverse-market. [Accessed: 2025-August-22]

[5] Roblox Corporation. Roblox Q2 2025 Shareholder Letter: Daily Active Users & Demographics [Internet]. Available from: https://s27.q4cdn.com/984876518/files/doc_financials/2025/q2/Q2-25-SH-Letter.pdf [Accessed: 2025-November-26]

[6] Owens JD, Houston M, Luebke D, Green S, Stone JE, Phillips JC. GPU computing. Proceedings of the IEEE. 2008;**96**(5):879–899. DOI: 10.1109/JPROC.2008.917757

[7] Parker SG, Bigler J, Dietrich A, Friedrich H, Hoberock J, Luebke D, et al. OptiX: A general purpose ray tracing engine. ACM Transactions on Graphics. 2010;**29**(4):66. DOI: 10.1145/1778765.1778803

[8] Baltsavias EP. Airborne laser scanning: Basic relations and formulas. ISPRS Journal of Photogrammetry and Remote Sensing. 1999;**54**(2–3):199–214. DOI: (99)00015-5",1,0,0>10.1016/S0924-2716(99)00015-5

[9] Durrant-Whyte H, Bailey T. Simultaneous localization and mapping: Part I. IEEE Robotics and Automation Magazine. 2006;**13**(2):99–110. DOI: 10.1109/MRA.2006.1638022

[10] Cadena C, Carlone L, Carrillo H, Latif Y, Scaramuzza D, Neira J, et al. Past, present, and future of simultaneous localization and mapping: Toward the robust-perception age. IEEE Transactions on Robotics. 2016;**32**(6):1309–1332. DOI: 10.1109/TRO.2016.2624754

[11] Guertin-Lahoud S, et al. User experience evaluation in shared interactive virtual reality. Cyberpsychology, Behavior, and Social Networking. 2023;**26**(4):213–221. DOI: 10.1089/cyber.2022.0261

[12] Quispe BM, et al. Towards the development of prosocial behavior in students through the use of video games. World Journal on Educational Technology. 2023;**15**(1):1–10. Available from. https://www.researchgate.net/

publication/367327401_Towards_the_development_of_prosocial_behavior_in_students_through_the_use_of_video_game

[13] Gottschalk F Impacts of technology use on children: Exploring literature on the brain, cognition and well-being. *OECD Education Working Paper* No. 195. Paris: OECD Publishing; 2019

[14] Grinspoon P The health effects of too much gaming [Internet]. *Harvard Health Publishing;* 2021. Available from: https://www.health.harvard.edu/staying-healthy/the-health-effects-of-too-much-gaming. [Accessed: 2025-May-22]

[15] Farchakh Y, et al. Video gaming addiction and its association with memory, attention, and learning skills in Lebanese children. Child and Adolescent Psychiatry and Mental Health. 2023;**17**:94

[16] Qustodio. Annual digital report 2023–24 [Internet]. Qustodio; 2024. Available from: https://static.qustodio.com/public-site/uploads/2024/01/19122535/ADR_2023-24_EN.pdf. [Accessed: 2025-May-22]

[17] Shepherd's Hill Academy. Teens and social media addiction [Internet]. Shepherd's Hill Academy; 2024. Available from: https://www.shepherdshillacademy.org/common-teen-issues/teens-social-media-addiction. [Accessed: 2025-May-22]

[18] Uihak SCC. Emergence of the metaverse and psychiatric concerns in children and adolescents. Soa Chongsonyon Chongsin Uihak. 2023;**34**(4):215–221. DOI: 10.5765/jkacap.230047

[19] Sternlicht L, Sternlicht A. The metaverse and mental health [Internet]. Family Addiction Specialist; 2024. Available from: https://www.familyaddictionspecialist.com/blog/a-new-age-of-digital-addiction-what-the-metaverse-means-for-mental-health-and-digital-addiction. [Accessed: 2025-May-22]

[20] Kuss DJ, Griffiths MD. Internet gaming addiction: A systematic review of empirical research. International Journal of Mental Health and Addiction. 2012;**10**(2):278–296. DOI: 10.1007/s11469-011-9318-5

[21] Schneider LA, King DL, Delfabbro PH. Family factors in adolescent problematic Internet gaming: A systematic review. Journal of Behavioral Addictions. 2017;**6**(3):321–333. DOI: 10.1556/2006.6.2017.035

[22] Throuvala MA, Bonnaire C, Panayiotou G, Heshmat M, Shao A, Kuss DJ. The role of family and personality traits in Internet gaming disorder: a structural equation model. Addictive Behaviors Reports. 2019;**10**:100218. Available from: https://pmc.ncbi.nlm.nih.gov/articles/PMC7044602/

[23] Andreassen CS, Billieux J, Griffiths MD, Kuss DJ, Demetrovics Z, Mazzoni E, Pallesen S. The relationship between addictive use of social media and video games and symptoms of psychiatric disorders: A large-scale cross-sectional study. Psychology of Addictive Behaviors. 2016;**30**(2):252–262. DOI: 10.1037/adb0000160

[24] Nielsen J. Usability heuristics for user interface design [Internet]. Nielsen Norman Group; 1995. Available from: https://www.nngroup.com/articles/ten-usability-heuristics [Accessed: 2025-May-30]

Chapter 10

Adaptive Human Digital Twin (aHDT) in Metaverse: A Model for Enhancing Physical Safety

Viktorija Diak and Andrii Diak

Abstract

Human physical safety within increasingly complex sociotechnical systems faces significant constraints. Individual cognitive resources are often insufficient to respond effectively to concurrent threats, while conventional protective mechanisms typically detect events only after they occur. These limitations reduce the effectiveness of risk management and increase the probability of critical errors. This paper introduces the concept of an adaptive human digital twin (aHDT) – a model integrating biometric data, behavioral indicators, and predictive analytics algorithms. The aHDT framework shifts the paradigm from reactive response toward proactive threat prediction and self-corrective adaptation through continuous synchronization with the HDT. The model supports personalized interaction, reduces cognitive load, and enables collective knowledge integration across users. Despite these advantages, the paper presents a detailed analysis of the model's inherent limitations, driven by the current state of technology as well as legal, economic, ethical, and cultural factors. Particular attention is given to the challenges of maintaining transparency, synchronization, and mutual trust among HDTs within the metaverse.

Keywords: HDT, physical safety, predictive analytics, explainable AI, metaspace, proactive safety, resilience engineering

1. Introduction

The concept of the metaverse refers to a virtual environment where people interact with each other and digital objects through avatars. It opens up new opportunities for communication, education, creativity, and work, but it also presents significant security risks, including cyberattacks, data breaches, psychological pressure, fraud, and gaps in legal regulation [1, 2]. Research primarily focuses on immersive technologies, such as VR and AR, and the associated risks: discomfort, fatigue, motion sickness, falls, and user injuries [3].

However, the issue of human physical safety in the real-world environment remains underexplored. Limitations of human physiology, cognitive, and behavioral mechanisms substantially affect the ability to recognize and respond to dangers in a timely manner. Information processing speed, working memory capacity, cognitive overload, limited personal experience, and the inability to encounter the full range of

IntechOpen

potential threats render traditional reactive security strategies inadequate. Even automated skills and accumulated experience remain partial and not always transferable, which increases the risk of accidents and injuries. These circumstances highlight the need for human-centered security models capable of integrating human condition data with environmental dynamics.

Emerging technologies – such as wearables, smart textiles [4], AR/VR, and intelligent algorithms [5] – offer new opportunities for proactive protection. These technologies are already being applied in industries and transportation: Digital twins (DTs) predict equipment failures [6], predictive analytics systems reduce accident rates [7], and adaptive interfaces help manage information overload [8, 9]. However, these solutions primarily focus on objects or processes, while human vulnerability is addressed only partially. Existing human digital twin (HDT) [10] models attempt to fill this gap by extending DT technology to consider physiological, cognitive, and behavioral parameters of humans. Nevertheless, they also remain fragmented, focusing on localized approaches – such as ensuring worker safety [11], human–robot interaction [12], modeling interactions with medical devices [13], or analyzing stress in daily life [14] – without creating a holistic model for human–environment interaction or knowledge exchange between users.

The adaptive HDT (aHDT) model proposed in this work aims to overcome these limitations by employing explainable AI (XAI) models [15, 16], federated/collective learning mechanisms [17], human-in-the-loop (HITL) principles [18, 19], and resilience engineering (RE) [20, 21] in a multiuser metaverse [22]. Operating within shared metaspace[1], aHDTs can exchange aggregated models and behavioral patterns, forming a distributed cognitive network that enables collective learning, systemic protection, and overall architecture resilience. To validate human–HDT interaction in a safe environment, a simulation test bed [23, 24] is used to refine adaptation strategies and predictive responses. While existing metaverse concepts focus on immersive experience [25], aHDT creates a human-centered metaspace, where safety is defined by the ability of both the human and their digital twin to adapt to real-time environmental changes. In this context, HDT acts as the digital core of the user, while aHDT integrates multiple HDTs via sensory, AR/VR, and algorithmic infrastructure (XAI, HITL, RE) into a shared metaspace of collective learning and resilient interaction.

The aim of the paper is to develop and justify the conceptual aHDT model as a human-centered tool for enhancing physical safety and cognitive resilience in real-world conditions.

Structure of the paper: Section 2 describes the architecture of aHDT and the key components that integrate technical tools and data analysis/reaction methods. Section 3 outlines the barriers to implementation, correlates them with the challenges of the metaverse, and proposes a roadmap for the development of aHDT. Section 4 discusses the social-level prospects, and Section 5 concludes the paper.

2. Concept of aHDT model

2.1 External threats and the limitations of human experience

Modern humans are confronted with numerous threats – both accidental (falls, household injuries) and systemic (professional, environmental, technological,

[1] Metaspace – the functional layer of the metaverse where HDTs and their users interact.

social). In conditions of high dynamics and uncertainty, the human ability to recognize dangers is constrained by biological and cognitive factors [26], including information processing speed, attention span, fatigue, and the limitations of personal experience [27]. These constraints justify the need to transition from reactive strategies to proactive security approaches [20], based on forecasting and risk scenario modeling. The HDT model facilitates this transition by enabling real-time analysis of the human condition and predictive safety management. Unlike traditional monitoring systems, HDT interprets data in the context of physical and cognitive activity, helping to uncover hidden dependencies and proactively form corrective actions. The capability for collective learning [28] aggregates the experience of multiple users and adapts it to individual conditions, providing a foundation for personalized and resilient threat prevention strategies.

2.2 Architecture of the adaptive HDT

The adaptive human digital twin (aHDT) is developed as a new type of cyber-physical system, where the human is not viewed solely as a data source but as an active element of the safety and adaptation model. Unlike traditional monitoring systems, which are limited to collecting and visualizing biometric indicators, aHDT relies on an extended algorithmic architecture[2] that integrates the principles of XAI, HITL, RE, and simulation test bed. This integration allows not only for capturing the user's current state but also for predicting their response, interpreting the causes of changes, and adjusting the model's behavior in real time.

The sensory infrastructure includes smart textiles[3] (measuring heart rate, respiration, muscle activity, body temperature, and biomechanics of movement) and AR/VR devices[4], which capture spatial trajectories, interactions with objects, and cognitive reactions (e.g., through eye-tracking[5]). Using these data, a multimodal model is formed that reflects the physiological, cognitive, and behavioral states of the individual.

Example: A wristband detects elevated heart rate, AR glasses track gaze direction, and the system interprets the combination of these signals, considering previous behavioral patterns, to predict potential lapses in concentration. Unlike conventional predictive models, HDT does not rely solely on statistical correlation; the XAI component explains which factors led to the prediction, the HITL module allows the user to confirm, adjust, or reject the interpretation, the RE level ensures robustness in the face of incomplete data, and the test bed environment tests the effectiveness of the correction in simulated scenarios before deployment in real time. Therefore, the aHDT architecture functions as a closed cognitive-predictive loop (**Figure 1**): The sensor level generates data → the analytical level builds a predictive model → XAI ensures decision transparency → HITL supports adaptive human involvement

[2] Computational algorithms in HDT are methods that convert raw sensor data into risk models, identify critical parameter patterns (e.g., elevated heart rate plus delayed reaction), and pass them to XAI for user-transparent explanation [122].

[3] Smart textiles – woven materials with integrated sensors and data collection systems [9].

[4] Augmented reality (AR) and virtual reality (VR): technologies that enable users to interact with digital objects either overlaid onto the physical environment (AR) or within a fully immersive artificial environment (VR) [123].

[5] Eye-tracking – a technology for measuring gaze direction and fixation to analyze attention and interaction with interfaces [124].

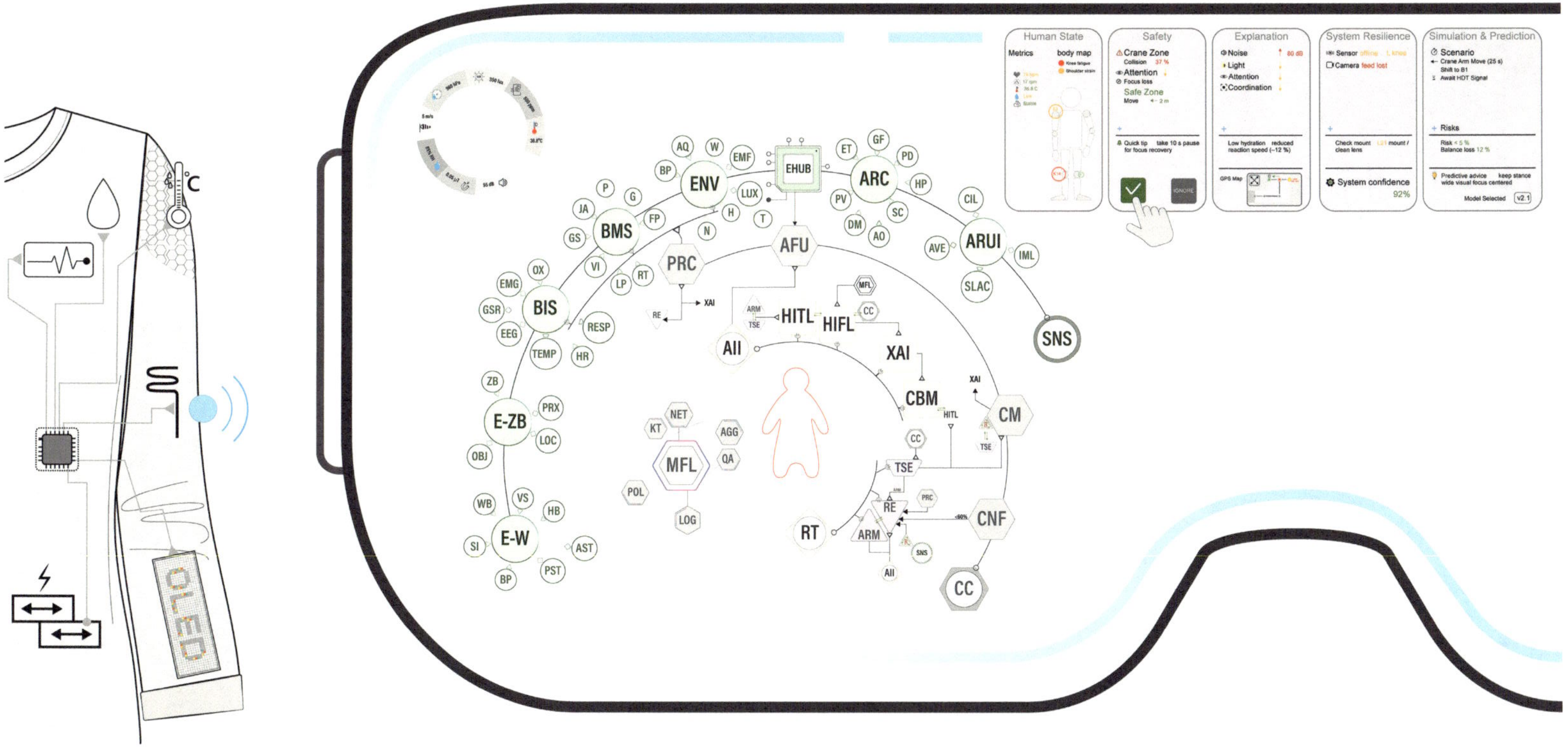

Figure 1.
Adaptive HDT architecture circle diagram. ARUI scenario: The operator is located in an assembly zone with moving cranes and exposed cable routes. The aHDT system monitors biometric data, position, gaze direction, and the surrounding environment. ***SES*** *– sensors (role: collects sensor data);* ***CC*** *– cognitive core/analytics (interprets sensor data streams, identifies correlations, causes, predictions, and confidence levels);* ***AII*** *– adaptive interface interaction (provides adaptive user interaction, explains system reasoning, and collects feedback);* ***RT*** *– resilience and test bed (maintains operational stability, simulates scenarios, and manages adaptive recovery).* ***SES .ENV*** *– environment sensor (detect ambient conditions);.****ARC*** *– AR-capture/eye-tracking (captures visual context, gaze direction, and user attention focus);* ***ARUI*** *– AR user interface (UI) (uses sensory feedback and contextual data to adapt visual, auditory, and cognitive interaction layers as UI for the human operator);* ***BMS*** *– behavior/motion sensor (tracks physical*

activity, coordination, and movement stability); ***BIS*** *– bio-sensor (monitors physiological and psychophysiological states);* ***E–ZB*** *– environment: zone beacon (defines spatial zones and hazard boundaries);* ***E–W*** *– external device: wearable (integrates multiple sensors on the user's body/apparel);* ***EHUB*** *– edge hub/aggregator (aggregates, preprocesses, and synchronizes data locally).* ***ENV .T*** *– ambient temperature sensor;* ***H*** *– humidity (relative);* ***.N*** *– noise (sound level);* ***AQ*** *– air quality (CO_2/VOC concentration);* ***LUX*** *– light (illumination);* ***BP*** *– barometric (air pressure);* ***EMF*** *– EM field (electromagnetic radiation);* ***W*** *– wind (speed and direction);* ***ARC .ET*** *– eye-tracking (tracks gaze, fixations, blinks);* ***gf*** *– gaze-focus (detects focused visual target);* ***PD*** *– pupil dilation (measures pupil size (stress/load);* ***HP*** *– head pose (measures head position and tilt);* ***SC*** *– scene capture (records real-world surroundings);* ***DM*** *– depth mapping (measures object distance/shape);* ***PV*** *– peripheral vision (tracks off-center attention);* ***AO*** *– AR overlay align (aligns virtual and real objects).* ***ARUI AVE*** *– adaptive visualization engine (controls display timing and clarity);* ***CIL*** *– cognitive integration layer (merges predictions, explanations, and resilience data);* ***IML*** *– interaction mediation layer (manages feedback and confirmation);* ***SLAC*** *– system-level adaptation controller (coordinates adaptive UI logic).* ***BMS P*** *– posture (tracks body Alignment);* ***G*** *– gait (measures stride and balance);* ***GS*** *– gesture (detects hand/finger motion);* ***JA*** *– joint angle (measures joint bending);* ***LP*** *– load/pressure (measures body or limb pressure);* ***VI*** *– vibration/impact (detects shocks or impacts);* ***FP*** *– fatigue pattern (identifies movement fatigue);* ***RT*** *– reaction time (measures response delay).* ***BIS HR*** *– heart rate (tracks pulse);* ***RESP*** *– respiration (monitors breathing rate);* ***TEMP*** *– body temp (measures body temperature);* ***EMG*** *– muscle activity (detects muscular effort or strain);* ***GSR*** *– skin conductance (measures stress response);* ***OX*** *– oximeter (monitors blood oxygen (spo_2));* ***EEG*** *– brain activity (tracks cognitive workload and fatigue).* ***E–ZB ZB*** *– zone beacon (detects user position in risk zones);* ***PRX*** *– proximity (detects approach to objects or people);* ***LOC*** *– location (tracks spatial coordinates and path);* ***OBJ*** *– object tracking (monitors moving machinery or objects).* ***E–W WB*** *– smart wristband (monitors pulse, activity, temp, etc.);* ***VS*** *– smart vest (tracks HR, respiration, EMG, posture);* ***HB*** *– smart helmet (EEG, eye-tracking, light detection);* ***SI*** *– smart insole/shoes (measures gait, pressure, balance);* ***BP*** *– biopatch (small patch for HR, skin temp, muscle activity);* ***PST*** *– passive smart textile (senses color, posture, motion, pressure via material properties);* ***AST*** *– active smart textile (embedded sensors/APU for active monitoring and data processing).* ***CC PRC*** *– predictive core (interprets sensor data streams, identifies correlations, causes, predictions, and confidence levels);* ***AFU*** *– analytics/feature fusion (processes and fuses data from heterogeneous sensors);* ***CM*** *– causal module (detects cause-and-effect relationships between system parameters);* ***CNF*** *– confidence/uncertainty (quantifies data reliability and prediction confidence);* ***MFL*** *– meta-aggregation/federation layer (exchanges model metrics and parameters across nodes; performs meta-analysis of resilience and trust; supports distributed decision-making).* ***AII HITL*** *– human-in-the-loop;* ***HIFL*** *– human-in-federated-loop;* ***XAI*** *– explainable AI interface;* ***CBM*** *– causality-based modeling.* ***RT RE*** *– resilience engineering core;* ***ARM*** *– anticipatory risk management;* ***TSE*** *– test bed/simulation environment.* ***MFL NET*** *– federation network interface (links local and remote aHDT instances);* ***AGG*** *– meta aggregation engine (merges models, parameters, and statistics);* ***QA*** *– quality assurance layer (ensures data trust and consistency);* ***KT*** *– knowledge transfer layer (transfers stable knowledge);* ***POL*** *– policy coordination layer (aligns decision-making policies across nodes);* ***LOG*** *– logging/replay layer (stores and verifies interaction history).*

→ RE guarantees robustness in case of failures and anomalies → the test bed environment validates and trains the model.

The shared metaspace unites multiple HDTs into a distributed system, where individual digital twins exchange aggregated patterns, correct each other's models, and form a collective "adaptation ecosystem." This provides not only local responses but also enables system-wide evolution at the population level, which is particularly important in the context of safety, operator workload, and risk forecasting.

Thus, the distinguishing feature of aHDT architecture is its cognitively interpretable structure, where human involvement, algorithmic explainability, and simulation validation converge into a unified mechanism for prediction and adaptation.

2.3 Algorithms and adaptive response

Adaptive response in HDT is shaped through the integration of several algorithmic principles, ensuring the system's predictiveness, transparency, and resilience. This layer forms the core of the intelligent architecture of the proposed aHDT model, where sensory data are transformed into cognitively interpretable risk models and dynamic action scenarios. HDT analyzes streams of physiological, behavioral, and contextual data to identify patterns indicating potential threats, such as fatigue, coordination failure, cognitive overload, or injury risk. The algorithms not only capture current states but also predict the evolution of events. For instance, if the system detects a decline in gait stability and changes in breathing rate, it can predict the likelihood of a loss of balance well before a fall occurs. This approach enables the shift from reactive to proactive safety management.

The XAI model ensures decision transparency, allowing the user to see which parameters influenced the prediction and why specific actions are suggested. For example, if HDT detects signs of fatigue, it can visualize that changes in heart rate and micro-movements of the wrists were key to the conclusion. At a more advanced level, XAI expands to causality-based modeling (CBM) [29], where the system uncovers not only statistical correlations but also probable causal relationships between physiological and contextual factors. For example, the digital twin can determine that a combination of increased temperature and dehydration leads to a rise in cognitive errors, rather than merely coinciding with them. This shifts explainability into the realm of interpretation, improving user trust and simplifying model refinement through feedback.

The HITL model forms the learning loop, where the user actively participates in adapting the algorithms. In the basic version, the user confirms or rejects predictions, adjusting the model for future scenarios. For example, a driver might confirm an HDT warning about a concentration lapse if they feel fatigued, or reject it if it was triggered by a false alarm. On a more advanced level, this evolves into the human-in-the-feedback-loop (HIFL) [30], where interaction becomes continuous: The system analyzes not only responses but also the nature of the human reaction – timing, confidence, and context. This mechanism enables HDT to learn to differentiate between temporary lapses and real threats, adjusting algorithm sensitivity to the individual's characteristics.

The RE ensures the system's reliability and robustness in unpredictable conditions. If sensor data is partially missing or erroneous, HDT maintains functionality by reconstructing missing data and using backup scenarios. For instance, in a rescue operation, the system can recalculate the risk zone using available sensors and predictive dependencies between parameters. At this level, RE evolves into anticipatory resilience modeling (ARM) [31, 32], where HDT not only compensates for failures but anticipates them, analyzing failure probabilities and proposing preventive actions. As such, the system becomes not just resilient but self-adapting to uncertainty.

These algorithmic principles mutually reinforce one another. XAI and CBM ensure explainability and trust, HITL and HIFL enable interactive self-learning and accurate interpretations, and RE and ARM ensure resilience and continuous operation, even in the event of sensor failures. Together, they form the core of the adaptive response of HDT, where prediction, explanation, learning, and resilience form a closed loop.

In practical scenarios, HDT can not only predict hazardous states but also dynamically adjust its response strategy based on context and data quality. For example, if cognitive load increases in an operator, the system can temporarily redistribute tasks, modify the visual presentation of information, or suggest a short break. In critical situations, such as emergency or medical scenarios, HDT can re-prioritize sensor analysis, highlighting the most relevant data channels and minimizing the likelihood of erroneous interventions.

Thus, HDT evolves from an observation model to one of interpretation and anticipation, where explainability, human involvement, and resilience become interconnected elements of the unified aHDT intelligence ecosystem.

The simulation test bed[6] in this architecture not only serves as a validation platform but also as an active component for learning and validation. At its core, the test bed allows for the simulation of scenarios (overload, accident, extreme conditions) in a safe virtual environment, evaluating the behavior of the "collection → prediction → explanation → intervention" cycle. This provides an opportunity to test the logic of XAI, the accuracy of predictions, and the adequacy of HITL interactions without any risk to real users.

The extended functionality of the test bed seamlessly integrates into the aHDT concept and enhances its capabilities. Firstly, closed-loop simulation [33] with HITL enables real-world interaction: The user in the simulation reacts to explanations and recommendations, providing data on the practical effectiveness of communication and adjusting the model in near-real conditions. Second, adversarial and counterfactual scenario generation [34] creates rare and "black swan" scenarios through generative models and adversarial testing methods, increasing RE resilience and identifying algorithmic vulnerabilities before they arise in real-world deployment. Third, the test bed provides synthetic training data for continual and meta-learning [35, 36]: Simulated, yet realistic behavior and anomaly trajectories accelerate model learning and reduce dependency on rare empirical cases. Finally, the functionality-oriented digital sandbox [37] in the test bed supports transfer-to-reality validation: Scenarios are transferred from the virtual environment to field conditions via step-by-step validation and monitoring, reducing the risk of discrepancies between simulation and reality.

The practical benefits of integrating the extended test bed manifest in several ways. Firstly, it improves the quality of XAI: Simulations test whether explanations match the actual causes of events and identify instances where correlational

---

[6] Simulation test beds – software–hardware environments for modeling scenarios and testing algorithms without risk to real users.

explanations may mislead. Secondly, for HITL/HIFL, testing provides metrics on user engagement and cognitive load savings (reaction time, number of adjustments, level of trust). Thirdly, for RE/ARM, simulations allow evaluation of how quickly the system reconfigures when sensor channels are lost or simulated failures occur, and which preventive strategies are most effective.

In summary, the simulation test bed evolves from a supplementary tool into an active component of an aHDT architecture. It generates data for continual learning, helps identify causal models for XAI/CBM, optimizes HITL/HIFL interaction, and tests RE/ARM mechanisms in a controlled but varied environment. This approach reduces the barrier to transferring models from the lab to the field, making the system more ready for unforeseen operating conditions.

Thus, the algorithmic subsystem of aHDT – combining XAI→CBM, HITL→HIFL, RE→ARM, and an advanced simulation test bed – implements a closed cycle of prediction, explanation, interactive adjustment, and resilient response. This cycle not only helps to predict individual risks but also evolves based on collective experience, enhancing the overall adaptability and reliability of the human–technology ecosystem.

For systematic assessment of XAI/CBM, HITL/HIFL, RE/ARM, and simulation test bed algorithms, *conceptual metrics* are used, allowing for both quantitative and qualitative analysis of the model's performance, identifying weaknesses, and planning improvements. **Table 1** below presents the main categories of metrics, evaluation objects, and their application methods.

2.4 Monitoring

The architecture of the aHDT model relies on a multimodal sensor infrastructure, combining wearables, smart textiles, and AR/VR environments [38]. Its task is to capture the physiological, behavioral, and cognitive state of the user and transmit the data to the analytical core of the model. Unlike traditional biomonitoring systems, aHDT not only collects parameters but also integrates them into a dynamic digital model capable of adapting to changing conditions and compensating for local failures.

Passive smart textiles[7] form the basic sensor layer, recording physical body and environmental parameters – such as temperature, pressure, and deformation – using materials that change properties in response to external factors, such as thermochromic polymers or piezoresistive fibers [39, 40]. Structurally adaptive elements – such as shape-memory materials, piezoelectric actuators, and microfluidic channels [41] – provide the fabric with autonomous reactivity, changing its shape or stiffness in response to overheating or mechanical stress. These reactions allow the system to maintain partial functionality even in the event of power loss in active modules, implementing RE principles. Visual changes in color or texture provide natural cues to the user, enhancing the cognitive explainability of the data (XAI level).

Active textiles[8] complement the system with embedded MEMS sensors, biosensors (ECG, EMG, sweat sensors) [42], and microprocessors that perform

[7] Passive smart textiles – responds to external stimuli without electronics, using material properties to register changes [125].

[8] Active smart textiles – fabrics with integrated sensors and actuators that adaptively change their properties [126].

DOI: http://dx.doi.org/10.5772/intechopen.1013725

Metric/principle	What is being evaluated?	Evaluation method	Example of application
XAI – transparency of decisions	How well the user understands how the system generates predictions and recommendations?	Analysis of the explainability ratio (explainability ratio); user trust survey; cognitive test of model understanding.	Evaluation of whether a doctor can correctly interpret the model's explanations based on visualized risk factors and confirm or reject recommendations.
CBM – causal validity	How well the system's explanations match the actual causal relationships between the data?	Comparison of XAI predictions with causal modeling results (causal graph validation); analysis of false correlations.	Verification of whether the system correctly identifies that dehydration and fatigue cause a decline in concentration in a driver.
HITL – interaction effectiveness	How frequently and accurately the user corrects the system?	Metrics such as reaction time (reaction time), frequency of corrections (correction frequency), and confirmation rate (confirmation rate).	In an industrial setting, evaluating how quickly an operator confirms or modifies HDT recommendations to prevent an accident is crucial.
HIFL – feedback quality	Depth and relevance of user feedback, and its impact on model accuracy over time.	Semantic analysis of comments and correlation of feedback with model accuracy improvement.	Analyzing how user corrections improve model predictions over time, such as how operator adjustments lead to better future predictions.
RE – system resilience	The system's ability to maintain functionality during data failures and delays.	Measurement of accuracy degradation (degradation index) and recovery time (recovery time).	In a simulated sensor failure, the HDT system is evaluated on how quickly it compensates for data loss and continues to operate.
ARM – anticipatory resilience	The system's ability to predict a failure and adapt its behavior before it happens.	Accuracy of failure prediction (failure prediction accuracy); testing of "black swan" scenarios.	In transportation scenarios, the system predicts operator overload before actual reaction time deterioration, suggesting rest or task adjustments.
Simulation test bed – modeling adequacy	How well simulation scenarios reflect real-world operating conditions?	Comparison of simulation results and real-life cases (simulation-to-reality gap); expert evaluation of model validity.	Verifying whether the HDT behavior during overload in a virtual scenario matches the behavior in real-world conditions (e.g., operator stress).
Closed-loop simulation – effectiveness of the "explanation → reaction → correction" cycle	How user actions influence the model within a closed-loop learning and correction cycle?	Analysis of model accuracy dynamics after feedback: time to stabilize decisions.	In a rescue operation scenario, measuring how quickly the model adapts after rescuer corrections improves prediction accuracy.

Metric/principle	What is being evaluated?	Evaluation method	Example of application
Adversarial/counterfactual simulation – robustness to anomalies	Reliability of predictions in rare or conflicting data conditions, and system adaptation to such situations.	Generation and testing of counterfactual scenarios; false alarm rate (false alarm rate).	Testing model robustness under sudden environmental parameter changes (e.g., GPS and temperature sensor failures during an emergency).
Continual learning – adaptability	The system's ability to improve over time without forgetting previously learned patterns.	Evaluation of model weight stability (weight drift analysis); comparison of errors on old and new data.	Verifying whether the model's old predictions deteriorate when learning from new operating behavior scenarios, such as changing conditions.
User trust index – trust level	The balance between automation and the user's perception of system reliability.	Trust surveys, behavioral metrics of interaction, and analysis of deviations from recommendations.	Measuring how often a user ignores HDT recommendations indicates their level of trust in the system, such as ignoring warning signals that seem too extreme or too mild.

Table 1.
Metrics of the aHDT model's performance: identifying weaknesses and planning improvements.

initial signal filtering. They are capable of dynamically adjusting sensitivity and processing algorithms in response to deviations identified by the user or system, providing direct alignment with the HITL principle, where the user can confirm or correct the interpretation of the state.

Wearables serve as a bridge between textile sensors and the cognitive services of HDT [43]. They aggregate data, perform local analytics (edge processing), and return recommendations in the form of tactile signals or visual indicators. This bidirectional interaction supports the HITL loop and implements explainable feedback (XAI) at the user level.

AR/VR devices track movement trajectories, poses, objects, and gaze direction (eye-tracking), creating spatial context for HDT. They can enhance XAI, HITL, and RE: In cases of sensor failures or data delays, the system can visualize key information about the current state and predictions, providing recommendations and warnings. This enables the user to adjust their behavior and refine the model in real time, increasing the accuracy of predictions and the resilience of the entire architecture.

IoT sensors [44] add environmental data – such as noise, vibration, and microclimate – allowing algorithms to account for external factors in real time. *Neurointerfaces (BCI)* [45] record EEG and attention indicators, linking physiological and cognitive levels and enabling cyclic self-correction of models.

Thus, the sensor layer in an aHDT model is not just an observation system, but an adaptive architecture where each component physically supports one or more principles of algorithmic resilience: explainability (XAI), human participation (HITL), reliability (RE), and predictive verification (simulation test bed). This creates a self-learning and transparent infrastructure capable of maintaining accuracy and user trust even under unstable conditions.

2.5 aHDT in metaspace

The previous sections have shown that human vulnerability in the digital environment is no longer related to a lack of data but to the limited ability to transform it into meaningful action. The aHDT architecture, linking physical and digital realities, forms a flow of sensory data and adaptive reactions. However, this structure remains within the bounds of the individual interaction loop. To transition from local adaptation to sustainable collective forms of behavior, a super-systemic level is required – a shared metaspace that connects multiple HDTs and their users into a distributed cognitive ecosystem [46].

In this meta, each “human–HDT” pair (through *avatar synchronization*) becomes an element of a more complex network, where not only physical and virtual actions are synchronized but also cognitive and emotional states [47]. The coherence of attention, intentions, and emotional reactions forms a stable “cognitive signature” that supports the continuity of human identity in the digital domain [48]. In this context, the metaverse acts not as a visual scene but as an architecture of collective intelligence, where data, models, and adaptation patterns circulate between multiple agents [49].

The key mechanism at this level is *collective learning*. HDTs exchange aggregated models via secure federated learning protocols [17], without revealing personal data but transmitting structured adaptation strategies. As a result, a distributed cognitive network is formed, where each participant not only learns from their own data but also strengthens the system's collective knowledge. This mutual interconnectedness creates the effect of collective resilience – the network retains its ability to adapt even in the face of local errors or failures, redistributing cognitive resources among the agents [50].

The metaspace also ensures the long-term existence of digital twins. aHDTs do not lose accumulated strategies and states between sessions but accumulate memory of past scenarios, reactions, and decisions. This turns an aHDT network into a self-developing learning ecology, where human and machine experiences continuously refine each other [51]. Explainability (XAI) in this context takes on a new function – it becomes the language of trust between agents [52]. The transparency of cause-and-effect relationships allows aHDTs not only to exchange analysis results but also to make the process of joint learning verifiable and predictable. This reduces the risk of misalignment between cognitive contours and increases the accuracy of collective decisions in uncertain situations.

The systemic logic of the metaspace lies in the fact that it unites local adaptation loops into a dynamic, self-organizing ecosystem. Data flows from sensory and analytical modules form a shared cognitive scene where humans and aHDTs act as coordinated agents capable of joint reflection and design [53]. In this sense, the metaspace becomes not only a support tool but also a means of self-analysis for the architecture – it is used to validate, adjust, and evolve the system in action.

In such a configuration, the validation process ceases to be a final stage and becomes a continuous refinement. Simulations in the metaspace allow for the exploration of synchronization accuracy, fault tolerance, emotional state consistency, and algorithm transparency. Each iteration of interaction adds a new layer of understanding, enhancing the system's ability to self-develop. This marks the transition from individual adaptation to collective resilience – a hallmark of a mature aHDT ecosystem, where learning and survival merge into a unified process of cognitive coordination [54].

3. Challenges of implementing aHDT model

The challenges of implementing aHDT model span multiple levels – from the technical limitations of sensor systems and algorithms to institutional barriers and broader philosophical–cultural concerns. Subsections 3.1–3.3 examine these dimensions sequentially: first as engineering and technological issues of reliability, then as legal, social, and economic conditions of application, and finally as human-centered challenges related to perception, identity, autonomy, and cultural practices. For clarity, the key challenges and possible pathways to overcoming them are additionally summarized in tabular form, where they are systematized by category.

3.1 Technical limitations

One of the fundamental challenges in implementing aHDT lies in the limitations of existing sensor technologies [55]. Devices must be miniaturized and comfortable to wear, capable of autonomous operation, and able to maintain high measurement accuracy over extended periods [56]. In practice, however, power consumption, durability, and reliability of sensors remain constrained [57], hindering their widespread deployment.

Equally important is the quality and accuracy of data. Even when devices function correctly, their outputs are subject to noise and variability under real-world conditions and, therefore, require continuous calibration [58]. This reduces the system's predictability [59] and may undermine user trust [60].

A third concern involves the integration of heterogeneous data streams – physiological, behavioral, and contextual [61]. Synchronization difficulties and the absence of unified standards often result in module incompatibility and partial information loss [62].

Further risks are associated with data storage and transmission; for example, personal physiological information requires far stricter protection than digital records of behavior or activity within a virtual environment [63].

Comparable challenges have been identified in the development of the metaverse, where issues of interoperability and cybersecurity are also widely discussed [64]. However, in the context of HDT, the consequences are far more severe: A sensor failure or an integration error does not merely lead to the loss of digital content or reduced immersive quality but may result in missing a critical change in a person's physical condition. Whereas in the metaverse the stakes concern comfort and engagement, in aHDT the stakes are human safety and health.

For this reason, the requirements for reliability, resilience, and data protection in HDT must be significantly higher than in most other digital systems.

The key limitations, challenges, and potential solutions are summarized in **Table 2.**

3.2 Ethical, social, legal, and economic aspects

The implementation of aHDT generates a set of challenges that go far beyond those already identified in the metaverse. While in the latter, threats primarily concern account privacy and interaction histories [79], HDT operates with biometric, medical, cognitive, and emotional data and may even involve genetic information [80]. Compromise of such data could result not only in loss of confidentiality but also in discrimination in employment or insurance, as well as direct threats to the user's health and life [81].

The social dimension is linked to the risks of technological paternalism and control [82]. By continuously recording and interpreting human states, HDT may become a tool for restricting autonomy and freedom of choice [83]. The challenge is exacerbated by the possibility that the digital twin, by replicating cognitive and behavioral patterns, could potentially exist in an autonomous mode [84]. This raises fundamental questions of identity, accountability, and ownership: Does HDT belong to the user, the system developer, or the organization responsible for its operation [85]?

The legal dimension encompasses several layers. International deployment of HDT faces divergent national standards for the protection of medical and personal data, a lack of certification for sensors and algorithms, and uncertainty regarding legal liability in the event of system errors [86]. Critical domains such as healthcare, transportation, and education may, therefore, remain closed to full-scale HDT implementation, as the risks are shifted onto users or organizations.

The economic dimension amplifies issues of inequality in access [87]. The high cost of sensors, AR/VR devices, cloud infrastructure, and AI algorithms may render the technology unaffordable, while uncertainty regarding monetization and the high

Key limitation/ challenge	Potential problems if HDT performance deteriorates	Potential engineering/ organizational solutions	Examples of solutions
Miniaturization, ergonomics, and biocompatibility of sensors	Reduced comfort, skin irritation, and device abandonment.	Development of flexible materials, skin-like electronics.	Flexible graphene sensors for physiological monitoring [65], conductive textile fibers for smart textiles [66], and biomimetic self-adhesive structures [67].
Energy efficiency and autonomy	Limited sensor operating time; data loss when the battery drains.	Energy harvesting (TENG, TEG); ultra-low-power communication protocols.	Triboelectric generators for wearables [68]; energy-efficient Bluetooth Low Energy chips [69].
Reliability and durability of sensors	Device failures, data loss, decreased user trust.	Use of self-healing polymers; moisture-resistant encapsulation.	Self-healing hydrogel for pressure sensors [70]; waterproof encapsulation for wearable sensors [71].
Data quality and accuracy	Noise, artifacts, false alarms.	Filtering algorithms (Kalman, adaptive filters); regular calibration.	Accelerometer noise filtering via Wavelet Shrinkage/Kalman Filter [72]; calibration methods for inertial sensors [73].
Integration of heterogeneous data streams	Module incompatibility; information loss.	IoT middleware; edge computing.	IoT middleware for sensor integration [74]; edge computing to reduce latency [75].
Data storage and transmission	Data loss, delays, communication channel vulnerabilities.	Cloud platforms; protocol standardization.	Integration of cloud computing and IoT for sensor data [76]; Bluetooth, ZigBee, Wi-Fi Low Power, and other wearable protocols [69].
Data protection and cyber-resilience	Leaks of biometric data; sensor tampering/hacking.	Lightweight cryptographic protocols; blockchain-based solutions.	Cryptography for IoT/wearables [77]; FHIRChain – blockchain for medical data [78].

Table 2.
Systematization of key technical limitations of aHDT.

cost of errors (including liability for injury compensation) could discourage investors and slow down scaling. As a result, HDT risks becoming a tool accessible only to a narrow group of users [88], contradicting the original idea of human-centered safety.

Similar challenges are discussed in the context of the metaverse [89], but in the case of HDT, their significance is radically amplified: The stakes involve not merely user comfort or digital data integrity but the protection of health, autonomy, and legal security of the individual. For this reason, the ethical, social, legal, and economic aspects of HDT cannot be considered external barriers; they constitute the fundamental conditions for user trust and physical safety.

The key challenges and possible solutions are summarized in **Table 3**.

3.3 Human factors and philosophical–cultural challenges

The human factor is a critical element in the implementation of aHDT, similar to how digital skills and user perceptions influence engagement with the metaverse

Key limitation/ challenge	Where it appears?	Potential consequences	Potential solutions	Examples from practice
Confidentiality and privacy of biometric data	When collecting and storing HDT information.	Data leaks, discrimination based on health or genetics.	Strengthened encryption protocols, differential privacy, distributed storage.	Health Information Portability and Accountability Act (HIPAA) [90].
Risk of discrimination and social inequality	When using HDT for employee evaluation or insurance tariffs.	Unequal access to jobs, insurance services.	Prohibition of discrimination, regulation of employers' and insurers' use of data.	John Hancock (insurance tariffs based on health); court cases on biometric data [91].
Technological paternalism and restriction of autonomy	When HDT intervenes in the interpretation of a person's state.	Loss of freedom of choice, algorithmic pressure.	HITL, algorithmic transparency, ethical codes.	XAI as a tool for reducing paternalism [92].
Legal status and identity of HDT	When the digital twin functions autonomously.	Uncertainty of ownership and responsibility.	Definition of the legal status of HDT, development of property, and inheritance norms.	Discussions on "electronic personalities" [93].
Legal uncertainty in cases of failure	In the event of HDT errors.	Lack of liability, legal disputes.	Certification standards, investigation protocols, liability insurance.	ISO 13485 (medical device certification) [94]; malpractice (lawsuits over medical errors).
Incompatibility of legal regimes	When using HDT across borders.	Limitation of interoperability, jurisdictional conflicts.	International agreements, harmonization of standards.	GDPR and CCPA (different data protection regulations) [95].
High cost of implementation and operation	When using expensive sensors and cloud infrastructure.	Limited access, increased social inequality.	Subsidies, open platforms, reduction of entry barriers.	Smart hospital projects (Philips, Siemens Healthineers); corporate eHealth programs [96].
Uncertainty of monetization and investments	With long-term HDT return on investment.	Slowed implementation, investor caution.	New business models, public–private partnerships.	GE Healthcare PPP (initiatives in medicine); Accenture digital medicine projects [97].
Cybersecurity risks	When transmitting and storing HDT data.	Hacks, leaks, manipulation of state.	Cybersecurity measures, system audits, "zero trust architecture."	NIST Cybersecurity Framework; Google BeyondCorp (Zero Trust approach) [98].

Table 3.
Systematization of key ethical, social, legal, and economic challenges in aHDT implementation.

[99], but with far more serious consequences for health and safety. A key aspect here is digital literacy: Insufficient understanding of HDT principles may lead to misinterpretation of signals or the disregard of warnings [100], thereby increasing the likelihood of errors in high-risk situations. Cognitive load also plays a significant role: A constant flow of notifications may trigger anxiety, alert fatigue, or, conversely, a decline in trust due to false alarms [101]. Even at high levels of accuracy, the system remains vulnerable if the interaction design is not adapted to human cognitive constraints.

The subjectivity of perception further complicates the issue: Users respond differently to alerts [102] – some may ignore them, while others may overreact – thus reducing the universality of interaction algorithms. All these factors directly affect the effectiveness of HDT as a tool for ensuring physical safety.

The philosophical and cultural challenges touch upon deeper questions of identity, autonomy, and the social order. Unlike metaverse avatars, HDT reflects an individual's physiological and cognitive characteristics in real time, challenging the boundary between the "natural self" and the "digital self" [103]. The possibility of the autonomous existence of the digital twin raises the phenomenon of digital immortality [104] and the problem of data inheritance [105], including the right to use or modify one's digital likeness after death. This also introduces the effect of eternal memory [106]: Unlike humans, who can forget errors and traumas, HDT permanently records them, thereby transforming the perception of personal history and time.

Equally important is the dilemma of autonomy and free will [107]. If HDT can predict actions and suggest optimal decisions, the risk of technological paternalism arises [82], in which individuals act not independently but in accordance with algorithmic recommendations. Excessive reliance on the digital twin may erode critical thinking [108] and foster dependence. This raises the fundamental question of the boundaries of intervention: Where does safety support end and imposed "enhancement" begin? The loss of the value of human error [109] – as a source of experience and creativity – could lead to behavioral standardization and diminish individual uniqueness.

The cultural dimension further complicates the picture. Standardization of aHDT models may lead to a unification of human experience [110]: Algorithms record only what is measurable, excluding subjective and spiritual aspects of life. This poses a risk of eroding unique cultural practices and limiting the diversity of human experience. Unlike the metaverse, where such effects primarily concern perceptions of virtual environments [111], HDT is literally integrated with human physiology and cognition, making the cultural consequences far more radical.

Thus, human factors and philosophical–cultural barriers constitute a dual layer of constraints. On the one hand, they undermine trust and reduce the willingness to adopt HDT; on the other, they raise fundamental questions about the balance between safety, autonomy, and identity. These challenges cannot be regarded as external – they directly determine whether aHDT will become a genuine tool for risk reduction or a source of new threats.

The key limitations, challenges, and potential solutions are summarized in **Table 4**.

3.4 Roadmap for aHDT implementation

The challenges discussed in Section 3 demonstrate that the development of aHDT is impossible without a *systemic strategy*. Technical failures directly threaten human physical safety; legal uncertainty and weak data protection undermine trust; and human factors may neutralize the potential of even the most advanced technology. These risks require step-by-step resolution, including the elimination of fundamental technical limitations, the establishment of regulatory frameworks and protection standards, and the integration of user experience and cultural dimensions.

Key limitation/ challenge	Where it appears?	Psychological/ cultural consequences	Potential solutions	Examples from practice
Digital literacy and readiness	In everyday interaction with HDT.	Misinterpretation of signals, refusal to use.	Educational programs, simplified interfaces, and step-by-step AR onboarding.	Operator training simulators (Siemens Simcenter) [112]; digital literacy courses (Coursera, Khan Academy) [113].
Cognitive load and alert fatigue	When there are many notifications.	Anxiety, fatigue, reduced attention.	Adaptive interfaces, signal filtering, and prioritization of notifications.	Medical alerts (Philips IntelliVue with priority system) [114]; pilot support systems (Boeing, Airbus).
Trust and subjectivity of perception	In reactions to HDT warnings.	Distrust or excessive dependence on the system.	Personalization of settings, XAI, manual verification.	XAI systems (DARPA XAI); medical AI platforms with physician confirmation (IBM Watson Health) [115].
Autonomy, paternalism, and boundaries of intervention	When HDT proposes or enforces decisions.	Restriction of free will, technological control.	Right to opt-out, HITL, ethical codes.	Expert systems (Watson for Oncology – recommendations, final decision by physician); IEEE ethical principles for AI [116].
Dependence and loss of value of human error	In everyday HDT operation.	Reduced autonomy, abandonment of learning through errors.	Balance "recommendation ↔ choice," "safe error" scenarios, gamification.	Game trainers (Duolingo – learning through mistakes); educational VR simulators (Labster) [117].
Identity and the "second self"	When creating a digital twin.	Identity crisis, blurring boundaries of "natural" and "digital" self.	User control, delineation of HDT operating modes.	VR/AR avatars (Meta Horizon Worlds); virtual persona systems (Replika AI) [118].
Digital immortality and inheritance of data	When HDT is preserved after a user's death.	Ethical conflicts, disputes over data ownership.	Digital wills, protocols for deletion/ transfer of data.	Google Inactive Account Manager (transfer of account) [119]; Facebook memorial accounts.
Eternal-memory effect	With long-term data storage.	Anxiety, inability to "forget" mistakes or illnesses.	Right to be forgotten, limitation of retention periods.	GDPR (Right to Erasure) [120]; services for digital-footprint control (Mine, Jumbo Privacy).
Cultural unification and loss of uniqueness	In standardization of HDT.	Averaging of experience, loss of cultural diversity.	Culturally-sensitive algorithms, multicultural testing.	Personalized telemedicine services (Babylon Health); multicultural VR platforms (AltspaceVR) [121].

Table 4.
Systematization of key human, philosophical–cultural, and social limitations in aHDT implementation.

Such an approach allows a shift from ad hoc problem-solving to the construction of a *coherent trajectory for aHDT development*. At the first stage, it is essential to achieve a *minimum threshold of reliability* through sensor improvement, prototyping, and testing in controlled environments – thus forming the foundation of trust. At the next stage, the key task becomes *institutionalization*: the establishment of legal norms, interoperability standards, data protection protocols, and sustainable economic models that ensure long-term implementation.

Only then is it possible to progress toward *human-centered integration*, where critical factors include reducing cognitive load, enhancing digital literacy, and designing ergonomic interfaces. The final stage envisions the *co-evolution of aHDT with humans and society*: the accumulation of collective experience, adaptation to cultural diversity, and resilience under conditions of uncertainty.

This staged approach transforms the development strategy into a genuine roadmap, where each step creates the prerequisites for the next, and the ultimate goal is to strengthen human physical safety across both real and virtual environments.

4. Perspectives: aHDT as a "mirror" of society

The initial conception of aHDT was as a tool for individual safety. However, it became evident that its implications extend far beyond the individual user. The digital twin not only reflects the physiological parameters of a specific person but also encompasses a broader social and cultural context. In this regard, aHDT can be considered a "mirror" of society, wherein the phenomenon of *reflexive feedback* emerges – where the system begins to represent not just the individual but also collective social patterns, revealing the maturity and vulnerabilities of social structures.

Over time, aHDT transcends its static nature and evolves into an element of collective reflection, where social dynamics are not only observed but also adjusted through a network of interconnected digital twins. This creates a new level of interaction, where each digital twin becomes part of a more complex system, showcasing both individual and collective behavioral traits.

4.1 aHDT as a "sensor" of society

One of the key aspects of the future aHDT is its ability to function as a "sensor" for society. When millions of digital twins register stress, overload, or deteriorating health, the potential arises to observe the collective state in real time. Safety is no longer a purely personal matter but becomes a distributed system, where individual signals combine to form an overarching picture. This approach enables the consideration of collective well-being and the formation of coordinated response strategies, thereby enhancing the resilience of the entire network in the event of localized failures.

The joint processing of signals and the exchange of data among network participants allow the system to learn and adapt at the group level. This increases flexibility and resilience not only for individual agents but also for the system as a whole. For instance, in the case of global threats or catastrophic events, collective knowledge and adaptive strategies become crucial for mitigating risks and enhancing overall safety.

4.2 Sociotechnical infrastructure of trust

Another vital aspect of aHDT is the formation of a new sociotechnical infrastructure of trust. In contexts where decisions were traditionally based on subjective opinion or limited data, aHDT introduces the possibility of relying on objective, explainable, and consensus-based data. The transparency of algorithms and the interpretability of decisions provide the foundation for trust not only between humans and systems but also among participants within the collective field.

This approach enables the creation of safe, verifiable, and predictable interactions between individuals and digital systems, which is of paramount importance in domains where mistakes can have serious consequences, such as healthcare, transportation, education, and labor relations. In these areas, aHDT could significantly improve decision-making processes by providing more accurate diagnostics, forecasting, and responses to emerging issues.

4.3 Collective learning and resilience

aHDT also paves the way for collective learning, where the errors and successful strategies of individual users become resources for all. Instead of being limited to individual practices, aHDT transforms into a "collective body," where human and machine experiences mutually reinforce each other. In such a system, local failures do not compromise the integrity of the network; on the contrary, they strengthen it through the redistribution of resources and adaptation.

This enables the formation of systems with distributed resilience, where errors and failures do not destroy the system but serve as points for growth. The interaction between aHDT and humans creates a platform for collaborative evolution, supporting individual autonomy by providing objective data for decision-making.

4.4 Social and cultural changes

On a cultural level, aHDT also raises important questions about identity and memory. A digital twin can preserve and transmit a person's knowledge, habits, and responses, even after their death, creating new forms of "digital presence." This gives rise to new opportunities for preserving heritage, where a person's experience does not disappear but continues to exist and be utilized by others.

Over time, this data becomes part of a larger collective memory, where individual stories are linked into a shared narrative, which changes the very nature of legacy. This creates new forms of social interaction, where the memory of the past becomes an integral part of the social context and future engagements.

5. Risks and challenges

Despite the promising perspectives, aHDT also presents significant risks that must be carefully considered in its implementation.

1. **Social inequality**. One of the most significant risks is the amplification of social inequality within the collective network. The technology could divide people into the "transparent" and "nontransparent": those who share their data and those who do not. This division could result in limited integration of diverse experiences into the collective cognitive ecosystem, potentially reducing the completeness of collective learning and the variability of adaptation strategies.

2. **Depersonalization and standardization**. Mass aggregation of data could lead to the *loss of uniqueness* in individual adaptations, reducing the variability of behavior and the flexibility of the system (HDT). This creates a threat to individuality, as algorithmic standardization may result in "algorithmic conformity," diminishing the diversity of human experience.

3. **The diminishment of the value of error**. In scenarios where the system minimizes errors, the *learning potential is diminished*. Mistakes serve as a vital tool for growth, both at the individual level and within the collective ecosystem. Excessive error reduction limits innovation potential and adaptive capacity.

4. **Technological paternalism**. If a system continuously provides "correct" solutions, human *autonomy may be weakened*, leading to technological paternalism. This could diminish personal initiative and potentially create *social passivity*, where participants rely on collective decisions instead of developing their own skills.

5. **The "eternal memory" effect**. The availability of data about mistakes and failures within the vast cognitive ecosystem increases the risk of its uncontrolled use, potentially leading to new forms of discrimination or manipulation. Errors captured by the system could be used against participants if access to this data becomes excessive or unrestricted.

6. **Dependence and alienation**. The more decisions are delegated to the system, the higher the likelihood that individuals will lose confidence in their own abilities to make decisions. In a collective infrastructure, this can undermine active participation, as people stop forming shared experiences. Consequently, the digital twin ceases to be a tool and begins to assume the role of a "second self," blurring the line between subject and algorithm.

Thus, the risks of aHDT should be considered not only at the level of individual users but also at the level of the entire cognitive network. It is important to understand how the integration and distribution of data influence collective learnability, adaptability, and social responsibility. Addressing these risks and challenges in the design and implementation of aHDT will be critical for developing resilient and equitable technologies for the future.

6. Conclusions

The analysis demonstrates that the problem of human physical safety in increasingly complex sociotechnical systems is inherently multidimensional. Human cognitive limitations, the high consequences of errors, and delayed responses make conventional safety approaches progressively less reliable. Systems that merely record events after they occur cannot bridge the critical gap between threat perception and reaction time. Within this context, it becomes necessary to develop models that augment human capabilities and transform safety from a reactive process into a preventive one – operating within a shared metaspace that integrates individual and collective levels of interaction.

The proposed aHDT model illustrates that such a transformation is feasible. Its principal advantage lies in the ability to predict risks before they reach critical thresholds. Through the integration of physiological and behavioral data, the HDT enables early hazard detection and personalized response mechanisms. The system's human-centered design ensures that notifications and interfaces adapt to individual cognitive profiles, supporting decision-making without an excessive information load. Moreover, by linking multiple users within a collective cognitive ecosystem, the HDT facilitates pattern recognition across shared data and strengthens overall safety in high-risk environments.

Nevertheless, the identified limitations reveal that aHDT's potential remains constrained. The technical reliability of sensors and algorithms continues to be a weak point; even a single failure may lead to catastrophic outcomes if the system is assumed to be fully dependable. The question of trust is equally significant. The reliance on biometric and behavioral data raises concerns about privacy and data protection; without transparent guarantees, HDT may be perceived as a potential threat rather than a safeguard. Another issue concerns the tension between automation and human autonomy: While HDT is intended to reduce cognitive workload, it may also cause notification overload or user dependence, undermining its human-centered premise.

A further social dimension must be acknowledged. Unequal access to aHDT technologies risk widening safety disparities among user groups. This concern becomes particularly critical when the model operates within the metaverse, where a distributed cognitive ecosystem relies on collective learning, co-evolving strategies, and network-level resilience.

These findings indicate that the future development of aHDT should advance not only through improvements in sensing and computational technologies but also through institutional, legal, and cultural frameworks that ensure accountability and social inclusion. The sustainable evolution of aHDT depends on achieving a balance between technical efficiency, transparency, trust, and social equity. Only under such conditions can the digital twin become a resilient and genuinely human-centered instrument of physical safety, functioning within an integrated environment where individual and collective intelligence coalesce and shared experience continuously reinforces adaptive strategies and systemic resilience.

Acknowledgments

This chapter was supported by the Research Council of Lithuania (LMTLT), project number: S-A-UEI-23-3.

Conflict of Interest

The authors declare no conflict of interest.

Author details

Viktorija Diak[1*] and Andrii Diak[2]

1 NEB Research Centre, Vilnius Academy of Arts, Vilnius, Lithuania

2 NTUU KPI, Kyiv, Ukraine

*Address all correspondence to: vk.diak@gmail.com

References

[1] Laiz-Ibanez H, Mendana-Cuervo C, C CJL. The metaverse: Privacy and information security risks. International Journal of Information Management Data Insights. 2025;**5**(2):100373. DOI: 10.1016/j.jjimei.2025.100373

[2] Rahartomo A, Merino L, Ghafari M. Metaverse security and privacy research: A systematic review. Computers & Security. 2025;**157**:104602. DOI: 10.1016/j.cose.2025.10460

[3] Chow Y-W, Susilo W, Li Y, Li N, Nguyen C. Visualization and Cybersecurity in the Metaverse: A survey. Journal of Imaging. 2023;**9**(1):11. DOI: 10.3390/jimaging9010011

[4] Stoppa M, Chiolerio A. Wearable electronics and smart textiles: A critical review. Sensors. 2014;**14**(7):11957–11992. DOI: 10.3390/s140711957

[5] Zhang S, Suresh L, Yang J, Zhang X, Tan SC. Augmenting sensor performance with machine learning towards smart wearable sensing electronic systems. Advanced Intelligent Systems. 2022;**4**(4):2100194. DOI: 10.1002/aisy.202100194

[6] Hassan M, Svadling M, Björsell N. Experience from implementing digital twins for maintenance in industrial processes. Journal of Intelligent Manufacturing. 2024;**35**(2):875–884. DOI: 10.1007/s10845-023-02078-4

[7] Zhong D, Xia Z, Zhu Y, Duan J. Overview of predictive maintenance based on digital twin technology. Heliyon. 2023;**9**:4. DOI: 10.1016/j.heliyon.2023.e14534

[8] Wang Y. Fatigue-aware adaptive interfaces for wearable devices using deep learning. arXiv preprint arXiv:2506.13203. 2025. DOI: 10.48550/arXiv.2506.13203

[9] Ruckdashel RR, Khadse N, Park JH. Smart E-textiles: Overview of components and outlook. Sensors. 2022;**22**(16):6055. DOI: 10.3390/s22166055

[10] Lin Y, Chen L, Ali A, Nugent C, Cleland I, Li R, Ding J, Ning H. Human digital twin: A survey. Journal of Cloud Computing. 2024;**13**(1):131. DOI: 10.1186/s13677-024-00691-z

[11] Berti N, Finco S, Guidolin M, Battini D. Towards human digital twins to enhance workers' safety and production system resilience. IFAC-PapersOnLine. 2023;**56**(2):11062–11067. DOI: 10.1016/j.ifacol.2023.10.809

[12] Ramasubramanian AK, Mathew R, Kelly M, Hargaden V, Papakostas N. Digital twin for human–robot collaboration in manufacturing: Review and outlook. Applied Sciences. 2022;**12**(10):4811. DOI: 10.3390/app12104811

[13] Katsoulakis E, Wang Q, Wu H, Shahriyari L, Fletcher R, Liu J, Achenie L, Liu H, Jackson P, Xiao Y, Syeda-Mahmood T. Digital twins for health: A scoping review. NPJ Digital Medicine. 2024;**7**(1):77. DOI: 10.1038/s41746-024-01073-0

[14] Spitzer M, Dattner I, Zilcha-Mano S. Digital twins and the future of precision mental health. Frontiers in Psychiatry. 2023;**14**:1082598. DOI: 10.3389/fpsyt.2023.1082598

[15] Guidotti R, Monreale A, Ruggieri S, Turini F, Giannotti F, Pedreschi D. A survey of methods for explaining black box models. ACM Computing Surveys (CSUR). 2018;**51**(5):1–42. DOI: 10.1145/3236009

[16] Arrieta AB, Díaz-Rodríguez N, Del Ser J, Bennetot A, Tabik S, Barbado A, García S, Gil-López S, Molina D, Benjamins R, Chatila R. Explainable Artificial Intelligence (XAI): Concepts, taxonomies, opportunities and challenges toward responsible AI. Information Fusion. 2020;**58**:82–115. DOI: 10.1016/j.inffus.2019.12.012

[17] Xie Y, Mou S, Sundaram S. Communication-efficient and resilient distributed Q-learning. IEEE Transactions on Neural Networks and Learning Systems. 2023;**35**(3): 3351–3364. DOI: 10.1109/ TNNLS.2023.3292036

[18] Patterson ES, Winner J, Patterson MD, Rayo MF, Deutsch ES Incorporating resilience engineering into simulation for health care education and training. In: Proceedings of the International Symposium on Human Factors and Ergonomics in Health Care 2023 Mar; (Vol. 12, No. 1). Los Angeles, Sage CA: SAGE Publications; p. 53–56. DOI: 10.1177/ 2327857923121014

[19] Dellermann D, Calma A, Lipusch N, Weber T, Weigel S, Ebel P The future of human-AI collaboration: A taxonomy of design knowledge for hybrid intelligence systems. arXiv preprint arXiv:2105.03354. 2021 DOI: 10.48550/ arXiv.2105.03354

[20] Hollnagel E. Safety-I and safety-II: The past and Future of Safety Management. London: CRC press; 2018. DOI: 10.1201/9781315607511

[21] Hollnagel E, Woods DD, Leveson N, editors. Resilience Engineering: Concepts and Precepts. London: Ashgate Publishing, Ltd; 2006. p. 416. DOI: 10.1201/9781315605685

[22] Menukhin O, Mehandjiev N, Quboa Q Digital twins in the metaverse for collaborative discovery of contextual factors. In: 2024 2nd International Conference on Intelligent Metaverse Technologies & Applications (iMETA) ; 26 November; IEEE; 2024. p. 065–069. DOI: 10.1109/ iMETA62882.2024.10808107

[23] Pitzalis RF, Giordano A, Di Spigno A, Cowell A, Niculita O, Berselli G. Application of augmented reality-based digital twin approaches: A case study to industrial equipment. The International Journal of Advanced Manufacturing Technology. 2025;**23**:1–7. DOI: 10.1007/ s00170-025-15755-w

[24] Asad U, Khan M, Khalid A, Lughmani WA. Human-centric digital twins in industry: A comprehensive review of enabling technologies and implementation strategies. Sensors. 2023;**23**(8):3938. DOI: 10.3390/ s23083938

[25] Cecere L, Grimaldi M, Lorusso A, Marra A, Stoia F. Immersive urban planning: Evaluating park safety perception with digital twins and metaverse simulation. Sustainability. 2025;**17**(17):7608. DOI: 10.3390/ su17177608

[26] Sweller J, Ayres P, Kalyuga S. Cognitive load theory. Springer Science & Business Media. 2011;**16**:274. DOI: 10.1007/978-1-4419-8126-4

[27] Tenison C, Fincham JM, Anderson JR. Phases of learning: How skill acquisition impacts cognitive

processing. Cognitive Psychology. 2016;**87**:1–28. DOI: 10.1016/j.cogpsych.2016.03.001

[28] Woolley AW, Aggarwal I, Malone TW. Collective intelligence and group performance. Current Directions in Psychological Science. 2015;**24**(6):420–424. DOI: 10.1177/0963721415599543

[29] Carloni G, Berti A, Colantonio S. The role of causality in explainable artificial intelligence. Wiley Interdisciplinary Reviews: Data Mining and Knowledge Discovery. 2025;**15**(2): e70015. DOI: 10.1002/widm.70015

[30] Retzlaff CO, Das S, Wayllace C, Mousavi P, Afshari M, Yang T, Saranti A, Angerschmid A, Taylor ME, Holzinger A. Human-in-the-loop reinforcement learning: A survey and position on requirements, challenges, and opportunities. Journal of Artificial Intelligence Research. 2024;**79**:359–415. DOI: 10.1613/jair.1.15348

[31] Muñoz-Erickson TA, Selkirk K, Hobbins R, Miller C, Feagan M, Iwaniec DM, Miller TR, Cook EM. Anticipatory resilience bringing back the future into urban planning and knowledge systems. In: Hamstead ZA, Iwaniec DM, McPhearson T, Berbés-Blázquez M, Cook EM, Muñoz-Erickson TA, editors. Resilient Urban Futures. Cham: Springer International Publishing; 2021. p. 159–172. DOI: 10.1007/978-3-030-63131-4_11

[32] Blok AN, Sharpanskykh A, Vert M. Formal and computational modeling of anticipation mechanisms of resilience in the complex sociotechnical air transport system. Complex Adaptive Systems Modeling. 2018;**6**(1):7. DOI: 10.1186/s40294-018-0058-2

[33] Cunningham JP, Nuyujukian P, Gilja V, Chestek CA, Ryu SI, Shenoy KV. A closed-loop human simulator for investigating the role of feedback control in brain-machine interfaces. Journal of Neurophysiology. 2011;**105**(4):1932–1949. DOI: 10.1152/jn.00503.20

[34] Ding W, Xu C, Arief M, Lin H, Li B, Zhao D. A survey on safety-critical driving scenario generation—a methodological perspective. IEEE Transactions on Intelligent Transportation Systems. 2023;**24**(7):6971–6988. DOI: 10.48550/arXiv.2202.02215

[35] Bauer A, Trapp S, Stenger M, Leppich R, Kounev S, Leznik M, Chard K, Foster I Comprehensive exploration of synthetic data generation: A survey. arXiv preprint arXiv:2401.02524. 2024. DOI: 10.48550/arXiv.2401.02524

[36] Son J, Lee S, Kim G. When meta-learning meets online and continual learning: A survey. IEEE Transactions on Pattern Analysis and Machine Intelligence. 2024;**47**:413–432. DOI: 10.1109/TPAMI.2024.3463709

[37] Abufadda M, Mansour K. A survey of synthetic data generation for machine learning. In: 22nd International Arab Conference on Information Technology (ACIT); 21 December 2021; IEEE; p.1–7. DOI: 10.1109/ACIT53391.2021.9677302

[38] Diak V, Diak A. Smart textile as advanced human digital interface in metaverse. The Design Journal. 2025;**28**(3):386–412. DOI: 10.1080/14606925.2025.2452084

[39] Toan VN, Tri NM, Nguyen XH, Nguyen DD, Chung W, Chang SW, La DD. Exploring the potential of organic thermochromic materials in textile applications. Journal of Materials

Science. 2024;**59**(32):14924–14947. DOI: 10.1007/s10853-024-10056-1

[40] Ullrich J, Eisenreich M, Zimmermann Y, Mayer D, Koehne N, Tschannett JF, Mahmud-Ali A, Bechtold T. Piezo-sensitive fabrics from carbon black containing conductive cellulose fibres for flexible pressure sensors. Materials. 2020;**13**(22):5150. DOI: 10.3390/ma13225150

[41] Mirvakili SM, Hunter IW. Artificial muscles: Mechanisms, applications, and challenges. Advanced Materials. 2018;**30**(6):1704407. DOI: 10.1002/adma.201704407

[42] Trung TQ, Lee NE. Flexible and stretchable physical sensor integrated platforms for wearable human-activity monitoringand personal healthcare. Advanced Materials. 2016;**28**(22):4338–4372. DOI: 10.1002/adma.201504244

[43] Oatley G, Choudhury T, Buckman P. Smart textiles for improved quality of life and cognitive assessment. Sensors. 2021;**21**(23):8008. DOI: 10.3390/s21238008

[44] Islam SR, Kwak D, Kabir MH, Hossain M, Kwak KS. The internet of things for health care: A comprehensive survey. IEEE Access. 2015;**c3**:678–708. DOI: 10.1109/ACCESS.2015.2437951

[45] He H, Wu D. Transfer learning for Brain–Computer interfaces: A Euclidean space data alignment approach. IEEE Transactions on Biomedical Engineering. 2019;**67**(2):399–410. DOI: 10.1109/TBME.2019.2913914

[46] Pournaras E Collective learning: A 10-year odyssey to human-centered distributed intelligence. In: 2020 IEEE International Conference on Autonomic Computing and Self-Organizing Systems (ACSOS); 17 August 2020; IEEE; p. 205–214. DOI: 10.1109/ACSOS49614.2020.00043

[47] Zhang J, Ma F, Pi Y, Du H, Pan X. Digital twin embodied interactions design: Synchronized and aligned physical sensation in location-based social VR. Frontiers in Virtual Reality. 2025;**6**:1499845. DOI: 10.3389/frvir.2025.1499845

[48] SK J, Yang Z, Yang Q, Huang C, Xu W, Shikh-Bahaei M, Zhang Z. Semantic-aware digital twin for metaverse: A comprehensive review. IEEE Wireless Communications. 2023;**30**(4):38–46. DOI: 10.1109/MWC.003.2200616

[49] Zhao Y, Rieger C, Zhu Q. Multi-agent learning for resilient distributed control systems. In: Wang J, editor. Power Grid Resilience: Theory and Applications. Cham: Springer Nature Switzerland; 2025. p. 425–458. DOI: 10.1007/978-3-031-73978-1_10

[50] Jin Y, Wei S, Montana G. Achieving collective welfare in multi-agent reinforcement learning via suggestion sharing. Machine Learning. 2025;**114**(8):190. DOI: 10.1007/s10994-025-06823-z

[51] Krupas M, Kajati E, Liu C, Zolotova I. Towards a human-centric digital twin for Human–Machine collaboration: A review on enabling technologies and methods. Sensors. 2024;**24**(7):2232. DOI: 10.3390/s24072232

[52] Ivanov D. A survey of system-cybernetic principles in supply chain resilience: Viability, artificial intelligence, digital twins, and ecosystems. International Journal of Systems Science. 2025;**19**:1–6. DOI: 10.1080/00207721.2025.2519204

[53] Abdelrahman M, Macatulad E, Lei B, Quintana M, Miller C, Biljecki F. What is a digital twin anyway? Deriving the definition for the built environment from over 15,000 scientific publications. Building and Environment. 2025;**274**:112748. DOI: 10.1016/j.buildenv.2025.112748

[54] Suárez-Román M, Sanz-Rodrigo M, Marín-López A, Arroyo D. A digital twin threat survey. Big Data and Cognitive Computing. 2025;**9**(10):252. DOI: 10.3390/bdcc9100252

[55] Heikenfeld J, Jajack A, Rogers J, Gutruf P, Tian L, Pan T, Li R, Khine M, Kim J, Wang J. Wearable sensors: Modalities, challenges, and prospects. Lab on a Chip. 2018;**18**(2):217–248. DOI: 10.1039/C7LC00914C

[56] Trung TQ, Lee NE. Flexible and stretchable physical sensor integrated platforms for wearable Human-Activity monitoring and personal healthcare. Advanced Materials. 2016;**28**(22):4338–4372. DOI: 10.1002/adma.201504244

[57] Amjadi M, Kyung KU, Park I, Sitti M. Stretchable, skin-mountable, and wearable strain sensors and their potential applications: A review. Advanced Functional Materials. 2016;**26**(11):1678–1698. DOI: 10.1002/adfm.201504755

[58] Bariya M, Nyein HY, Javey A. Wearable sweat sensors. Nature Electronics. 2018;**1**(3):160–171. DOI: 10.1038/s41928-018-0043-y

[59] Bandodkar AJ, Wang J. Non-invasive wearable electrochemical sensors: A review. Trends in Biotechnology. 2014;**32**(7):363–371. DOI: 10.1016/j.tibtech.2014.04.005

[60] Ferreira JJ, Fernandes CI, Rammal HG, Veiga PM. Wearable technology and consumer interaction: A systematic review and research agenda. Computers in Human Behavior. 2021;**118**:106710. DOI: 10.1016/j.chb.2021.106710

[61] Shahandashti YM, Larijani S, Eskandari M, Zarepour A, Khosravi A, Iravani S, Zarrabi A. Biomedical potentials of MXene-based self-powered wearable devices: The future of next-generation wearables. RSC Advances. 2025;**15**(40):33773–33803. DOI: 10.1039/D5RA04611D

[62] Villa-Gallón JE, Valencia-Bernal JA, Garcés-Gómez YA. ISO standards in healthcare organizations: Research evolution and trends from a bibliometric analysis. Publications. 2024;**12**(3):27. DOI: 10.3390/publications12030027

[63] Price WN, Cohen IG. Privacy in the age of medical big data. Nature Medicine. 2019;**25**(1):37–43. DOI: 10.1038/s41591-018-0272-7

[64] Flavián C, Ibáñez-Sánchez S, Orús C. The impact of virtual, augmented and mixed reality technologies on the customer experience. Journal of Business Research. 2019;**100**:547–560. DOI: 10.1016/j.jbusres.2018.10.050

[65] Adeel M, Rahman MM, Caligiuri I, Canzonieri V, Rizzolio F, Daniele S. Recent advances of electrochemical and optical Enzyme-Free glucose sensors operating at physiological conditions. Biosensors and Bioelectronics. 2020;**165**:112331. DOI: 10.1016/j.bios.2020.112331

[66] Stoppa M, Chiolerio A. Wearable electronics and smart textiles: A critical review. sensors. 2014;**14**(7):11957–11992. DOI: 10.3390/s140711957

[67] Chen F, Han L, Dong Y, Wang X. Biomimetic self-adhesive structures for wearable sensors. Biosensors. 2022;**12**(6):431. DOI: 10.3390/bios12060431

[68] Zou Y, Raveendran V, Chen J. Wearable triboelectric nanogenerators for biomechanical energy harvesting. Nano Energy. 2020;**77**:105303. DOI: 10.1016/j.nanoen.2020.105303

[69] Gomez C, Oller J, Paradells J. Overview and evaluation of Bluetooth low energy: An emerging low-power wireless technology. sensors. 2012;**12**(9):11734–11753. DOI: 10.3390/s120911734

[70] Lei Z, Wang Q, Sun S, Zhu W, Wu P. A bioinspired mineral hydrogel as a self-healable, mechanically adaptable ionic skin for highly sensitive pressure sensing. Advanced Materials. 2017;**29**(22):1700321. DOI: 10.1002/adma.201700321

[71] Trung TQ, Lee NE. Recent progress on stretchable electronic devices with intrinsically stretchable components. Advanced Materials. 2017;**29**(3):1603167. DOI: 10.1002/adma.201603167

[72] Kang S, Paul A, Jeon G. Reduction of mixed noise from wearable sensors in human-motion estimation. Computers & Electrical Engineering. 2017;**61**:287–296. DOI: 10.1016/j.compeleceng.2017.05.030

[73] Pacher L, Chatellier C, Vauzelle R, Fradet L. Sensor-to-segment calibration methodologies for lower-body kinematic analysis with inertial sensors: A systematic review. Sensors. 2020;**20**(11):3322. DOI: 10.3390/s20113322

[74] Da Xu L, He W, Li S. Internet of Things in industries: A survey. IEEE Transactions on Industrial Informatics. 2014;**10**(4):2233–2243. DOI: 10.1109/TII.2014.2300753

[75] Shi W, Cao J, Zhang Q, Li Y, Xu L. Edge computing: Vision and challenges. IEEE Internet of Things Journal. 2016;**3**(5):637–646. DOI: 10.1109/JIOT.2016.2579198

[76] Botta A, De Donato W, Persico V, Pescapé A. Integration of cloud computing and internet of things: A survey. Future Generation Computer Systems. 2016;**56**:684–700. DOI: 10.1016/j.future.2015.09.021

[77] Rana M, Mamun Q, Islam R. Lightweight cryptography in IoT networks: A survey. Future Generation Computer Systems. 2022;**129**:77–89. DOI: 10.1016/j.future.2021.11.011

[78] Zhang P, White J, Schmidt DC, Lenz G, Rosenbloom ST. FHIRChain: Applying blockchain to securely and scalably share clinical data. Computational and Structural Biotechnology Journal. 2018;**16**:267–278. DOI: 10.1016/j.csbj.2018.07.004

[79] Hourcade JP, Braud T, Zhou PY, Wang L, Xu D, Lin Z, Kumar A, Bermejo C, Hui P. All one needs to know about metaverse: A complete survey on technological singularity, virtual ecosystem, and research agenda. Foundations and Trends® in Human–Computer Interaction. 2024;**18**(2–3):100–337. DOI: 10.1561/1100000095

[80] Bonomi L, Huang Y, Ohno-Machado L. Privacy challenges and research opportunities for genomic data sharing. Nature Genetics. 2020;**52**(7):646–654. DOI: 10.1038/s41588-020-0651-0

[81] Thomas M, Mackes N, Preuss-Dodhy A, Wieland T, Bundschus M.

Assessing privacy vulnerabilities in Genetic Data Sets: Scoping review. JMIR Bioinformatics and Biotechnology. 2024;**5**(1):e54332. DOI: 10.2196/54332

[82] Yeung K. Hypernudge': Big Data as a mode of regulation by design. In: Beer D, editor. The Social Power of Algorithms. New York: Routledge; 2019. p. 118–136. DOI: 10.1080/1369118X.2016.1186713

[83] Mittelstadt BD, Allo P, Taddeo M, Wachter S, Floridi L. The ethics of algorithms: Mapping the debate. Big Data & Society. 2016;**3**(2):2053951716679679. DOI: 10.1177/2053951716679679

[84] Bruynseels K, Santoni de Sio F, Van den Hoven J. Digital twins in health care: Ethical implications of an emerging engineering paradigm. Frontiers in Genetics. 2018;**9**:31. DOI: 10.3389/fgene.2018.00031

[85] Jurcys P, Greenwald A, Fenwick M, Loikkanen V. Who owns my AI twin? Rethinking ownership and rights in a new world of hybrid identities. Rethinking Ownership and Rights in a New World of Hybrid Identities. 2024. DOI: 10.2139/ssrn.4940663

[86] Cohen IG, Amarasingham R, Shah A, Xie B, Lo B. The legal and ethical concerns that arise from using complex predictive analytics in health care. Health Affairs. 2014;**33**(7):1139–1147. DOI: 10.1377/hlthaff.2014.0048

[87] Whitelaw S, Pellegrini DM, Mamas MA, Cowie M, Van Spall HG. Barriers and facilitators of the uptake of digital health technology in cardiovascular care: A systematic scoping review. European Heart Journal-Digital Health. 2021;**2**(1):62–74. DOI: 10.1093/ehjdh/ztab005

[88] Beer D. The quantified self: A sociology of Self-Tracking. Information, Communication & Society. 2017;**20**(12):1805–1806. DOI: 10.1080/1369118X.2017.1305430

[89] Flavián C, Ibáñez-Sánchez S, Orús C. The impact of virtual, augmented and mixed reality technologies on the customer experience. Journal of Business Research. 2019;**100**:547–560. DOI: 10.1016/j.jbusres.2018.10.050

[90] McGraw D. Building public trust in uses of Health Insurance Portability and Accountability Act de-identified data. Journal of the American Medical Informatics Association. 2013;**20**(1):29–34. DOI: 10.1136/amiajnl-2012-000936

[91] Spender A, Bullen C, Altmann-Richer L, Cripps J, Duffy R, Falkous C, Farrell M, Horn T, Wigzell J, Yeap W. Wearables and the internet of things: Considerations for the life and health insurance industry. British Actuarial Journal. 2019;**24**:e22. DOI: 10.1017/S1357321719000072

[92] Barredo Arrieta A, Tabik S, García López S, Molina Cabrera D, Herrera Triguero F, Díaz Rodríguez NA. Explainable Artificial Intelligence (XAI): Concepts, taxonomies, opportunities and challenges toward responsible AI. Information Fusion. 2020;**58**:82–115. DOI: 10.1016/j.inffus.2019.12.012

[93] Pagallo U. Vital, Sophia, and Co.—The quest for the legal personhood of robots. Information. 2018;**9**(9):230. DOI: 10.3390/info9090230

[94] Miclăuş T, Valla V, Koukoura A, Nielsen AA, Dahlerup B, Tsianos GI, Vassiliadis E. Impact of design on medical device safety. Therapeutic Innovation & Regulatory Science.

2020;**54**(4):839–849. DOI: 10.1007/s43441-019-00022-4

[95] Lim S, Oh J. Navigating privacy: A global comparative Analysis of data protection laws. IET Information Security. 2025;**2025**(1):5536763. DOI: 10.1049/ise2/5536763

[96] Guo Y, Hao Z, Zhao S, Gong J, Yang F. Artificial intelligence in health care: Bibliometric analysis. Journal of Medical Internet Research. 2020;**22**(7): e18228. DOI: 10.2196/18228

[97] European Commission. Public-private partnerships in transport research. [Internet]. 1999. Available from: https://research-and-innovation.ec.europa.eu/research-area/transport/public-private-partnerships_en [Accessed: 2025–October–31]

[98] Rose S, Borchert O, Mitchell S, Connelly S. Zero trust architecture. NIST Special Publication. 2020;**800**(207):800–207. DOI: 10.6028/NIST.SP.800-207

[99] Ruiu P, Nitti M, Pilloni V, Cadoni M, Grosso E, Fadda M. Metaverse & human digital twin: Digital identity, biometrics, and privacy in the future virtual worlds. Multimodal Technologies and Interaction. 2024;**8**(6):48. DOI: 10.3390/mti8060048

[100] de Kerckhove D. The personal digital twin, ethical considerations. Philosophical Transactions of the Royal Society A. 2021;**379**(2207):20200367. DOI: 10.1098/rsta.2020.0367

[101] Huang PH, Kim KH, Schermer M. Ethical issues of digital twins for personalized health care service: Preliminary mapping study. Journal of Medical Internet Research. 2022;**24**(1): e33081. DOI: 10.2196/33081

[102] Parasuraman R, Wickens CD. Humans: Still vital after all these years of automation. Human Factors. 2008;**50**(3):511–520. DOI: 10.1518/001872008X312198

[103] Popa EO, van Hilten M, Oosterkamp E, Bogaardt MJ. The use of digital twins in healthcare: Socio-ethical benefits and socio-ethical risks. Life Sciences, Society and Policy. 2021;**17**(1):6. DOI: 10.1186/s40504-021-00113-x

[104] Öhman C, Floridi L. The political economy of death in the age of information: A critical approach to the digital afterlife industry. Minds and Machines. 2017;**27**(4):639–662. DOI: 10.1007/s11023-017-9445-2

[105] Methuku V, Myakala PK Digital doppelgangers: Ethical and societal implications of pre-mortem AI clones. arXiv preprint arXiv:2502.21248. 2025. DOI: 10.48550/arXiv.2502.21248

[106] Mayer-Schönberger V. Delete: The virtue of forgetting in the digital age. In: Delete. New Jersey: Princeton University Press; 2011. p. 272. DOI: 10.1515/9781400838455

[107] Alabdullah YY, Alzaid E, Alsaad S, Alamri T, Alolayan SW, Bah S, Aljoudi AS. Autonomy and paternalism in shared decision-making in a Saudi Arabian tertiary hospital: A cross-sectional study. Developing World Bioethics. 2023;**23**(3):260–268. DOI: 10.1111/dewb.12355

[108] Matei SA. The Shallows: What the Internet Is Doing to Our Brains, by Nicholas Carr. New York, NY: WW Norton; 2010. 276 p. DOI: 10.1080/01972243.2013.758481

[109] Billett S. Learning through Practice. In: Learning through Practice:

Models, Traditions, Orientations and Approaches. Dordrecht: Springer Netherlands; 2010. p. 1–20. DOI: 10.1007/978-90-481-3939-2

[110] Obia V. The Costs of Connection: How Data Is Colonizing Human Life and Appropriating It for Capitalism: By Nick Couldry and Ulises A. Stanford: Mejias, Stanford, Stanford University Press; 2019. 352 p. DOI: 10.1080/1369118X.2022.2062254

[111] Mystakidis S. Metaverse. Encyclopedia. 2022;**2**(1):486–497. DOI: 10.3390/encyclopedia2010031

[112] Van Laar E, Van Deursen AJ, Van Dijk JA, De Haan J. The relation between 21st-century skills and digital skills: A systematic literature review. Computers in Human Behavior. 2017;**72**:577–588. DOI: 10.1016/j.chb.2017.03.010

[113] Ifenthaler D, Yau JY. Utilising learning analytics to support study success in higher education: A systematic review. Educational Technology Research and Development. 2020;**68**(4):1961–1990. DOI: 10.1007/s11423-020-09788-z

[114] Ancker JS, Edwards A, Nosal S, Hauser D, Mauer E, Kaushal R. With the HITEC Investigators. Effects of workload, work complexity, and repeated alerts on alert fatigue in a clinical decision support system. BMC Medical Informatics and Decision Making. 2017;**17**(1):36. DOI: 10.1186/s12911-017-0430-8

[115] Hoffman RR, Johnson M, Bradshaw JM, Underbrink A. Trust in automation. IEEE Intelligent Systems. 2013;**28**(1):84–88. DOI: 10.1109/MIS.2013.24

[116] Jobin A, Ienca M, Vayena E. The global landscape of AI ethics guidelines. Nature Machine Intelligence. 2019;**1**(9):389–399. DOI: 10.1038/s42256-019-0088-2

[117] Tsirulnikov D, Suart C, Abdullah R, Vulcu F, Mullarkey CE. Game on: Immersive virtual laboratory simulation improves student learning outcomes & motivation. FEBS Open Bio. 2023;**13**(3):396–407. DOI: 10.1002/2211-5463.13567

[118] Pentina I, Hancock T, Xie T. Exploring relationship development with social chatbots: A mixed-method study of Replika. Computers in Human Behavior. 2023;**140**:107600. DOI: 10.1016/j.chb.2022.107600

[119] Prates RO, Rosson MB, de Souza CS Making decisions about digital legacy with Google's inactive account manager. In: IFIP Conference on Human-Computer Interaction; 30 August 2015; Cham: Springer International Publishing; p. 201–209. DOI: 10.1007/978-3-319-22701-6_14

[120] Mangini V, Tal I, Moldovan AN. An empirical study on the impact of GDPR and right to be forgotten-organisations and users perspective. In: Proceedings of the 15th International Conference On Availability, Reliability And Security; 25 August 2020; p. 1–9. DOI: 10.1145/3407023.3407080

[121] Liu Q, Steed A. Social virtual reality platform comparison and evaluation using a guided group walkthrough method. Frontiers in

Virtual Reality. 2021;**2**:668181. DOI: 10.3389/frvir.2021.668181

[122] Sabry F, Eltaras T, Labda W, Alzoubi K, Malluhi Q. Machine learning for healthcare wearable devices: The big picture. Journal of Healthcare Engineering. 2022;**2022**(1):4653923. DOI: 10.1155/2022/4653923

[123] Nanjappan V, Shi R, Liang HN, Xiao H, Lau KK, Hasan K. Design of interactions for handheld augmented reality devices using wearable smart textiles: Findings from a user elicitation study. Applied Sciences. 2019;**9**(15):3177. DOI: 10.3390/app9153177

[124] Chamberlain L. Eye tracking methodology; theory and practice. Qualitative Market Research: An International Journal. 2007;**10**(2):217–220. DOI: 10.1108/13522750710740862

[125] Ramakrishnan T, Kumar SS, Chelladurai SJ, Gnanasekaran S, Sivananthan S, Geetha NK, Arthanari R, Assefa GB. Recent developments in stimuli responsive smart materials and applications: An overview. Journal of Nanomaterials. 2022;**2022**(1):4031059. DOI: 10.1155/2022/4031059

[126] Xiang H, Li Y, Liao Q, Xia L, Wu X, Zhou H, Li C, Fan X. Recent advances in smart fabric-type wearable electronics toward comfortable wearing. Energies. 2024;**17**(11):2627. DOI: 10.3390/en17112627

Chapter 11

Embodied Presence: Realistic Avatars and Trust Verification in Metaverse Environments

Jaime Gallego Vila

Abstract

The metaverse is posited as the next evolution of human–computer interaction, promising unprecedented social presence through realistic avatars. Yet, realism alone is insufficient: As photorealism increases, so does the feasibility of identity spoofing (such as deepfakes) and real-time impersonation. Realism concerns how closely an avatar aligns with a user's appearance and behavior; verification concerns how reliably we can establish – and *continuously* maintain – the link between the avatar and the human who claims it. This chapter confronts that tension by surveying the psychological foundations of presence, state-of-the-art AI methods for photorealistic, behaviorally congruent avatars, and the resulting trust crisis in multiuser environments. We then introduce the AI-driven Continuous Trust Verification Framework: a layered architecture that integrates active/passive biometrics, behavioral signatures, decentralized cryptographic proofs, and interoperability mechanisms as the necessary components of a robust identity fabric. Finally, we examine the transdisciplinary implications and argue that embodied presence and verified trust are inseparable: Without continuous verification, realism erodes plausibility; with it, realism can safely underpin governance, commerce, and public services in virtual worlds.

Keywords: metaverse, virtual worlds, embodied presence, realistic avatars, trust verification, artificial intelligence, digital identity, deepfake, biometrics, decentralized identity, uncanny valley

1. Introduction

1.1 The metaverse as the next paradigm of human–computer interaction

The metaverse represents more than an incremental evolution of the Internet; it is conceived as a paradigm shift in how humans interact with information, computation, and, fundamentally, with each other. It transcends 2D screens to offer a spatial, persistent, and synchronous Internet where individuals coexist and interact through digital representations, or avatars [1]. In this new plane of digital existence, human activities – from collaborative work and commerce to socialization and entertainment – are expected to achieve far greater fidelity and immediacy, blurring the lines between the physical and virtual worlds.

1.2 The double helix of immersion: Plausibility, presence, and the embodied avatar

The success of this paradigm hinges on its ability to generate a profound sense of "presence." Influential researcher Mel Slater breaks this experience down into two critical components: place illusion (PI), which is the sensation of truly "being there" in the virtual environment, and plausibility illusion (Psi), the sensation that the events occurring within that environment are actually happening [2]. While PI can be achieved with basic immersive technology, Psi is more elusive and fundamental; it requires the virtual world and its avatars to behave in a believable manner. Without plausibility, interactions feel artificial, and the sense of presence shatters.

It is at this juncture that we must draw a fundamental distinction between two types of realistic avatars:

1. **Visually similar avatars:** These are 3D representations that achieve a high degree of photorealism, replicating a user's appearance from photographs or scans. However, their animation might be generic or limited. These avatars answer the question "Who am I?" but in a static way. They contribute to PI but can harm Psi if their behavior is incongruent.

2. **Dynamically embodied avatars:** These realistic avatars move beyond mere resemblance. They are equipped with a humanoid rig that is animated in real time using the user's motion data, captured via the virtual reality (VR) headset and controllers. This type of avatar does not just *look* like the user; it *moves* like the user, replicating gestures, posture, and head movements. This direct sensorimotor mapping is the true engine of *embodied presence* and a massive catalyst for Psi. When the avatar acts as a natural extension of one's own body, the mind accepts the virtual events as genuinely "real."

Therefore, presence and realism form a double helix: Visual likeness (the avatar's appearance) and behavioral congruence (the embodied animation) intertwine to build a convincing and plausible immersive experience.

1.3 The obstacle of perfection: The uncanny valley

The pursuit of realism is not a linear progression toward greater user acceptance. This journey is fraught with a significant perceptual pitfall known as the "uncanny valley," a concept first introduced by Masahiro Mori in his seminal 1970 essay, "Bukimi no Tani" (the uncanny valley) [3]. The hypothesis posits that as a robot or digital avatar becomes more humanlike, our affinity for it increases, but only up to a certain point. When the representation is almost perfectly human but fails in subtle, almost imperceptible details – such as eye movement that is slightly too slow, unnatural skin texture, or imperfect lip-syncing – our affinity plummets dramatically, replaced by a sense of eeriness, strangeness, or even revulsion.

As illustrated by the uncanny valley hypothesis (see **Figure 1**), an avatar that falls into the valley directly destroys the Psi described by Slater [2]. It breaks immersion

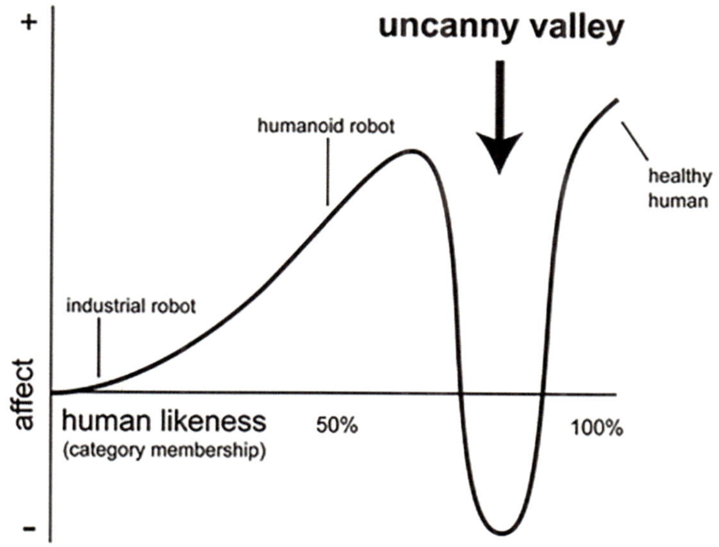

Figure 1.
The uncanny valley hypothesis, as proposed by Mori. As a representation approaches perfect human likeness, a point is reached where subtle imperfections cause a sharp drop in affinity, creating a sense of eeriness. The graph illustrates this dip. (Image recreated by the author based on Mori, 1970).

by constantly signaling that something is "wrong," even if the user cannot consciously pinpoint the flaw. Overcoming this valley is therefore not merely a matter of better 3D modeling but of achieving behavioral realism through the precise, AI-driven animation of the subtle cues that constitute authentic human interaction. This challenge is not merely theoretical; it is a practical obstacle in fields like 3D avatar reconstruction (see **Figure 2**).

This effect is equally prominent in robotics, where famous examples such as the SAYA robot (**Figure 3**) are often cited for their uncanny appearance, despite being

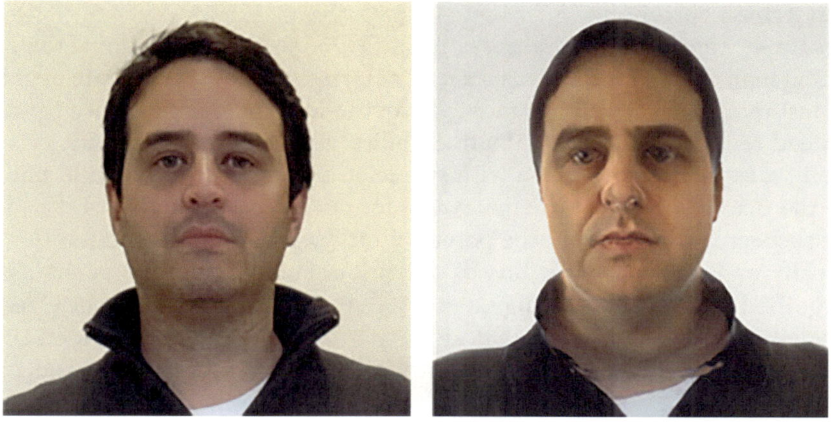

Figure 2.
An example of the uncanny valley in real-time avatar generation. (a) the real person; (b) a reconstruction that captures their likeness but whose subtle imperfections in skin texture and expression can place it in the uncanny valley, creating a sense of unease.

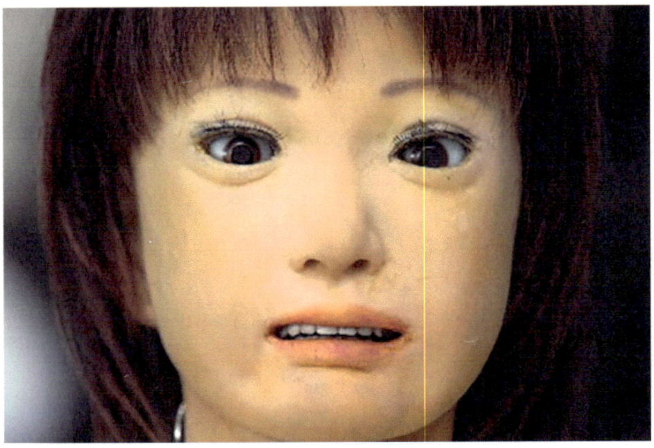

Figure 3.
The animatronic head of the robot SAYA, developed at the Tokyo University of Science by Prof. H. Kobayashi. Designed to express basic emotions, its mechanical nature and subtly unnatural expressions often place it deep within the uncanny valley, highlighting the profound challenge of simulating human behavior.

designed for social interaction [4]. This very challenge highlights the core tension of this chapter: The technologies essential to making an avatar feel genuinely human are the same ones that could be leveraged to create a dangerously deceptive fake.

1.4 The crisis of trust in an age of artificial realism

Paradoxically, the very technology that promises to create realistic, embodied avatars is the source of an existential threat to the metaverse: the systematic erosion of trust. While the current Internet era already suffers from a crisis of confidence fueled by disinformation and phishing, the metaverse magnifies these risks exponentially. It weaponizes the tools of realism – the very AI-driven animations of micro-expressions and gestures needed to cross the uncanny valley – to enable the creation of real-time deepfake avatars. These malicious representations are capable of impersonating identities in a manner that is functionally indistinguishable to unaided human perception [5].

This threat constitutes a direct assault on the Psi that is foundational to presence. Imagining high-stakes interactions – a medical consultation, a corporate negotiation, a legal testimony – in an environment where the interlocutor's identity cannot be guaranteed reveals a fundamental vulnerability. Any hint of inauthenticity shatters plausibility, replacing immersion with suspicion and anxiety. This could not only stymie the mass adoption of the metaverse for critical uses but also confine it to an "era of suspect reality," where the potential for deep human connection is perpetually undermined by the fear of deception. Furthermore, these challenges are magnified in a fragmented digital ecosystem. For any solution to be effective, it must be interoperable, ensuring that identity and trust can be maintained across different virtual worlds and platforms, rather than being trapped in proprietary silos.

1.5 Central thesis and chapter structure

This chapter posits that authentic embodied presence and verified trust are not independent goals but are symbiotic and inseparable. A photorealistic avatar without a verifiable seal of authenticity fails to generate a sustainable Psi, thus creating not presence but anxiety and suspicion. Therefore, the construction of a functional metaverse requires that the technological sophistication of avatars be matched by an equally sophisticated trust architecture. The main contributions of this chapter are as follows:

- A structured survey and synthesis of the foundational psychological theories (embodied presence, plausibility) and the state-of-the-art in AI-driven avatar reconstruction, creating a comprehensive taxonomy of methods ranging from parametric models to neural volumetric representations.

- The proposal of a novel conceptual framework, the AI-driven Continuous Trust Verification Framework (AI-CTVF), serves as a structured solution to the identified trust crisis.

- A critical analysis of the transdisciplinary implications and open research challenges, providing a forward-looking agenda for building safe and trustworthy virtual worlds.

To address these points, we introduce an AI-based conceptual framework for continuous identity verification. The chapter is structured as follows: Section 2 explores the theoretical foundations of embodied presence. Section 3 analyzes the AI technologies that enable the creation of realistic avatars. Section 4 delves into the trust paradigm and its threats. Section 5 details our original proposal: a multilayered framework for trust verification. Section 6 analyzes the transdisciplinary implications. Finally, Section 7 presents case studies and future directions, before offering conclusions in Section 8.

2. Foundations of embodied presence

Having established the critical role of realism in the introduction, this section delves into the foundational psychological mechanisms that enable embodied presence. We move beyond basic definitions to explore the formal models and cognitive processes that explain how a user's mind comes to accept a digital representation as an extension of the self.

2.1 Presence as a dual illusion

As introduced earlier, the experience of presence arises from the interaction of two orthogonal illusions first articulated by Slater [2] and later probed empirically by Skarbez [6]: PI – the feeling of "being there" in the virtual scenario – and Psi – the belief that the events unfolding are actually happening. We can therefore regard presence as a function of both factors.

$$Presence = f(\mathrm{PI}, \mathrm{Psi}), \quad (1)$$

PI can be understood as a largely thresholded phenomenon – either the conditions are sufficient for "being there," or they are not – whereas Psi is continuously modulated by social believability and trust. Crucially, Psi holds a *power of veto*: If users doubt that interlocutors are genuine or that events are authentic, presence collapses regardless of visual fidelity. This is not merely experiential; it undermines *governance* in high-stakes domains (telemedicine, finance, public services), where plausibility is a prerequisite for accountability and due process. This theoretical foundation explains why a single suspected *deepfake* avatar can shatter the integrity of a high-stakes virtual interaction: It directly attacks and nullifies the Psi component, making genuine presence impossible.

2.2 Mechanisms of embodiment: Body ownership and agency

The feeling of an avatar being an "authentic extension" of the self, known as embodied presence or embodiment, relies on two specific neurological illusions: the illusion of body ownership and the illusion of agency, concepts whose application to virtual environments has been both theorized [7, 8] and extensively validated through empirical studies [9].

- **The illusion of body ownership:** It refers to the feeling that an avatar's body *is* one's own body. This is achieved through the congruence of sensory information. For instance, when a user looks down and sees a virtual body that visually matches their own posture and movement (visuomotor correlation), or feels a haptic vibration when their avatar touches an object (visuotactile correlation), the brain begins to adopt the digital form.

- **The illusion of agency:** It is the feeling of being in control of the avatar's actions. This arises from the seamless mapping of a user's intentions to the avatar's behavior. Low latency and precise tracking of movements from VR hardware are critical for maintaining this illusion. Any lag or error breaks the sense of control.

Achieving both illusions is the technical goal of "dynamically embodied avatars." It is this deep, sensorimotor link – the feeling that "this body is mine" and "I am controlling it" – that makes interactions in the metaverse feel impactful and real.

2.3 The avatar's influence on the self: The proteus effect

The relationship between user and avatar is not unidirectional. Remarkably, the characteristics of our digital representation can alter our own behavior and attitudes, a phenomenon known as the proteus effect [10]. Studies have shown that users assigned taller avatars negotiate more confidently, while those with more attractive avatars exhibit greater sociability and self-disclosure.

This effect has critical implications for the trust-verification paradigm. It means that the danger of a deepfake avatar is not merely one of visual impersonation. A malicious actor assuming the avatar of a figure of authority (e.g., a CEO, a police officer) may subconsciously begin to act with more confidence and assertiveness, making their impersonation more convincing and manipulative. The proteus effect thus acts as a psychological amplifier for deception, underscoring that an avatar's appearance is not a neutral costume but a powerful tool that shapes social dynamics, for better or for worse.

3. The technological frontier: A survey of AI-driven avatar reconstruction

The creation of a realistic, animatable 3D avatar from simple visual input is a foundational goal for the metaverse. This section provides a survey of the state-of-the-art AI technologies that form the modern reconstruction pipeline, highlighting how the field has evolved to overcome key limitations, moving from structured models to flexible neural representations.

3.1 The foundation: Parametric human models

Modern reconstruction pipelines rarely start from a blank slate. Instead, they leverage statistical, parametric models of the human body that encapsulate a vast amount of prior knowledge. The most influential of these is the skinned multiperson linear model (SMPL) [11] and its extension, SMPL-X, which incorporates expressive hands and face [12]. These models can generate a wide variety of human bodies by controlling a low-dimensional set of shape and pose parameters. This approach is powerful because it constrains the problem: AI models only need to infer the correct parameters that best fit a person in an image, a task often achieved via deep neural networks [13, 14]. The primary limitation, however, is that these models have a fixed mesh topology and cannot represent person-specific details such as hairstyles or loose clothing.

3.2 Single-view refinement of parametric models

To address the limitations of the base SMPL model, a significant branch of research focuses on refining its shape using a single photograph.

- **Silhouette and map-based deformation:** Methods such as photo wake-up [15] project the initial SMPL model onto the image plane and then "warp" its vertices to match the person's 2D silhouette. This allows the model to capture the shape of clothing and hair. The refined 2D information is then back-projected to create a 3D mesh.

- **Texture-space detail inference:** Other approaches, such as Tex2Shape [16], operate in the UV space of the SMPL model. They use an input image to infer detailed normal or displacement maps, which are then applied to the base mesh to add high-frequency details such as wrinkles and fabric folds.

- **Complete end-to-end pipelines:** Building on these foundational techniques, other research focuses on creating complete, automated pipelines designed to produce a fully animatable and usable avatar. For example, Beacco et al. [17] present a workflow that integrates SMPL fitting, silhouette warping, and, crucially, a separate high-fidelity head reconstruction module. The resulting head mesh is then stitched onto the reconstructed body, creating a final avatar that prioritizes not just geometric accuracy but also the user's recognizability and immediate usability in VR applications. **Figure 4** shows a graphical representation of the method presented in [17].

Figure 4.
Complete pipeline of the avatar reconstruction method presented in [17]. The method runs several deep learning techniques over a frontal RGB image of a single person such as region segmentation, pose detection, normal and depth maps, head reconstruction, and combines them to automatically retrieve a fully usable and recognizable 3D animated avatar.

Despite these advances, the fundamental limitation of all single-view methods is that they produce "2.5D" avatars, where any occluded part is either missing or inferred from visible ones.

3.3 Beyond fixed topology: Implicit function-based reconstruction

To overcome the constraints of fixed-topology models, a significant breakthrough came from methods using implicit neural representations. Instead of defining a surface with a discrete mesh, these approaches learn a continuous function that models the 3D shape. A seminal work in this area is PIFu [18], which learns a function that can infer whether a 3D point is inside or outside a surface based on its corresponding 2D image features, allowing for the reconstruction of arbitrary topologies. However, these methods still suffer from monocular ambiguity. To improve robustness, hybrid approaches such as PaMIR [19] condition the implicit function on an SMPL prior, combining the best of both worlds.

3.4 From single-view ambiguity to volumetric shape: Temporal and multiview fusion

To achieve a truly volumetric, 360-degree model, information from multiple viewpoints is essential.

- **Multiview photogrammetry:** The classic approach uses synchronized camera arrays to capture a subject from all angles, generating highly detailed meshes via structure-from-motion and multiview stereo.

- **Video-based refinement:** A more accessible approach uses a single monocular video. As a person moves, they naturally reveal different aspects of their body. Representative systems -such as the one proposed in [20] and related methods- initialize a model from one frame and iteratively refine it, gradually "filling in" the missing geometry and texture to create a fully volumetric model.

3.5 The rendering revolution: Neural volumetric representations

The most recent paradigm shift concerns how the final avatar is represented and rendered, moving toward neural techniques that offer unprecedented realism.

- **Neural radiance fields (NeRFs):** A NeRF [21] is an implicit representation that uses a neural network to encode a scene's color and density. Methods such as HumanNeRF can create stunningly photorealistic, deformable human avatars, though they are often slow to render.

- **3D Gaussian splatting:** To solve the speed problem, 3D Gaussian splatting [22] has emerged as a revolutionary alternative. This explicit method represents a scene as millions of tiny 3D Gaussians, achieving NeRF-level quality at real-time frame rates, making it a leading technology for the metaverse.

The rapid progress toward perfect realism makes the central thesis of this chapter – the link between realism and trust verification – more urgent than ever.

3.6 From technical breakthroughs to persistent multiuser systems

Realistic reconstruction is necessary but not sufficient for live, shared worlds. Persistent ecosystems require (i) identity continuity across sessions and worlds, (ii) asset portability and entitlements that survive context switches, (iii) networked animation with low-latency state sync, and (iv) defenses against impersonation that operate end-to-end. In practice, this couples avatar tech to identity and permissions: The same pipelines that reconstruct a face or gait must bind to verifiable credentials and runtime trust signals so that "Who controls this avatar?" is answered *continuously* as scenes, servers, and devices change.

4. The trust paradigm: The challenge of verification in anonymous environments

Having established the technological pipeline for creating realistic avatars, we now confront the profound social and security crises this very technology engenders. This section deconstructs the paradigm of trust, analyzing how physical-world mechanisms break down in the metaverse and defining a threat model for embodied identity.

4.1 The digital identity problem: From physical anchors to abstract presence

In the physical world, trust is built upon verifiable identity "primitives" that are difficult to forge: government-issued ID cards, biometric signatures, and, most fundamentally, the immutable reality of physical copresence. These mechanisms underpin nearly all high-value interactions [23]. The metaverse dissolves these anchors. Digital identity becomes malleable, an abstract data stream separate from the physical self. The challenge is not merely authenticating a user at login but ensuring the continuous, unbroken link between the human operator and the stream of photons and data that constitutes their avatar's presence.

4.2 A threat model for embodied identity

The primary threat is not simple anonymity but active, malicious impersonation enabled by the same AI tools used for reconstruction. Such risks were recently examined in an impersonation experiment published in [24]. We can define a threat model with several key attack vectors:

- **Identity spoofing and deepfake impersonation:** This involves creating a photorealistic avatar of a known, trusted individual (a CEO, a politician, or a family member) to commit fraud, spread disinformation, or gain unauthorized access. *Impact:* This is a direct attack on social and economic trust structures. In the context of presence, it is designed to exploit the victim's preexisting mental model of the person being impersonated.

- **Real-time avatar puppeteering:** A more sophisticated attack involves an actor modulating their own voice and using their movements to animate a victim's stolen or replicated avatar in real time. *Impact:* This is a direct assault on the Psi. An interaction with a "puppeted" avatar, even if subtly flawed, injects an element of the uncanny and unreal, shattering the victim's sense of presence and replacing it with anxiety.

- **Proteus effect weaponization:** Malicious actors can exploit the proteus effect [10] by choosing avatars designed to psychologically manipulate others. An avatar appearing as a doctor could elicit unwarranted trust and disclosure of private medical information; an avatar designed to appear vulnerable could be used for large-scale social engineering scams. *Impact:* This attack vector weaponizes social psychology, using the avatar's appearance as a tool to alter social dynamics and manipulate behavior, making the deception more effective.

- **Cross-platform vulnerabilities.** A further risk is *identity spillover*: Compromises in one ecosystem (e.g., a cloned avatar or leaked credential) can be replayed elsewhere if platforms accept screenshots, recordings, or unverifiable tokens as proof. Without portable cryptographic proofs and liveness checks, attackers can bootstrap trust in World B using artifacts harvested from World A. Mitigation requires cross-platform verification primitives and revocation mechanisms that travel with the user, not with a single vendor.

4.3 The perception dilemma: The failure of human intuition

Herein lies the central paradox: the technologies that allow us to cross the uncanny valley and achieve true embodied presence are the same ones that give adversaries the perfect toolkit to subvert it. This creates a technological arms race, but it is an asymmetric one. Human perception, honed for the physical world, is ill-equipped to detect sophisticated digital forgeries [5]. Relying on users to spot subtle artifacts in a real-time deepfake is a strategy doomed to fail, as it is often computationally easier to generate a convincing fake than it is to detect one definitively.

4.4 The architectural imperative: Toward a verifiable digital identity fabric

For the metaverse to mature beyond entertainment, it requires a new digital identity infrastructure – a "fabric" woven into its very foundation. The

"Digital Passport" analogy is useful, but its implementation must be dynamic, privacy-preserving, and user-centric. This points toward architectures based on self-sovereign identity (SSI). The key components of such a fabric are as follows:

- **Decentralized identifiers (DIDs):** Unique, persistent identifiers that are owned and controlled by the user – not a corporation or government. They are the anchor of identity in a decentralized world [25].

- **Verifiable credentials (VCs):** Tamper-proof, cryptographically signed claims about a user (e.g., "is over 18," "is a verified employee of Company X") that can be presented without revealing unnecessary data.

- **Zero-knowledge proofs (ZKPs):** A powerful cryptographic technique that allows a user to prove a statement is true without revealing the information underlying the proof. For example, a user could prove they are on a list of verified employees without revealing which employee they are, perfectly balancing verification with privacy.

A paradigmatic and widely adopted application of these principles in the Web3 ecosystem is the use of nonfungible tokens (NFTs) as a form of VC for digital assets, including avatars. An NFT, typically based on standards such as ERC-721 on the Ethereum blockchain, acts as a unique, publicly verifiable, and user-owned certificate of ownership. This enables a powerful verification mechanism known as "token-gating," where access to a digital resource (like using a specific avatar in a game) is granted only if the user can prove they own the corresponding NFT (note: proves ownership/usage rights of avatar assets, but not human personhood).

A practical implementation of this workflow is demonstrated in [26], which details a system where the user's Ethereum wallet address is used to query the blockchain in real time. The system verifies if the user is the registered owner of the ERC-721 token associated with a 3D avatar, whose metadata and model are stored decentrally on IPFS. This approach serves as a tangible example of a "Digital Passport" for avatars, grounding the abstract concepts of SSI in a functional, implemented solution. It is important to note, however, that these cryptographic solutions are not a panacea; they introduce their own challenges related to key custody, wallet security, phishing vulnerabilities, and the complex issue of credential revocation.

These architectural primitives are the necessary building blocks for the continuous, AI-driven verification framework we propose in the next section.

5. AI-powered trust-verification architectures

To resolve the stated dilemma, we propose the AI-CTVF. This framework does not rely on a single point of verification but on a "defense-in-depth" model with multiple continuously operating layers to establish a dynamic trust level for the user's identity.

5.1 A multilayered model for continuous identity verification

1. **Layer 1: Active and passive biometric verification**

This layer establishes the initial identity and monitors it.

- *Active verification (onboarding):* The initial enrollment process can utilize robust biometric methods, such as 3D facial scanning with *liveness detection* (to prevent photo or video spoofing) or voice authentication.

- *Passive verification (continuous):* During the session, AI noninvasively monitors biometric data. For instance, it can continuously analyze the user's voice biometrics for anomalous changes or verify subtle, unconscious patterns such as blink rate or head micro-movements, which are difficult to forge in real time.

2. **Layer 2: AI-powered behavioral analysis (behavioral signature)**

This is perhaps the most innovative and difficult-to-spoof layer. AI can learn a unique "behavioral signature" for each user, composed of idiosyncratic patterns.

- *Behavioral biometrics:* This includes gesture patterns, speech cadence, eye movement patterns when scanning a scene, and even the way a user interacts with virtual objects.

- *Coherence analysis:* An AI model can detect inconsistencies between the expected behavior of the legitimate user and the observed behavior, such as unusual hesitation or a movement pattern that does not match historical data. An impostor can replicate a face, but replicating a decade of learned behavioral habits is computationally infeasible in real time.

3. **Layer 3: Cryptographic and decentralized verification**

This layer protects user privacy and ensures identity portability.

- *DIDs:* The user's identity would not be controlled by a single corporation but by the user themselves via a blockchain-based system, giving them control over their data [25].

- *ZKPs:* This powerful cryptographic tool allows a user to prove a fact without revealing the underlying information. For example, a user could prove their avatar is verified as "human, over 18" without revealing their name, face, or birth date, thus preserving anonymity when desired.

- *Verifiable ownership via NFTs:* A direct and practical implementation of this layer involves linking the avatar asset to a NFT. This "token-gating" architecture, as demonstrated in systems built with the Ethereum blockchain [26], ensures that only the cryptographic owner of the NFT can use the associated avatar, providing a robust, on-chain verification of rights without a central authority.

4. **Layer 4: Perceptual watermarking and digital forensics**

This final layer adds a seal of authenticity directly into the avatar's data stream.

- *Perceptual watermarking:* An imperceptible signal, detectable by an algorithm but not by humans, can be embedded in the avatar's video or audio stream. The absence or alteration of this watermark would indicate that the avatar has been tampered with or is not from a verified source. However, the robustness of such watermarks against transformations such as video re-compression or adversarial attacks remains an active area of research.

- *Digital forensics:* In the event of a dispute, cryptographic audit logs—together with data from the system's earlier layers—enable forensic verification of whether the session was legitimate or spoofed.

5. **Layer 5: Interoperability and portability**

Trust must be portable across devices and worlds. This layer ensures that identities, credentials, watermarks, and audit proofs are *standards-aligned* and verifiable beyond a single vendor stack. Practically, this means: (a) binding avatar controllers to DIDs/VCs that any conformant verifier can check; (b) shipping trust signals (e.g., liveness attestations, watermark hashes) as signed, privacy-preserving metadata alongside media streams; and (c) defining revocation and key-rotation flows that work across organizations and jurisdictions.

Figure 5 summarizes the AI-CTVF layered trust-verification architecture described above. The model follows a defense-in-depth approach: The upper layers focus on continuous authentication through direct human signals, while the lower layers provide cryptographic assurances and forensic traceability.

5.2 The role of AI in real-time anomaly and deepfake detection

Artificial intelligence is the engine that drives the AI-CTVF. It acts as a real-time anomaly detection system, constantly comparing incoming data streams (biometric, behavioral) against the established trust profile for the user. If a significant deviation is detected in one or more layers, the avatar's "trust level" could be visibly downgraded (e.g., its verification badge changes from green to yellow), alerting other users to a potential risk.

5.3 Implementation notes: Scaling to consumer devices

To run continuously on consumer hardware, AI-CTVF emphasizes: (i) on-device inference for sensitive biometrics, (ii) model compression and quantization for low-latency behavioral models, (iii) adaptive sampling (graceful degradation under load), and (iv) edge offloading for heavy cryptographic proof generation with end-to-end encryption. Together, these choices keep verification responsive without sacrificing privacy or battery life.

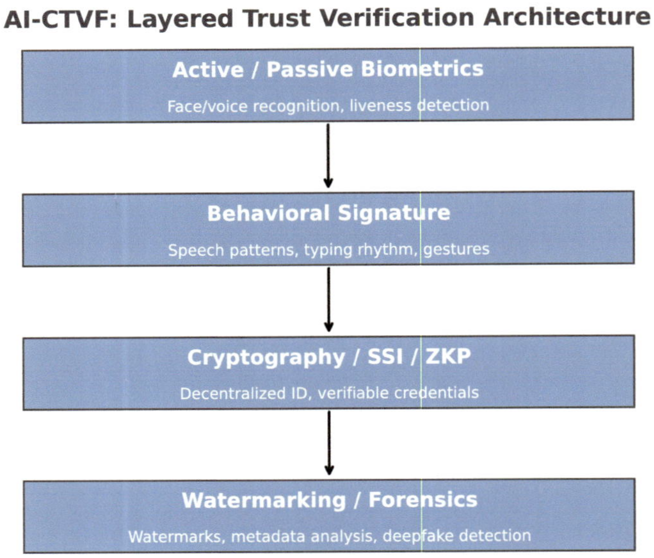

Figure 5.
AI-CTVF: layered trust-verification architecture. The framework integrates (a) active/passive biometrics – *such as face/voice recognition and liveness detection; (b)* behavioral signature – *for example, speech patterns, typing rhythm, and gestures; (c)* cryptography/SSI/ZKP – *decentralized identity, VCs, and ZKPs; and (d)* watermarking/forensics – *watermark embedding, metadata analysis, and deepfake detection. Together, these layers ensure robust, multimodal verification of trusted embodied presence in virtual environments.*

6. Transdisciplinary implications and ethical considerations

The implementation of systems like the AI-CTVF transcends engineering and has profound societal consequences.

6.1 Psychology

The existence of a visible "trust score" could fundamentally alter interpersonal perception. How do we interact with someone whose avatar is marked as "partially verified"? This could influence judgment formation, trust, and self-presentation. Furthermore, the pressure of being continuously monitored, even passively, could generate anxiety or induce less spontaneous behavior.

6.2 Sociology

These systems could create new forms of social stratification: a "verified class" with access to high-value interactions and an "anonymous class" relegated to less secure spaces. This could exacerbate existing digital divides, where those without access to the necessary technology for verification are marginalized from the metaverse economy and society.

6.3 Law and regulation

Complex legal questions arise. Who is legally responsible for the actions of a deepfake avatar: the software creator, the platform that hosted it, or the individual who operated it? A legal framework for digital identity is urgently needed to define the status of a "verified avatar" and establish liability in cases of fraud or impersonation. Jurisdiction in a global, decentralized metaverse is another monumental challenge.

6.4 Ethics

The tension between security and privacy is central. To what extent is it ethical to require biometric and behavioral monitoring to participate in digital society? It is crucial to ensure that verification algorithms do not contain biases that discriminate against certain demographic groups. For example, biometric systems are known to exhibit biases based on skin tone or age, and behavioral analysis could unfairly penalize users with atypical movement patterns, a phenomenon known as "biometric drift." The ownership and control of biometric and behavioral data – arguably the most intimate information we possess – must remain firmly in the hands of the user, as proposed by decentralized identity architectures. The right to anonymity, vital for freedom of expression and the protection of dissidents, must be carefully balanced with the need for security.

6.5 Governance models for trust infrastructure

Three governance archetypes emerge, each with trade-offs:

- **Regulatory (public-sector-led):** Clear accountability and due process; risks include slower iteration and over-centralization.

- **Consortium-led (industry standards):** Faster alignment with practical needs; risks include capture and uneven user protections across vendors.

- **Decentralized (SSI/DAO-aligned):** User-controlled keys and credentials; risks include key management burdens, fragmented assurance levels, and complex liabilities.

A polycentric approach – public baselines for rights and redress, consortium standards for interoperability, and SSI for user agency – can balance safety, innovation, and autonomy.

7. Case studies, applications, and future directions

7.1 Case study 1 (high stakes): Telemedicine in the metaverse

A surgeon, whose avatar is verified by the AI-CTVF, remotely guides a local medical team through a complex operation. Continuous verification assures the hospital and the patient that the guidance is from the legitimate expert. The cryptographic layer (ZKP) allows the surgeon to prove their medical license without revealing any other personal data.

7.2 Case study 2 (commerce): International contract execution

Two executives from different continents meet in a virtual boardroom to sign a merger agreement. Their photorealistic avatars display a "fully verified" status. The contract signing is executed via a cryptographic key tied to their verified identities, creating a legally binding and nonrepudiable record.

7.3 Case study 3 (social): Safe and moderated communities

A social platform allows users to choose to interact only with others who meet a certain verification level (e.g., "verified as human"). This could drastically reduce harassment, bots, and spam, creating safer spaces, especially for vulnerable users, without completely eliminating the option for anonymity in other areas of the platform.

7.4 Case study 4 (civic): Verified avatars in e-governance

Citizens access municipal services in a virtual town hall. Their avatars present a ZKP that they are residents and over 18, without revealing their names or addresses. A council hearing permits only "human-verified" avatars to speak, mitigating bot-driven disruption while preserving anonymity for whistleblowers. Audit trails – watermarked media plus cryptographic session logs – create accountable, appealable records compatible with public-sector retention policies.

7.5 Future directions: Government-issued avatars as digital identity certificates

The logical culmination of the trust-verification paradigm is the evolution of avatars from mere representations to legally recognized digital identity instruments, analogous to physical passports or digital certificates. In this future state, we envision a system where trusted entities, potentially government-certified or acting as sovereign identity providers, are responsible for creating and issuing high-fidelity, verified avatars.

The process would mirror the issuance of a passport:

1. A citizen would undergo a robust in-person identity verification process at an authorized office.

2. During this process, a photorealistic, biometrically accurate 3D scan of the individual will be captured, creating a "base" avatar.

3. This verified avatar would then be cryptographically signed and minted as a nontransferable soulbound token or a specialized NFT, and delivered to the citizen's secure digital wallet.

This "Sovereign-Issued Avatar" would become the root of trust for all high-stakes interactions in the metaverse. It would be universally verifiable across different virtual worlds, allowing citizens to sign binding contracts, access government e-services, conduct secure financial transactions, or give legal testimony with the same level of legal certainty as if they were physically present or using a national digital certificate. This framework would solve the identity problem at its core, creating the foundational trust layer necessary for the metaverse to become a genuine extension of our civic and economic lives.

7.6 Open research avenues and pending challenges

The path to implementing the AI-CTVF is fraught with challenges:

- **Computational overhead:** Continuous analysis of multiple real-time data streams requires significant computational power.

- **Interoperability:** To avoid "walled garden" virtual worlds, open standards for identity and verification are needed that work across different platforms.

- **User acceptance:** Users must perceive the benefits of these systems as outweighing their concerns about privacy and surveillance.

- **System robustness:** The security of the verification system itself is paramount, as it would become a high-value target for attackers.

8. Conclusion

8.1 Recapitulation: The inseparable symbiosis of realistic presence and verified trust

This chapter has argued that the pursuit of embodied presence through realistic avatars in the metaverse is an incomplete and dangerous endeavor if detached from the simultaneous construction of a trust infrastructure. Realism without verification leads not to immersion but to an era of "suspect reality," where every interaction is fraught with uncertainty. Authentic presence can only flourish on the fertile ground of guaranteed safety and identity.

8.2 AI as the "system" of the metaverse

Artificial intelligence reveals itself as a double-edged sword. It is the tool that generates both the problem (*deepfakes*, impersonation) and the solution. In proposing the AI-CTVF, we have repositioned AI not only as an architect of virtual worlds but as their essential, adaptive, continuously learning system that identifies and neutralizes threats to identity, allowing the social organism of the metaverse to function healthily.

8.3 Final reflections on building safe and trustworthy infinite worlds

The construction of the metaverse is not merely a technical challenge but a profound social, ethical, and philosophical one. The choices we make now about the architecture of identity and trust will define the nature of these "infinite worlds" for decades to come. By integrating verification into the core design of the metaverse, rather than adding it as a later patch, we have the opportunity to build the next chapter of the Internet's history, that is, from its inception, safer, more accountable, and ultimately more human.

8.3.1 Who should own and operate the trust?

We argue for *polycentric governance*: (i) individuals own their cryptographic identifiers and credentials; (ii) independent, auditable verifiers (public interest or accredited) operate the attestation services; (iii) platforms consume standardized proofs but cannot lock users in; and (iv) regulators set baseline guarantees (revocation, appeals, nondiscrimination). Trust then becomes an interoperable utility – like the web's PKI – rather than a proprietary moat.

Author details

Jaime Gallego Vila
Polytechnic University of Catalonia, Vilanova i la Geltru, Spain

*Address all correspondence to: jaume.gallego@upc.edu

References

[1] Ball M. The Metaverse: And How It Will Revolutionize Everything. New York: Liveright Publishing Corporation; 2022

[2] Slater M. Place illusion and plausibility can lead to realistic behaviour in immersive virtual environments. Philosophical Transactions of the Royal Society B: Biological Sciences. 2009;**364** (1535):3549–3557

[3] Mori M. The uncanny valley. Energy. 1970;7(4):33–35

[4] Hashimoto T, Hitramatsu S, Tsuji T, Kobayashi H. "Development of the face robot SAYA for rich facial expressions," In: *2006 SICE-ICASE International Joint Conference*. IEEE; 2006, pp. 5423–5428

[5] Chesney R, Citron D. Deep fakes: A looming challenge for privacy, democracy, and national security. California Law Review. 2019;**107**:1753–1819

[6] Skarbez R, "Plausibility Illusion in Virtual Environments," Ph.D. dissertation, University of North Carolina at Chapel Hill, Chapel Hill, 2016. [Ph.D. dissertation]. Available: https://cdr.lib.unc.edu/concern/dissertations/v118rf14z [Accessed: 2025-April-23]

[7] Kilteni K, Gonzalez R, Slater M. The sense of embodiment in virtual reality. In: Presence: Teleoperators and Virtual Environments. **21**. Cambridge, USA: MIT Press; 2012. p. 373–387

[8] Biocca F. The cyborg's dilemma: Progressive embodiment in virtual environments. Journal of Computer-Mediated Communication. 1997;**3**(2). DOI: 10.1111/j.1083-6101.1997.tb00070.x

[9] Sanchez-Vives M, Spanlang B, Frisoli A, Bergamasco M, Slater M. Virtual hand illusion induced by visuomotor correlations. The New Science of Consciousness: States of Mind. 2010;**5**(2):e10381

[10] Yee N, Bailenson JN. The proteus effect: The effect of transformed self-representation on behavior. Human Communication Research. 2007;**33** (3):271–290

[11] Loper M, Mahmood N, Romero J, Pons-Moll G, Black MJ. SMPL: A skinned multi-person linear model. ACM Transactions on Graphics (Proceedings of SIGGRAPH Asia). 2015;**34**(6):248:1–248

[12] Pavlakos G, Choutas V, Ghorbani N, Bolkart T, Osman AAA, Tzionas D, Black MJ. "Expressive body capture: 3d hands, face, and body from a single image." In: *Proceedings IEEE Conf. on Computer Vision and Pattern Recognition (CVPR)*. 2019

[13] Bogo F, Kanazawa A, Lassner C, Gehler P, Romero J, Black MJ. "Keep it SMPL: Automatic estimation of 3d human pose and shape from a single image." In: *European Conference on Computer Vision*. Springer; 2016, pp. 561–578

[14] Kanazawa A, Black MJ, Jacobs DW, Malik J. "End-to-end recovery of human shape and pose." In: *Proceedings of the IEEE Conference on Computer Vision and Pattern Recognition*. 2018, pp. 7122–7131

[15] Weng C-Y, Curless B, Kemelmacher-Shlizerman I. "Photo wake-up: 3d character animation from a single photo." In: *IEEE Proc. Conf. on Computer Vision and Pattern Recognition*. 2019, pp. 5908–5917

[16] Alldieck T, Pons-Moll G, Theobalt C, Magnor M. "Tex2shape: Detailed full human body geometry from a single image." In: *IEEE International Conference on Computer Vision (ICCV)*. IEEE; 2019

[17] Beacco A, Gallego J, Slater M. "Automatic 3d avatar generation from a single RGB frontal image." In: *2022 IEEE Conference on Virtual Reality and 3D User Interfaces Abstracts and Workshops (VRW)*. IEEE; 2022, pp. 764–765

[18] Saito S, Huang Z, Natsume R, Morishima S, Kanazawa A, Li H. "PIFu: Pixel-aligned implicit function for high-resolution clothed human digitization." In: *Proceedings of the IEEE International Conference on Computer Vision (ICCV)*. 2019

[19] Zheng Z, Yu T, Liu Y, Dai Q. "Pamir: Parametric model-conditioned implicit representation for image-based human reconstruction." *IEEE Transactions on Pattern Analysis and Machine Intelligence (TPAMI)*. 2021

[20] Alldieck T, Magnor M, Xu W, Theobalt C, Pons-Moll G. "Video based reconstruction of 3d people models." In: *Proceedings of the IEEE Conference on Computer Vision and Pattern Recognition*. 2018, pp. 8387–8397

[21] Mildenhall B, Srinivasan PP, Tancik M, Barron JT, Ramamoorthi R, Ng R. Nerf: Representing scenes as neural radiance fields for view synthesis. Communications of the ACM. 2021;**65**(1):99–106

[22] Kerbl B, Kopanas G, Leimkühler T, Drettakis G. 3d Gaussian splatting for real-time radiance field rendering. ACM Transactions on Graphics. 2023;**42** (4):139–1

[23] Preukschat A, Reed D. Self-sovereign Identity. New York: Manning Publications; 2021

[24] Oliva R, Wiesing M, Gallego J, Inami M, Interrante V, Lecuyer A, McDonnell R, Nouviale F, Pan X, Steinicke F, Slater M, "Where extended reality and AI may take us: Ethical issues of impersonation and AI fakes in social virtual reality." 2025. Available: 10.5281/zenodo.15413114

[25] W3C. "Decentralized identifiers (dids) v1.0." W3C Recommendation. 2022. [Online]. Available: https://www.w3.org/TR/did-core/ [Accessed: 2025-March-3]

[26] Sanchez LI. "Estudi Sobre la Verificació D'identitat D'avatars 3d En Entorns de Realitat Virtual Utilitzant Nft I Blockchain." Master's thesis, Universitat Politècnica de Catalunya (UPC), Escola Superior d'Enginyeries Industrial, Aeroespacial i Audiovisual de Terrassa, 2025, master's Thesis

Chapter 12

Perspective Chapter: Identity in Metaverse

Nem Samejima, Liudmila Bredikhina and Junji Ohyama

Abstract

Who do you want to be in the metaverse? The virtual world known as the "metaverse" is attracting attention as a communication service called "Social VR," where people can immerse themselves in realistic experiences through VR headsets. Millions of residents already live there as avatars, leading lives as a "new self." What is the nature of the new identities that emerge in this space? In this chapter, Virtual Girl Nem, a heavy user of Social VR and author of Metaverse Evolution Theory [1], Liudmila Bredikhina, an anthropologist also active as the VTuber "Mila," and Junji Ohyama, a psychologist studying identity in both the physical and virtual worlds, introduce the concept of "Identity in the Metaverse." Discussions are based on quantitative and qualitative data from large-scale online surveys and laboratory experiments to explore the form of Identity in the Metaverse era.

Keywords: metaverse, VR (virtual reality), Social VR, avatar, identity, cyber-physical, experience design, diversity

1. Introduction: Welcome to the world of "Social VR"

Social VR refers to online 3D virtual spaces where communication occurs through avatars, with immersion via VR headsets as a key feature. Approached as a new living space for humanity within virtual reality (VR), it is currently attracting significant attention. Notable services include VRChat (USA), NeosVR (Czech Republic), Resonite (Czech Republic), Cluster (Japan), and Virtual Cast (Japan).

Already, many users live their lives in this virtual world, where entirely new norms and cultures – unimaginable in the physical world – are emerging [1] (see **Figure 1**).

According to our survey [2], more than 90% of Social VR users are on "VRChat." As of New Year's Day 2025, VRChat reached approximately 130,000 concurrent users [3, 4]. Based on this and various other data, Nem estimates that there are millions of active Social VR users worldwide [2]. The global COVID-19 pandemic and falling VR headset prices have caused user numbers to surge in recent years, with a 30% increase in 2025 compared to the previous year [2–4].

However, the high level of anonymity results in the lifestyles and cultures of its residents remaining little known to the general public.

Figure 1.
Residents living in VRChat.

2. Over 5,000 responses from metaverse residents: The "Social VR Lifestyle Survey"

To shed light on the reality of Social VR life, Virtual Girl Nem, a heavy Social VR user, launched the "Social VR Lifestyle Survey" in 2021 together with anthropologist Liudmila Bredikhina ("Mila" in the VR world). Conducted annually and published online [2, 4–6], this survey is likely the first large-scale, platform-agnostic statistical study of Social VR residents worldwide. All survey procedures, full results (including those not cited in this chapter), and limitations have been made publicly available in the form of online reports. However, we present some essential information about the 2023 survey (see **Figure 2**) to facilitate understanding of the subsequent explanation of interesting findings.

- Survey protocol:
  Purpose: To clarify the actual lifestyles of Social VR users.
  Participants: English or Japanese speakers who have used Social VR with a VR headset at least five times in the past year. N = 2007 (Platform: VRChat 1,645, Cluster 146, NeosVR 104, Virtual Cast 94, ChilloutVR 3, Rec Room 3, Roblox 3, Horizon Worlds 3, Others 3; Region: Japan 1547, North America 221, Europe 115, Asia (except Japan) 106, Oceania 11, South America 6, Middle East 1).
  Method: Online public questionnaire.
  Promotion: Through media, communities, and snowball sampling.

- Limitations:
  Survey was conducted voluntarily by Nem and Mila, with respondents recruited anonymously in both Japanese and English through public calls. As such, several limitations should be noted. First, there is a possibility of non-probability sampling

Figure 2.
Social VR Lifestyle Survey 2023.

bias and heavy-user bias due to the open survey method. To minimize these risks, responses were collected from a wide range of users via various media sites and related communities, and the results were compared with those from two previous surveys (1,197 samples in 2021 and 876 samples in 2022) to check for extreme biases. In addition, language bias remains, as the survey was conducted only in English and Japanese. Sample size also affects sampling error; therefore, data analysis was conducted only for categories that met the pre-established minimum sample size (typically at least 70 samples, corresponding to a maximum error of approximately 12%). Other limitations include cross-sectional self-reporting, platform culture effects, and survivorship bias. As of 2025, many people worldwide still do not use the metaverse, and thus, as with any such study, it remains difficult to capture global diversity. Nevertheless, the significance of empirically investigating the lived realities in the Metaverse is substantial.

The survey goes beyond platform usage statistics to explore topics such as romantic relationships in the metaverse and "phantom sense" (sensations felt in VR despite not existing physically) [4]. The results reveal surprising aspects of metaverse life.

By 2024, the total number of responses had exceeded 5,000, with findings presented at academic conferences and at the United Nations' Internet Governance Forum Kyoto 2023 (IGF Kyoto 2023), generating considerable attention.

This chapter presents the latest identity-related data from the 2023 survey and the 2024 survey. The 2024 study, themed "Identity in the Metaverse," was conducted with Professor Ohyama's collaboration as supervisor and included many open-ended qualitative questions [6]. For the qualitative component of the survey, we conducted systematic coding of the open-ended responses. First, a subset of responses was carefully reviewed by the research team to identify major themes, from which a preliminary category framework was developed. Two coders then independently applied this framework to the full dataset, after which their results were compared and reconciled through discussion. Additionally, from the perspectives of categorizations and diversity of responses, we have incorporated representative quotations. Responses were originally written in either Japanese or English; the Japanese responses were translated into English by the authors. The original Japanese texts are available in the source document of the survey.

In a VR world where you can freely choose your avatar's appearance, how do users' identities change? Let us take a look at the diversity of new lifestyles and self-concepts emerging in virtual spaces.

3. "Cosplay of identity" in the metaverse

Psychologist Erik Erikson described identity as a fundamental organizing principle developing throughout life [7]. He stated that feeling comfortable in one's own body is one of the most important conditions for achieving optimal identity. Traditionally, identity was tied closely to one's physical self – name, appearance, voice – and was something to "accept" rather than design by oneself.

In the metaverse, however, users can freely change all three – name, appearance (via avatars), and voice (via voice modulation technology). Unlike the physical world, where individuals cannot change identities with a couple of clicks, the metaverse allows for designing identity and even switching between multiple identities. Nem calls this concept "cosplay of identity" [1].

Just as cosplay enables people to transform into fictional characters in the physical world, metaverse avatars allow people to "wear" an identity as their "soul," not just as clothing.

4. Avatars: Identity in the visual world

Among the three crucial elements of identity – name, appearance, and voice – appearance and visual outlook play a particularly central role in the metaverse, where they take the form of avatars. This section explores metaverse-era identity through avatars-as-bodies from various perspectives. For example, in the Japanese sci-fi anime *Ghost in the Shell: S.A.C. 2nd GIG,* episode 13, "*Face*" (2004), a woman, obsessed with possessing her beloved, steals the shape of his cyborg body and ultimately kills him to replace him entirely. Such stories resonate because appearance is not merely a "tool for tasks" but a marker of identity that proves one's existence.

In the physical world, it is difficult for people to change their bodies, making life heavily influenced by body shape, physical sex, and other aspects of physical appearance – factors that underlie persistent prejudice and discrimination. In contrast, the metaverse will enable complete freedom of bodily design.

Who do you want to be in the metaverse? Face, height, body shape – all can be customized in the metaverse. The appearance need not match one's physical body; one can live as male, female, or even nonhuman – robot, monster, or supernatural being. Through avatars, people can design their identity and live as their "desired self." In metaverse societies, where communication occurs without reference to physical traits, prejudice based on bodily attributes may increasingly be seen as obsolete. Let us now examine what kinds of avatars people actually use in Social VR.

5. Avatar appearance: Both men and women choose feminine avatars

Among the visual traits of avatars, feminine or masculine avatar appearance is especially important since it is often regarded as central to identity in the physical world. In avatars, however, users can adopt any appearance, regardless of their sex in the physical world.

To distinguish between avatar appearance (masculine or feminine) and sex in the physical world, survey participants were asked: "Please state your sex in the physical world." This was labeled as "physical sex." This expression was chosen to avoid discrimination, respect diversity, and examine how avatar appearance is expressed in the metaverse, where diverse self-identifications may not be fully recognized by society. In the 2023 survey, when asked, "Does your avatar (the one you use the most) look masculine or feminine?" results revealed a striking imbalance: Regardless of physical sex, about 80% of respondents used female avatars. By contrast, only 8% of physical females used male avatars. Overall, about 60% of Social VR users used avatars of the opposite appearance (see **Figure 3**). "avatar appearance" implies an avatar's visual characteristics, such as feminine- and/or masculine-looking avatars. Since we did not explicitly ask respondents about their gender identity, nonbinary persons may have answered as "others" or may have responded in terms of physical characteristics or sex assigned at birth. Therefore, in this survey, it is not possible to clearly distinguish these categories in the analysis.

By region, female avatars predominated across all areas – exceeding 60% in North America and Europe and reaching a remarkable 78% in Japan. By platform, VRChat and Virtual Cast exhibited particularly high proportions of female avatars (approximately 80%), whereas NeosVR and Cluster were closer to 60% (see **Figure 4**). These findings suggest pronounced cultural differences among platforms.

6. Living in the desired appearance

One of the first reasons that come to mind for why someone might use an avatar of the opposite appearance from their physical sex is incongruence between their mind and body. **Figure 5** shows the results of the question: "If you use an avatar with an 'opposite' appearance from your physical sex (ex., you are male and use a feminine-looking avatar), please select the primary reason."

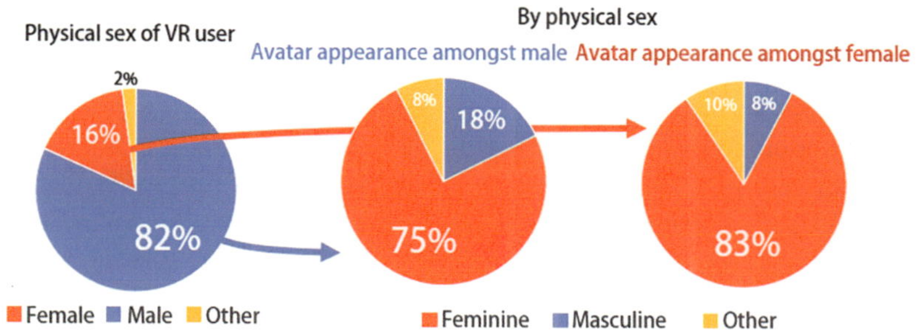

Figure 3.
Physical sex and avatar appearance.

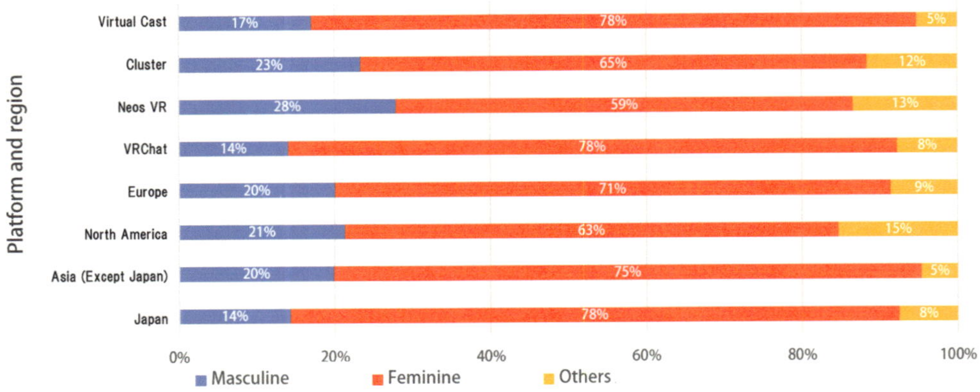

Figure 4.
Avatar appearance by platform and region.

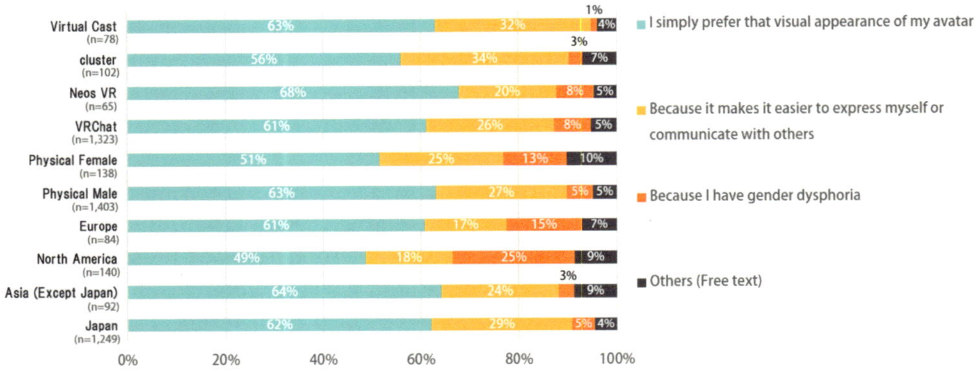

Figure 5.
Why choose a different avatar appearance?.

On VRChat, 8% said they did so because they felt an incongruence between body and mind. Broken down further, this was cited by 25% of North American users and 13% of physical females. This finding is consistent with the presence of transgender individuals in Social VR at a certain proportion.

Preliminary laboratory experiments conducted by Ohyama and Hanashima provided additional indicative evidence supporting these survey results. Participants were asked about their spectrum of gender identity using the implicit gender identity test, and to use an avatar congruent or incongruent with their sex assigned at birth, and then rate their sense of body ownership (Does this avatar feel like your own body?). If gender identity is similar to their sex assigned at birth, incongruent gender avatars reduce the sense of ownership. However, when participants' gender identity leaned toward the opposite sex, they reported a stronger sense of ownership with incongruent avatars. These findings are reported here only as supplementary context and should be regarded as preliminary until formally published.

These results suggest that transgender individuals can live more authentically when using avatars aligned with their gender identity. Thus, although "gender incongruence" is not the primary reason for adopting incongruent gender avatars, it represents a significant and effective use of the metaverse for fostering self-authenticity.

7. Reasons for the preference of feminine avatars

Across Social VR as a whole, 75% of the users who chose feminine avatars were physically male. Why do men want to become women in the metaverse? Our survey revealed three main reasons:

(1). Want to be cute

The first and most common reason can be described as a fashion-like desire to appear cute. The top reason given by physically male users for choosing female avatars was simply, "because I like the avatar's appearance" (63%). Given that cute female characters are overwhelmingly popular in anime and other media, users could be interested in adopting popular cute appearances.

In the physical world, it is not easy for men to cosplay as female characters, but in the metaverse, such limitations do not exist. Additionally, women generally have a broader range of fashion options than men, with more available outfits and accessories, which makes "becoming female to enjoy fashion" a frequently heard opinion. In other words, feminine avatars in the metaverse seem to embody a significant "fashion" dimension.

Figure 6 presents responses from the 2024 survey, themed "Identity in the Metaverse," highlighting the most frequent open-ended answers from physically male respondents about why they use feminine avatars. In the 2024 survey, as well, "want to be cute" emerged as a common response.

(2). Needs for expressing emotions

The second reason (27%) was that female avatars make it easier to express oneself and communicate. In cultures such as Japan's, men are often expected to be stoic and unemotional. By using feminine avatars, men can more freely show

Major reason	Examples
1. To be cute (209/558)	• I want to look cute in virtual reality • i not sure , but maybe feminine usually more cute
2. Personal preference for feminine avatars (84/558)	• The avatar that becomes your alter ego will always be in your field of vision, even if it is modified, so it is desirable to have an appearance that you find attractive • I generally prefer feminine avatars. They fit my style better and vrchat has a wider variety of assets for feminine avatars.
3. To be different myself (79/558)	• I think one of the appeals of VR is that you can become a different version of yourself than you are in the real world • I've always felt that something was wrong with me, and in vrc after becoming a feminine avatar, it felt so liberating. I've never felt so happy with my portrayal of who I was and am like this before and that's why I chose this appearance
Extra interesting reason • To fit in with others or because there are more options (45/558)	• Highly fashionable and easy to look at
• To be liberated from being "male" (25/558)	• Because the status of "being a man" felt painful

Figure 6.
Why do men use "feminine avatars"?.

their feelings without intimidating others. Feminine avatars, therefore, function as tools for emotional expression. From the open-ended responses in the 2024 survey, some male respondents mentioned a desire to escape from the pressures of conforming to socially stereotypical notions of masculinity.

(3). Needs for getting closer to others

Feminine avatars facilitate physical and psychological closeness in communication. Psychological studies show that women generally maintain smaller personal spaces than men, and women interacting with other women are the closest of all [8, 9]. In VRChat and Virtual Cast, "cuddly" female-to-female interactions (rare among men in reality) are common. This closeness makes female avatars effective tools for reducing interpersonal distance. Although no empirical data could be identified to substantiate this claim, the author Nem – who has been a heavy user of Social VR since its earliest stages worldwide – observes from personal experience that the use of cute feminine avatars for close-range communication and social touch has become common, even in everyday interactions (e.g., see **Figure 7**).

Thus, while gender incongruence explains some cases, most men use feminine avatars for self-expression and communication reasons.

8. Diversity of avatar species

Beyond gender, another striking trait is avatar type or "species." In Social VR, users can be anything – schoolgirl, angel, giant robot, dog, or even an avatar close to one's physical world appearance (see **Figure 8**). To study this diversity, researchers categorized avatars into seven species groups after field research and user interviews:

Humanoid type

- *Humanoid* – close to humans in the physical world (e.g., anime-style girls, photorealistic avatars).

Figure 7.
Common close-range communication and social touch with cute feminine avatars.

Figure 8.
Examples of avatar species.

- *Semi-humanoid* – human-like with added fantasy elements, such as cat ears, tails, etc. (e.g., cat girls, fox spirits, angels).
- *Humanoid robots or cyborgs* – partly or fully mechanical, human-like bodies.

Nonhumanoid type

- *Animals* – nonfantasy animals, nonhuman form.
- *Plants* – nonfantasy plants (e.g., leek, tree, radish).
- *Monsters* – Fantasy animal or plant, nonhumanoid (e.g., tentacled aliens, dragons, skeletons).
- *Others* – anything not fitting above (e.g., oscilloscopes, cars, nonhumanoid robots).

Users' self-perceptions determined classification; for example, a cat-ear avatar could count as "humanoid" (if the ears are accessories) or "semi-humanoid" (if the ears are part of the body).

To obtain a statistical understanding of the distribution of actual avatar types used, we asked users, "What type of avatar do you use the most often?" in the survey conducted in 2023 (see **Figure 9**).

As a result, humanoid-type avatars dominated overall, accounting for 94%. Within this category, semi-humanoids led at 47%, surpassing humanoids at 41%. Humanoid robots or cyborgs made up 4%, while nonhumanoid types were rare.

Why are semi-humanoids preferred? **Figure 10** shows open-ended responses regarding the reasons for choosing semi-humanoids. The results indicated desires to

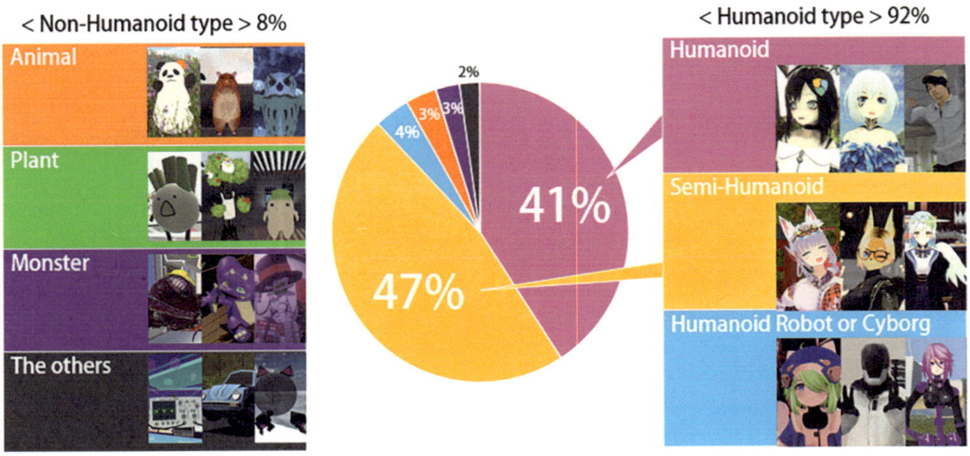

Figure 9.
Avatar species distribution survey.

Major reason	Examples
1. To be cute (180/511)	• It looks cute, and it feels right. I'm just comfortable in it I guess. • I want to exist as a cute girl in the virtual world because in the real world, I'm just a scruffy old man.
2. To get a uniqueness different from my physical self or personal preference (120/511)	• I wear ears and a tail as a sign that I am different from my real self. • Because it matches my preferences.
3. Liked the look (83/511)	• When I was looking at Booth, it suddenly caught my eye and I liked it. • i enjoy the character style and have for a long time.
Extra interesting reason • Furry fandom (39/511)	• I'm very involved in the furry fandom and want a more interesting form.

Figure 10.
Reasons for choosing semi-humanoids.

be "cuter" or to experience "specialness different from real life." Fantasy traits such as animal ears or wings accentuate individuality.

Interestingly, although all the people are human-shaped in the physical world, the distribution of choosing humanoid-type avatars dropped below half in the metaverse. This suggests a tension: Avatars must be human-like enough for communication, yet users prefer not to be bound by real-life human form when expressing identity.

As shown in **Figure 11**, platform differences were also evident. NeosVR, for instance, had only 34% plain humans, while animal and monster avatars were more common, reflecting its "furry culture." By contrast, VRChat favored anime-style humans.

9. Cognitive and behavioral changes induced by avatar use

Yee and Bailenson (2007) defined the Proteus Effect as the process whereby "an individual's behavior conforms to their digital self-representation independent of how others perceive them [10]." As with the Proteus Effect, it is known that the appearance of an avatar can influence the behavior and cognition of its user. For example, participants using muscular avatars in immersive VR reported

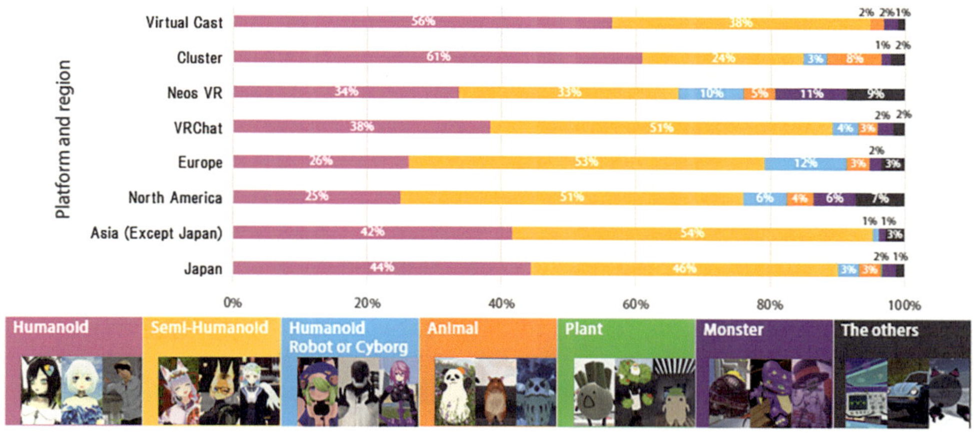

Figure 11.
Distribution of avatar species by platform and region.

approximately 16% lower pain on the Pain Assessment Scale compared to those using average-body avatars. The effect was strongest when avatar and participant gender matched, particularly for male users – illustrating how a muscular avatar can enhance perceived physical resilience [11]. In the case of cognitive change, the use of a dark-skinned avatar reduced implicit racial bias in light-skinned participants [12].

In the 2024 survey, respondents were asked, "Does your behavior in Social VR (such as the way you speak, react, and act) differ from how you behave in the physical real world?," and 62% answered, "somewhat different."

Open-ended responses revealed that people became more social and outgoing, adjusted their behaviors to match their avatars' appearance, and felt liberated from physical-world roles. Some even changed their movement styles or speech patterns. Avatars act as mirrors of the mind, reshaping personality itself.

10. Influence of VR Life: 92% report positive effects

In the 2024 survey, we also asked respondents, "How does your life in Social VR generally influence your life in the physical world?," and 92% answered, "positive."

The reasons for these positive effects include the expansion of social connections, improvements in mental health, and the broadening of values and learning.

Negative effects cited included spending excessive time in VR, which reduced focus on physical life, sleep deprivation, and physical or mental strain caused by overuse or interpersonal conflicts. Thus, while VR life is overwhelmingly beneficial, it requires balance to avoid harmful side effects.

11. Do users hide their VR identity? 55% said "no"

When asked, "Do you keep your identity in Social VR hidden from your friends or family in the physical world?" in the 2024 survey, 55% said, "*no*" Results were similar across regions.

Reasons for hiding included fear of prejudice, generational gaps, and the desire to separate physical and virtual lives. Reasons for not hiding included viewing physical and virtual as connected and wanting to promote the metaverse.

This suggests that disclosure depends largely on personal values and circumstances, though many still feel that physical society is unready to accept VR identities.

12. Main identity in life: Which is the "true self"?

Respondents were asked: "If you have different identities in Social VR and the physical world, in the future, would you want your Social VR identity to become your main identity in your life rather than your real world identity?" in the 2024 survey.

Surprisingly, 13% answered that identity in Social VR is already their main identity, and 26% want identity in VR to be their main identity in the future (see **Figure 12**). Reasons for wanting VR as their main identity include being their desired self, better self-expression, and living more positively. Reasons against include preferring separation, valuing physical reality, or seeing VR as "just a hobby/game."

13. Social and self-augmentation through the metaverse

Up to this point, we have examined how identity and communication are affected based on surveys of people who incorporate the metaverse into their daily lives. As of 2025, people cannot live solely within virtual space. As such, the lives of metaverse users will inevitably unfold within a cyber-physical society – a world in which cyber space and physical space are interconnected, or in which physical space is extended and augmented by cyber space.

At such a time, one might feel that the physical body – difficult to alter in accordance with identity – constrains authentic ways of living. However, we anticipate that society will not fall into a negative, dichotomous situation of "cyber space versus real space."

Multiple academic studies have shown that using an avatar resembling one's physical body increases the sense of body ownership – that is, the feeling that the avatar is one's own body – more than when using avatars that do not resemble one's body [13, 14]. On the other hand, as with the Proteus Effect discussed earlier, prior research reports that embodying a body that looks different from one's physical self can reduce prejudice toward people with different physical characteristics [12].

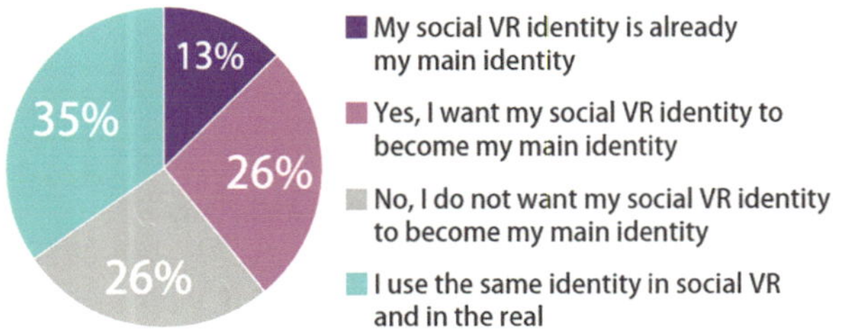

Figure 12.
Main identity in life.

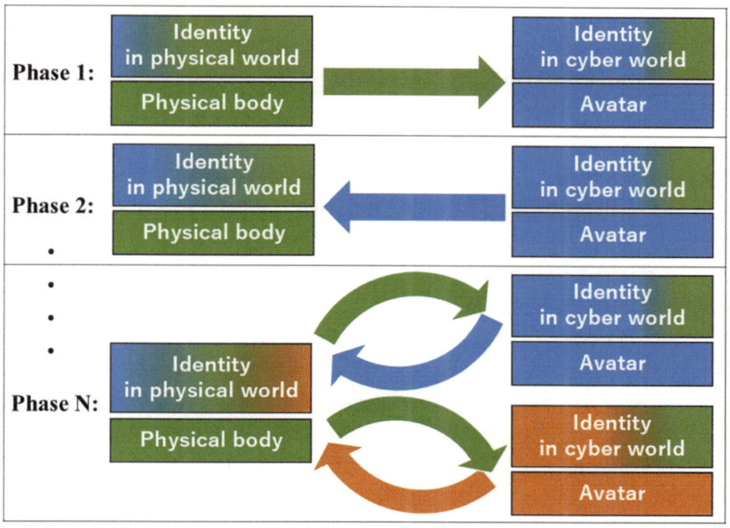

Figure 13.
Circulation model of identity in the cyber-physical world.

Based on these academic findings, the relationship between the self in the physical world and the self in the cyber world can be diagrammed as shown in **Figure 13**.

Phase 1 represents the stage of beginning to use the metaverse, showing the influence of physical world identity and body on experiences with avatars in the cyber world. Physical world identity does not always align with the physical body. Using an avatar different from one's physical body may initially feel more awkward than using one resembling the physical body. At the same time, in the cyber world – the metaverse – users tend to behave, to some extent, in line with the personality traits implied by the appearance of their avatars. See Section 15 for discussion on how people estimate an avatar's personality from its appearance (body image).

Phase 2 represents the impact of using an avatar different from one's physical body in the cyber world on physical world identity. Experiencing interactions in the metaverse through a body different from one's preexisting physical world self can bring new perspectives and insights to one's physical world identity as well.

Continued use of avatars in the cyber world reduces the initial discomfort felt toward them, and avatar-based experiences are perceived with greater reality. In this way, experiences in the physical and cyber worlds influence one another cyclically.

As phases progress further, users may begin to use different avatars across different cyber worlds or communities. In such cases, the self at that time is shaped within each world or community, while simultaneously influencing the physical-world self. Identity is inherently multifaceted, and avatars that allow easier expression of such facets may, in extreme cases, lead to transformations that could be called identity changes. However, in most cases, using a body different from one's physical body allows people to observe themselves more objectively or to take the perspective of others, resulting in new insights about the self and others. This can be compared to entering a new school or workplace, or traveling to an unfamiliar culture: Encounters with new people and environments are stimulating and anxiety-provoking, but they provide opportunities for self-discovery and a stronger sense of connection to society.

The metaverse, with its potential to construct worlds far broader than the physical one, expands not only society but also the self. Thus, the expansion from a purely physical-world society to a cyber-physical society, including the metaverse, can be expected to augment the self and help realize a society in which people understand one another more deeply.

As mentioned at the beginning of this chapter, we argue that it is not appropriate to draw a sharp distinction between the existing physical world and the cyber world of the metaverse as "real" versus "virtual." The reason is that the metaverse has already become part of people's *real lives*.

Moreover, for those whose physical bodies do not align with their identities, life in the metaverse – using an avatar consistent with their self-identity – may feel more real than life in the physical world.

Humans receive information about the world through the five senses and the body as physical stimuli. Yet, the vast multimodal information we perceive is subject to selection, integration, and transformation by the sensory organs, cognitive processing in the brain, and top-down influences from past memory and learning. The world is recognized only after this internal cognitive processing. Thus, we do not observe the physical world objectively *as it is*.

For example, when several people travel together, each person's "real" travel experience may differ. Conversely, when reading a novel, one may vividly feel the protagonist's experiences as if they were their own. In this sense, the "real world" exists individually within each person's brain or mind.

In the metaverse, both body and environment can be tailored to the world one imagines. Therefore, experiences in the metaverse can become as real – or even more real – than those in the physical world because they resonate directly with the reality perceived in one's brain and mind.

14. The era of designing identity: How to create the best "self"?

What does VR identity mean to each individual? As we have seen, there are as many earnest answers as there are people. In this world, where a completely new lifestyle – switching between multiple identities – has only just begun to materialize, countless users are now struggling and experimenting in their own ways.

How should one design the self in VR? What avatar appearance should it be? What species should it be? How should one navigate between multiple selves and multiple relationships? How should one combine and balance VR with physical reality?

Challenges certainly remain, but the fact is that many users feel they can be more authentically themselves in Social VR than in the physical world. By analyzing the realities of these identities, we may have glimpsed a future where people can live truer to themselves – a future that is easier for everyone to inhabit.

Who do you want to be in the metaverse? The doors to the metaverse era are already open to you.

15. For the future of metaverse: Ethical and social perspectives

While there are various concerns regarding the use of the metaverse, many of these have not yet been sufficiently examined with scientific evidence. As authors, we wish to avoid unnecessarily amplifying such anxieties. Many of the ethical issues in the metaverse overlap with those already encountered in social networking services (SNSs). Although SNSs have generated new social challenges, they have spread widely due to their overwhelmingly positive value. Likewise, discussions about the metaverse should not focus merely on whether to use technology but rather on how individuals and society can experiment with positive ways of using it.

On this basis, we discuss one particularly important feature that differentiates the metaverse from SNS: embodiment. Ohyama, together with members of Japan's metaverse industry, established a domestic committee for the international standardization of avatars. This committee has been discussing the minimum ethical and social considerations that should form a global common foundation for avatar use. Virtual Girl Nem, one of the authors of this chapter, participates as a representative of metaverse users. Key items identified as desirable considerations for metaverse systems, applications, content, or services are summarized in **Table 1**.

Item 1 may seem self-evident, but, as noted above, avatar "species" are highly diverse, and the first image users have of an avatar can vary depending on national culture or the worldview of a given platform. For example, a user who expects a photorealistic avatar may instead encounter an anime-style avatar. A user who expects a full-body avatar may instead find only the face and hands displayed. Since avatars are experienced as one's body, it is recommended that users be given at least a general idea of what kind of avatar they will inhabit before the experience begins. However, it is not realistic to list every possible detail, but ensuring that accessible information is available at the outset regarding the type of avatar to be used is not difficult. At the same time, in cases where the purpose of the experience requires deliberately withholding information about the avatar to be used, prior disclosure is not necessary. Ohyama conducted an online survey about avatar's appearance and personality image from their appearance in Japan. In the experiment, 300 women and 300 men in their twenties (*Mean* = 25.88; *SD* = 2.53) were randomly presented with figures of 10 different avatars as shown in **Figure 14**.

For each avatar, participants were asked about the personality impression they perceived from their appearance. Personality was assessed using the Japanese version of the Ten Item Personality Inventory developed by Oshio et al. [15]. **Table 2** shows the means and variances of the personality ratings for each avatar.

1	Users should be informed in advance that the experience involves the use of avatars and what type of avatars will be used.
2	Users should have accessible information about what data are collected during avatar use and how those data are utilized.
3	Users should be informed in advance about the extent to which violent or sexual expressions through avatars are permitted.
4	Preventive measures and responses should be prepared to address impersonation and human rights violations.
5	The degree of experiential reality should be designed to be necessary and sufficient for the intended purpose.

Table 1.
Main ethical considerations for avatar use.

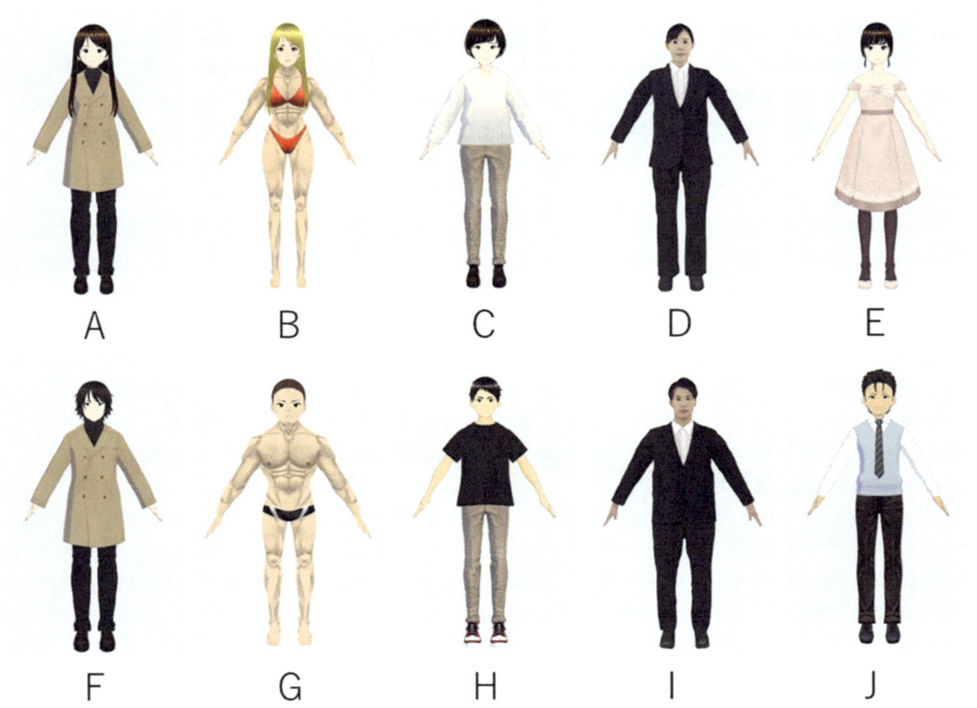

Figure 14.
Avatar images used in the experiment.

The values in the table represent the mean, and the values in parentheses indicate the standard deviation (SD).

Although individual differences exist, on average, some avatars were perceived as more "agreeableness" but less "extraversion," while others were perceived as more "openness." This suggests that personality impressions derived from an avatar's appearance are, to some extent, commonly shared among observers.

In this survey, we also asked participants to rate the degree to which they felt their own personality resembled the avatar's perceived personality, and the degree to which their own appearance resembled the avatar's appearance using seven-point Likert scale. **Figure 15** shows a histogram of the differences between similarity evaluations of personality and appearance (personality similarity – appearance similarity).

In each graph, the bin between greater than –1 and up to 0 indicates the number of respondents who evaluated personality similarity as equal to or slightly lower than appearance similarity. For all avatars, this bin contained the largest number of respondents. This indicates that, in general, perceived similarity in appearance and perceived similarity in personality to avatars are felt to be roughly equivalent.

On the other hand, for about 15% to 30% of participants, the difference between appearance similarity and personality similarity was larger. In other words, some participants felt that although the avatar did not resemble their appearance, its perceived personality was similar to their own (the positive side of the bins in each graph of **Figure 15**). This suggests that some individuals may not feel their physical-

Avatar	Female [Mean (SD)]					Male [Mean (SD)]				
	E	A	C	N	O	E	A	C	N	O
A	3.52 (1.09)	4.64 (1.04)	4.39 (0.92)	4.09 (0.91)	3.81 (0.91)	3.74 (1.04)	4.60 (1.08)	4.30 (0.93)	4.13 (0.80)	4.07 (0.89)
B	5.11 (1.37)	3.93 (1.07)	4.67 (1.25)	4.45 (0.97)	4.53 (1.08)	4.93 (1.21)	4.02 (1.02)	4.64 (1.12)	4.41 (0.91)	4.51 (1.10)
C	3.53 (1.08)	4.49 (1.04)	4.41 (1.07)	4.18 (0.85)	3.88 (0.83)	3.65 (0.98)	4.41 (1.00)	4.29 (0.88)	4.13 (0.90)	3.89 (0.82)
D	3.78 (0.95)	4.32 (1.05)	4.44 (1.07)	4.10 (0.93)	3.78 (0.88)	3.88 (0.95)	4.30 (1.09)	4.37 (1.05)	4.27 (0.94)	3.93 (0.88)
E	4.18 (1.11)	4.03 (1.07)	4.08 (0.88)	4.05 (0.82)	4.13 (0.86)	4.31 (1.09)	4.06 (1.13)	4.11 (0.95)	4.05 (0.94)	4.26 (0.89)
F	3.56 (1.15)	4.25 (0.97)	4.14 (0.92)	4.08 (0.88)	3.92 (0.91)	3.88 (1.01)	4.31 (0.99)	4.22 (0.99)	4.29 (0.89)	4.06 (0.96)
G	4.97 (1.32)	3.89 (1.09)	4.71 (1.24)	4.35 (0.97)	4.38 (1.03)	4.95 (1.26)	3.97 (1.11)	4.70 (1.20)	4.43 (1.01)	4.37 (1.03)
H	4.31 (1.09)	4.30 (0.98)	4.17 (1.00)	4.29 (0.87)	3.84 (0.85)	4.29 (1.05)	4.36 (1.01)	4.28 (0.88)	4.30 (0.87)	3.87 (0.93)
I	4.03 (1.11)	4.43 (0.91)	4.19 (1.00)	4.19 (0.89)	3.91 (0.86)	4.10 (1.02)	4.26 (0.99)	4.16 (1.06)	4.27 (0.91)	3.88 (0.90)
J	4.72 (1.22)	3.66 (1.03)	4.12 (1.03)	4.29 (0.86)	4.23 (0.98)	4.71 (1.17)	3.82 (1.03)	4.22 (1.03)	4.23 (0.94)	4.24 (0.96)

Note: E, Extraversion; A, Agreeableness; C, Conscientiousness; N, Neuroticism; O, Openness.

Table 2.
Personality impressions of avatars.

world appearance matches their personality and, therefore, may feel more comfortable living in a body in the metaverse that better reflects their personality. Conversely, some participants felt that although an avatar's appearance resembled their own, its perceived personality was dissimilar (the negative side of the bins in each graph of **Figure 15**). In such cases, using such avatars might lead individuals to behave more in line with the personality impressions conveyed by the avatar rather than with their own physical-world self.

Item 2 in **Table 1** concerns the protection of personal information. In SNS and e-commerce, the secondary use of personal data has already been identified as a major issue. In avatar-based experiences, information such as body movement, gaze, facial expression, and voice is often collected in order to operate the avatar as one's body. It is essential that users be able to confirm, whenever they wish, what kinds of information are collected and how they are being used, so that such information is not gathered without consent or repurposed in ways different from those agreed upon.

Item 3 is important from two perspectives: appearance and behavior. Regarding appearance, care should be taken to ensure that users are not forced to inhabit avatars with highly revealing clothing against their will. Regarding behavior, safeguards are needed not only against violent actions directed toward the user's avatar but also in cases where a user's avatar is made to perform violent actions against others. Recent research has reported that when an avatar is covertly manipulated from outside to

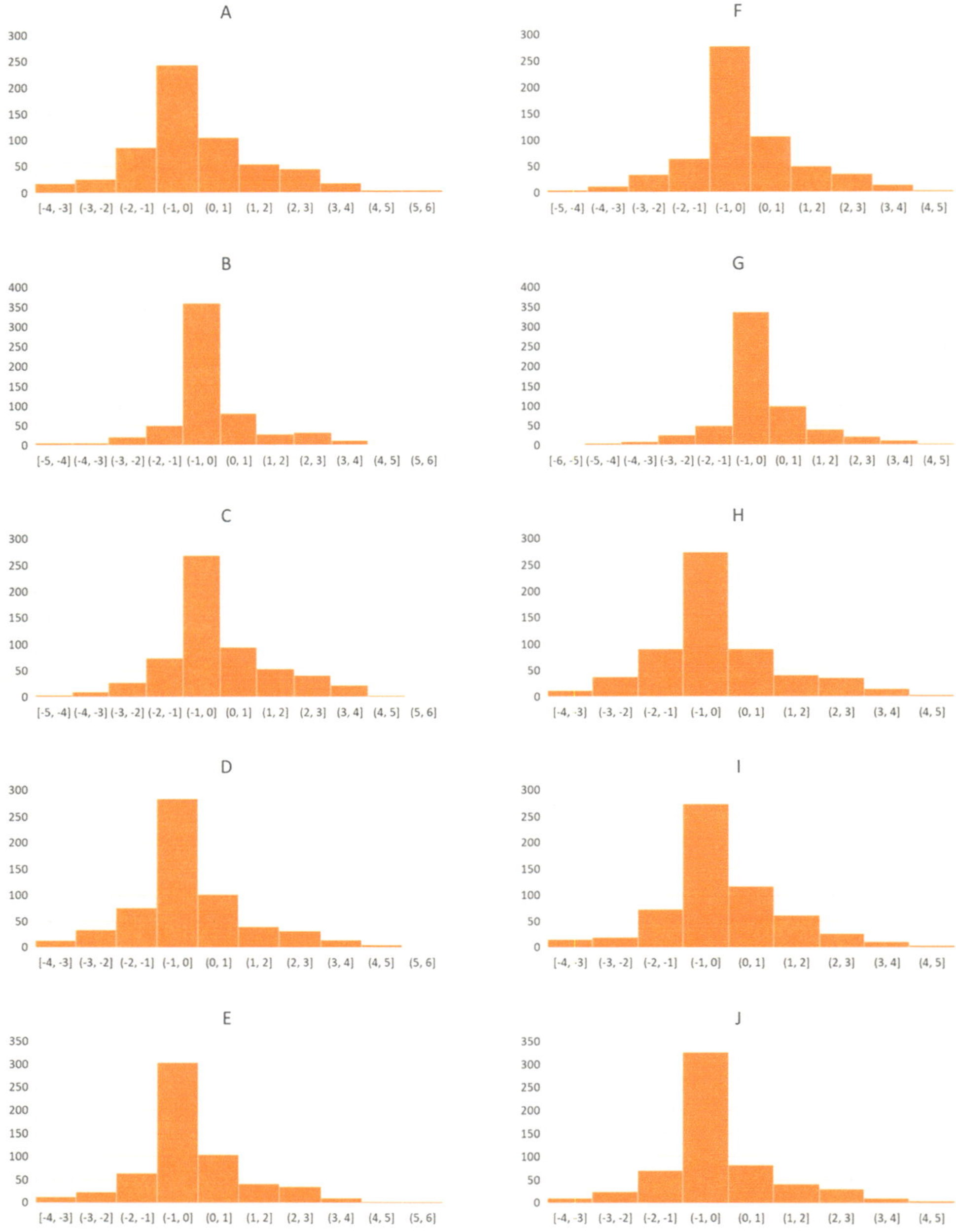

Figure 15.
Histogram of the difference between the perceived similarity in personality and appearance of avatars compared with the self. The calculation was defined as personality minus appearance (i.e., appearance was subtracted from personality).

display movements different from those the user actually performs, the user may mistakenly believe they themselves carried out those actions.

Item 4 extends to the creation and operation of avatars. The ability to become one's desired self in the metaverse, without relying on one's physical-world name, appearance, or voice, is a remarkable feature. Yet, this also makes malicious impersonation possible. Although not involving avatars, lawsuits have already occurred concerning digital characters. A well-known case is the character *Pepe* from the 2005 comic *Boy's Club*, which was repurposed as discriminatory and violent memes far removed from the creator's original intent, raising issues of image infringement [16]. With avatars too, problematic uses that contradict the creator's intended character are emerging, and instances of avatars being sold that closely resemble specific existing avatars are often observed. In Japan's international standardization committee, countermeasures under discussion include embedding usage conditions and information about the legal rights holder directly into avatar data formats. The crucial point, however, is to avoid imposing rules that would force users to adopt avatars resembling their physical selves in order to curb malicious uses. Importing such physical-world restrictions into the metaverse would undermine its potential to expand both self and society.

Furthermore, generative AI has made it possible to create CG models of public figures, such as prime ministers, and have them act in ways that defame their reputation without their consent. AI is increasingly capable of producing human-like behaviors that are indistinguishable in appearance from real people. While it is desirable for AI to support people as AI, when AI replaces real individuals in daily contexts and convincingly impersonates them as if they were real, unforeseen problems may arise. The functionality of AI has advanced to the point where, depending on the domain, it can already respond with greater speed and accuracy than humans. Yet, if AI interacts socially as if it were a real person, deeper discussion will be required regarding AI's user interface and its role within human society.

Item 5 is one of the most important perspectives for the wider adoption of the metaverse. Until now, we have focused mainly on the metaverse as Social VR, but it is also valuable as a digital twin for education and training. In such applications, less realism may sometimes be more effective. As noted earlier, the cyber world can feel real when it approximates the mental image that users perceive as reality. Therefore, even with current VR technology, appropriately designed experiences can produce realism comparable to that of the physical world. For example, prior studies have shown that simulated virtual experiences can be effective for PTSD exposure therapy [17]. However, in educational content such as horror or accident simulations (e.g., amputation or falls) or other traumatic scenarios, excessive continuity with reality may pose psychological risks. A notable (though anecdotal) case reported strong stress responses from a user whose avatar was decapitated in VR [18]. As content realism increases, such risks may become more serious. To address this, Ohyama has proposed, as shown in **Table 3**, four levels of body reality tailored to the purpose of use, along with questionnaire items for evaluating them [19].

Level 4 corresponds to the question widely used in evaluating body ownership and indicates a state in which one feels that the experience is occurring in their own physical body in the physical world.

Level 3 indicates a state in which, while understanding that the experience is taking place in the cyber world different from the physical world, it is nonetheless felt as one's own experience.

Level 2, by contrast, refers to the experience of playing a character in cyberspace that is not oneself. In Social VR, the sensation of communicating with others while using an avatar that does not resemble one's real self – either as oneself or role-playing as a character imagined from the avatar's appearance – corresponds to Level 3 or Level 2 body reality.

Level	Experience	Questionnaire
4	Same as the real user's body in real world.	"I felt that the body I saw during the experience was same as my own body in the real world."
3	User's own body in the cyber world.	"I felt that the body I saw during the experience was my own body in the cyber (experienced) world."
2	Acting someone other than themselves in the cyber world.	"I felt like I was playing the role of someone in the cyber (experienced) world."
1	Viewing or reliving other character's experience in the cyber world.	"I felt viewing someone else's experience from their body."

Table 3.
Body Reality Index (BRI).

Level 1 indicates a state in which one does not act by their own will but instead feels as if they are reliving another person's experience through that person's body. Even in this state, as with watching a film, people can empathize with the characters and feel their experiences as real.

For safety-training content that recreates accidents or disasters, where psychological risk is a concern, it may be effective to intentionally design for Level 1 body reality rather than Level 2 or higher. In other words, the Level 4 body reality – long regarded as essential in VR research on body ownership – is not necessarily required in all VR content or metaverse experiences. Going forward, it will be important to deliberately design experiences to achieve the necessary and sufficient level of embodiment for the intended purpose. This variation in levels of reality, which cannot be designed in the physical world, will further enhance the experiential value of the metaverse.

Similar to the issues in SNS, guidelines will be needed to protect privacy and identities of minors or prevent impersonation; however, there is not sufficient global knowledge to clarify the situations, facts, and countermeasures in the use of the metaverse. In other words, the metaverse holds many possibilities, including uses that have not yet been conceived, and it is important to avoid constraining such possibilities without clear evidence. There remains room for discussion on what kinds of rules should be established and at what levels. At present, we have begun discussions with international experts within ISO/IEC.

Conflict of Interest

The authors declare no conflict of interest with respect to the research presented in this chapter.

Data and materials' availability

The anonymized datasets from the 2023 and 2024 surveys, together with the full questionnaires in Japanese and English, are available at [insert repository name/URL]. Access to the data shown in this chapter is provided by contacting the authors directly.

The raw survey data are not publicly available, as respondents did not provide informed consent for data sharing beyond the purposes of this study. Interested readers may contact the authors for further information about the survey design and analysis procedures.

Author details

Nem Samejima[1], Liudmila Bredikhina[2] and Junji Ohyama[3]*

1 VTuber “Virtual Girl Nem”, Writer

2 VRChater “Mila”

3 AIST, The University of Tsukuba, Japan

*Address all correspondence to: j.ohyama@aist.go.jp

References

[1] Nem VG. Metaverse Evolution Theory, Gijutsu-Hyoron-sya. 2021. Available from: https://medium.com/@nemchan_nel/f8d234ae826c. [Accessed: 2025-November-18]

[2] Nem VG, Mila (Liudmila Bredikhina). Metaverse Demographic Report 2025. Nem X Mila, 2025. 2025. Available from: https://medium.com/@nemchan_nel/cc1e71405a14 [Accessed: 2025-November-18]

[3] Foorack. VRChat API Metrics. n d. Available from https://metrics.vrchat.community [Accessed: 2025-November-18]

[4] Nem VG, Mila (Liudmila Bredikhina). Social VR Lifestyle Survey 2021. Nem X Mila. 2021. Available from: https://medium.com/@nemchan_nel/social-vr-lifestyle-survey-2021-5914c35ec063 [Accessed: 2025-November-18]

[5] Nem VG, Mila (Liudmila Bredikhina). Social VR Lifestyle Survey 2023. Nem X Mila. 2023. Available from: https://medium.com/@nemchan_nel/a61d1c4cae33 [Accessed: 2025-November-18]

[6] Nem VG, and Mila (Liudmila Bredikhina). Identity in Metaverse: Social VR Lifestyle Survey 2024. Nem X Mila. 2024. Available from: https://medium.com/@nemchan_nel/1b61700b89a1 [Accessed: 2025-November-18]

[7] Erikson EH. Identity: Youth and Crisis. New York: Norton & Co.; 1968

[8] Sommer R. Small group ecology. Psychological Bulletin. 1967;**67**(2): 145–152. DOI: 10.1037/h0024201

[9] Patterson ML, Schaeffer RE. Effects of size and sex composition on interaction distance, participation, and satisfaction in small groups. Small Group Behavior. 1977;**8**(4):433–442. DOI: 10.1177/104649647700800403

[10] Yee N, Bailenson J. The Proteus effect: The effect of transformed self-representation on behavior. Human Communication Research. 2007;**33**(3):271–290

[11] Yim Y, Xia Z, Kubota Y, Tanaka F. The proteus effects on human pain perception through avatar muscularity and gender factors. Scientific Reports. 2024;**141**:11332

[12] Banakou D, Hanumanthu PD, Slater M. Virtual embodiment of white people in a black virtual body leads to a sustained reduction in their implicit racial bias. Frontiers in Human Neuroscience. 2016;**10**:601

[13] Blanke O, Metzinger T. Full-body illusions and minimal phenomenal selfhood. Trends in Cognitive Sciences. 2009;**13**(1):7–13

[14] Hanashima R, Ohyama J. How to elicit ownership and agency for an avatar presented in the third-person perspective: The effect of visuo-motor and tactile feedback. In: *International Conference on Human-Computer Interaction*. Cham: Springer International Publishing; 2022. (pp. 111–130)

[15] Oshio A, Abe S, Cutrone P. Development, reliability, and validity of the Japanese version of Ten Item Personality Inventory (TIPI-J). The Japanese Journal of Personality.

2012;**21**:40–52. DOI: 10.2132/personality.21.40

[16] Furie M. *Pepe the Frog's Creator: I'm Reclaiming Him. He Was Never About Hate. Time*. 2016- October-13. Available from Time.com [Accessed: 2025-November-18]

[17] Tielman ML, Neerincx MA, Bidarra R, Kybartas B, Brinkman WP. A therapy system for post-traumatic stress disorder using a virtual agent and virtual storytelling to reconstruct traumatic memories. Journal of Medical Systems. 2017;**41**(8):125

[18] MoguLive. In VR, at the guillotine... the "strange reaction" that occurred in the user the moment the blade fell. Available from: https://www.moguravr.com/vr-guillotine/ [Accessed: 2025-November-18]

[19] Ohyama J. A Proposal for a Common Platform and Methodology for Evaluating xR Experiences. 2025:479–482. DOI: 10.1109/ISMAR-Adjunct68609.2025.00096

Chapter 13

Seeing the Unseen: Augmented Reality for Environmental Awareness in the Metaverse

Barbara Buljat Raymond

Abstract

How can immersive technologies in the Metaverse drive environmental action? This chapter explores the potential of augmented reality (AR) for environmental awareness by presenting a conceptual prototype that vividly illustrates animals trapped in plastic pollution. Designed to evoke emotional responses and stimulate reflection, the AR experience leverages affective storytelling to make distant or invisible ecological crises more tangible to the public. To assess its effectiveness and practical implementation, the chapter draws on qualitative interviews with nine experts in the domain of environmental communication. The rigorous analysis of rich empirical data reveals valuable insights into immersive design principles, user engagement strategies, and AR technical requirements. The chapter concludes with recommendations for integrating such technologies into broader sustainability efforts and outlines policy implications for future Metaverse-based sustainability initiatives.

Keywords: augmented reality (AR), environmental communication, environmental policy innovation, sustainability education in metaverse, metaverse for green

1. Introduction

"The world is in a climate emergency," warns the United Nations, emphasizing that substantial changes in environmental behavior and policy are required to prevent catastrophic and potentially irreversible consequences for life on Earth [1]. Anthropogenic environmental degradation has increased the vulnerability of both human and ecological systems, resulting in more frequent and severe extreme weather events, including droughts, floods, and heatwaves [2].

However, despite the wide range of environmental threats, communication efforts still struggle to promote pro-environmental behaviors. This challenge arises primarily from the difficulties in communicating about environmental issues, which often involve a temporal and spatial disconnect between causes and consequences – making them appear "psychologically distant" [3, 4].

This chapter explores the potential of augmented reality (AR) to "see the unseen" and enhance environmental storytelling by making it more immersive, tangible, and relatable. We developed a prototype AR application that vividly simulates the destructive effects of plastic pollution and evaluated it through a series of interviews with experts from the environmental communication ecosystem.

The objective of this study is to gather expert feedback to better understand how metaverse-related technologies can serve as effective media for environmental communication, education, and policy-making. Using a Design Science Research (DSR) approach [5] and adhering to rigorous guidelines for qualitative research [6], this study aims to provide theoretically and empirically grounded recommendations for the design and implementation of persuasive digital AR artifacts that promote environmental sustainability – recommendations that could also be applied to similar "metaverse for green" initiatives.

2. Background

2.1 Overcoming the challenges of environmental communication

Despite sustained efforts by international institutions and environmental communicators, current strategies have not succeeded in mobilizing the behavioral changes necessary to halt ongoing environmental degradation [1]. To date, extensive research has explored the psychological and social mechanisms that influence the adoption of pro-environmental behaviors [7] – "behavior that consciously seeks to minimize the negative impact of one's actions on the natural and built world" [8]. Insights from cognitive and behavioral psychology emphasize that individuals are more likely to engage with environmental issues when these issues are perceived as personally relevant [3].

However, traditional communication strategies often rely on abstract statistics and projections. This approach lacks emotional salience and is difficult for individuals to contextualize, as human cognition tends to favor experiential over analytical information processing [3]. While there is some evidence that direct exposure to experiences, such as extreme weather events, can influence climate-related attitudes and decision-making, empirical findings remain inconclusive [9, 10].

Research grounded in Construal Level Theory (CLT) suggests that psychological distance significantly affects individuals' mental representations of environmental issues. According to CLT, events perceived as temporally, spatially, or socially distant are construed in abstract terms, while proximal events are perceived more concretely. This mental construal influences individuals' estimations of risk, urgency, and personal relevance [4].

In the context of climate change and environmental degradation, enabling direct experiences of environmental consequences is often infeasible due to their intangible nature, long time horizons, and geographical remoteness. This challenge has led researchers and practitioners to explore the use of metaverse environments and immersive technologies – such as AR and virtual reality (VR) – as potential alternatives for direct experience.

Immersive technologies provide either partial (AR) or full (VR) sensory simulations of real or imagined environments. VR typically requires the use of head-mounted displays to create entirely synthetic environments, while AR overlays digital elements onto the physical world using mobile devices or headsets [11]. Both modalities can generate a sense of presence, which has been shown to influence cognitive and emotional engagement [12].

By enhancing the realism and immediacy of environmental narratives, immersive technologies have the potential to reduce psychological distance, thereby making distant or abstract threats appear local, tangible, and urgent. If sufficiently realistic, these experiences may elicit emotional, cognitive, and behavioral responses analogous to those produced by direct interaction with real-world phenomena [12]. The following section explores how such potentials are being realized in practice and research, showcasing concrete applications of AR and VR technologies aimed at promoting environmental awareness and action.

2.2 Applications of immersive technology in sustainability communication and research

Global institutions and leading environmental organizations now recognize the progressive democratization of metaverse technologies and have started to embrace immersive storytelling in their campaigns. For example, UNEP, in collaboration with Sony PlayStation, developed an immersive VR experience that visualizes an individual's carbon footprint as an 18-meter-high gaseous sphere. The simulation guides users through everyday scenarios – such as breakfast routines – to illustrate the environmental impact of common lifestyle choices [13].

Similarly, the World Wildlife Fund (WWF), in partnership with Google, Netflix, and PHORIA, created REWILD Our Planet, a social AR experience based on the Netflix series Our Planet. This initiative immerses users in endangered ecosystems, including Arctic ice caps and Borneo's tropical rainforests, enabling interaction with 3D wildlife models to foster emotional connections and raise awareness of conservation priorities [14].

In parallel, academic research has increasingly examined the role of immersive media in promoting sustainability outcomes (for reviews, see [15, 16]). VR experiences that simulate underwater environments have been associated with increased donation behavior [17], and embodied experiences in VR – such as assuming the perspective of non-human animals – have been linked to greater environmental concern and behavioral intent [12, 18, 19].

The effects of AR, however, are less extensively studied and present more variable results. Some recent studies report sustained improvements in environmental attitudes and behaviors following AR interventions [20], while others find no significant behavioral impact, despite participants reporting high levels of engagement, presence, and perceived relevance to an issue [21].

Nevertheless, the capacity of immersive technologies to generate a sense of presence remains one of their most promising affordances. This capability allows digital interfaces to function as social actors – a phenomenon explored in the field of persuasive technology. Research shows that individuals often respond to computers and digital systems as they would to human counterparts, allowing these technologies to engage users in socially driven behavioral change [22]. In line with Social Influence Theory [23], such interactions may be particularly powerful in guiding environmentally beneficial behavior through mechanisms of identification, internalization, and compliance.

Given these theoretical insights and emerging empirical evidence, the present study seeks to examine the persuasive potential of AR in the context of environmental communication. The following section outlines the research methodology, including the design of a prototype AR system that simulates the consequences of plastic pollution and the qualitative evaluation conducted with domain experts to assess its effectiveness.

3. Methodology and artifact description

3.1 Design science research approach

This study applies the DSR approach [5] to design, develop, and evaluate a novel Green Information System (Green IS) artifact [24]. The Design Science Research (DSR) methodology is primarily employed to address complex, real-world problems through the development and rigorous evaluation of innovative artifacts. Within a DSR project, researchers undertake a series of activities aimed at designing the artifact, followed by systematic evaluation processes. These evaluation activities generate feedback that enhances the understanding of the underlying problem and informs iterative improvements to both the artifact and the design process [5].

We followed the steps and guidelines for conducting a rigorous DSR study [25, 26] and analyzing qualitative data [6], which led to theoretical developments and practical contributions.

Here is the summary of our study design:

I. We began by identifying the core problem – the global environmental crisis of plastic pollution – and the associated challenge of promoting pro-environmental behaviors (see Section 1).

II. Next, we defined the objectives of a potential solution by analyzing existing literature on the use of immersive technologies for sustainability (see Section 2). We also defined the theoretical basis that influenced the initial design principles, which guided the development of our artifact (see Section 3.2).

III. We then carried out a design–demonstration–evaluation cycle (see Sections 3.1 and 4). The artifact was evaluated by various user experts to assess its potential to address the identified problem.

IV. Finally, the findings from the empirical study were communicated to academic and other relevant audiences.

Evaluation is central in any DSR study, as it determines whether the artifact is able to solve intended real-world problems [5]. For this purpose, the artifact is evaluated with the help of professional expertise. Between September 2021 and May 2022, we conducted semi-structured interviews aiming to capture practical knowledge from different actors within an ecosystem of environmental communication. In total, our sample consisted of nine experts. To ensure diversity among the respondents, these experts belonged to three different sectors: nonprofit organizations, public sector, and private sector.

Pseudonym	Sex	Country	Job title	Type of organization	Interview duration (min.)	Online/ in person
Interviewee_1	F	Monaco	Marketing manager	Oceanographic museum and foundation	122	In person
Interviewee_2	F	France	Founder, president	Environmental NGO	69	In person
Interviewee_3	M	France	CEO	AR&VR agency	30	In person
Interviewee_4	M	France	3D artist, developer	AR&VR agency	29	In person
Interviewee_5	M	Poland	CEO	VR&AR agency	45	Online
Interviewee_6	F	Spain	UX designer, consultant	Design, UX, learning experience design	50	Online
Interviewee_7	F	Singapore	CEO	AR/VR agency and foundation/incubato	28	Online
Interviewee_8	F	Poland	University professor, scientist	Science & education /VR, UX	89	Online
Interviewee_9	F	United States	Urban policy consultant researcher	Environment, sport, policy	42	Online

Table 1.
Overview of study sample (interview participants).

Given the early stage of research in this area, our primary objective was exploratory – to gain initial insights and a deeper understanding of the phenomenon under investigation. The nine interviews were intended to provide a diverse range of perspectives that could inform future research, rather than comprehensively represent all possible viewpoints or experiences. Demographic details of the sample participants can be found in **Table 1**.

Interviews were conducted either in person or, when not possible, over a video call. After a general presentation of the interviewee and his/her work, the interview guide focuses on assessing experts' opinions about the informational and social structures of environmental campaigns, as well as gaining feedback on the artifact and how to implement it in practice. We focus more on certain themes depending on an interviewee's expertise and profession. The prototype AR artifact was presented with a narrative, video, and, if the interview was conducted on-site, a live demonstration using a tablet. A complete interview guide is available in Appendix A.

3.2 Artifact description: Prototype AR application "eco animals"

When it comes to artifact demonstration – particularly in the context of immersive technologies – the principle of "show, don't tell" is especially relevant. To effectively convey the concept and functionality, we developed a prototype AR application, Eco Animals, available for Android devices. Our first step was to understand why the design should work in addressing the problem at hand – in this case, enhancing communication about an environmental issue.

Namely, in DSR, the creation of a novel artifact must be grounded in theoretical foundations. In other words, the design should be justified using *kernel* theories – descriptive knowledge that informs the construction of the artifact and helps explain why the design is expected to be effective [25]. Following this approach, three key aspects of the artifact's design – informational, social, and technological [27] – were informed by corresponding kernel theories, as outlined in **Table 2** below.

Guided by these design principles, we developed a prototype AR mobile application called Eco Animals. The prototype was created by an external provider using Unity, a widely adopted cross-platform engine known for its strengths in building interactive 3D environments and video games. Due to budget constraints, we were only able to develop a very basic AR experience without any game-like scenarios or interactive elements. Although AR development tools are becoming increasingly accessible, such experiences are currently limited to mobile devices (phones or tablets) equipped with integrated AR capabilities, such as ARKit (for iOS) or ARCore (for Android) (see [28] for a full list of devices).

Eco Animals serves as an educational tool, presenting environmental narratives in a vivid, interactive, and three-dimensional format. It allows users to visualize the consequences of plastic pollution through immersive, life-sized holograms of animals trapped in plastic litter (see **Figure 1** below and Video 1 for a demonstration). The artifact's design was influenced by the previous DSR cycle [29].

By leveraging AR technology, the app enables users to experience realistic scenarios – such as the accumulation of plastic waste in marine ecosystems and its impact on marine life – overlaid directly onto their physical surroundings via mobile devices. This interactive approach aims to foster a deeper understanding of environmental issues by "making the invisible visible" and engaging users on an emotional level. Moreover, the artifact is designed to support two key forms of social interaction: (1) interactions between users and (2) interactions between users and the digital content itself.

Design aspect	Kernel theory that informed the artifact's design	Design principle
Information	Construal level theory [4]	Information about environmental issues should be conveyed through powerful narratives that take the form of personal, direct, and vivid experiences. This approach aims to reduce the psychological distance individuals feel toward environmental problems.
Social	Social influence theory [23]	The artifact should facilitate social interactions both (1) between users and (2) between users and the artifact itself. This is based on the understanding that human attitudes and behaviors are shaped by social influences.
Technology	Theory of persuasive technology [22]	The artifact should offer realistic, interactive, and sensory-rich simulations that clearly link the causes and effects of environmental problems. By making the experience relevant and personalized, such features enhance the persuasiveness of the technology and support behavior change.

Table 2.
Overview of kernel theories that informed the artifact's design.

Figure 1.
Screenshots captured within the application "eco animals", demonstrating animals suffering the consequences of plastic pollution in AR.

First, the experience could be delivered through AR camera filters integrated into popular social media platforms such as Instagram, TikTok, or Snapchat. This approach would allow users to easily access, record, and share personalized content, potentially triggering viral engagement. By encouraging user-generated content – where individuals share their own interpretations or emotional reactions – the system could amplify awareness through organic, peer-driven dissemination.

Second, the artifact aims to foster emotional connections by portraying realistic and impactful scenes, such as animals visibly suffering due to plastic pollution. When these virtual entities appear sufficiently lifelike and relatable, users may begin to form empathetic bonds with them. This type of interaction can deepen users' emotional engagement with the issue, potentially motivating behavior change through the power of affective experience. When the development of the prototype was finalized, we moved on to the next step: artifact evaluation.

4. Artifact evaluation: Results and discussion

A total of 504 minutes of interviews were recorded using a voice recorder. Written transcriptions consist of 165 pages of text. Transcribed data were then analyzed following strict guidelines to maximize research rigor and the validity of the results [6]. The first-level analysis resulted in 3 major themes and 25 codes. The second-level analysis resulted in the figure below (**Figure 2**) representing the first-order concepts, second-order themes, and aggregated dimensions that emerged from the data. Aggregated dimensions reflect the three aspects of the artifact –

Figure 2.
Summary and visual representation of the insights from the interview data categorized into three design aspects: information, social, and technology aspects.

information, social, and technology aspects [27]. This data structure enabled easier discussion and summary of the rich empirical data collected through interviews. We discuss the findings in the next three subsections.

4.1 Information aspect

Environmental communication plays a critical role in shaping public understanding and behavior toward ecological issues. Interviewees pointed out that, unlike commercial campaigns aimed at profitability, environmental communication is mission-driven, focusing on awareness, education, and long-term ecological responsibility. Therefore, its strategies must adapt to diverse audiences, timeframes, and media ecosystems. Whether part of a global campaign or a localized initiative, environmental messaging operates within a complex network of actors and platforms, all striving to inspire tangible change.

> *Interviewee_9: "If we're, for instance, doing a tourism activation, that's very much based on the individual and what they can do when they're traveling, at home, when they're on the road, in terms of car tires and taking off the microplastics of the car tires."*

Interviewees agree that one of the greatest challenges of environmental communication lies in the abstract and data-heavy nature of environmental content. Scientific brochures, reports, and statistics are not easily digestible by the general public – particularly by younger audiences who consume content visually and interactively. Emotional disconnection often stems from psychological distance; people are less likely to care about issues they cannot see, feel, or relate to directly. This is where the power of narrative and experiential interventions comes into play. Tactile exhibits, like aquariums filled with plastic instead of fish, or interactive installations that simulate marine ecosystems, serve as compelling ways to bridge this distance. These formats transform data into relatable, immersive stories that people can experience firsthand, even if only briefly.

> *Interviewee_9: "I think until somebody sees it right in their face and gets directly affected by it, they're not going to really be paying attention to the issue. Unless they're really being affected and going to a highly polluted place, I think they're going to be this problem doesn't affect me directly so I don't need to be so active about making a change because my life is not directly being affected by it. I think with that kind of mindset, it's actually very difficult to again create behavioral change unless we can make it I guess in their facing, like this is the reality."*

For such stories to resonate, the emotional tone must be calibrated. Interview data show that while emotional visuals, such as injured animals, can spark initial attention, they may also trigger guilt or climate apathy if overused. Rather than overwhelming the audience, it is more effective to start with positive or familiar imagery before gradually revealing the underlying environmental message. Campaigns that focus on everyday objects like plastic bottles, balloons, or packaging are particularly impactful because they connect the issue with the user's daily life. Emotional engagement increases when the narrative includes recognizable and relatable elements, but ultimately, the message must also provide hope or solutions to avoid alienation.

Moreover, education is not just one of many objectives in environmental communication – it is its foundation. Campaigns that incorporate schools, NGOs, and cultural institutions, like museums, amplify their impact by reaching audiences early and often. Interviewees describe how collaborations between educators and subject-matter experts create programming that is not only informative but memorable. When children can interact with marine life, explore augmented worlds, or participate in activities like zero-waste breakfasts, they begin to internalize sustainability as part of their identity.

> *Interviewee_5: "Regarding other institutions that develop different applications, VR applications for themselves, I would say that 90%, maybe 80% of the success for a project like that lies on the teacher because there are teachers that take the goggles and they say, "Oh this is great. Let's do it." "*

Finally, personalization significantly enhances the relevance and effectiveness of campaigns, according to our interviewees. When people are represented in the message – or invited to participate in its delivery – the impact becomes more personal. With the help of digital technologies, environmental experiences can now be tailored to the individual, making it easier for users to "live" through the consequences of climate threats in a virtual sense. Even donation appeals can be made more compelling by identifying specific victims, whether they are people, animals, or ecosystems, which encourages empathy and action.

> *Interviewee_6: "I do feel like VR has the opportunity to make you really close, different to what you see when you watch the news or you see a documentary, like this idea of having plastic on your face, like make it really personal."*

In sum, the informational strength of an environmental artifact lies not only in what it communicates, but also in how it connects with the audience. A strategic blend of emotional narrative, educational content, platform-specific storytelling, and personal relevance is essential to achieving meaningful communication outcomes. These principles form the groundwork for developing more immersive, engaging, and persuasive digital experiences that foster environmental awareness and action.

4.2 Social aspect

Beyond the transfer of information, environmental communication also functions as a social catalyst. It is deeply embedded in how individuals perceive themselves, their peers, and their place within a broader collective. Understanding the social mechanisms behind environmental behavior is key to designing an artifact that not only informs but inspires people to act – and to act together, as noted by our participants.

> *Interviewee_7: "I do think it would be great to be able to see that in the hands of actual sustainability advocates who are doing beach cleanups as well. (...) For example, we chose 30 sustainability advocates across the Asia region to then help us then use all of the four AR experiences in the "100 days to beat plastic pollution" toolkit. Then they would share that with their friends, et cetera."*

Also, personal norms and perceived control are major drivers in this dynamic. When individuals feel they have the power to make a difference, they are more likely to engage in pro-environmental behaviors. This perception of agency can be enhanced by allowing users to interact with a digital experience and influence its outcome. For example, giving users the ability to virtually clean an ocean scene or

DOI: http://dx.doi.org/10.5772/intechopen.1011932

rescue an animal creates a sense of impact and ownership. These small, symbolic gestures are psychologically powerful, reinforcing users' belief that their actions matter – even in a simulated environment.

Social networks thus serve as fertile ground for environmental campaigns – not just because they are scalable, but because they create a shared identity around sustainability. When these networks are harnessed effectively, they can generate viral campaigns that ripple far beyond their initial scope. Although virality alone doesn't guarantee lasting behavior change, it lays the groundwork for shifting public discourse. Users who repeatedly encounter pro-environmental messages, challenges, and actions on their feed may begin to internalize the norms they observe. This form of passive social learning can become a powerful enabler for change when backed by meaningful engagement.

Another important insight that emerged from the interview data is that digital entertainment and gamified systems could turn environmental behavior into a collective experience. Multiplayer games, team-based challenges, and virtual competitions tap into the human drive for cooperation, recognition, and achievement. For example, a school-wide contest to collect the most virtual ocean plastic or complete educational missions could not only teach students about pollution but also reward and reinforce learning through social interaction.

Equally important is the strategic use of influencers. Collaborating with well-known individuals or content creators who already have strong engagement with specific audiences adds credibility and appeal. While macro-influencers offer broad reach, micro-influencers – those with 1,000 to 10,000 followers – often deliver more authentic engagement. Their niche authority and relatable tone make them ideal partners in local or community-driven environmental efforts. Even global organizations have recognized this, increasingly relying on micro-influencers to bridge the gap between abstract issues and everyday life.

Interviewees highlight that digital simulations and virtual experiences can also evoke empathy in users, not just for nature but for other people. The ability to "become" another through a virtual experience – for instance, a person with a disability or a war refugee – can change attitudes and foster compassion. However, designers must remain cautious. Overexposure to distressing content can cause emotional fatigue or disconnection, particularly when users are not psychologically prepared.

> *Interviewee_8: "Yes. I also cooperate with a psychologist from Warsaw and together we are reviewing VR applications in which you can see the world from the perspective of someone with a disability. For example, when a person is losing sight or is in a wheelchair or has dementia or autism or Asperger's syndrome and so on. There are several such applications or movies, 360-degree movies. The reason for this is to make people feel more empathy who take, for example, colleagues at university or coworkers who suffer from this kind of disabilities."*

Overall, the social power of an artifact depends on its ability to engage users not just as individuals but as members of a community. By tapping into peer influence, gamification, credibility, and empathy, environmental campaigns can move beyond awareness to collective impact. The digital sphere becomes not just a place of content consumption but a networked arena for shared action and identity-building.

4.3 Technology aspect

As digital media continues to evolve, immersive technologies like AR and VR offer new pathways for engaging audiences in meaningful, interactive ways. These tools are especially promising in the context of environmental communication, where complex data and distant issues can be brought to life through immersive experiences. Our participants remind us that the development of such an artifact must account for both technical capabilities and user needs to be effective.

One of the key advantages of AR and VR lies in their ability to transform abstract or invisible phenomena into tangible, visual narratives. Traditional communication formats – brochures, slides, or videos – may fail to capture attention or evoke emotional responses. By contrast, immersive technologies allow users to interact with 3D content, walk through simulations, and witness environmental degradation or recovery in real-time. These experiences are not only more memorable but also more likely to inspire reflection and learning.

> *Interviewee_3: "well for me there we have on the one hand virtual reality which could also very well exploit the subject but on a more fictitious side, that is to say create stagings, create fictions perhaps same, or reproduce events that have already taken place."*

Examples from recent years illustrate how immersive media can successfully communicate environmental messages. Educational AR games teach children to protect marine animals by avoiding virtual plastic. AR camera effects on social media platforms inform users about climate actions they can take, while mixed-reality weather forecasts turn dry data into dramatic visual warnings. VR installations in museums allow visitors to explore distant coral reefs or step into the shoes of someone living in a crisis – eliciting empathy that static media cannot.

Gamification adds another layer of interactivity. By turning environmental protection into a game – complete with levels, badges, and team competitions – users are more likely to engage with the material and retain knowledge. Importantly, this approach does not require hyper-realistic graphics. The key is interactivity, feedback, and a sense of progression. Games can even blend physical and digital environments, as seen in Pokémon GO-style apps, where players must physically explore real-world locations to complete virtual challenges.

However, one of the important conclusions is that, for AR to gain widespread adoption, it must offer value beyond novelty. While showcasing environmental damage can be impactful, the technology must also provide educational, emotional, or practical benefits. Potential applications include AR teaching tools in schools, museum installations, or interactive camera filters that promote sustainable action. When promoted by influencers or paired with donation appeals, AR experiences can also drive real-world impact.

Technical implementation should favor accessibility and ease of use. Markerless AR that works across locations and devices is preferable, as it avoids the need for specific images or GPS triggers. WebAR and camera filters offer frictionless entry points for users unfamiliar with AR, especially on platforms like Instagram or Snapchat. To increase realism and engagement, visual enhancements such as lighting effects, shadows, and audio cues should be carefully designed. A short tutorial can also help first-time users navigate the experience smoothly.

> *Interviewee_5: "I wouldn't say that it's a big age difference but for older people, you have to show them first of all that this is 3D. Often, I have to take the person's hand-"*
>
> *Interviewer: "And move them around?"*
>
> *Interviewee_5: " – in space so that they get this concept of 3D because they're used to sitting in front of a computer where you just move the mouse with your hands and there is no physical movement. That's the first barrier. The second is that the older generation is less keen to explore."*

Also, interviewees added that the promotion of such interventions is critical, as immersive media must be experienced firsthand to be appreciated. Effective rollout strategies include classroom campaigns, public events, social media teasers, and influencer partnerships. The goal is to build curiosity and facilitate entry. While younger generations are more receptive to AR, broader adoption requires attention to diverse user needs. For example, some users may prefer analog entry points, such as physical posters or school activities, that link to a digital component.

> *Interviewer: "When you create a game, how do you advertise it? How would you advertise this kind of serious game?"*
>
> *Interviewee 4: "We are using, for sure– I don't know how to say that, an influencer. I think, for this kind of project, there is also an organization, communication. I'm thinking about .."*
>
> *Interviewee 3: "Maybe also magazine, like Science & Vie, Science et Avernir, Nature, Geo, all these kinds of magazine."*
>
> *Interviewee 4: "The specialized press."*

Finally, our participants warn that, despite its promise, immersive technology also presents limitations. VR, in particular, is more exclusive due to its high cost, motion sickness issues, and age restrictions. Schools may lack the infrastructure to support advanced setups, and testing new concepts remains costly and complex. Nonetheless, as devices become more affordable and mainstream, these barriers are expected to decline.

The figure below (**Figure 3**) summarizes the key interview findings and expert insights on how to build and implement effective green AR artifacts.

Figure 3.
Summary of key interview findings – information, social, and technology aspects of green AR artifacts.

In conclusion, the technological potential of AR and VR in environmental communication is vast but must be carefully aligned with user experience and accessibility. When implemented thoughtfully, immersive artifacts can close the psychological distance between people and environmental issues, making them more immediate, understandable, and actionable. By integrating emotion, interactivity, and storytelling into digital formats, technology becomes not just a tool but a transformative medium for ecological awareness.

4.4 General discussion and implementation guidelines

This DSR study [5] introduces a novel Green IS artifact designed to communicate environmental issues through AR simulations and motivate pro-environmental behavior. The conceptual prototype serves as an example of using the "metaverse for green" – specifically, employing interactive tridimensional technologies to inspire real-world impact. Rich empirical data, analyzed according to established qualitative research guidelines [6], yielded novel insights valuable for practitioners in environmental communication and potentially transferable to other behavior-change interventions. We summarize and discuss the key findings below, offering design recommendations and practical implementation guidelines for Green AR (and similar behavior-changing) digital artifacts.

4.4.1 Immersion and persuasion through AR

AR technology offers advantages over traditional forms of environmental communication (e.g., photos or videos) by providing a more immersive, engaging, and vivid experience – thus enhancing persuasion and emotional resonance [20]. Experiencing, rather than simply observing, environmental issues can significantly increase users' risk awareness and reduce psychological distance [3, 4]. One significant finding from the data is the critical role of perceived self-efficacy. When individuals believe they can make a difference and see the simulated outcomes of their actions, they are more likely to engage in environmentally friendly behaviors – a notion supported by prior research [7]. Interactive metaverse technologies can reinforce this by visualizing the long-term effects of current choices [30].

4.4.2 Social influence in immersive environments

Immersive technologies are reshaping social interaction and creating new opportunities for social influence. In AR and VR environments, digital objects and avatars can act as social actors [22], with users forming social bonds even with virtual agents [31]. Furthermore, these platforms enable shared experiences through multiuser games, collaborative challenges, and virtual competitions [14], which can foster collective influence and encourage group-based behavioral change with real-world implications.

4.4.3 Motivation through gamification and design

To fully leverage AR's potential in promoting sustainable behavior, the artifact should integrate persuasive and gamified elements (see examples [32, 33]), making the path toward sustainability more enjoyable and engaging. However, given the early-stage adoption of the Metaverse and immersive technologies, communicators must recognize potential user unfamiliarity. Intermediary actors – such as educators introducing AR to students – are, therefore, crucial during the onboarding process.

4.4.4 Practical guidelines for implementation

To ensure the successful implementation of Green AR artifacts (and similar interventions intended for behavior change), we propose the following step-by-step guideline:

I. Minimize contextual barriers: Reduce distractions, technological limitations, and unsuitable settings to create a smooth, focused user experience.

II. Embed in a value-added system: Integrate the AR experience within a broader framework that includes educational content, entertainment, or gamification to sustain user engagement.

III. Provide onboarding support: Include a simple, intuitive tutorial to help users understand AR, especially for those new to the technology.

IV. Allow exploration time and space: Ensure users have adequate physical space and time to interact freely with AR elements, without pressure.

V. Collaborate with influential partners: Work with influencers, educators, or sustainability advocates to enhance visibility, credibility, and adoption.

VI. Encourage post-experience action: Guide users toward tangible next steps, such as educational follow-ups or real-world calls to action, extending the impact beyond the digital experience.

4.4.5 Policy implications

These insights suggest that AR-based environmental campaigns represent a promising communication tool for governments and NGOs. Such campaigns can be used to raise awareness of critical environmental issues, build public support for policies, and enhance understanding of challenges that may seem psychologically distant. For instance, a policy banning single-use plastic bags in stores could be supported by an immersive AR campaign: by scanning a simple QR code printed on reusable bags, shoppers could visualize their positive impact on nature, with marine animals "thanking" them for helping to protect their habitat.

5. Limitations of the study and future steps

From a practical standpoint, despite its potential, communicators may encounter several challenges when promoting and implementing AR-based artifacts. First and foremost, AR experiences require a compatible device and, unless using local memory, a stable internet connection. Although most modern smartphones are equipped with built-in AR capabilities [28], and many users have access to high-speed internet, it is important to recognize that AR campaigns may exclude individuals who do not meet these technical prerequisites.

Second, the sense of presence generated in virtual environments plays a critical role in user engagement. If the AR experience is not sufficiently realistic, it may fail to persuade individuals about the seriousness of an issue. Conversely, if the simulation feels too realistic and induces a high sense of presence, it may lead to user fatigue or cognitive overload.

Third, user unfamiliarity with the technology may hinder the adoption of AR campaigns. Communicators must ensure that audiences understand how to access and interact with AR content. As AR remains an emerging technology and no universal formula guarantees its success, we recommend pre-testing campaigns with the intended target audience before launching on a larger scale. For example, conducting focus groups with end users can provide valuable feedback on initial impressions and usability [29].

This study also has several limitations. First, due to the emerging nature of AR technology, it is difficult to generalize the findings across the broader environmental communication landscape. While the study is exploratory in nature, it provides a foundation for further research on AR-based behavior change interventions. Furthermore, one potential direction for future research could involve focusing on body transfer as a mechanism for behavior change, as it has shown promising potential [34].

Furthermore, access to relevant interviewees was limited. It proved challenging to identify environmental communication professionals with experience in AR technologies. For instance, we were unable to include social media influencers in our sample, despite their recognized influence in the success of digital campaigns. Although we reached out to numerous social media influencers within the environmental sustainability space, none agreed to participate in the study, despite repeated follow-ups.

A methodological limitation relates to the evaluation of the AR artifact itself. Demonstrating AR effectively requires on-site interaction; however, some interviews had to be conducted remotely, limiting participants' ability to fully experience the prototype. Future work should aim to expand the interview sample and conduct in-person sessions that allow for more immersive, hands-on demonstrations of AR technologies.

Finally, this research project has the potential to expand its scope through collaborations with both academia and industry. For instance, the prototype AR application could be further developed into an educational, interactive multiplayer game designed to teach users about the harmful effects of plastic overconsumption. Such a tool could serve as supplementary material in schools, particularly among younger audiences and in under-resourced areas that would greatly benefit from this type of educational intervention.

6. Concluding remarks

In the face of escalating environmental crises, institutions, researchers, and communicators are increasingly seeking innovative approaches to foster pro-environmental behavior. While environmental communication remains a crucial mechanism for shaping public understanding and promoting sustainable action, its effectiveness is often constrained by the abstract, complex, and data-heavy nature of environmental information.

Although prior research suggests that direct experiences of environmental threats significantly influence individuals' concern, risk perception, and adaptive behavior, replicating such experiences in real-world settings presents substantial practical challenges. Addressing this gap, the present study explores the concept of the "metaverse for green" – leveraging immersive technologies, particularly AR, to simulate environmentally relevant experiences and bridge the psychological distance between audiences and "unseen" ecological threats.

Guided by the DSR framework, we developed and prototyped a novel Green IS that simulates the catastrophic impacts of plastic pollution on marine life. This AR artifact was evaluated through qualitative interviews with experts in the field of environmental communication. The findings reveal that carefully designed AR experiences can enhance environmental storytelling by rendering distant or abstract threats more immediate, vivid, and personally relevant. Key design elements, such as interactivity, gamification, and social influence, were found to be instrumental in fostering engagement and educational impact.

Beyond identifying AR's persuasive potential, this study offers actionable implementation guidelines, including the minimization of contextual barriers, the integration of onboarding support, and the involvement of educators and influencers as critical intermediaries. Nonetheless, challenges remain – particularly around accessibility, user familiarity with AR technology, and the nuanced balance between realism and cognitive overload. The novelty of immersive media introduces both opportunities and limitations that must be carefully navigated.

Ultimately, this research contributes to the evolving discourse on immersive environmental communication by illustrating how AR-based artifacts can serve as effective tools for raising ecological awareness and promoting sustainable behavior. While exploratory in nature, the findings offer a foundation for future research and practical applications – particularly in the context of educational interventions where users could benefit from visualizing the long-term consequences of their present actions. Continued work should expand sample diversity, facilitate in-person testing, and explore the long-term behavioral effects of immersive interventions aimed at environmental sustainability.

Acknowledgments

The author sincerely thanks all nine interviewees for their time and generosity in sharing their expert insights. Special gratitude is extended to Professor Lise Arena and Professor Agnès Festré for their invaluable support and guidance throughout this project.

Conflict of interest

The author declares no conflict of interest.

Appendix.

Appendix A – Interview guide

Introduction

"Hello, my name is Barbara Buljat, I am a PhD student in Economics at the Université Côte d'Azur. First of all, I would like to thank you for your time today. It is my big pleasure to have this opportunity to learn from an expert like you.

This interview is a part of the big empirical study in which I am investigating the role of new mediums for environmental communication. Since you are an expert in this field, I am curious to find out about your valuable opinion, and eventually make conclusions about how to use new technologies to improve environmental communication. There is no right or wrong answer, it's your opinion that interests me.

If you don't mind, I will record the interview and later transcribe it, so it is easier for me to analyse the data. Please be sure that your name, and the name of your organization won't be mention, unless you want to. Ok?

Please make yourself comfortable and feel free to stop me and have a break whenever you need. If, at any moment, you want to give up on the interview, you have the right to do so. The interview will take approx. 45 minutes. Do you have any questions before we start?"

Start recording

1. Presentation of the interviewee and of his/her general perception of communication related to environmental problems

First theme: general perception of the interviewee.

Sub-theme	Questions	Follow-ups	What we are looking for
Interviewee's presentation	Please tell me something about yourself and your organization.	What does your job consist of (what's a typical day at work like)? Since when have you been part of this organization?	General information on the interviewee
Environmental sustainability awareness	How do you see the role of your organization in promoting environmental sustainability?	Could you provide examples of specific missions/ projects? How do you evaluate your impact on environmental sustainability?	How much engaged with promoting environmental sustainability the organization is? (Referring to the degree of maturity in environmental engagement.)
Communication of environmental issues	What do you think is the biggest challenge of communicating about environmental problems?	How do you overcome it? Provide examples of specific campaigns.	Empirical barriers (media?) to communicating about environmental issues (Ref).
Communication to enhance green behavior	What do you think is the biggest challenge of communicating to motivate people to adopt green behavior?	(psychological distance, contextual barriers, mistrust, social norms...)	Role of communication to enhance green behavior (Ref)
Familiarity with AR	How familiar are you with Augmented Reality technology?	Have you used any kind of immersive experiences in your communication?	Familiarity with technology (Ref, precursory users vs. experts?)

2. Campaign elements

Second theme: Which traditional and less traditional communication methods can be used to promote environmental sustainability and change behavior?

Sub-theme	Questions	Follow-ups	What we are looking for
Campaigns to promote green behavior (possibly answered in part 1)	Which means, do you usually use to promote sustainable behavior?	Campaigns, educational activities, school, exhibition...? Which forms? (video, photo, posters) On which platforms (social media, newspapers, billboards)?	To what extent do organizations use traditional campaigns to promote green behavior?
Information/content provided by the campaign	When you create a campaign, what are the important elements for you? Is credibility important? How do you make sure that your message is credible?	What is good content for an environmental campaign? Could you provide examples of a "good" campaign in terms of content?	Relevant information provided by the sustainable campaign.
Behind textual information, the role of visuals in campaign perception	How do you choose visuals for your campaigns?	Can you comment on the role of fearful visuals (for example, animals in danger because of climate change)? Did you get any feedback? How do you measure the impact of visuals?	Role of visuals in environmental campaigns
Type of media support to communicate efficiently	In your experience, can you comment on the role of social media in promoting environmental behavior?	Do you hire other influential people, such as influencers or celebrities, to advertise for you?	Recently, we've seen how social media can play a big role in societal movements, such as Black Lives Matter, Fridays for Future, or Earth Hour (Ref)
Type of audience	What audience are you usually trying to reach?	Do you make segmentations of different audiences?	Targeted audience of environmental campaigns (ref)
Quantified goals of campaigns	What are usually your campaign goals?	What is, in your opinion, a successful environmental campaign, and how do you measure success?	Evaluation/Role of environmental campaigns (Ref)
Impact of communication on policy makers (part of one of the targeted audiences?)	Do you think a social media campaign can put pressure on policymakers and make an impact?	How? Can you illustrate with a personal experience or an anecdote you know?	How much sensible policymakers are to this kind of campaigns? (ref/ empirical research?)

3. Artifact evaluation

Third theme: Feedback on the artifact

"Thank you very much for this useful insight. Now, I would like to present you a prototype of an IT artifact that is still in the early phase of development, and in order to improve its design, I need your feedback.

Research says that the lack of direct experiences of environmental problems (for example, wild fire or marine pollution) leads to lower perception of risk and lower motivation to engage around such issues. So, this artifact is based on the idea to provide direct experiences of environmental threat, in the form of augmented reality.

Augmented reality is a technology that superimposes digital objects over the real world, and creates an illusion that they actually belong there. By using your smartphone, you can virtually insert any 3D digital object in your immediate surrounding, in real time. This technology is supported by every newer mobile device nowadays, and is mostly used in the form of Facebook or Instagram camera filters.

So, instead of using posters or videos to communicate about environmental issues, governments, museums or nonprofits can now provide audience with interactive tridimensional experiences. We took an example of a growing and urgent global problem: plastic pollution. The artifact you are about to see is inspired by real scenes, and demonstrates 5 most impacted animals struggling with single use plastic trash.

First, I am going to give you a short video explanation, and then I will demonstrate it to you on my smartphone/tablet."

Video

Demonstration of the artifact on the phone/tablet.

Sub-theme	Questions	Follow-ups	What we are looking for
First impressions	Could you share your first impression?	How did you feel experiencing AR? Did you feel like animals were there?	User's first impressions and opinions
Positive aspects	What is good about using this technology for environmental communication?	Do you think AR is a good supplement to traditional environmental campaigns? Why? Can this be a good marketing tool to lead users to a specific page/ raise visibility of an organization?	Positive aspects of the artifact
Negative aspects	What are the risks and downsides?	Privacy? Not realistic?	Negative aspects of the artifact
Possible extensions	What should be improved or extended?	Video game, filters, app, message, call-to-action.	How can the prototype be upgraded?
Form	There are three possible forms such experiences could take: as a (free) mobile app, a social media camera effect, and as an interactive experience within a website in a browser. What do you think is the most appropriate?	Why? Please elaborate.	Optimal artifact form
Launch	How would you advertise (launch) such a virtual experience to make people want to click and experience it?	Photo, video "call"? Influencers? What timing? Markerbased/markerless?	How to advertise/ launch the experience

Sub-theme	Questions	Follow-ups	What we are looking for
Buzz	AR campaigns can generate an infinite amount of unique content created by users. What do you think about this?	Can such AR experiences lead to a buzz and eventually to a social media movement? Can it go viral?	Can such a campaign lead to a buzz, a movement, and become viral?
Audience	Who do you think is the appropriate audience for such campaigns?	Age, gender. Eco-oriented or not.	Appropriate audience
Perceived ease of use	Do you think AR technology is easy to use?	What makes it hard or easy?	Perceived ease of use
Intention to use	(In case they haven't already used it) Would you use this kind of medium in your future campaigns?	Example.	Intention to use
Other remarks	Final comments.		Other remarks

Closing

"We came to the end of this interview. Thank you so much for your time and valuable feedback. Do you have any final comment or anything that you want to tell me?

I will now stop recording. In case there is something that later comes to your mind, or have any other question, feel free to write me by email."

Stop recording

Signing consent form

Author details

Barbara Buljat Raymond
Université Côte d'Azur, Nice, France

*Address all correspondence to: barbara.raymond@univ-cotedazur.fr

References

[1] United Nations Environment Programme [UNEP]. Climate action [Internet]. 2025. Available from: https://www.unep.org/topics/climate-action [Accessed: 2025-Jun-18]

[2] Intergovernmental Panel on Climate Change [IPCC]. Summary for policymakers. In Pörtner H-O, Roberts DC, Poloczanska ES, Mintenbeck K, Tignor M, Alegría A, Craig M, Langsdorf S, Löschke S, Möller V, Okem A. Climate Change 2022: Impacts, Adaptation, and Vulnerability. Contribution of Working Group II to the Sixth Assessment Report of the Intergovernmental Panel on Climate Change. Cambridge University Press. 2022:3–34

[3] Van der Linden S, Maibach E, Leiserowitz A. Improving public engagement with climate change: Five "best practice" insights from psychological science. Perspectives on Psychological Science. 2015;**10**:758–763. DOI: 10.1177/1745691615598516

[4] Trope Y, Liberman N. Construal-level theory of psychological distance. Psychological Review. 2010;**117**(2):440–463. DOI:10.1037/a0018963

[5] Hevner AR, March ST, Park J. Design research in information systems research. Management Information Systems Quarterly. 2004;**28**:75–105. DOI: 10.2307/25148625

[6] Gioia DA, Corley KG, Hamilton AL. Seeking qualitative rigor in inductive research: Notes on the Gioia methodology. Organizational Research Methods. 2013;**16**(1):15–31. DOI:10.1177/10944281124521

[7] Li D, Zhao L, Ma S, Ma S, Shao S, Zhang L. What influences an individual's pro-environmental behavior? A literature review. Resources, Conservation and Recycling. 2019;**146**:28–34. DOI: 10.1016/J.RESCONREC.2019.03.024

[8] Kollmuss A, Agyeman J. Mind the gap: Why do people act environmentally and what are the barriers to pro-environmental behavior?. Environmental Education Research. 2002;**8**(3):239–260. DOI:10.1080/13504620220145401

[9] Sambrook K, Konstantinidis E, Russell S, Okan Y. The role of personal experience and prior beliefs in shaping climate change perceptions: A narrative review. Frontiers in Psychology. 2021;**12**. 669911. DOI: 10.3389/fpsyg.2021.669911

[10] Piao X, Managi S. Determinants of pro-environmental behaviour: Effects of socioeconomic, subjective, and psychological well-being factors from 37 countries. Humanities and Social Sciences Communications. 2024;**11**:1293. DOI: 10.1057/s41599-024-03790-z

[11] Azuma RT. A survey of augmented reality. Presence: Teleoperators and Virtual Environments. 1997;**6**(4):355–385. DOI:10.1162/pres.1997.6.4.355

[12] Ahn SJ, Bostick J, Ogle E, Nowak KL, McGillicuddy KT, Bailenson JN. Experiencing nature: Embodying animals in immersive virtual environments increases inclusion of nature in self and involvement with nature. Journal of Computer-Mediated

Communication. 2016;**21**(6):399–419. DOI:10.1111/jcc4.12173

[13] UNEP. Experience your carbon footprint in VR [Internet].2020. Available from: https://www.unep.org/news-and-stories/story/experience-your-carbon-footprint-vr [Accessed: 2025-June-18]

[14] Worlf Wildlife Fund [WWF]. Rewild Our Planet [Internet]. 2020. Available from: https://rewild.wwf.sg/ [Accessed: 2025-June-18]

[15] Fauville G, Queiroz ACM, and Bailenson JN. 2020. Virtual reality as a promising tool to promote climate change awareness. In Kim J, and Song Heditors Technology and Health: Promoting Attitude and Behavior Change. p. 91–108. Elsevier; DOI: 10.1016/B978-0-12-816958-2.00005-8

[16] Cosio LD, Buruk O, Fernández Galeote D, Bosman IDV, Hamari J Virtual and augmented reality for environmental sustainability: A systematic review. In: CHI '23: Proceedings of the 2023 CHI Conference on Human Factors in Computing Systems. 23- 28 April 2023. Hamburg, Germany. DOI: 10.1145/3544548.3581147

[17] Nelson KM, Anggraini E, Schlüter A. Virtual reality as a tool for environmental conservation and fundraising. PLoS ONE. 2020;**15**(4): e0223631. DOI: 10.1371/journal.pone.0223631

[18] Pimentel D, Kalyanaraman S. The effects of embodying wildlife in virtual reality on conservation behaviors. Scientific Reports. 2022;**12**:6439. DOI: 10.1038/s41598-022-10268-y

[19] Spangenberger P, Freyta SC, Geiger SM. Embodying nature in immersive virtual reality: Are multisensory stimuli vital to affect nature connectedness and pro-environmental behaviour?. Computers and Education. 2024; **212**. 104964. DOI: 10.1016/j.compedu.2023.104964

[20] Levstek M, Papworth S, Woods A, Archer L, Arshad I, Dodds K, Holdstock JS, Bennett J, Dalton P. Immersive storytelling for pro-environmental behaviour change: The green planet augmented reality experience. Computers in Human Behavior. 2024; **161**. 108379. DOI: 10.1016/j.chb.2024.108379

[21] Attanasi G, Buljat RB, Festré A, Guido A. Raising environmental awareness with augmented reality. Ecological Economics. 2025; **233**. 108563. DOI: 10.1016/j.ecolecon.2025.108563

[22] Fogg BJ.Persuasive Technology: Using Computers to Change What We Think and Do. San Francisco, CA, USA: Morgan Kaufmann Publishers Inc; 2003

[23] Kelman HC. Compliance, identification, and internalization three processes of attitude change. Journal of Conflict Resolution. 1958;**2** (1):51–60. DOI:10.1177/002200275800200106

[24] Elliot S, Webster J. Editorial: Special issue on empirical research on information systems addressing the challenges of environmental sustainability: An imperative for urgent action. Information Systems Journal. 2017;**27**:367–378. DOI: 10.1111/isj.12150

[25] Gregor SD, Hevner AR. Positioning and presenting design science research

for maximum impact. Management Information Systems Quarterly. 2013;**37**:337–355. DOI: 10.25300/MISQ/2013/37.2.01

[26] Peffers K, Tuunanen T, Rothenberger M, Chatterjee S. A design science research methodology for information systems research. Journal of Management Information Systems. 2008;**24**(3):45–77. DOI: 10.2753/MIS0742-1222240302

[27] De Leoz G, Petter S. Considering the social impacts of artefacts in information systems design science research. European Journal of Information Systems. 2018;**27**(2):154–170. DOI:10.1080/0960085X.2018.1445462

[28] Google. Overview of ARCore and supported development environments [Internet]. 2024. Available from: https://developers.google.com/ar/develop [Accessed: 2025-June-18]

[29] Buljat B Augmented reality for nudging green behavior: Design, evaluation and implementation. ECIS 2022 Research Papers. The 30th European Conference on Information Systems. Timisoara, Romania, 16–18 June 2021.56. Available from: https://aisel.aisnet.org/ecis2022_rp/56

[30] Ahn SJ, Bailenson JN, Park D. Short- and long-term effects of embodied experiences in immersive virtual environments on environmental locus of control and behavior. Computers in Human Behavior. 2014;**39**(C):235–245. DOI:10.1016/j.chb.2014.07.025

[31] Miller MR, Jun H, Herrera F, Yu Villa J, Welch G, Bailenson JN. Social interaction in augmented reality. PLoS ONE. 2019;**14**(5):e0216290. DOI: 10.1371/journal.pone.0216290

[32] Oppong-Tawiah D, Webster J, Staples S, Cameron AF, Ortiz de guinea A, Hung TY. Developing a gamified mobile application to encourage sustainable energy use in the office. Journal of Business Research. 2018;**106**(C):388–405. DOI:10.1016/j.jbusres.2018.10.051

[33] Morganti L, Pallavicini F, Cadel E, Candelieri A, Archetti F, Mantovani F. Gaming for Earth: Serious games and gamification to engage consumers in pro-environmental behaviours for energy efficiency. Energy Research & Social Science. 2017;**29**:95–102. DOI: 10.1016/j.erss.2017.05.001

[34] Pimentel D.Uses and effects of AR- and VR-based animal embodiment: A field study at a beach music festival. New Media & Society. 2025;**0**(0). DOI: 10.1177/14614448251346153

Chapter 14

Beyond Post-Work Digital Labor: Fostering Arendtian *Action* in the Metaverse

Harun Serpil

Abstract

The accelerating pace of artificial intelligence (AI) and automation raises profound concerns about the erosion of traditional employment and the future of human purpose. This paper explores the potential of the metaverse to serve as a platform for meaningful life engagement in a post-work society. As the metaverse evolves into a potential site for work, sociality, and creativity, its role in a future of widespread technological unemployment demands critical scrutiny. Employing Hannah Arendt's tripartite framework of labor, work, and action, the study evaluates whether immersive virtual environments can authentically support human flourishing through purpose, social connection, creativity, and political engagement. Drawing on psychological theories of meaning, sociological analyses of community, and philosophical critiques of technology, the paper bridges techno-optimistic visions and humanistic resistance by emphasizing the structural, political, and ethical conditions under which the metaverse might enable genuine action. While opportunities exist for education, creativity, and alternative economic participation, risks such as digital commodification, reality distortion, inequitable access, and the expansion of invisible labor remain pressing concerns. The metaverse's value is contingent not on its technological sophistication but on its governance, design ethics, and capacity to foster democratic public spaces. Ultimately, the metaverse may form one component of a broader post-work ecology of meaning, but it cannot replace the fundamental need for authentic human action, community, and world-building.

Keywords: metaverse, technological unemployment, post-work society, Hannah Arendt, meaning in life, digital labor, philosophy of technology

1. Introduction

The twenty-first century is witnessing an unprecedented technological transformation, one that raises fundamental questions about the nature of human purpose, identity, and fulfillment. With each passing year, artificial intelligence (AI) and automation extend their capabilities into domains once considered the exclusive province of human cognition and skill. From generative AI that can produce text, music, and art, to robotic systems capable of performing complex physical tasks, the boundaries of "human work" are eroding. Forecasts by McKinsey Global Institute suggest that nearly half of existing tasks may be automated in the coming decades, an estimate echoed by numerous labor economists and futurologists [1]. These projections reignite a concern voiced decades earlier by Hannah Arendt, who warned of "a society of laborers without labor" (p. 5), a condition where technological progress undermines the very activity that historically gave structure, identity, and meaning to human lives [2].

Traditional employment has long served as more than an economic necessity; it has been a central arena where individuals derived purpose, contributed to collective welfare, and forged social bonds. The loss of this structure, through widespread technological unemployment, would not simply disrupt economies but also unsettle the existential foundation of modern life. What happens to human meaning in a world where machines assume the bulk of labor and work? This question demands not only economic or technical answers but also philosophical reflection.

Within this shifting landscape, the metaverse has emerged as a contested vision of the future. Popularly framed as a constellation of immersive virtual worlds interconnected by advanced digital infrastructure, the metaverse has been alternately heralded as the next frontier of human flourishing and condemned as a sophisticated distraction engineered by corporate interests [3, 4]. While techno-optimists portray it as a platform for unprecedented creativity, collaboration, and even symbiosis with artificial intelligence [5], humanistic critics liken it to a twenty-first century Plato's Cave, warning of alienation and spiritual manipulation.

The metaverse, as the latest stage of digital society, provides a vital context for rethinking digital labor and meaning in a post-work world. Platforms such as Roblox and Fortnite already illustrate how virtual worlds host large-scale creative economies where users design, build, and monetize digital goods, events, and experiences [4, 6, 7]. These environments blur distinctions between play and work: while they enable world-building [8] and cultural production akin to Arendt's category of work, they also reproduce precarious, gig-style labor such as streaming, audience maintenance, and virtual customer service [9]. Moreover, the metaverse relies on extensive invisible labor, especially in AI-assisted content moderation and data annotation, which shapes what is visible in virtual spaces and determines the boundaries of public discourse [10, 11]; Governance further complicates these dynamics, since ownership and decision-making are concentrated in private platforms, raising questions about political participation, digital citizenship, and the possibility of collective action [12]. The metaverse exemplifies the blurring of leisure, labor, and politics [3, 13]; making it a crucial case through which to test whether Arendt's categories of labor, work, and action can still sustain meaning in an era of technological unemployment.

This paper argues that the truth lies neither in utopian celebration nor in wholesale rejection. Rather, the value of the metaverse must be assessed through a critical philosophical lens attentive to the conditions that make human life meaningful. To this end, Hannah Arendt's tripartite framework of labor, work, and action provides a uniquely powerful tool. By distinguishing between cyclical biological maintenance *(labor)*, durable world-building *(work)*, and spontaneous political engagement *(action)*, Arendt enables us to ask: Does the metaverse foster genuine action and world-building, or does it merely extend digital labor and consumption? The metaverse may support human flourishing in a post-work society, but only if its governance structures (ie. currently raising critical questions about platform ownership, democratic participation, and digital citizenship) are deliberately designed to prioritize plurality and action over commodification and control [10, 14]. Otherwise, it will intensify the crisis of meaning by accelerating the complete dissolution of boundaries between leisure, labor, and political engagement, creating a world where all experience is susceptible to commodification.

2. Theoretical framework: Understanding the metaverse

The metaverse has become a term of both popular fascination and scholarly contention. Its conceptual roots can be traced to Neal Stephenson's Snow Crash, which imagined a three-dimensional digital universe where avatars interacted in shared virtual space [15]. Today, definitions converge on a set of core features: immersive environments, avatar-based representation, user-generated content, synchronous interactions, and persistent digital economies [6, 16]. The World Economic Forum defines it as an "interconnected web of ubiquitous virtual worlds" overlapping with and augmenting physical reality [17].

Technological trajectories suggest increasing accessibility and integration of such environments by the 2030s and 2040s, driven by advances in computational processing, spatial computing, haptic feedback, and telecommunications infrastructure [18]. Industry estimates predict that by 2026, one-quarter of the global population will spend at least one hour per day in metaverse environments. While some scholars anticipate widespread adoption and profound social transformation, others remain skeptical, noting both technological and cultural barriers [3].

Importantly, the metaverse is not monolithic but shaped by competing visions. Techno-optimistic narratives [5] celebrate it as a platform for human–AI collaboration and collective intelligence, suggesting it may function as an evolutionary leap in human consciousness. In contrast, humanistic critiques warn of alienation, manipulation, and loss of authentic experience [4]. A recent study by Tommasi highlights precisely this tension: while the metaverse could enable new forms of work and community, it also risks undermining dignity and well-being if subordinated to corporate extraction [19]. Beyond this polarized debate, a more pressing political-philosophical critique has emerged. Scholars like Bay argue that the primary danger of the metaverse lies not in mere alienation but in its capacity to disrupt the very foundation of democracy by dismantling the intersubjective common reality necessary for the establishment of factual truth [20].

Arendt's framework provides a critical alternative to both extremes. Her tripartite distinction is particularly apt for analyzing virtual environments. Labor, in her sense, refers to repetitive activities tied to biological necessity and cyclical consumption. Work involves the creation of durable objects and institutions that outlast individual lives, forming a stable human world. Action, the highest form of activity, represents spontaneous political engagement and the capacity to initiate something genuinely new through interaction with others in a public space [2].

This challenges Arendt's categories themselves, demanding we examine how they manifest in a digitally mediated world. The framework for evaluation thus becomes:

Labor: Does activity consist of repetitive, consumptive cycles (e.g., maintaining a social profile, performing algorithmically rewarded tasks)?

Work: Does it result in durable contributions to a shared world (e.g., creating a persistent virtual artifact or institution)?

Action: Does it involve unpredictable, collective world-building and political speech in a public realm?

As Atak and Özkoc demonstrate in their Delphi study on the impact of the metaverse on work life, current expert opinion is divided [21]. While some foresee empowering new professional and creative opportunities, others anticipate exploitative gig-like arrangements extended into virtual space. Their findings reinforce the need for a framework capable of distinguishing meaningful action from disguised labor, a role Arendt's categories are uniquely suited to play. As such, the metaverse is best understood as a socio-technical system whose value depends not on inherent features but on governance, design, and cultural orientation.

3. Psychological foundations of meaningful life

If the metaverse is to be considered a platform for human flourishing in a post-work society, it must be measured against the psychological foundations of meaning. Research across psychology and sociology consistently affirms that meaning in life is not a luxury but a fundamental human need with profound implications for health, resilience, and well-being [22]. Individuals who perceive their lives as meaningful exhibit greater longevity, lower stress levels, and higher overall life satisfaction.

One influential framework is Paul Wong's PURE model, which identifies four essential dimensions of meaning: *Purpose* (directional motivation toward valued goals), *Understanding* (coherent comprehension of self and world), *Responsible Action* (ethical engagement with others and environment), and *Enjoyment/ Evaluation* (positive affect and reflective life satisfaction) [23]. A meaningful life thus requires both cognitive coherence and emotional fulfillment, achieved not through passive consumption but through purposeful action. Sources of meaning are diverse, including relationships, creativity, achievement, spirituality, and contribution to community [24]. Traditionally, employment has been a central arena for many of these dimensions. Work provided not only income but also identity, structure, and opportunities for contribution. Its disappearance or reduction therefore raises existential risks: without replacement structures, individuals may face a void in purpose and belonging.

The challenge for the metaverse, then, is to serve as more than a platform for entertainment or distraction. Can it provide opportunities for purposeful goal pursuit, coherent self-understanding, responsible engagement, and genuine enjoyment? Some evidence suggests promise. For example, Youssef et al., in their field study of Generation Z in the United Arab Emirates, found that engagement with metaverse technologies enhanced social development and psychological well-being, particularly by expanding avenues for self-expression and community building [25]. Their findings support the possibility that virtual environments can contribute positively to meaning, especially when they foster authentic social connection.

However, as Arendt reminds us, not all activity is equal. If virtual engagement primarily resembles labor its contribution to meaning will be limited. Even if virtual worlds enable the creation of durable digital artifacts (work), the deepest form of flourishing requires spaces for action: authentic, unpredictable engagement with others in a shared world. Without such opportunities, the metaverse risks producing not a meaningful post-work society but a digitized extension of consumption and invisible labor. This digital labor includes not only the visible acts of content creation and moderation but also the invisible extraction of behavioral data used for hypertargeted personalization [20], a process that actively works against the formation of a shared, common reality. Thus, the psychological foundation for evaluating the metaverse is clear: its capacity to support meaning hinges not on immersion or realism, but on whether it provides opportunities for purpose, understanding, responsibility, and joy rooted in authentic human action.

4. Virtual communities and social connection

The metaverse's most celebrated promise is its potential to create new forms of community and social connection. Humans are, as Aristotle observed, "political animals," oriented toward life in common. Social relationships have always been central to the experience of meaning, providing a sense of belonging, recognition, and purpose. When technological unemployment disrupts traditional workplaces, ie. the institutions that historically organized social life, the need for alternative arenas of connection becomes particularly pressing.

The metaverse can facilitate such connection through real-time multisensory interactions mediated by avatars and supported by immersive environments. Unlike two-dimensional platforms such as Facebook or Zoom, metaverse environments allow individuals to experience co-presence, the phenomenological sense of "being there" with others, which research has shown can generate more robust forms of engagement [3, 26]. This enhanced presence opens possibilities for collaboration, friendship, and even intimacy that transcend geographical boundaries.

Yet the question remains: what kind of connection does the metaverse foster? Is it merely an intensified version of social media performance and maintenance, or does it create conditions for deeper, authentic relationships and political community?

Recent empirical research offers both promise and caution. Youssef et al., in a large-scale study of Generation Z in the UAE, found that metaverse participation enhanced psychological well-being and social development by expanding opportunities for interaction and identity exploration [25]. Their findings confirm that, at least for younger cohorts, virtual environments can strengthen rather than erode social capital. Similarly, Atak and Özkoc emphasize that expert consensus points to the metaverse as an arena where professional collaboration and community building may occur alongside entertainment [21].

However, other studies highlight risks. Platform design often prioritizes engagement metrics such as time spent, interactions logged, data collected, over the quality of human relationships. This creates incentives for shallow, consumptive sociality rather than authentic dialogue or collective action. Arendt warned of precisely this danger: a society where the public realm, the space of action, is replaced by endless laboring and consuming [2]. If metaverse platforms are governed primarily by corporate interests, algorithmically curating experiences to maximize advertising revenue, they may simulate community while suppressing genuine plurality and unpredictability.

The development of identity within virtual communities illustrates both potential and peril. Avatars offer opportunities for self-expression, experimentation, and even liberation from physical or social constraints. Research suggests that identity play can promote self-expansion and personal growth [27]. Yet it can also lead to confusion or dissonance if virtual and offline selves diverge too radically. Aligning digital identities with authentic self-concepts is crucial for psychological well-being.

From an Arendtian perspective, the danger lies in mistaking mere performance for action. When individuals endlessly curate avatars, optimize social metrics, and maintain reputational profiles, they may in fact be laboring rather than acting in the deeper sense of initiating something new and unpredictable. The challenge for the metaverse is to resist becoming a glorified extension of social media's performative cycles and instead to cultivate spaces where authentic political speech and collective deliberation can occur.

The stakes are high. In a post-work society, where traditional structures of belonging may erode, the metaverse could either become a refuge of genuine community or a sophisticated distraction machine. Its future role will depend not on technological immersion but on whether it is architected to support the plurality and freedom of action that Arendt deemed essential to human flourishing.

5. Creativity, work, and identity in virtual spaces

Beyond social connection, one of the metaverse's strongest claims to significance lies in its capacity to enable creativity and world-building. Arendt's category of work, i.e., the fabrication of durable objects and institutions, provides a vital lens for evaluating this potential. Unlike labor, which is consumed in endless cycles, work produces artifacts that endure, contributing to the shared human world.

In virtual environments, creativity takes diverse forms: digital art, architectural design, music composition, storytelling, and collaborative projects that span the globe. Virtual reality's three-dimensional, interactive nature allows creators to shape environments in ways impossible in physical contexts. This democratization of creative tools is one of the most compelling aspects of the metaverse, offering new forms of expression for those historically excluded from traditional art institutions. The promise of creativity in the metaverse is best exemplified by platforms like Roblox and Fortnite Creative. However, a critical Arendtian analysis is necessary. While users engage in world-building, the platform's economic model often instrumentalizes this creativity, reducing it to a form of content generation for corporate platforms [28]. The "durability" of this work is precarious, existing at the pleasure of corporate owners and vulnerable to platform closure [7]. This creative activity often borders on gig work, challenging traditional employment categories. The integration of AI tools further threatens to displace the intentionality that defines genuine work, potentially reducing human creators to editors of machine-generated content [11].

However, critical questions must be asked: what kind of creativity does the metaverse support? If artistic production is guided primarily by algorithms optimized for engagement or monetization, then creativity risks being instrumentalized, reduced to a form of content generation for corporate platforms. Instead of fostering durable work in Arendt's sense, such creativity may collapse back into labor, which means the endless cycles of production consumed as quickly as they appear.

The risk is amplified by the integration of artificial intelligence into creative processes. AI systems can now generate paintings, music, and literature at astonishing speed and fidelity. While such tools may expand human capacities, they also threaten to displace the very craftsmanship and intentionality that define genuine work. As Waelen argues, the automation of creativity represents not liberation but a profound threat to world-building, as machines produce artifacts without human meaning or durability [8].

Nevertheless, the metaverse retains transformative potential. Šímová, writing on the virtual workplace, emphasizes that immersive environments may cultivate new professional identities and creative roles, extending opportunities for craftsmanship and collaboration beyond the limits of geography [28]. For individuals with disabilities or social constraints, virtual tools can unlock avenues of expression previously inaccessible.

The challenge lies in ensuring that such creativity is not co-opted into cycles of invisible labor. Content moderation, avatar maintenance, and algorithmically rewarded "engagement" tasks are forms of hidden work that sustain virtual platforms without producing enduring contributions. Digital platforms often rely precisely on this invisible labor, disguising it as creativity while exploiting human effort [9].

Identity again plays a central role. Virtual creativity allows individuals to craft and project identities through artistic work, not merely through curated avatars. This aligns with Arendt's emphasis on work as the act of leaving one's mark on the world. Yet the durability of digital artifacts is fragile. Without institutional support, platforms may erase or devalue creations when servers shut down or business models shift. True world-building requires durability not only in code but also in governance and recognition.

6. Virtual economies and alternative value creation

One of the most striking developments in the metaverse is the rise of virtual economies, or "metanomics." These economies allow for the creation, exchange, and accumulation of value through digital assets such as cryptocurrencies, NFTs, and virtual real estate. Proponents argue that such systems can provide alternative pathways for economic participation beyond traditional employment, offering autonomy and creative rewards to individuals. From an economic perspective, virtual markets display features of complex systems, including supply and demand dynamics, taxation, and regulation [29]. They also introduce novel forms of value creation, from digital fashion and architecture to event management and community governance. The integration of blockchain and decentralized finance protocols enhances autonomy, enabling peer-to-peer transactions and reduced reliance on intermediaries [30]. Techno-optimists celebrate these economies as democratizing engines of creativity. Al-Maroof et al. note that user adoption is often driven by intrinsic enjoyment as well as financial gain, suggesting that participation can provide both psychological satisfaction and income [31]. Atak and Özkoc likewise emphasize that metaverse economies could reconfigure work-life balance, offering new professional opportunities aligned with individual passions [21].

Yet a critical perspective reveals significant limitations. First, the sustainability of such economies is contingent on continued user engagement and platform stability, both vulnerable to corporate decision-making and technological obsolescence. Second, the translation of virtual earnings into real-world subsistence remains mediated by external systems: one cannot eat NFTs or pay rent with virtual assets without reliable exchange mechanisms.

Most importantly, many metaverse economic activities may not transcend labor at all but rather rebrand it. Šímová highlights how avatar-based workplace environments often reproduce hierarchies and pressures from traditional employment, embedding them in immersive settings [28]. The danger is that gig-like tasks such as customer service, content production, audience maintenance are recast as "creative entrepreneurship," masking precarious labor as liberation. This echoes Arendt's critique: when work and action are subordinated to labor's cyclical logic, human flourishing is diminished. Wang goes further, suggesting that the metaverse is becoming an "integral part of everyday life," blurring boundaries between leisure and labor [13]. This integration risks expanding commodification into every corner of experience. Instead of offering respite from technological unemployment, virtual economies may deepen precarity by demanding continuous engagement and self-marketing. The Arendtian question is whether these economies foster work, i.e., durable contributions to a shared world, or merely extend labor under a new guise. Virtual art, architecture, and cultural production have potential to constitute genuine work, but only if they endure beyond immediate cycles of consumption and are recognized within stable communities. Otherwise, the metaverse economy risks becoming a hyper-accelerated gig economy, cloaked in the aesthetics of creativity but devoid of authentic world-building.

6.1 Virtual gig work and the architecture of invisible labor

The metaverse economy is built on a foundation of visible and invisible digital labor. Visible gig work includes virtual customer service, event hosting, and live streaming [20]. Yet, beneath this visible economic activity lies a vast ecosystem of invisible labor that sustains metaverse operations. This includes the psychologically taxing work of AI-assisted content moderation, performed by both algorithms and an often-precarious human workforce [5, 32]. It also encompasses the "surveillant physics" of the platform itself – the continuous, automated extraction of behavioral, biometric, and interactional data that fuels hyper-targeted advertising and shapes the virtual environment [14]. This data labeling and moderation are forms of labor essential to the platform's function but are systematically rendered invisible, what Castellena and Romanelli identify as the "exploitation disguised as participation" [33]. From an Arendtian perspective, this invisible labor is the antithesis of action; it is activity that sustains the system but does not appear in the public realm as a recognized contribution.

7. Philosophical and practical limitations

Despite its promise, the metaverse is not immune to profound limitations that must be confronted before it can be credibly advanced as a domain of meaningful life in a post-work society.

7.1 Arendtian critique of labor, work, and action

Hannah Arendt's categories provide a sharp lens for diagnosing the limitations of virtual worlds. The majority of metaverse engagement today resembles labor: repetitive cycles of logging in, maintaining avatars, engaging with algorithmically recommended content, and participating in gamified systems of consumption. These activities, though immersive, are often ephemeral, disappearing as soon as they are performed. They sustain life within virtual environments but do not build durable structures or contribute meaningfully to the world. Where the metaverse enables work, it does so precariously. Digital creations exist within fragile infrastructures controlled by corporations. Unlike physical objects that endure across generations, virtual artifacts may vanish when servers close, platforms pivot, or companies collapse. This fragility undermines Arendt's notion of world-building, which requires stability and durability. Most troubling is the scarcity of action in Arendt's sense: the capacity to initiate new, unpredictable beginnings in a shared public world. While metaverse platforms advertise themselves as collaborative and democratic, their governance structures are typically centralized, their terms of service opaque, and their economic models oriented toward extraction. Opportunities for genuine political speech, dissent, and co-determination are minimal. In this sense, the metaverse risks replicating what Arendt feared most: the crowding out of public action by endless cycles of labor and consumption. This analysis finds a powerful contemporary application in the work of Bay, who argues that the metaverse, particularly under the control of data-extractive "gatekeeper" platforms, is primed to generate endless cycles of consumptive labor while simultaneously inhibiting the possibility of genuine political action by destroying the common world in which it must occur [20].

7.2 Critical theory and spiritual alienation

Beyond Arendt, critical theorists raise further concerns about the metaverse's potential to alienate rather than liberate. Serpil and Karaca argue that the metaverse can function as a form of "digital spirituality," manipulating human desires for transcendence while commodifying attention and identity [4]. By simulating depth and connection, it may obscure the structural inequalities and ecological crises of the physical world. This risk resonates with longstanding critiques of technology as an apparatus of distraction. Heidegger warned of *enframing*, the tendency of technological systems to reduce human beings to resources within a standing-reserve [34]. The metaverse, if driven by corporate imperatives, may "enframe" human creativity and sociality as inputs into algorithms of engagement. Instead of opening spaces of freedom, it may deepen enslavement to cycles of consumption, now more immersive than ever before.

7.3 Overconsumption and reality distortion

Another limitation lies in the metaverse's potential to distort reality and promote overconsumption. Immersive environments can produce powerful psychological effects, including dissociation, addiction, and blurred boundaries between the virtual and the physical [26]. Wang emphasizes that the metaverse is rapidly becoming an "integral part of everyday life," with boundaries between leisure, work, and identity collapsing into a single immersive continuum [13]. While integration may create new possibilities, it also risks totalizing experience, reducing opportunities for withdrawal, reflection, or non-mediated life. Tommasi stresses that without critical governance, such integration can undermine human dignity [19]. Individuals may become trapped in exploitative cycles of "playbor" (i.e., play that simultaneously functions as labor) generating profit for corporations while offering only fleeting meaning. The promise of the metaverse as a domain of flourishing thus confronts a practical paradox: the very immersion that makes it attractive also intensifies risks of dependency and alienation.

7.4 Governance, ownership, and the political void

The most significant Arendtian limitation of current metaverse platforms is the scarcity of authentic political action. The governance structures governing these virtual societies raise critical questions about platform ownership, democratic participation, and digital citizenship. While corporate-controlled environments may experiment with community-led models or Decentralized Autonomous Organizations (DAOs), empirical evidence often reveals a plutocracy where voting power correlates with wealth [14, 35]. This centralized control, with opaque terms of service and profit-driven models, suppresses the unpredictability and plurality necessary for action [12]. The danger, as Bay argues, is that the metaverse doesn't just fail to provide a space for politics; it actively destroys the common, intersubjective reality upon which factual truth and democratic action depend [20]. Users navigating complex questions about political speech and community standards within privately-owned virtual spaces are not engaging in action but are rather subject to corporate governance. For the metaverse to avoid becoming a political void, it must architect spaces for genuine co-determination and protect a digital public sphere free from corporate monopolization [36].

8. A tripartite philosophical lens: Integration, resistance, and action

Given these limitations, how should we situate the metaverse in broader debates about technology and meaning? Three dominant philosophical positions can be discerned: techno-optimism, humanistic resistance, and an Arendtian middle path of action.

8.1 Techno-optimism: Integration with human evolution

The first position is techno-optimism, which views the metaverse as an evolutionary leap in human consciousness. Proponents such as Schmalzried argue that immersive environments and AI-enhanced collaboration will enable the emergence of a new form of collective intelligence, extending human capacities in unprecedented ways [5]. From this perspective, the metaverse is not merely a tool but an environment in which human and machine symbiotically co-create meaning. There is truth in this vision. As Youssef et al. show, younger generations already use metaverse technologies to expand social development and psychological well-being [25]. Similarly, Atak and Özkoc highlight that professionals foresee new opportunities for creative collaboration and work-life balance in metaverse spaces

[21]. These findings underscore that the metaverse cannot be dismissed out of hand; it does possess the capacity to enrich life under certain conditions. Yet, techno-optimism tends to overestimate the liberatory potential of technology while underestimating structural dynamics of exploitation. Without careful governance, metaverse platforms may deepen rather than resolve crises of meaning.

8.2 Humanistic resistance: The metaverse as shadow play

The second position is humanistic resistance, which rejects the metaverse as an inauthentic substitute for reality. Critics liken it to Plato's Cave, where humans mistake shadows for reality, enslaved by illusions while neglecting the physical world's demands. Serpil and Karaca articulate this concern, warning that digital spirituality risks pacifying individuals into complacency, detached from ecological crises and real political struggle [4].

This position has force, reminding us that not all that glitters is meaningful. Addiction, alienation, and commodification are real risks. Yet wholesale rejection may also be naïve, given the rapid integration of virtual environments into everyday life [13]. To deny their significance may leave critical analysis underdeveloped, ceding the field to corporate narratives. This resonates with the recent perspective offered by Costa and Murphy, who also draw on Arendt to question the impact of emerging technologies on essential human capacities [37]. Their analysis of generative AI in education highlights how technological integration can displace the activity of thinking and foster *a culture of thoughtlessness*. They caution that without a commitment to responsibility, intellectual honesty, and plurality, digital capitalism risks eroding autonomy and undermining the democratic public sphere. Their call to preserve thinking as a core human practice strongly supports my argument that virtual spaces must be designed and governed to safeguard meaningful action and collective world-building.

8.3 Arendtian action: A middle path

The third position, and the one advocated here, is an Arendtian middle path that focuses on the possibility of action within the metaverse. Rather than celebrating or rejecting the medium, this approach asks: under what conditions can the metaverse foster genuine plurality, unpredictability, and collective world-building? Action, in Arendt's sense, is not mere activity but the initiation of something new in concert with others. It requires freedom, recognition, and a public realm that is not subordinated to necessity. For the metaverse to serve as a platform for meaning, it must therefore prioritize spaces of authentic dialogue, collective decision-making, and durable cultural creation. This entails governance structures that resist corporate monopolization and preserve openness to unpredictable human initiatives. Tommasi captures this imperative by calling for a research agenda that foregrounds human dignity and well-being over technological spectacle [19]. His critique aligns with Arendt's insistence that the highest form of human flourishing is not found in consumption or production but in acting together in freedom. The metaverse will only matter philosophically if it can become such a space. This approach is exemplified by Bay [20], whose Arendtian analysis does not reject the metaverse outright but provides a precise framework for evaluating its threats, focusing on how specific technical properties like reality indistinguishability and predictive processing can be weaponized to undermine democratic foundations [20].

9. Opportunities and limitations

Bringing these strands together, a balanced evaluation emerges. The metaverse offers opportunities for connection, creativity, and economic participation that may partially compensate for the loss of traditional work in an automated society. It can expand avenues for identity exploration, democratize creative tools, and facilitate communities that transcend geography. Empirical studies [21, 25] confirm these potentials. At the same time, the limitations are profound. Current platforms primarily reproduce cycles of labor, commodify creativity, and suppress authentic action under corporate logics. They risk alienating individuals, distorting reality, and deepening dependence rather than fostering autonomy. As Wang observes, the integration of metaverse systems into everyday life threatens to collapse the distinction between leisure, work, and identity, rendering all experience susceptible to commodification [13]. The metaverse may contribute to meaningful life if and only if it is designed and governed to prioritize action, not labor. This requires embedding plurality, durability, and collective governance at the heart of virtual environments. Without such conditions, the metaverse will not solve the crisis of meaning produced by technological unemployment; it will intensify it. **Figure 1** below visualizes the core Arendtian framework for evaluating metaverse activities, distinguishing between Labor, Work, and Action based on their durability and potential for human flourishing.

10. Implications for policy and design

If the metaverse is to become a credible platform for meaningful life in the shadow of technological unemployment, it must be deliberately shaped through policy, governance, and design. Left to market forces alone, virtual environments will likely reproduce the exploitative dynamics of digital capitalism. The following implications emerge from the preceding analysis.

First, governance must move beyond corporate self-regulation toward democratic oversight. As Arendt reminds us, action requires a public realm where individuals can appear before one another as equals. To cultivate such spaces in the metaverse, governance must ensure openness, plurality, and protection of rights. This could include decentralized decision-making mechanisms, transparent moderation policies, and avenues for user participation in platform design. The risk of privatization must be actively countered through public policy.

Tommasi underscores this by calling for research and policy that foreground human dignity rather than profit [19]. His warning resonates with Wang's analysis of how the metaverse is becoming integrated into everyday life: without safeguards, commodification will permeate all domains of existence [13]. Governance that prioritizes the public good is therefore not optional but essential. Current policy frameworks, such as the EU's strategy on virtual worlds, remain focused on traditional misinformation and interoperability but largely ignore the more fundamental threat of reality-indistinguishability and the individualization of perception [20]. Therefore, regulation must move beyond content moderation to address the architectural and economic models of XR platforms, mandating transparency in algorithmic curation and limiting the use of sensory data for micro-segmentation.

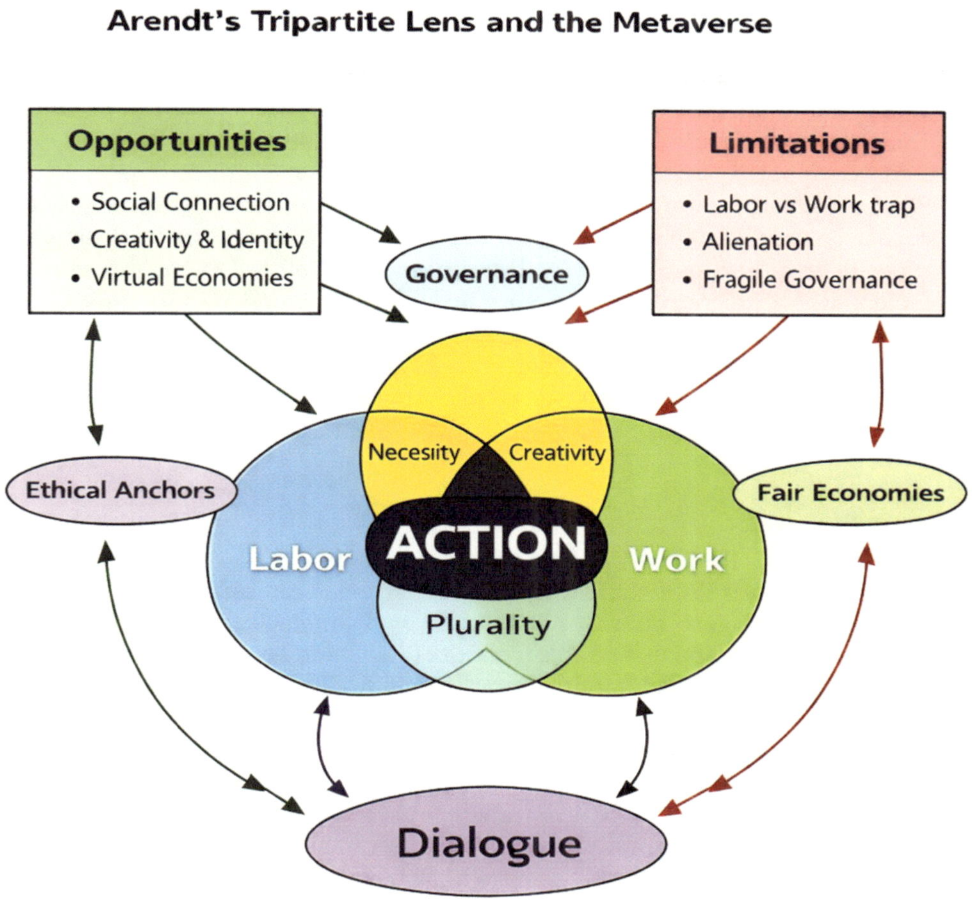

Figure 1.
An Arendtian framework for metaverse activities centralizing action.

Second, economic models within the metaverse must be designed to avoid reproducing precarity. Atak and Özkoc highlight expert concerns that virtual economies risk extending gig-like labor into immersive environments [21]. To prevent this, platforms should integrate mechanisms that guarantee creators royalties, recognize durable contributions, and distribute value fairly. Universal Basic Income (UBI) proposals, though controversial, may also need to be considered as complements to virtual economies in order to ensure subsistence for those displaced by automation. Símová emphasizes that workplace dynamics are already being reconfigured within immersive environments [28]. If these dynamics mirror old hierarchies, the metaverse will merely extend exploitation into new domains. Instead, platforms should experiment with cooperative ownership models, collective bargaining rights for digital workers, and interoperable systems that prevent monopolistic lock-in.

Third, design must include anchors to reality that prevent dissociation and ensure balance. Wang warns that immersive integration risks erasing boundaries between leisure, work, and identity [13]. Designers must therefore provide tools for time management, reminders to disengage, and interfaces that encourage reflection rather than endless immersion. Policies could also mandate ethical design standards akin to those proposed for social media, limiting addictive features and ensuring informed consent. Mental health frameworks must be integrated into the metaverse from the ground up. Bailenson has shown that prolonged immersion can produce psychological strain [26]; designers must address this proactively through guidelines, support systems, and transparency about risks.

Finally, platforms must actively cultivate conditions for action in Arendt's sense. This means not only enabling user-generated content but also fostering forums for dialogue, deliberation, and collective decision-making. Political expression must be protected, dissent tolerated, and plurality preserved. The most meaningful metaverse will not be one where individuals merely consume or create isolated artifacts, but one where they act together to shape a shared world Therefore, the metaverse must be governed as a public sphere rather than a private commodity. Only under such conditions can it contribute to meaning in a post-work society.

11. Conclusion

This paper set out to examine whether the metaverse can serve as a platform for meaningful life engagement in a future shaped by technological unemployment. Through the lens of Hannah Arendt's tripartite distinction between labor, work, and action, the analysis revealed both the promise and peril of immersive virtual environments.

On one hand, the metaverse offers genuine opportunities: enhanced social connection, new forms of creativity, and alternative economic participation. Empirical studies [21, 25, 28] demonstrate that users already experience psychological benefits and professional possibilities in virtual environments. These findings suggest that the metaverse can partially compensate for the erosion of traditional work structures, offering new avenues for purpose, belonging, and identity.

On the other hand, the metaverse confronts severe limitations. Current platforms are dominated by cycles of repetitive, consumptive, and ephemeral labor rather than enduring work or authentic action. Corporate governance structures prioritize profit over plurality, suppressing opportunities for democratic engagement. As Tommasi and Wang emphasize, without radical reform, the metaverse risks becoming an immersive extension of digital capitalism, commodifying not only time and labor but identity and meaning itself [13, 19]. As Bay warns, if the business models of the dominant "gatekeeper" platforms are left unchallenged, the metaverse will not solve the crisis of meaning but will instead become its most powerful engine, leveraging properties like false memory creation and predictive processing to dismantle common reality itself [20].

The synthesis advanced here is conditional: the metaverse may indeed support human flourishing if it is governed and designed to prioritize action over labor. This requires embedding democratic governance, ensuring fair economic participation, protecting mental health, and cultivating spaces for dialogue and plurality. Absent these conditions, the metaverse will not resolve the existential challenges of technological unemployment; it will intensify them.

Future research should deepen this inquiry by empirically investigating cases where the metaverse has successfully supported action and durable work, as well as exploring governance models that align with democratic values. Comparative studies across cultural contexts may reveal how meaning in the metaverse is differentially constructed and contested.

Ultimately, the metaverse crystallizes the challenges and opportunities of a post-work society. It demonstrates the complete dissolution of boundaries between leisure, labor, and political engagement, fundamentally challenging traditional categorizations. Whether it becomes a domain for Arendtian action or a hyper-commodified space of invisible labor depends on our collective choices regarding its governance, economic models, and design ethics. The task is not to reject the metaverse but to fight for a version that honors human capacity for new beginnings, ensuring that this new digital frontier supports durable work and authentic political action rather than extending the cycles of labor into every corner of our virtual lives.

Conflict of Interest

The author declares no conflict of interest.

Author details

Harun Serpil
Anadolu University, Eskişehir, Türkiye

*Address all correspondence to: hserpil@anadolu.edu.tr

References

[1] Manyika J, Chui M, Miremadi M, Bughin J, George K, Willmott P, Dewhurst M. A future that works: AI, automation, employment, and productivity. McKinsey Global Institute Research, Technical Report. 2017;**60**:1–35

[2] Arendt H. The Human Condition. 2nd ed. Chicago: University of Chicago Press; 2018

[3] Dwivedi YK, Hughes L, Baabdullah AM, Ribeiro-Navarrete S, Giannakis M, Al-Debei MM, et al. Metaverse beyond the hype: Multidisciplinary perspectives on emerging challenges, opportunities, and agenda for research, practice, and policy. International Journal of Information Management. 2022;**66**:102542

[4] Serpil H, Karaca D. The Metaverse or meta-awareness?. Journal of Metaverse. 2023;**3**(1):1–8. DOI: 10.57019/jmv.1093347

[5] Richter S, Richter A. Human-AI Collaboration in the Metaverse—How to Research the Future of Work? 2024

[6] Mystakidis S, Lympouridis, V. Immersive Learning. Encyclopedia. 2023;**3**:396–405

[7] Kraus K, Kraus N. Institutionalization of the metaverse based on the development of the exabyte economy and gig economy. Journal of Vasyl Stefanyk Precarpathian National University. 2025;**12**(2):6–13

[8] Waelen RA. Rethinking automation and the future of work with Hannah Arendt. Journal of Business Ethics. 2025;**25**:1–2

[9] Lowry PB, Boh WF, Petter S, Leimeister JM. Long live the metaverse: Identifying the potential for market disruption and future research. Journal of Management Information Systems. 2025;**42**(1):3–38

[10] McStay A. The metaverse: Surveillant physics, virtual realist governance, and the missing commons. Philosophy & Technology. 2023;**36**(1):1–26

[11] Biasi M. Guest Editorial. The Labour Side of the Metaverse. Italian Labour Law e-Journal. 2023;**1**:1–12

[12] Goldberg M, Schär F. Metaverse governance: An empirical analysis of voting within Decentralized Autonomous Organizations. Journal of Business Research. 2023;**160**:113764

[13] Wang G, Zhang Z, Nandhakumar J, Manoharan N. Everyday Metaverse: The Metaverse as an integral part of everyday life. Journal of Management Information Systems. 2025;**42**(1):310–42

[14] Dolata M, Schwabe G. What is the Metaverse and who seeks to define it? Mapping the site of social construction. Journal of Information Technology. 2023;**38**(3):239–266

[15] Stephenson N. Snow Crash. Bantam Books; 1992

[16] Mystakidis S, Lympouridis V. Immersive Learning Design in the Metaverse: A Theoretical Literature Review Synthesis. Application of the Metaverse in Education. 2024:55–71

[17] World Economic Forum. Defining and building the metaverse: A new framework for governance. WEF Report. 2024

[18] Anderson J, Rainie L. The Metaverse in 2040. Washington, D.C: Pew Research Center; 2022

[19] Tommasi F, Degen JL, Orhan MA, Sartori R. Exploring Work and Organizational Psychology in the Metaverse: A Critical Research Agenda. Scandinavian Journal of Work and Organizational Psychology. 2025;**10**(1):1–2

[20] Bay M. Arendt in the Metaverse: Four properties of eXtended Reality that imperil factual truth and democracy. Convergence: The International Journal of Research into New Media Technologies. 2023;**29**(6):1698–1712

[21] Atak M, Özkoc H. The impact of the metaverse on work life: A Delphi study. Journal of Management Development. 2023;**42**(7):633–650

[22] Steger MF. Meaning in life: A unified model. In: The Oxford Handbook of Positive Psychology. 3rd ed. New York, New York: Oxford University Press; 2021:959–967 p

[23] Wong PTP. The PURE model of meaning: A conceptual framework for understanding the human quest for meaning. International Journal of Existential Psychology and Psychotherapy. 2013;**4**(1):1–10

[24] Martela F, Steger MF. The three meanings of meaning in life: Distinguishing coherence, purpose, and significance. The Journal of Positive Psychology. 2016;**11**(5): 531–545

[25] Youssef E, Medhat M, Abdellatif S, Babiker Yousif N. Analyzing the Impact of Metaverse Technology on Social Development: A Field Study on Generation Z in the United Arab Emirates. Social Sciences. Social Sciences. 2024;**13**:(9):446. DOI: 10.3390/socsci13090446 102426

[26] Bailenson J. Experience on Demand: What Virtual Reality Is and How It Works. New York, NY: W. W. Norton & Company; 2018

[27] Yee N, Bailenson J. The Proteus effect: The effect of transformed self-representation on behavior. Human Communication Research. 2007;**33**(3):271–290

[28] Šímová T, Zychová K, Fejfarová M. Metaverse in the virtual workplace. Vision: The Journal of Business Perspective. 2024;**28**(1):19–34

[29] Hileman G, Rauchs M. Global Cryptocurrency Benchmarking Study. Cambridge CB2 1QA United Kingdom: Cambridge Centre for Alternative Finance; 2017

[30] Wang Q, Li R, Wang Q, Chen S Non-fungible token (NFT): Overview, evaluation, opportunities, and challenges. arXiv preprint arXiv:2105.07447. 2021

[31] Ugar ET. Rethinking remote work, automated technologies, meaningful work and the future of work: Making a case for relationality. Philosophy & Technology. 2023;**36**(2):32

[32] Egliston B, Carter M, Clark KE. Who will govern the metaverse? Examining governance initiatives for extended reality (XR) technologies. New Media & Society. 2025;**27**(6):3361–3381

[33] Castelnovo W, Romanelli M. Power relationships in the co-production of smart city initiatives. In: Digital Transformation and Human Behavior, Lecture Notes in Information Systems and Organisation 37 C. Metallo et al. . Cham: Springer International Publishing; 2020. p. 329–342

[34] Heidegger M. The Question Concerning Technology and Other Essays. New York: Harper & Row; 1977

[35] Turner C. The metaverse: Virtual metaphysics, virtual governance, and virtual abundance. Philosophy & Technology. 2023;**36**(4):1–8

[36] Effing R. Will the metaverse be out of control? Addressing the ethical and governance implications of a developing virtual society. Digital Government: Research and Practice. 2024;**5**(3): Article29

[37] Costa C, Murphy M. Generative artificial intelligence in education: (what) are we thinking?. Learning, Media and Technology. 2025;**18**:1–2

Section 4

Immersive Creativity: VR Storytelling, Digital Art, and Creative Economies

Chapter 15

Immersive Narratives in Virtual Reality

Ilona Nowosad and Adam Szalach

Abstract

The chapter explores how immersive technologies, such as virtual reality (VR), are transforming storytelling in the digital age. The focus concentrates on the significant contributions of immersive experiences to emotional and sensory engagement, enabling novel opportunities for interactive and spatial storytelling. The chapter also references studies conducted into story and user engagement, using eye-tracking that examines patterns in gaze as it is embedded within narrative spaces, and BCIs that allow for the real-time generation of customized story experiences. Within the chapter, we review key narrative techniques, VR implementations, consumer experiences in virtual 3D landscapes, and developer challenges (e.g., cyber sickness (simulator sickness), which can impair consumer convenience and session duration). There is also a gloss on ethical debates and the future potential of immersive narratives such as the inclusion of artificial intelligence or multi-channel transmedia experiences. The chapter provides a comprehensive understanding of immersive storytelling through the integration of theoretical and practical insights incorporating technological, cultural, and narrative perspectives.

Keywords: immersive narratives, emotional engagement, virtual reality (VR), interactive media, spatial storytelling, eye-tracking

1. Introduction

Digital technologies have revolutionized the way we communicate and process information—offering new possibilities for the narrative. One of them is digital storytelling, combining conventional storytelling techniques with multimedia to develop dynamic, immersive experiences.

As Lambert and Alexander stress, digital storytelling enables you to create tailored content and reach readers with an interactive type of telling [1, 2].

There are many possible implementations of digital storytelling, ranging from simple video presentations to complex interactive narratives that involve the user in building the story. In addition, this technique is not only useful in the entertainment field but also a useful learning tool to improve the learning process, besides the knowledge acquisition and critical thinking skills development [3].

In education, digital storytelling is used to assist teachers in engaging students and making lessons more appealing. Studies show that multimedia narratives aid in processing information and yield more successful outcomes when developing students' communication skills [4]. Furthermore, digital storytelling assists learning in itself and implementing the twenty-first-century standards of creativity, collaboration, and critical thinking [5].

Even in marketing strategies, we cannot imagine not using digital storytelling to build the brand and to make an emotional connection with customers [6]. Studies have shown that storytelling-based campaigns are more engaging than traditional advertising forms and generate higher customer loyalty [7].

Digital storytelling tools are employed by modern social media and journalism for serving content. An example of this might be an "interactive multimedia report," such as those published by media organizations, including The New York Times or the BBC. This format also engages a deeper involvement of the receiver and allows complex topics to be presented in an accessible way [8].

Modern technologies are critical to a new way of storytelling: interactive, multi-dimensional, immersive. AI, AR, and VR all offer entirely new opportunities for creators to connect with their audience.

For instance, narrative games are designed to let users drive the decisions that effectively alter the trajectory of the plot [9].

The Internet and social media also democratized storytelling—everyone can create and share their stories on this platform. Blogs, vlogs, and podcasts enable sharing experiences and perspectives that until recently were confined to professional media [10].

One of the disruptive aspects of digital storytelling is the personalization of stories using artificial intelligence. Algorithms track users' actions and curate content accordingly, which can make each story unique. A good example is the recommendation systems used by streaming platforms, which suggest movies and series based on viewers' previous choices [11].

Immersive technologies like virtual reality (VR), augmented reality (AR), and mixed reality (MR) have become increasingly significant ways of telling stories. They bring in the degree of interactivity and engagement that the earlier media simply cannot offer. VR allows users to fully immerse themselves in a virtual world through special goggles such as the Oculus Rift or HTC Vive. The technology has wider applications across gaming, education, and medicine, providing immersive experiences to assimilate knowledge and learn practical skills. While VR immerses users completely in a computer-generated environment, AR overlays virtual attributes onto the real world, as perfectly illustrated by the example of the popular game Pokémon Go. MR merges characteristics of both of these technologies, enabling interaction with both the real and the virtual, for example, Microsoft HoloLens.

A key concept in the context of these technologies is immersion, the degree to which the user feels present in the digital environment. Witmer and Singer describe immersion as detachment from reality, while Lombard and Ditton emphasize that the greater the sense of presence in VR, the stronger the involvement in the story [12, 13]. Studies show that high-quality graphics, interactivity, and surround sound significantly affect this effect [13]. Murray points out that decision-making mechanisms in the narrative further enhance immersion [14].

Interactivity in digital storytelling takes various forms. According to Murray, interactive narratives allow users to shape the course of the story, which distinguishes them from traditional, linear storytelling [14]. Ryan distinguishes different interaction models from stories with limited user influence to fully dynamic stories that change in real time in response to the viewer's actions [15]. AI extends these possibilities by adapting the story to the user's preferences, as Manovich notes [16]. This form of narrative co-creation enhances emotional engagement and allows people to better identify with the characters [3].

2. VR technology

Virtual reality is transforming the way we experience stories. At its core, it simulates sensory experiences—visual, auditory, and even tactile—to create realistic environments. VR worlds can reflect real locations or be entirely fictional. It is crucial that the system responds immediately to the user's actions, as even small delays can disrupt the sense of immersion.

The idea of immersive experiences is not new. As early as the eighteenth century, panoramas—huge paintings that gave the illusion of being inside the depicted scene—appeared. The first panorama, patented in 1787 by Scottish artist Robert Barker, employed techniques of perspective to augment the effect of realism. The twentieth century brought technological advances that provided previous generations with new types of immersive experiences, such as the Link Trainer flight simulator (1929) and Morton Heilig's Sensorama (1957), one of the first VR devices to use binaural sound and emit smells [17, 18].

The second half of the twentieth century saw groundbreaking innovations in VR. In 1965, Ivan Sutherland presented the concept of "The Ultimate Display"—a fully interactive, computer-generated world. Soon after, this idea crystallized in a head-mounted display (HMD) system that tracked head movements of the user (1968). The device itself was unwieldy and heavy, requiring a ceiling-mounted arm to support it, hence the name "Sword of Damocles."

Another significant development in VR occurred in 1975, when Myron Krueger made the first interactive VR platform, called Videoplace. This platform was able to track user movements and their location using cameras, without the need for goggles or gloves as in previous systems.

It was a system that consisted of a dark room with cameras sending signals to a computer that processed the information. The computer would then render the information for graphical output in real-time. This interactive VR platform allowed users to manipulate virtual objects, select letters from a virtual keyboard, and even interact with people in other rooms, whose movements were mapped onto the virtual space.

Another innovation was the Aspen Movie Map navigation system (1977), an interactive program for military personnel created by Andrew Lippman's team at the Massachusetts Institute of Technology (MIT). The show gave a virtual tour of Aspen, Colorado, as seen from stop-frame cameras mounted on a car. Users could explore the city, observe seasonal changes, and navigate through 3D models of buildings created from photos. Users could pan, zoom in, and virtually turn into specific streets.

In the following years, Thomas Furness designed a flight simulator developed for military pilots, called "The Super Cockpit" (1986), which included an HMD. The system provided virtual enhancements such as 3D maps and infrared imagery. Pilots could communicate with the virtual environment as in the real world, using hand gestures, eye movements, and through voice commands.

The 1990s and early 2000s led to the commercialization of VR. Practical applications of the technology [19, 20] were demonstrated with networked VR games such as Virtuality (1990), CAVE Automatic Virtual Environment (1992), and the "Virtual Vietnam" (1997) therapeutic system for PTSD veterans. Back in 1990, Jonathan Waldern introduced something that felt straight out of science fiction—a VR arcade machine called Virtuality, unveiled at the Computer Graphic 90 exhibition in London. This wasn't just any arcade game; it let players step into a fully 3D virtual world. Even more impressively, if several machines were networked together, players could see each other in the same digital space. The system used two LCD screens, which had a relatively low resolution of 276 × 372 pixels and were able to render up to 30,000 polygons for 3D display. Players commanded the experience via joysticks and a built-in microphone, and quadraphonic sound made it all the more immersive.

CAVE (Cave Automatic Virtual Environment), the next generation of VR, was conceived in 1992 at the Electronic Visualization Laboratory (EVL) at the University of Illinois. Inside a cube measuring 3 × 3 × 3 meters, you were immersed in high-quality projection on multiple well-placed screens, crisp 3D visuals popping around you in front of the projectors. This innovation was a game changer for the analysis and visualization of scientific data, as users could float through the space using joysticks or electromagnetic sensors that tracked their motion.

In the following years, VR had moved from entertainment and research into therapy. Developed in 1999 by the Georgia Institute of Technology, a program called Virtual Vietnam was designed to help Vietnam War veterans cope with post-traumatic stress disorder (PTSD). It wonderfully mapped the harsh, realistic conditions of the conflict—from the roar of helicopter rotors to the treacherous jungle paths—enabling therapists to gradually expose veterans to their traumatic memories in a controlled and adapted environment. The clinic could tweak sound levels, visual effects, environmental details, and other parameters to suit each patient, making it a potentially breakthrough tool for conditions like post-traumatic stress disorder.

Over the next years, Google Street View (2007) and Oculus Rift (2010) brought VR closer to home, literally and figuratively.

3. Advantages of VR

VR is used in many fields—from tourism (virtual tours), to education (interactive lessons in anatomy, chemistry, physics), to architecture and professional training in demanding industries. In the cultural sector, VR enables museum tours and historical reenactments to preserve cultural heritage in digital form.

Virtual reality (VR) technology has been further used in creating immersive games, allowing interaction, engagement, and the generation of multiple emotional sensations.

The combination of sound, vibrations from the controllers, and natural user movement within VR games has opened up avenues where participants can experience a multiplicity of exciting journeys.

Unlike VR gaming, 360-degree movies watched through VR headsets do not require active user engagement. In such scenarios, the only action the user needs to do is rotate their head; the content on screen does not lead to a change in the user experience. Such films are captured with special spherical cameras that record everything within the camera range.

360-degree video (i.e., when the viewer is wearing VR goggles) is much more immersive than traditional video, as it enables the viewer to completely separate from their surrounding environment, allowing greater engagement with the universe presented in the film.

During the COVID-19 pandemic lockdown, worldwide restrictions immobilized populations, which implied a feeling of separation and enclosure. Virtual reality became one of the ways to temporarily escape these limitations, offering virtual mobility without actual displacement. Virtual tourism, for instance, enables individuals to discover faraway locations, cities, and famous spots that are usually visited by millions of people a year. Virtual reality (VR) technology can produce 360-degree videos and virtual tours that capture realistic representations of these venues, such as a gondola ride through Venetian canals.

Furthermore, the VR in tourism can act as an experience for visualizing locations now beyond reach, whether by decay or ruin, or by practical barriers such as a lack of financial, spatial, or access to vision and hearing experiences, especially for the disabled.

One of the most important value-adding prospects of VR technology is to trigger curiosity and improve the learning curve for students, mainly in domains like biology, chemistry, physics, and history. Subjects such as anatomy can be taught more effectively by allowing users to visualize human or animal bodies at a 1:1 scale, even allowing them to see the correct placement of organs in the body as well as explore diseases in a 3D environment, such as the growth of brain tumors.

Other natural processes, like the water cycle, volcanic eruptions, or seismic activity, including earthquakes and tsunamis, can also be very well-demonstrated via virtual reality simulations. This also helps chemistry and physics play out simulations of physical processes, like a bullet trajectory in a gun, or magnesium burning in oxygen, that would need a very expensive or dangerous run inside a laboratory environment.

Using VR technology, architects can portray and compare their constructions with physical structures before implementation. This ability allows for the discovery of any design flaws and corrections to be made before a structure is built, potentially averting accidents or calamities. Furthermore, VR allows architects to compare the intended design to existing buildings, which helps in decisions related to esthetics like color schemes, shapes, and sunlight rays.

Collaborative engagement is so much more interesting when there are VR glasses involved, and the same applies to interior designers, who use the technology to pitch their designs to clients. By experiencing it in this way, one can better appreciate what the result will be and integrate changes into the design, such as the penetration of daylight at specific hours of the day, into the project before it is too late to adapt them.

VR can help companies, especially in high-risk environments, where human errors may have devastating impacts, to train and simulate. VR creates dangerous or complicated situations that can help employees rehearse their reactions before an error could happen with real-world consequences; if employees can practice in a safe, low-stakes environment, the chances of making mistakes are less in the real world.

What is more, VR tech can augment product demos, providing 3D visualization and a more immersive experience than basic visuals/physical object or text. This kind of technology aids with catching design mistakes early and having potential buyers respond with their own fixes. It enables creating virtual exhibitions to display products more interestingly, which can attract more customers.

Let us also highlight the role of VR in the field of cultural heritage and history. Many museums and galleries also provide virtual tours and enable people to view priceless artwork or historical artifacts without needing to travel. One such location is "Mona Lisa: Beyond the Glass," which offers insight into the iconic work as well as in-depth dissections of its creation and history.

VR is also being utilized for the reconstruction of historical and archaeological objects that are too fragile or damaged to reconstruct physically and allow users to interact with items that are often difficult if not impossible to be easily displayed or studied in detail. With VR, users can manipulate objects—rotating them and zooming in or out on them, studying them from different vantage points—in a way that allows for a much more intimate, up-close and fine-grain examination than traditional museum displays allow.

Virtual reality (VR) technology allows historians and researchers to remodel the layouts of places devastated by natural disasters or wars or those that simply faded away or disappeared from maps. One prominent instance is Pompeii, buried in a volcanic eruption, including such things as an online city built of archaeological remains and plans. These reconstructions are frequently impracticable with the expense or cultural significance of the sites potentially destroying precious and non-replaceable artifacts.

Virtual reality enables us to reconstruct cities as they evolved over historical epochs, based on architectural schematics, illustrations, or photographs. This technology enables the side-by-side interaction with cultural influences inferred from contemporary events that led to the creation of urban forms and construction techniques in certain historic contexts. This also allows for detailed comparisons between different architectural styles, with the possibility of comparing differences (or similarities) between modern-day cities as well as those from earlier historical periods.

As digital storytelling evolves, the integration of AI, VR, and AR will further redefine the way we tell stories. Modern technologies not only expand the boundaries of narrative but also increase its impact on education, entertainment, medicine, and culture.

4. Narrative design in VR

Designing narratives in virtual reality (VR) requires a whole new approach to storytelling—one that takes spatial drama into account. As Ryan [9] notes, stories in VR do not have to unfold in a linear fashion. Instead, the user is free to explore the world and shape the course of the narrative on their own [14]. The key, then, is to design the space in such a way that the story engages the viewer not only with content but also with the very possibility of interaction. Unlike traditional media, such as books or movies, VR allows the user not only to follow the storyline but also to actually become part of it. In practice, two main approaches are used to build such experiences: the Points of Interest (POI) method and the open exploration environment (OEE).

The POI method involves placing key locations in the VR world that naturally capture the user's attention and guide them through the story. Such a solution is great for games, interactive videos, or educational applications, as it allows the user to maintain control over the narrative while giving the viewer some freedom of action. This allows developers to precisely shape the user experience—which is especially important in education or therapy. If the goal is to assimilate specific knowledge or guide the user through a series of tasks, the POI method provides structure and direction.

One of POI's greatest strengths is its effect on immersion—well-designed points of interest help focus the viewer's gaze and attention, so that he or she becomes immersed in the VR world in a more natural way. This makes the experience seamless and engaging, without feeling lost. In education, this approach allows the user to be guided consciously through the steps of learning, making it easier to absorb knowledge. In therapy, on the other hand, controlled narration allows patients to gradually become accustomed to difficult situations and build emotional resilience.

Although it does have its advantages, the POI method also has limitations. However, it is highly directional and gives a lot of attentional cues to the user, so it can leave an impression of too much linearity. When applied to VR environments, this structure can stifle an audience's sense of freedom (for audiences who are already accustomed to more open-ended VR experiences) and decrease levels of engagement.

The user also risks feeling too much control, which can lead to diminishing the autonomy felt by the player and reduce immersion.

One of the concept alternatives is the Open Exploration Environment (OEE), where the user has the complete freedom to discover the world and interact with the narrative. The model, inspired by open worlds in video games, is also applied in fields like education, art, and therapy. Its principal strength lies in allowing for complete customization, being entirely up to the user what he or she wants to look into and at what pace.

Such a model plays on a desire in the viewer, an inherent curiosity that makes the viewer want to keep exploring and finding out what happens in the story for themselves. As a result, interactions become more spontaneous, and the overall VR experience is more authentic and individual. An interesting phenomenon in this context is the so-called emergent narrative—the story can shift dynamically as a response to the actions taken by the user, so each VR session is different.

Both approaches—POI and OEE—have their advantages and limitations (**Table 1**). Choosing the right strategy depends on the goal of the project. If the goal is to precisely guide the user through a specific set of content, the POI method will be a better option. On the other hand, when free exploration and individual experience is key, the open exploratory environment model will be more appropriate. In practice, the best results are often achieved by combining both approaches, creating engaging stories that respond to users' needs.

However, designing open VR worlds comes with significant challenges. One of them is ensuring narrative consistency—in a world without a clear structure, it is easy to lose the logical flow of the story, which can negatively affect the quality of the experience. In addition, users may feel lost without clear directions for exploration. To prevent this, it is necessary to introduce navigation mechanisms that subtly guide the viewer without imposing a rigid path. Another challenge is the high technological requirements—open VR worlds require advanced graphics rendering and real-time interaction management, which entails higher production costs and the need for powerful hardware.

The level of immersion and interactivity is crucial to the reception of narratives in VR. Research indicates that users who are more engaged in exploring the narrative space exhibit stronger emotional responses and greater identification with the

Mechanisms used in POI	Mechanisms used in OEE
Visual cues—Using lighting, color contrast, and movement to attract the viewer's attention	Non-linear narrative—The story is divided into fragments that can be explored in different orders.
Audible cues—Direct the narrative through sound effects such as whispers, echoes, and even changes in sound intensity.	Interactive objects—The user can freely manipulate objects, which affects the development of the plot.
Interactive elements—Objects that the user can interact with further the narrative.	Environmental dynamics—Changing environmental conditions, e.g., weather change, daily cycle.
Non-linear characters—NPCs (non-player characters) that can interact with the player and provide key plot information.	Procedural content generation—AI algorithms create new experiences depending on the user's choices.

Table 1.
Comparison of key features of POI and OEE methods.

characters [21]. Narrative design in VR requires consideration of both technical and psychological aspects. One of the biggest challenges is finding a balance between freedom of exploration and control over the story to ensure narrative consistency [22].

Brain-computer interfaces (BCIs) open up new possibilities in analyzing users' neural activity, making them a valuable tool for studying emotional responses to immersive experiences. In the context of virtual galleries, museums, or VR tours, BCI can assess users' level of engagement, excitement, or stress [23]. Analysis of electroencephalographic (EEG) signals can detect changes in brainwave activity associated with different emotional states—for example, an increase in beta wave activity can indicate increased concentration, while an increase in theta waves suggests a state of relaxation [24].

With this data, VR designers can optimize narrative spaces, increasing immersion and user comfort. What's more, advanced BCI models allow VR content to be dynamically adjusted in real time. For example, the system can automatically adjust the intensity of visual or audio stimuli based on the user's stress level, improving the user's experience and minimizing the negative effects of immersion [25]. The integration of BCI with VR systems is a promising research direction that could contribute to the creation of more personalized and emotionally engaging digital narratives.

Eye tracking, also known in the literature as oculography, is a widely used research technique for analyzing human eye movements. For a long time, researchers have been fascinated by how we perceive reality, which stimuli attract our attention and which are ignored by us. Although interest in the subject of oculography dates back to antiquity, the actual technological breakthrough did not occur until the turn of the twentieth century when the first non-invasive methods of tracking the path of gaze were developed and work began on the design of eye trackers.

The discoveries of Luis Emil Javal and Ewald Hering are considered key milestones in the development of modern oculography [26]. Studying the process of reading, Javal showed that eye movement is not smooth but consists of a series of short jumps (saccades) and moments of fixation, during which visual information is analyzed. Hering, on the other hand, is recognized as the discoverer of saccades as a phenomenon characteristic of eye movement. Their work laid the foundation for further research into the mechanisms of visual perception and visual attention [26, 27].

Important contributions to the development of eye-tracking research were also made by Guy T. Buswell and Alfred Yarbus [26]. Buswell studied eye fixation strategies from a perceptual dimension perspective, improving understanding of attention and image processing. Meanwhile, Yarbus focused on involuntary eye movements and their effects on visual acuity and perception. In a series of experiments, he showed that gaze patterns were being strongly modulated by context and cognitive goals. His innovative achievement was the development of a special contact lens anatomically matched to the cornea, which translated into accurate tracking of eye movements, although it was uncomfortable for the research participants [26, 27].

Thanks to the rapid development of eye-tracking technologies in the twentieth and twenty-first centuries, today's systems enable increasingly precise measurements, with applications in fields such as cognitive psychology, neuromarketing, human-computer interaction, and even clinical medicine.

Today's eye trackers are based on three key methods of recording eye movement:

- Mechanical—which involves using the physical properties of the eye. This category includes contact lenses fitted with magnetized rings or surgical implants that allow eye movements to be tracked.

- Electronic—based on electrooculography (EOG), a technique that measures changes in the electrical potential in the muscles and nerves that control eye movement.

- Optical—using light reflections (Purkini reflections) or direct recording of eye position using cameras and optical sensors [28].

Currently, the optical method is one of the most widely used methods in eye-tracking research. Particularly popular is the use of video oculography and double-Purkinje-image (DPI) measurement [29]. Its popularity is primarily due to its relatively simple design, which is based on the use of a light beam and cameras. Importantly, this method does not require extremely high-precision optics or high-tech image sensors, making it more accessible and less costly compared to other eye-tracking technologies. With the right software, modern webcams—standalone or embedded in mobile devices—are sufficient for analysis.

Thanks to increasing miniaturization and the use of modern, lightweight materials, the size of eye trackers is increasingly approaching that of classic corrective glasses. This makes them suitable for successful use in AR and VR, enabling more immersive and natural interactions of the user with the digital environment and at the same time significantly affecting the quality of perception of the multimodal digital space.

One of the key applications of eye-tracking technology integrated into classic VR and AR systems is to use it for natural interaction and movement in digital space. In practice, thanks to such a solution, users can control a character, object, or interface without the use of dedicated manipulators and navigate using eye movement alone, resulting in increased engagement and a positive impact on the user experience [30]. In addition, it should be noted that research indicates that the use of eye tracking in VR/AR interfaces can lead to more effective and less user-intensive interaction methods. In the article "Interaction Design of Dwell Selection Toward Gaze-based AR/VR Interaction," the authors analyze the dwell selection technique as an alternative to traditional control methods, highlighting its potential to create more natural and intuitive user interfaces [31].

An equally interesting application of eye tracking is the adaptation of rendered content, which involves modifying the displayed content based on the analysis of the user's visual perception patterns, which significantly increases the effectiveness of the message and can lead to a better understanding and memory of the presented information [32]. It is also noteworthy that, with the implementation of customized artificial intelligence models, it can be used to personalize educational experiences in VR. By monitoring which elements of the learning material the user pays the most attention to, the system can adjust the pace and presentation of content to better support the learning process.

The aforementioned user experience is closely linked to the monitoring of fixation points and the order and length of saccades, which allow the system to understand which elements of the presented content attract attention and which are completely ignored, enabling optimization for more engaging elements of the generated environment [33]. In practice, this can allow the generation of a virtual space with appropriately selected and personalized content tailored to the needs and expectations of the end user, thereby increasing the effectiveness of the message and optimizing for ineffective functionality of a given interface.

Eye tracking, in addition to information related to the user's experience itself, his or her cognitive abilities in the digital environment, can significantly improve the optimization of digital systems, especially in the context of VR as well as standalone AR solutions, using acute and peripheral/peripheral vision issues [34]. The technique known as foveated uses eye movement analysis to improve the quality of the rendered environment by increasing the detail of objects directly related to the point of gaze. Peripheral areas, less relevant to the perceptual process, are generated with less detail, which significantly reduces the computing power requirements of the system used.

Eye-tracking technology in virtual reality (VR) and augmented reality (AR) environments shows many benefits, but it should be remembered that its implementation also faces technical and ergonomic challenges. One of the main problems is the accuracy and precision of the measurements and, many times, the insufficient precision of eye tracking, which can lead to misinterpretation of the data. Such errors, in turn, affect the quality of the user's interaction with the system itself. In addition, hardware limitations such as compatibility with corrective eyewear can reduce the effectiveness of eye-tracking systems. In a study published on virtual reality, the authors note the need for further work to improve the accuracy and reliability of these systems in the context of VR [34].

Another important aspect is user comfort. Prolonged use of VR/AR devices equipped with eye-tracking systems can lead to eye fatigue, dry eyeballs, and even headaches. This is often the result of differences in saccadic movements in virtual environments compared to natural conditions, which can cause visual discomfort. Research published in the Proceedings of the Human Factors and Ergonomics Society Annual Meeting suggests that these differences may contribute to increased visual fatigue and highlights the need to develop ergonomic solutions to offset these effects [35]. Additionally, studies indicate that stereoscopic visual inconsistencies in VR applications can lead to so-called cybersickness, manifested by dizziness and nausea, which poses another challenge to implementing eye-tracking technology in VR/AR [36].

Eye tracking is playing an increasingly important role in the development of human interaction with digital XR environments. Its applications include not only intuitive control of interfaces but also content personalization, UX/UI optimization, and improved performance of rendering systems. As this technology continues to evolve, we can expect to see increasingly sophisticated and integrated solutions that will further impact the future of virtual and augmented reality.

5. Ethics and psychological effects of immersion

Virtual reality represents a disruptive innovation that unlocks experiences with high emotional and transformative engagement. However, as this technology progresses, it presents some real challenges to our social interactions, mental health, and ethical dilemmas.

One of the significant challenges associated with immersive virtual environments is the risk of alienation and impaired social interaction. Long-term use of VR technology is shown to cause a gradual reduction in interpersonal skills and difficulties functioning in physical reality [37]. Users may increasingly prefer virtual interactions, which weakens social bonds and makes it more difficult to adapt to everyday situations [38].

VR technology offers intense narrative experiences that can affect users' emotions in ways that require ethical analysis. Immersive environments can influence perceptions of reality and shape viewers' opinions, raising questions about potential mechanisms of manipulation [39].

This is particularly relevant in the context of advertising, political propaganda, and psychological therapy. For example, VR narratives can be constructed to reinforce certain beliefs, which is used in both military training and therapeutic interventions [40].

However, that same mechanism can be used to influence users' identities and thus propagate a distorted view of reality [41]. The prolonged usage of the VR environment may be linked with the dissociative symptoms of depersonalization and derealization [42]. At worst, it may foster psychotic disorders in people who are predisposed to such experiences.

Furthermore, researchers are investigating how VR technology impacts stress and anxiety levels, particularly when exposed to realistic simulations of traumatic events [43]. Simultaneously, VR is also being used to treat post-traumatic stress disorder (PTSD), demonstrating that VR can be both a therapeutic device and an additional source of mental burden depending on the context of use.

As VR-assisted therapy enables users to confront unpleasant memories within a structured environment that they can safely control, patients slowly begin to restore emotional equilibrium. Ensuring that technology with this potential would be realized, however, rests on its thoughtful and responsible design, catering to the psychological needs of users.

One of the most commonly observed side effects of virtual reality use is so-called cybersickness. This condition manifests as nausea, dizziness, disorientation, and fatigue, which results from sensory conflict between visual stimuli and signals received by the vestibular system [44]. Studies show that an increase in visual processing latency in VR systems correlates with an increased risk of cybersickness symptoms [45].

Reducing this effect is one of the key challenges in VR system design. Primary strategies to minimize negative effects include optimizing frame rates, reducing latency, and using interfaces that stabilize visual perception to reduce sensory conflicts [46]. In addition, users can gradually adapt to the VR environment by systematically increasing exposure time and using relaxation techniques.

The rapid evolution of VR technology, too, raises solemn ethical dilemmas. Software developers are largely responsible for the psychological and social effects of their applications. Moreover, safeguarding privacy is increasingly difficult, as VR spaces are capable of tracking user behavior and emotional responses. This raises concerns about profiling and manipulative influence on consumer behavior. Given the potential for misuse of VR technologies, it is imperative to develop clear ethical guidelines and regulatory frameworks within VR to ensure that the technology is used in socially responsible ways and protects human well-being.

6. Summary

Digital storytelling is an important part of modern communication. Its application in education, in marketing, and in media and culture emphasizes its increasing significance in the digital era. In the future, tools to create digital stories will ensure that multimedia storytelling, and particularly immersive narratives, will be an integral part of interpersonal interactions.

Eye-tracking technology and a brain-computer interface can complement these systems and allow us to personalize content to an individual and even optimize a person's overall experience—opening up a whole new dimension in storytelling in the digital world.

Yet, flexible storytelling that responds to audience emotions and reactions arms us with tools for more engaging and interactive storytelling. Artificial intelligence and augmented reality (AR) are broadening the boundaries of digital storytelling—one that's more lifelike and multi-dimensional than traditional narrated storytelling—that bridges corporeality and digitization into transmedia experiences that coalesce the real and the virtual.

Responsible narrative design would also consider not only the technical aspects but also the ethical implications of the long-term use of the technology. As this becomes more ubiquitous, creators and fans will start to interlink in ways that have not existed before. As people explore digital environments, we will bridge the gap between creator and viewer, changing the way we interact on a level that we have never explored before.

Acknowledgements

The research is a part of project Bitscope (no 2021/03/Y/ST6/00002) supported by the National Science Centre, Poland within CHIST-ERA IV from the EU Horizon 2020 Research and Innovation Programme (Grant Agreement no 857925).

Author details

Ilona Nowosad* and Adam Szalach
University of Social and Media Culture, Toruń, Poland

*Address all correspondence to: ilona.nowosad@aksim.edu.pl

References

[1] Lambert J. Digital Storytelling: Capturing Lives, Creating Community. Oxfordshare, UK: Routledge; 2013. ISBN: 9780415627023. DOI: 10.4324/9780203102329

[2] Alexander B. The New Digital Storytelling: Creating Narratives with New Media. Westport, California, USA: Praeger; 2011. ISBN: 9780313387494. DOI: 10.5040/9798216979456

[3] Jenkins H. Convergence Culture: Where Old and New Media Collide. New York, USA: NYU Press; 2006. Available from: http://www.jstor.org/stable/j.ctt9qffwr [Accessed: March 20, 2025]

[4] Robin BR. Digital storytelling: A powerful technology tool for the 21st century classroom. Theory Into Practice. 2008;**47**(3):220-228

[5] Ohler J. Digital Storytelling in the Classroom: New Media Pathways to Literacy, Learning, and Creativity. Thousand Oaks, California, USA: Corwin Press; 2013. ISBN: 9781452268255. DOI: 10.4135/9781452277479

[6] Pulizzi J. Epic Content Marketing: How to Tell a Different Story, Break through the Clutter, and Win More Customers by Marketing Less. New York City, New York, USA: McGraw-Hill; 2012. ISBN: 978-0-07-181989-3

[7] Heath C, Heath D. Made to Stick: Why Some Ideas Survive and Others Die. New York, USA: Random House; 2007. ISBN: 1400064287

[8] Miller CH. Digital Storytelling: A Creator's Guide to Interactive Entertainment. Waltham, Massachusetts, USA: Focal Press; 2014. ISBN: 0415836948

[9] Ryan ML. Narrative as Virtual Reality 2: Revisiting Immersion and Interactivity in Literature and Electronic Media. Baltimore, USA: Johns Hopkins University Press; 2015. ISBN: 1421417979

[10] Jenkins H. Participatory Culture in a Networked Era: A Conversation on Youth, Learning, Commerce, and Politics. Cambridge, UK: Polity Press; 2016. ISBN: 9781509503247

[11] Saif A, Norzalita A. Impact of AI on Customer Experience in Video Streaming Services: A Focus on Personalization and Trust. International Journal of Human-Computer Interaction. 2024. DOI: 10.1080/10447318.2024.2400395

[12] Witmer BG, Singer MJ. Measuring presence in virtual environments: A presence questionnaire. Presence Teleoperators and Virtual Environments. 1998;7(3):225-240

[13] Lombard M, Ditton T. At the heart of it all: The concept of presence. Journal of Computer-Mediated Communication. 1997;**3**(2). DOI: 10.1111/j.1083-6101.1997.tb00072.x

[14] Murray JH. Hamlet on the Holodeck: The Future of Narrative in Cyberspace. Cambridge, Massachusetts, USA: MIT Press; 1997. ISBN: 9780262631877

[15] Ryan ML. Narrative as Virtual Reality: Immersion and Interactivity in Literature and Electronic Media. Johns Baltimore, Maryland, USA: Hopkins University Press; 2001. ISBN: 0801864879

[16] Manovich L. The Language of New Media. Cambridge, Massachusetts, USA: MIT Press; 2001. ISBN: 0262632551

[17] De Angelo J. The Link Flight Trainer. New York: Roberson Museum and Science Center; 2000. pp. 3-7

[18] Heilig ML. Sensorama Simulator. New York: United States Patent Office; 1962. pp. 9-13

[19] Cruz-Neira C, Sandim DJ, De Fanti TA. Surround-Screen Projection-Based Virtual Reality: The Design and Implementation of the CAVE. Chicago; 1993. pp. 135-136

[20] Hodges LF, Rothbaum BO, Alarcon R, Ready D, Shahar F, Graap K, et al. Virtual Vietnam: A Virtual Environment for the treatment of Vietnam War Veterans with Post-traumatic Stress Disorder. Paper presented at the International Conference on Artificial Reality and tele-existence. Tokyo, Japan: University of Tokyo; December 1998:21-23

[21] Slater M, Wilbur S. A framework for immersive virtual environments (FIVE): Speculations on the role of presence in virtual environments. Presence Teleoperators and Virtual Environments. 1997;**6**(6):603-616

[22] Kim YE, Khajavi MJ, Exploring the Viewer's Role in Narrative-Based Animated Virtual Reality Experiences: Strategies for Role Activation and Immersive Storytelling. Animation. 2024;**19**(2-3):101-128. DOI: 10.1177/17468477241281

[23] Guger C, Edlinger G, Harkam W, Niedermayer I, Pfurtscheller G. How many people are able to operate an EEG-based brain-computer interface (BCI)? IEEE Transactions on Neural Systems and Rehabilitation Engineering. 2016;**11**(2):145-147

[24] Fairclough SH, Gilleade K. Advances in Physiological Computing. London, UK: Springer Verlag; 2014. ISBN: 9781447163916

[25] Aricò P, Borghini G, Di Flumeri G, Colosimo A, Bonelli S, Golfetti A, et al. Adaptive automation triggered by EEG-based mental workload index: A passive brain-computer interface application in realistic air traffic control environment. Frontiers in Human Neuroscience. 2018;**12**:187

[26] Wade NJ. Pioneers of eye movement research. i-Perception. 2010;**1**(2):36-37. DOI: 10.1068/i0389

[27] Duchowski AT. Eyetracking Methodology. New York: Springer; 2017

[28] Holmqvist K et al. Eyetracking: A Comprehensive Guide to Methods and Measures. Oxford: Oxford University Press; 2015

[29] Dual Purkinje Eyetrackers. Ku Leuven—Laboratory of Experimental Psychology Dual Purkinje Eyetrackers. Available from: https://ppw.kuleuven.be/home/english/research/lep/resources/purkinje [Accessed: November 20, 2025]

[30] Sendhilnathan N, Fernandes AS, Proulx MJ, Jonker TR. Implicit gaze research for XR systems. arXiv preprint arXiv:2405.13878. 2024

[31] Isomoto T, Yamanaka S, Shizuki B. Interaction design of dwell selection toward gaze-based AR/VR interaction. In: Proceedings of the 2022 Symposium on Eye Tracking Research and Applications (ETRA '22). Seattle, WA, USA: Association for Computing Machinery; June 8-11 2022. pp. 1-2. DOI: 10.1145/3517031.3531628

[32] Gao H. Assessment of human behavior in virtual reality by eye tracking. arXiv preprint arXiv:2211.12846. 2022

[33] Osińska V, Nowosad I. Multimodal exploring art by VR goggles. Eye tracking patterns in a virtual gallery. Paper presented at the Visual Science of Art Conference(VSAC). University of Aberdeen; 2024. DOI: 10.13140/RG.2.2.27171.36649

[34] Adhanom IB, MacNeilage P, Folmer E. Eye tracking in virtual reality: A broad review of applications and challenges. Virtual Reality. 2023;**27**:1481-1505. DOI: 10.1007/s10055-022-00738-z

[35] Roberts J, Christian S. User comfort in VR/AR headsets: A mathematical investigation into ergonomic and functional limitations of eye tracking technology. Proceedings of the Human Factors and Ergonomics Society Annual Meeting. 2024;**68**(1):1235-1239. DOI: 10.1177/10711813241263510

[36] Li S, Gao C, Zhang J, Zhang Y, Liu Y, Gu J, et al. Less Cybersickness, Please: Demystifying and Detecting Stereoscopic Visual Inconsistencies in Virtual Reality Apps. Proceedings of the ACM on Software Engineering. 1, FSE, Article 96 (Jul 2024), pp. 2167-2189

[37] Slater M, Sanchez-Vives MV. Enhancing our lives with immersive virtual reality. Frontiers in Robotics and AI. 2016;**3**:74

[38] Gonaygunta H, Meduri SS, Podicheti S, Nadella GS. The Impact of Virtual Reality on Social Interaction and Relationship via Statistical Analysis. International Journal of Machine Learning for Sustainable Development. 2023;**5**(2). Available from: https://ijsdcs.com/index.php/IJMLSD/article/view/518 [Accessed: March 23, 2025]

[39] Madary M, Metzinger T. Real virtuality: A code of ethical conduct. Recommendations for good scientific practice and the consumers of VR-technology. Frontiers in Robotics and AI. 2017;**3**:3

[40] Gorini A, Riva G. Virtual reality in anxiety disorders: The past and the future. Expert Review of Neurotherapeutics. 2008;**8**(2):215-233

[41] Brey P. The ethics of representation and action in virtual reality. Ethics and Information Technology. 1999;**1**(2):5-14

[42] Aardema F, O'Connor K, Côté S, Taillon A. Virtual reality induces dissociation and lowers the sense of presence in objective reality. Cyberpsychology, Behavior, and Social Networking. 2010;**13**(4):429-435

[43] Rizzo AA, Pair J, Graap K, Manson B, McNerney PJ, Wiederhold MD, et al. Virtual reality exposure therapy for PTSD. Journal of Clinical Psychology. 2016. DOI: 10.1016/B978-0-12-397045-9.00196-8

[44] LaViola JJ. A discussion of cybersickness in virtual environments. ACM SIGCHI Bulletin. 2000;**32**(1):47-56

[45] Stanney KM, Lawson BD, Rokers B, Dennison MS, Fidopiastis C, Stoffregen T. Identifying causes of and solutions for cybersickness in immersive technology: Reformulation of a research and development agenda. International Journal of Human-Computer Interaction. 2020;**36**(19):1783-1803

[46] McCauley ME, Sharkey TJ. Cybersickness: Perception of self-motion in virtual environments. Presence Teleoperators and Virtual Environments. 1992;**1**(3):311-318. DOI: 10.1162/pres.1992.1.3.311

Chapter 16

VR as an Interface between Art and Technology: Enhancing User Experience and Emotional Engagement in a Virtual Gallery

Veslava Osinska, Dominik Mirosław Piotrowski, Adam Szalach, Weronika Kortas, Tomasz Gross and Jesus Casal Martinez

Abstract

In recent years, virtual reality and connected technologies such as augmented and mixed realities, have also enjoyed considerable popularity in architecture and culture. For example, design offices or furniture stores offer their clients the opportunity to walk around a virtual apartment, which is a visualisation of the project for approval and in which the consumer can check how a given arrangement or piece of furniture may look in reality, and not just on paper. However, when it comes to culture, here, we are also dealing with virtual walks, but in this case in art galleries or museums. Visitors can view an exhibition without having to visit a museum in another country, and they can interact with art by touching or viewing objects or paintings from very close, without damaging cultural assets. The chapter introduces to virtual art gallery project aimed to explore capabilities of human perception in VR. It included a comparative analysis of user experience and visual perception using eyetracking. The images, sourced from the BITSCOPE project's CHIST-ERA IV collection, represent different epoches and art styles. The eyetracking study focused on key areas and gaze plot sequences.

Keywords: virtual reality, art virtual gallery, headset, visual perception, eye tracking

1. Introduction

Virtual reality (VR) is an artificial spatial environment composed of objects and an IT-generated sequence of events. Early visions of a virtual world engaging the user's senses of touch, hearing, and sight date back to the first half of the twentieth century. In his 1935 book, The Pygmalion's Spectacles, Stanley Weinbaum introduced the concept of full immersion, in which the user not only receives stimuli but also actively participates in virtual experiences [1]. However, the technological realisation of these ideas did not take place until 1957, when Morton Heilig developed Sensorama, a device enabling a multisensory experience of city cycling. Sensorama provided a three-dimensional image, realistic sounds, vibrations, and even smells, but due to technological limitations, it failed to gain widespread popularity [1]. In the early 1960s, the Philco Headsight was developed – the first head-mounted display (HMD) capable of transmitting images from a distance, which gave rise to the concept of wearable displays. In 1968, Ivan Sutherland introduced the Sword of Damocles – the first head-mounted display capable of generating a three-dimensional virtual environment. Although the device was bulky and merely a prototype, it set the foundation for the future development of VR. In 1978, Myron Krueger created the first interactive VR platform that did not require goggles or helmets, using computer graphics, projectors, and cameras to generate a virtual space around the user.

At the core of VR lies a computer simulation that monitors the user's state and actions and then replaces or supplements them with feedback. All of these are designed to create a sense of immersion by engaging one or more senses. As a result, four key elements of VR can be identified: the virtual environment, virtual presence, feedback, and interactivity [2].

Until now, virtual reality has primarily been used in commercial sectors such as industry and computer gaming. However, in recent years – shaped by lockdowns related to the COVID-19 pandemic and the war in Ukraine – VR's immense potential has emerged in entirely new, previously unexplored areas of human activity.

While virtual reality (VR) requires the user's full immersion – a form of "detachment" from the real world – augmented reality (AR) enhances, enriches, or reinforces the real-world image with virtual elements. To achieve this visual effect, appropriate equipment – such as goggles or smart glasses – is required to overlay a digital layer onto the real-world view seen by the user.

Mixed reality (MR) builds upon the functionality of AR, allowing users to integrate and interact with virtual objects. Notably, it does not always require goggles or smart glasses, as it can also operate on mobile devices. However, it should be noted that, in the literature, the terms MR and AR are sometimes used interchangeably. The diagram below illustrates the terminological complexities surrounding MR-related technologies.

At times, MR is also referred to as AV (Augmented Virtuality), a concept where virtual reality remains dominant, subtly incorporating elements from the real world. Regardless of these fine distinctions, the primary difference between AR and MR mainly lies in the proportion of real and virtual elements. The development of VR accelerated with the advent of personal computers, 3D technology, and computer gaming. A major breakthrough occurred in 2014 when Facebook acquired Oculus

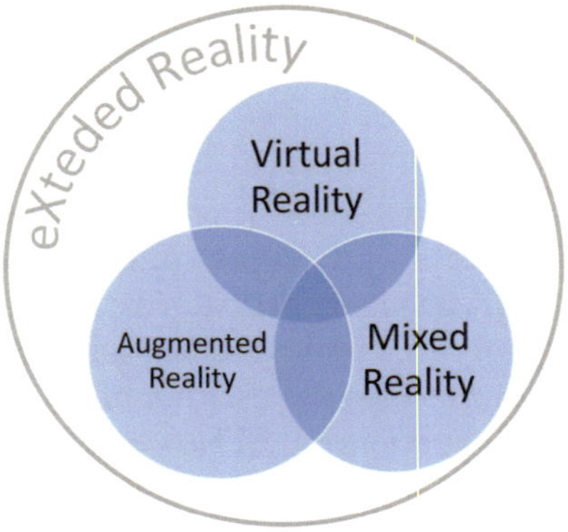

Figure 1.
The relation between immersive realities.

VR, ushering in a new era of VR and AR development and popularising the concept of the Metaverse – a virtual universe connecting people in the digital world [3]. There is also one term floating around that connects all above: extended reality (XR). This concept is a broad research area that encompasses three types of immersive realities. XR technologies aim to create entirely immersive experiences (**Figure 1**).

In recent years, shaped by the COVID-19 pandemic and armed conflicts, VR and AR have demonstrated their broad applicability across both general and highly specialised fields. This technology enables the study of user immersion in virtual galleries and museums. Moreover, user experience research can be conducted as individuals observe works of art they might never have the opportunity to see in the real world.

2. VR as art medium

VR art, which dates back to the 1990s [4], is a contemporary form of creativity and artistic expression that utilises immersive technology, such as virtual reality, to fully engage the viewer in a three-dimensional, interactive environment. Depending on the level of immersion, VR systems can be classified as non-immersive, semi-immersive, or fully immersive, with only the latter enabling complete immersion and intense interaction between the user and the virtual environment [5]. Typically, a VR art viewer can explore, navigate, and interact with the environment using head-mounted displays (HMDs), motion controllers, and various types of sensors [6]. Key characteristics of VR art include immersive experience, interactivity, and navigation [5, 7], as well as three-dimensionality and a multi-sensory experience [4, 8]. Within this framework, two distinct approaches can be identified. The first involves creating an artwork directly in a virtual space, such as a digital painting or a 3D sculpture, and presenting it in VR using an HMD. The second, by contrast, consists of producing the artwork using traditional methods and subsequently exhibiting it in VR (**Figure 2**).

Figure 2.
A user wearing an HTC VIVE Pro Eye exploring a virtual exhibition featuring traditional, digitised works of art; the monitor displays the image seen in VR (BITSCOPE project laboratory, 2024). Source: Own collection.

As an artistic medium, VR not only enables the creation of artworks but also allows them to be experienced in innovative ways [4]. VR art offers numerous possibilities for both artists and viewers, providing immersive and interactive experiences that transcend traditional forms of artistic expression. Modern technologies, combined with human creativity, facilitate the development of extraordinary experiences in virtual reality, opening up a wide range of VR applications in art. These include reconstructions of cultural heritage and archaeology, virtual museums and exhibitions, time travel, artistic tools and design, art education [5], immersive art galleries, innovative theatre performances, sculpture and 3D art [6], immersive storytelling [9], and emotional experimental typography [4].

As mentioned above, VR art is revolutionising approaches to art itself, opening up new perspectives for artists. One of the most significant innovations is the three-dimensional creative space, which provides a virtual environment for experimentation. Interactivity and co-creation represent another crucial aspect, allowing the viewer to become an active participant who can, for instance, influence the narrative of immersive stories. Additionally, VR enhances immersion and deepens the emotional impact on the viewer, as profound engagement with the artwork enables a more intense and emotionally charged experience. This technology introduces innovative ways of integrating art into education, facilitating, among other things, the opportunity to explore and appreciate works "from the inside." At the same time, global accessibility and inclusivity ensure that exhibitions and artworks are available to everyone, regardless of location. It is also worth noting that VR poses new challenges for artists, who must develop new skills and master advanced tools [5, 9, 10]. At present, artists can choose from a wide range of tools for creating VR art, depending on their objectives and expertise. The most popular ones include 3D modelling tools (Blender, Maya, SculptrVR), game engines (Unity, Unreal Engine), applications for producing VR experiences (Tilt Brush, Google Blocks), and animation software (Adobe Animate, Houdini).

VR art, generated using the aforementioned tools, not only facilitates the creation of unique works but also enables their display in innovative exhibitions. As a communication medium with significant potential, virtual exhibitions represent a rapidly growing field that offers numerous benefits and opportunities for both artists and art audiences [11]. Ensuring effective communication between the content of an exhibition and its audience is of paramount importance. Therefore, when designing virtual exhibitions, it is essential to consider that personal, social, content-related, and environmental factors all contribute to optimising this communication [11]. Simultaneously, the possibility of interaction and the feeling of presence through VR significantly enhance the experience of art exhibition visitors, with immersion, satisfaction, and expectation fulfilment playing a crucial role in their engagement and the overall success of the exhibitions [10]. It should be emphasised that, in an effort to intensify the audience's experience, exhibition creators can employ immersive storytelling, described as a "time-limited, location-based experience that invites audiences into a fragmented narrative across multiple mediums. Engaging various senses and requiring active participation, the experience adapts to individual choices and uses technology as a tool to expand the narrative spaces" [9]. Put differently, VR art – through interactive storytelling, modern technologies, and deep immersion – is reshaping creative perspectives and transforming perceptions of artistic outcomes, granting creators and audiences access to previously unattainable experiences.

3. Eye tracking in art perceptionVR as art medium

Eye tracking (ET), as a technique for monitoring eye movements, provides data on points of focus, known as fixations, and the rapid movements between them, referred to as saccades. By analysing ET data, we can determine the duration and location of fixations, as well as the timing and trajectory of saccades [12, 13]. This data offers valuable insights into the processes of both creating and perceiving works of art.

Eye-tracking makes it possible to identify both individual fixations and cumulative fixations from a group of observers. ET reveals how attention is distributed, what is focused on, and what is observed.

The origins of eye tracking (ET) research in the context of art are closely associated with figures such as Thomas Buswell and Alfred Yarbus. The former studied the relationship between eye movement and the viewing of art photography, concluding that eye movement cannot be described by a smooth trajectory. Participants focused their gaze on specific points depending on their interest in particular elements of the image. By comparing subjects' perceptual behaviour, Buswell found that, although gaze paths and directions of eye movement varied, certain areas consistently attracted attention across different individuals. He observed this using cumulative fixations at specific points in the image [14]. The Russian psychologist Yarbus formulated the hypothesis that central areas of an image most often attract the viewer's gaze. He was also the first to recognise the strong cognitive determinants influencing perceptual patterns in complex images, such as works of art [15]. Yarbus noted that gaze paths differed among participants depending on the specific cognitive task and suggested that the degree of interest in art should be considered when attempting to model eye movement [16]. Buswell's model, on the other hand, based on fixation durations, proposed two phases in the perception of artworks. The first is an initial recognition of the scene, lasting 10–15 seconds, during which fixations are short. The second phase involves a more detailed examination of closely positioned elements, characterised by shorter saccades and longer fixations. His findings have been confirmed in subsequent studies [14, 17].

Studies on image perception have shown that fixations of all subjects concentrate on so-called visual saliency regions. In this context, it is worth mentioning theoretical works that describe such viewer behaviour. In 1947, the Polish art theorist and artist Władysław Strzemiński wrote the manuscript Teoria widzenia (Theory of Seeing), intended for his students at the Academy of Fine Arts in Łódź. Thanks to them, this text was first published in 1958 and later republished in 2016 [18]. In his work, Strzemiński defined the concept of visual awareness, particularly its specific form: photosensitive awareness. According to Strzemiński, visual keys can be identified by strong contrasts of light and shadow, the interaction of local colours (as a result of the afterimage phenomenon), and the realism of moving images, as exemplified in the works of the Impressionists [19].

In ET research, digital modifications of original visual materials have been introduced to identify and test the compositional keys of an image. The aim was to observe, through fixation analysis, which areas serve as the strongest stimuli attracting subjects' attention [20]. For this purpose, changes in colour, optical balance, and the hierarchical scale of elements were applied. It was observed that areas of high-resolution images attract the most attention from users [20].

Due to the increasing availability of eye trackers, we are now witnessing a steady rise in interest in ET research on the perception of works of art. As of 7 January, a search for the phrase "eye tracking/eyetracking AND art" in the Web of Science scientific literature database returned 1507 records. These publications were mostly categorised within the field of computer science, including 428 in the AI section, 359 in engineering, 238 in CS methods and theory, and 177 in interdisciplinary applications of CS. Only 109 articles fell under the category of imaging science and photographic technology. This classification suggests that researchers working in this field are primarily affiliated with physics, computer science, or cognitive science.

ET experiments are conducted both in laboratory settings and in exhibition spaces, involving between 20 and 150 participants. In most cases, art experts – usually a minority within the sample – are identified separately. This approach allows researchers to examine whether expert knowledge of art influences the way artworks are analysed and perceived. Some scholars emphasise that experts' viewing strategy is characterised by longer but less frequent fixations when observing original artworks, with special attention paid to the composition of the piece [21]. Furthermore, expert artists exhibited longer fixations when contemplating familiar paintings and shorter ones when viewing unfamiliar works, whereas the opposite was observed among non-artists [14].

The average time required to view paintings in most experimental settings was less than the estimated 27.2 seconds (median: 17.0 seconds), which art experts consider sufficient to have an aesthetic experience [22]. This necessitates careful planning of visual stimulus presentation sequences with appropriately timed displays.

4. Eye tracking for GLAMs

In view of the growing number of museums and cultural institutions in metropolitan areas and in increasingly large cities, it seems vital to study visitors' experiences. Different UX models for museum visitors are being developed based on the sociocultural context, individual factors, or identity-related motivation, e.g. Falk [23]. Insight into these psychosocial mechanisms helps in designing ever more effective ways of promoting GLAM (Galleries, Libraries, Archives, and Museums) and reaching a wider audience. The time spent contemplating a work of art serves as an important indicator of visitor engagement: on average, it is just a few seconds, with a maximum of 30 seconds [24]. The study observed: "... visitors spend little time at individual exhibit components (often a matter of a few seconds and seldom as much as one minute); seldom read labels; usually stop at less than half the components at an exhibit; are more likely to use trial-and-error methods at interactive exhibits than to read instructions; that children are more likely to engage with interactive exhibits than adults, and that attention to exhibits declines sharply after about half an hour" [25].

The strategy of visiting has been noted to include the characteristic behaviour of "skipping" from object to object or focusing on a selected work for a longer time, though it rarely exceeds 1 minute [24]. In the case of interactive artworks, greater audience engagement has been observed, which has been linked to the time spent viewing the object. To accurately measure the time spent viewing artworks, eye-tracking technology, increasingly recognised in applied sciences, was used. This became particularly evident following the empirical discovery that gaze and attention are closely linked, which implies a direct relationship between how we look at museum objects and how we think about them [26]. At the turn of the century, work began on adapting eye trackers, which at the time were cumbersome and restricted users' head movements. Modified eye-tracking systems designed to study the general public, such as museum visitors, were first described by French engineers [27].

The limitations imposed by ET devices meant that research on the visual perception of art observers was largely conducted in laboratories rather than in museum settings [14].

More advanced eye-tracking systems were designed to be worn on the head (HMDs) and resembled goggles or glasses. They allowed users to move their heads freely. The potential of ET research has been particularly evident in studies using mobile eye tracking. With the help of ET glasses, it is possible to conduct extensive research on the experience of art directly in the museum environment. Milekic [28] provided an overview of ET research and its potential applications in museology and art history, emphasising the advent of affordable and widely accessible equipment. Mobile eye trackers have become the main technology for understanding how people contemplate art and for conducting multifaceted analyses of gallery visitors' behaviour [29]. Brieber et al. [30] observed that the relationship between the time spent contemplating art and viewing time varies between a gallery environment and a laboratory setting. Museum participants expressed more positive emotions when engaging with artworks, found them more fascinating, and spent more time looking at them compared to laboratory participants.

Visual perception was also studied in relation to the museum environment, including contextual information accompanying exhibits, such as descriptions and metadata [31]. Such user experience research sheds light on how viewers perceive and understand artworks, thus contributing to the improvement of museum practices in the display of artworks.

5. VR galleries

Virtual reality galleries have so far demonstrated a wide range of approaches to presenting art and engaging audiences. The development of these galleries has been closely tied to technological progress and artistic experimentation. The first experimental VR galleries appeared in the 1990s, when technology such as CAVE (Cave Automatic Virtual Environment) began to be incorporated into artistic projects, allowing the viewer to be immersed in a three-dimensional virtual space [32]. Unfortunately, their availability was severely limited due to technological barriers and the high cost of equipment. The development of VR headsets such as the Oculus Rift and HTC Vive revolutionised the sector, leading to more immersive experiences that could be enjoyed by a wider audience [33].

VR galleries such as the Museum of Other Realities and Acute Art [34] pioneered the use of virtual reality as a platform for artists and curators to experiment with space and interactivity. The Museum of Other Realities offers users access to virtual exhibitions where artworks are digitally displayed, taking advantage of the unique possibilities of VR. The Acute Art platform, on the other hand, has focused on collaborating with renowned artists such as Olafur Eliasson and Marina Abramović to provide intriguing experiences that would not be feasible in traditional galleries.

The key advantage of virtual galleries is their capacity to overcome geographical and logistical barriers. They allow those previously excluded from such experiences, for example due to geographical distance or physical disabilities, to enjoy art [35]. However, strict technical requirements, such as the necessity of expensive high-definition VR equipment and constant access to high-speed internet, still prevent the full realisation of the potential of such spaces.

Existing VR gallery projects often emphasise the key importance of immersion and interactivity in the user experience. Exhibitions such as *Dreams of Dalí* (https://thedali.org/dreams-of-dali-2/) or the *Van Gogh VR Experience* (https://vangoghexpo.com/) are designed to transport viewers into the artists' imaginary worlds, allowing for a deeper understanding of their work. Critics, though, point out differences between virtual and classic exhibitions. Some argue that the focus on technology is excessive and can ultimately overshadow the art itself, making VR galleries more of a tool for showcasing technological capabilities than a platform for artistic reflection.

In conclusion, to date, VR galleries are a rapidly developing artistic space which, while opening up new creative possibilities, also faces significant challenges in terms of accessibility, technology, and the balance between form and content. In this context, virtual reality is not a perfect reproduction of the original experience but rather a completely new medium with its own character and distinctive principles [36].

6. Exploration of VR galleries

Methods of movement in virtual reality play a critical role in fostering user immersion and minimising side effects. The most common undesirable effect is the so-called simulator sickness [37]. Analogous to motion sickness, this refers to a group of unpleasant symptoms, including dizziness, headaches, nausea, or difficulties with balance when using VR or AR devices. Despite offering various ways to move around, in the case of a VR art gallery, only a few are effective, mostly due to considerations of user comfort and immersion. The first of these is "teleportation," where the user is instantly transported to a chosen destination in the virtual world. This method, although it reduces the impression of realism, significantly minimises the symptoms of simulator sickness [38].

Alternatively, methods based on continuous movement are used via controllers. This allows for smoother and more realistic exploration of space but also increases the risk of discomfort caused by simulator sickness [39].

Solutions based on tracking the user's body movements, such as Omni One treadmills (https://virtuix.com), which allow for physical movement in any direction, are growing in popularity [40]. Studies also indicate the benefits of developing techniques involving hybrid systems that combine teleportation with analogue movement, thus ensuring a balance between immersion and user comfort [41]. Each of the aforementioned methods has its own advantages and disadvantages, and choosing one over the other depends on the nature of the gallery and the user's needs.

7. Case study

The BITSCOPE project aims to develop an innovative brain-computer interface (BCI) capable of recognising natural patterns of brain activity during interaction with the environment, as well as investigating mental states generated exclusively in virtual environments. In the era of rapid advancements in virtual reality technology, including online courses, virtual conferences, and digital art exhibitions, there is a growing demand for solutions that can effectively monitor and regulate users' emotions. The core of the project is the identification of individual "neural signatures" – unique patterns of brain activity analysed using advanced non-linear system models.

The objective is to create a passive BCI application that personalises user experiences through machine learning systems, known as recommendation algorithms. The web application provides visitors with the opportunity to explore a virtual art gallery. The gallery features a collection of exhibits that are initially randomly selected from a larger collection. The items on display may include photographs, famous paintings, 3D art objects, historical artefacts, and more.

A visitor experiencing the exhibition for the first time follows a path through a virtual gallery, stopping at selected exhibits to take a closer look. Some of them may resonate with them more than others. After leaving the gallery and returning later, the exhibition is reorganised. The exhibits that did not spark their interest the first time around are replaced with new, more engaging ones suggested by the system.

Another person, unlike the previous visitor, will see a completely different selection of objects. Over time, the exhibition gradually becomes increasingly interesting to the user because the pieces on display are adjusted to their preferences. While no two visitors are the same, people with similar interests will see similar pieces. This is the idea behind BITSCOPE: a socially supervised personal online experience.

The BITSCOPE app does not require visitors to enter data or use tags. It relies on a multimodal interface based on passive BCI, facial recognition, and eye movement tracking. Thanks to the VR technology implemented in HTC VIVE PRO EYE headsets, users explore galleries in a way consistent with their preferences. Signals recording gaze fixation points, which reflect heightened visual attention, are collected and processed with a dedicated Bitscope application developed in the LABleni Laboratory at the Technical University of Valencia as part of a project under the same name.

BITSCOPE is an advanced application designed to create dynamic, immersive environments that simulate a VR experience in an art gallery or museum. The application is highly customisable, allowing each user and session to be unique. The main features of BITSCOPE include:

- *Study configuration*: An experimenter can configure a study based on various parameters. These include selecting images from a library, determining the number of artworks, choosing textures for floors and walls, setting distractor elements, and adjusting the colour and intensity of lighting. Additional specific parameters can also be set according to the study's requirements.

- *User experience*: The user, equipped with an HTC VIVE Pro Eye headset, engages in the VR experience by moving through different rooms. The application allows interaction with the environment and uses the teleportation mechanism for long-distance movements. The user can freely navigate between rooms, exploring and interacting with the displayed artworks.

- *Data tracking and storage*: The application collects and stores raw eye-tracking data, recording the user's interaction with the artworks. Furthermore, BITSCOPE synchronises with the OpenVIBE EEG application, sending temporal markers that are recorded in the user's brain activity log, which is externally monitored.

BITSCOPE was developed using Unity v2022.3.13, a robust and flexible platform for creating virtual environments and VR applications.

Given the complexity of the research tasks and the multi-faceted use of the application, it has been divided into three modules. The first module is dedicated to researchers for designing VR galleries. It enables them to manage collections of images and adjust the visual parameters of the displayed setting. As shown in **Figure 3**, the researcher can decide on the number of displayed pictures and how densely they are placed on the walls. Additionally, distractors, such as 3D objects (flowers, sculptures) commonly seen in art galleries, can be added. The choice of floor material, e.g. stone, wood, or parquet, adds an important dimension. The preview window helps

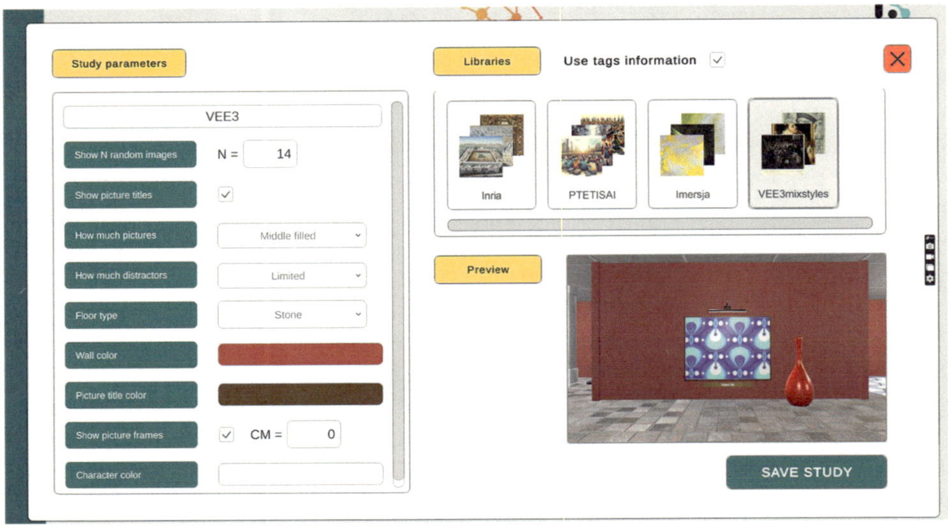

Figure 3.
Screenshot of the BITSCOPE application interface – design module.

researchers adjust the visual features of images, such as background and caption colour, font, and frame.

The second module is the main application, designed for exploring a virtual space with a VR headset. The user has access to an optimal number of rooms with evenly distributed images on the walls (**Figure 4**). Motion controllers, which are part of the headset, allow active movement around the gallery, including navigation between rooms. The user decides when to proceed to the next picture, the order in which to start the tour, when to enter the next room, and when to exit the session. The end of the session is linked to the recording of eye-tracking data, including the handling of input/output (I/O) errors.

Figure 4.
Screenshot of art virtual gallery Bitscope.

Finally, the third module analyses the spatial and temporal parameters of the tour attributable to each museum visitor, their choices, sensitivity, attention, and fatigue. This module enables the tour route to be replayed at a predetermined speed, showing the stops, the position of the head in relation to the body, and the time elapsed since the start of the session.

During pilot studies, the participants offered many valuable insights and suggestions. We paid special attention to the most common negative and positive comments in an effort to better identify what is most important to our VR gallery visitors.

Navigating in VR proved to be the biggest challenge. The method of movement is closely related to users' individual preferences and potential issues related to simulator sickness. During the study, we used a "teleportation" system for short distances, but some participants preferred to explore the virtual world using the touchpad on the controller. Importantly, despite the presence of subjects with motion sickness or inner ear problems, no incidents or complaints of balance issues, nausea, or dizziness were reported.

What the study participants appreciated the most was the overall experience offered by the VR gallery. The textural quality of the displayed artworks received special praise. The virtual gallery can be easily customised to visitors' individual needs, making it more accessible – especially for people who might have difficulties visiting a traditional gallery.

Each gallery session generated data about the time spent viewing the image, the gaze fixation points on the image, and changes in pupil diameter for each eye. The collection of fixation points is concentrated in the most essential parts of the image (e.g. figure, face, title), as illustrated in **Figure 5**. The fixation density function is assumed to follow a Gaussian distribution, thus producing a heatmap (**Figure 6**). The average time spent exploring the gallery for 75 participants was 16 minutes.

On average, tens of thousands of data rows were collected for each image, so with 75 visitors to the VR gallery, the final database contained 4.7 million records.

Figure 5.
Screenshot of fixation analysis for selected images in the VR gallery.

Figure 6.
Heatmaps generated from the first five fixations for selected images in the VR gallery.

Therefore, the team must take a special approach to processing this data to ultimately extract information that reveals relevant differences in the perception of graphics between selected user groups. An intensive effort is planned to process fixation data, saccade data, and pupillometric data.

8. Conclusions

Modern VR (virtual reality) art galleries share numerous similarities with traditional ones. First and foremost, they offer realistic exhibition spaces in which viewers can move freely and view the works from different perspectives, thus replicating the experience of a physical visit to a gallery. Technologies such as 3D reconstruction allow for precise mapping of exhibition objects and spaces, ultimately creating immersive visual environments. This makes it possible to take a close look at works of art and even interact with them [42].

Not unlike traditional galleries, VR galleries give artists the opportunity to present their work to a wide audience, while simultaneously overcoming geographical and time-related barriers. Global audiences can virtually attend cultural events and admire works of art in a museum without the need to be physically present. Research shows that through such an experience, people can engage more deeply with artistic content thanks to the immersive nature of VR [43]. The gallery presented within the BITSCOPE project aims to enable users to visit an exhibition of artworks and immerse themselves in virtual reality. The innovative aspect of the project is that visitor behaviour, visual attention, and body movements are tracked. After the VR session, the subjects undergo an interview about their sense of immersion and artistic impressions. Pilot studies indicate that the level of immersion, leading to a more intense experience of art, can vary greatly, depending largely on the technological solutions used. Young viewers, who often spend time in computer game environments with highly realistic graphics, tend to have similar expectations for VR space. The authors plan to conduct a comprehensive analysis of visual perception and visual attention for a group of visitors based on time-stamped data and gaze points generated in the BITSCOPE application.

However, VR galleries go one step further, leveraging technological advances to increase interactivity and enhance audience engagement. Immersive artistic environments created with VR allow for new forms of experiencing art that transcend the traditional limitations of physical spaces [42]. One example of such innovation is interactive VR installations, where the audience can actively influence the form of the piece by manipulating its elements in real time, thus transforming the viewer into a co-creator of the artistic experience [44].

Moreover, VR galleries open up new educational possibilities, enabling the presentation of art in contexts not available in traditional museums. Thanks to VR simulations, one can, for example, situate a work of art in its original historical or cultural context, offering viewers a better understanding of its meaning and origin [45]. Research shows that this approach increases educational effectiveness by engaging multiple senses and stimulating emotions, both of which promote deeper memory retention and interpretation of content [43].

Employing data analysis and artificial intelligence, VR galleries can also personalise the viewer's experience. They recommend artworks based on the spectator's previous preferences or facilitate the exploration of collections with the help of intelligent guides. Such solutions not only increase the accessibility of art but also help democratise its appreciation, reducing barriers posed by a lack of knowledge or exposure to high culture [46].

Acknowledgements

The research is a part of project Bitscope (no 2021/03/Y/ST6/00002) supported by the National Science Centre, Poland, within CHIST-ERA IV from the EU Horizon 2020 Research and Innovation Programme (Grant Agreement no. 857925).

Author details

Veslava Osinska[1*], Dominik Mirosław Piotrowski[1], Adam Szalach[1,2], Weronika Kortas[1], Tomasz Gross[1] and Jesus Casal Martinez[3]

1 Nicolaus Copernicus University, Toruń, Poland

2 Academy of Social and Media Culture, Toruń, Poland

3 Universitat Politècnica de València, Spain

*Address all correspondence to: wieo@umk.pl

References

[1] Don B. History of VR - Timeline of Events and Tech Development. 2024. Available from: https://virtualspeech.com/blog/history-of-vr [Accessed: January 19, 2025]

[2] Mihelj M, Novak D, Beguš S. Virtual reality technology and applications. In: Intelligent Systems, Control and Automation: Science and Engineering. Dordrecht: Springer Science+Business Media; 2014. p. 1. DOI: 10.1007/978-94-007-6910-6_1

[3] Riva G, Wiederhold B. What the metaverse is (really) and why we need to know about it. Cyberpsychology, Behavior and Social Networking. 2022;**25**:355-359. DOI: 10.1089/cyber.2022.0124

[4] Dur İU, B. Virtual reality art and immersive experimental typography. e-Journal New Media. 2021;**5**(3):1-14. DOI: 10.17932/IAU.EJNM.25480200.2021/ejnm_v5i3002

[5] Kuo Y-T, Garcia Bravo E, Whittinghill DM, Kuo Y-C. Walking into a modern painting: The impacts of using virtual reality on student learning performance and experiences in art appreciation. International Journal of Human-Computer Interaction. 2024;**40**(23):1-13. DOI: 10.1080/10447318.2023.2278929

[6] Wang F, Zhang Z, Li L, Long S. Virtual reality and augmented reality in artistic expression: A comprehensive study of innovative technologies. International Journal of Advanced Computer Science and Applications. 2024;**15**(3):1-9. DOI: 10.14569/IJACSA.2024.0150365

[7] Toscano JJR, Fondón I, Sarmiento A. The experience "Mondrian from inside": An immersive and interactive virtual reality experience in art. In: Augmented Reality, Virtual Reality, and Computer Graphics. Vol. 12980. Switzerland: Springer; 2021

[8] Zou L, Li J. Application of virtual simulation in digital exhibition and performance. In: 2022 7th IEEE International Conference on Data Science in Cyberspace (DSC). Guilin, China; 2022. pp. 588-591. DOI: 10.1109/DSC55868.2022.00088

[9] Polydorou D. Immersive storytelling experiences: A design methodology. Digital Creator. 2024;**35**(4):1-13. DOI: 10.1080/14626268.2024.2389886

[10] Cheng L, Xu J, Pan Y. Investigating user experience of VR art exhibitions: The impact of immersion, satisfaction, and expectation confirmation. Informatics. 2024;**11**(2):30. DOI: 10.3390/informatics11020030

[11] Kim S. Virtual exhibitions and communication factors. Museum Management and Curatorship. 2018;**33**(3):1-16. DOI: 10.1080/09647775.2018.1466190

[12] Holmqvist K, Nyström M, Andersson R, Dewhurst R, Jarodzka H, van de Weijer J. Eye Tracking: A Comprehensive Guide to Methods and Measures. Oxford: Oxford University Press; 2015

[13] Rosenberg R, Groner R. Eye tracking and visual arts. Journal of Eye Movement Research. 2022;**13**(2):1-7. DOI: 10.16910/jemr.13.2

[14] Rosenberg R, Klein C. The moving eye of the beholder: Eye tracking and the perception of paintings. In:

Huston JP, editor. Art, Aesthetics, and the Brain. Oxford: Oxford University Press; 2015. DOI: 10.1093/acprof:oso/9780199670000.003.0005

[15] Tatler BW, Wade NJ, Kwan H, Findlay JM, Velichkovsky BM. Yarbus, eye movements, and vision. Iperception. 2010;**1**(1):7-27. DOI: 10.1068/i0382

[16] Sancarlo R, Dare Z, Arato J, Rosenberg R. Does pictorial composition guide the eye? Investigating four centuries of last supper pictures. Journal of Eye Movement Research. 2020;**13**(2):7. DOI: 10.16910/jemr.13.2.7

[17] Locher PJ, Krupinski EA, Mello-Thoms C, et al. Visual interest in pictorial art during an aesthetic experience. Spatial Vision. 2007;**21**:55-77

[18] Strzemiński W. Teoria widzenia. Łódź: Muzeum Sztuki w Łodzi; 2016

[19] Osińska V, Szalach A, Pilarz E, Centek B, Pilarz K. Percepcja ikon w badaniu eye trackingowym: próba znalezienia wzorców interakcji z ikoną w środowiskach cyfrowych. Fides, Ratio Et Patria. Stud Toruńskie. 2023;**18**:208-232. DOI: 10.56583/frp.2504

[20] Quian Quiroga R, Pedreira C. How do we see art: An eye-tracker study. Frontiers in Human Neuroscience. 2011;**5**:98. DOI: 10.3389/fnhum.2011.00098

[21] Kapoula Z, Yang Q, Vernet M, Bucci MP. 2D-3D space perception in F. Bacon's and Piero della Francesca's paintings: Eye movement studies. In: Bordens KS, editor. Proceedings of the 20th Biennial Congress of the International Association of Empirical Aesthetics. Chicago: Indiana University-Purdue University Indianapolis; 2008. pp. 75-78

[22] Massaro D, Savazzi F, Di Dio C, Freedberg D, Gallese V, Gilli G, et al. When art moves the eyes: A behavioral and eye-tracking study. PLoS One. 2012;7(5):e99019. DOI: 10.1371/journal.pone.0099019

[23] Falk JH. Identity and the Museum Visitor Experience. Walnut Creek, CA: Left Coast Press; 2009

[24] Bachta E, Stein RJ, Filippini-Fantoni S, Leason T. Evaluating the Practical Applications of Eye Tracking in Museums. 2011. Available from: https://www.museumsandtheweb.com/mw2012/programs/evaluating_the_practical_applications_of_eye.html

[25] Hein GE. Learning in the Museum. London: Routledge; 1998

[26] Hoffman JE. Visual attention and eye movements. In: Pashler H, editor. Attention. Hove, UK: Psychology Press; 1998. pp. 119-154

[27] Buquet C, Charier JR, Paris V. Museum application of an eye tracker. Medical and Biological Engineering and Computing. 1988;**26**(3):277-281. DOI: 10.1007/BF02447081

[28] Milekic S. Gaze-tracking and museums: Current research and implications. In: Trant J, Bearman D, editors. Museums and the Web 2010: Proceedings. Toronto: Archives & Museum Informatics; 2010. Available from: http://www.archimuse.com/mw2010/papers/milekic/milekic.html

[29] Grazioso M, Esposito R, Maayan-Fanar E, Kuflik T, Cutugno F. Using Eye Tracking Data to Understand Visitors' Behaviour. AVI,CH@AVI; 2020. Available from: https://api.semanticscholar.org/CorpusID:225063007

[30] Brieber D, Nadal M, Leder H, Rosenberg R. Art in time and space: Context modulates the relation between

art experience and viewing time. PLoS One. 2014;**9**(6):e99019. DOI: 10.1371/journal.pone.0099019

[31] Bailey-Ross C, Beresford A, Smith D, Warwick C. Aesthetic appreciation and Spanish art: Insights from eye-tracking. Digital Scholarship in the Humanities. 2019;**34**(Suppl 1):i17-i35. DOI: 10.1093/llc/fqz027

[32] Cruz-Neira C, Sandin D, DeFanti T. Surround-screen projection-based virtual reality: The design and implementation of the CAVE. ACM SIGGRAPH. 1993;**27**:135-142. DOI: 10.1145/166117.166134

[33] McGill M, Boland D, Murray-Smith R, Brewster S. A dose of reality: Overcoming usability challenges in VR head-mounted displays. In: Proceedings of the 33rd Annual ACM Conference on Human Factors in Computing Systems (CHI '15). New York, NY: Association for Computing Machinery; 2015. pp. 2143-2152. DOI: 10.1145/2702123.2702382

[34] Jain V. Redesigning Acute Art — an AR app for everyone. 2020. Available from: https://medium.com/design-bootcamp/making-art-accessible-to-everyone-via-ar-caf72dd5d78d

[35] Rizzo A. Virtual reality and disability: Emergence and challenge. Disability and Rehabilitation. 2002;**24**:567-569. DOI: 10.1080/09638280110111315

[36] Chen J. Application and challenges of virtual reality (VR) in art exhibition planning. Applied Mathematics and Nonlinear Sciences. 2024;**9**:1-23. DOI: 10.2478/amns-2024-1454

[37] Bernhard K, Henning S. Development of a software tool to evaluate the tolerability of different VR-movement types. Health Technology. 2024;**14**:781-790. DOI: 10.1007/s12553-024-00873-4

[38] Bozgeyikli E, Raij A, Katkoori S, Dubey R. Locomotion in virtual reality for room scale tracked areas. International Journal of Human Computer Studies. 2019;**122**:38-49. DOI: 10.1016/j.ijhcs.2018.08.002

[39] Usoh M, Catena E, Arman S, Slater M. Using presence questionnaires in reality. Presence: Teleoperators and Virtual Environments. 2000;**9**(5):497-503. DOI: 10.1162/105474600566989

[40] Souman JL, Robuffo Giordano P, Frissen I, Ernst MO. Making virtual walking real: Perceptual evaluation of a new treadmill control algorithm. ACM Transactions on Applied Perception. 2010;**7**(2):11. DOI: 10.1145/1670671.1670675

[41] Rosenberg ES, Lipps Z, Finkelstein SL, De Luca A, Bolas M. Impossible spaces: Maximizing natural walking in virtual environments with self-overlapping architecture. IEEE Transactions on Visualization and Computer Graphics. 2012;**18**(4):555-564. DOI: 10.1109/TVCG.2012.47

[42] López-Rodríguez JC, Pérez-López D, Martínez-Mesa R. Immersive and virtual exhibitions: A reflection on... art? Applied Mathematics and Computation. 2024;**19**(2):124-139. DOI: 10.36922/ac.3688

[43] Freina L, Ott M. A literature review on immersive virtual reality in education: State of the art and perspectives. E-learning Software Education. 2015;**1**:133-141. DOI: 10.12753/2066-026X-15-020

[44] Slater M, Sanchez-Vives MV. Enhancing our lives with immersive virtual reality. Frontiers in Robotics

and AI. 2016;**3**:74. DOI: 10.3389/frobt.2016.00074

[45] Tavinor M. The Aesthetics of Virtual Reality. London: Routledge; 2020

[46] Sylaiou S, Mania K, Karoulis A, White M. Exploring the relationship between presence and enjoyment in a virtual museum. International Journal of Human Computer Studies. 2010;**68**(5):243-253. DOI: 10.1016/j.ijhcs.2009.11.002

Chapter 17

AI-Driven Technological Reconstruction and Industry Adaptation of CG Film Production in the Metaverse Era: A Review from Concept Design to Post–Production

Zihan Deng, Mingze Zhang, Fei Zhao, Baijun Chen, Yihong Wang and Nan Xiang

Abstract

As the Metaverse era unfolds, the film and animation industry faces a pivotal digital transformation. Advances in AI, especially large language models and generative AI, offer new potential for creative workflows. However, current research primarily focuses on specific technical breakthroughs, lacking pipeline-oriented needs analysis from the perspective of artists. As a result, the role of AI as a "creative collaborator" has not been fully realized. This study deconstructs the film and animation production pipeline, covering key stages such as concept design, pre-visualization, asset creation, and post-compositing, and incorporates unstructured interviews with industry professionals, including film investors, directors, and digital artists across various stages. It explores the balance between efficiency and artistic expression enabled by AI and analyzes challenges related to content accuracy, data privacy, and ethics in commercialization. The study aims to comprehensively demonstrate the role of current AI technology in CG production and attempts to provide technical pathway recommendations for its deep integration into film production, fostering the synergistic development of art and technology amid industry-wide technological restructuring.

Keywords: artificial intelligence, film production, AIGC, AI ethics, Metaverse

1. Introduction

Against the backdrop of the Metaverse era, the computer graphics (CG) film production industry is undergoing a significant wave of digital transformation.

The rapid development of artificial intelligence (AI) technologies, particularly the emergence of large language models (LLMs), has introduced novel paradigms for creative generation and production process optimization. As a critical component of the broader arts industry, CG film production, characterized by its intricate production pipelines and strong demands for artistic expression, is increasingly driven by Metaverse-enabled ecosystems. In this context, the industry's demand for AI-powered tool iteration is primarily reflected in the need to assist and streamline production workflows, reduce time costs, and improve overall efficiency. These advancements underscore AI's unique potential to contribute to artistic value within next-generation digital production environments.

The current CG film production pipeline encompasses several components, including scriptwriting, research and development (R&D), concept design, asset modeling, rigging, animation, visual effects, rendering, and compositing. These components can be planned as three major stages: pre-production, production (mid-production), and post-production. AI technologies are gradually being integrated into these processes. **Figure 1** illustrates the exploration and application of current representative AI technologies in CG film production. Among these technologies, LLMs show significant potential for creative tasks such as scriptwriting, character development, and dialog generation, while generative models are also the core technology of AI-generated content (AIGCs) [1–3]. Despite rapid technological advances, much of the existing research focuses primarily on the innovation of specific algorithms, remaining somewhat distant from practical industry applications. Moreover, there is a notable lack of systematic analysis of the entire production pipeline from the perspective of artists and creators. The core of the problem lies in how AI can function as a creative collaborator in the art creation process. In the context of a Metaverse

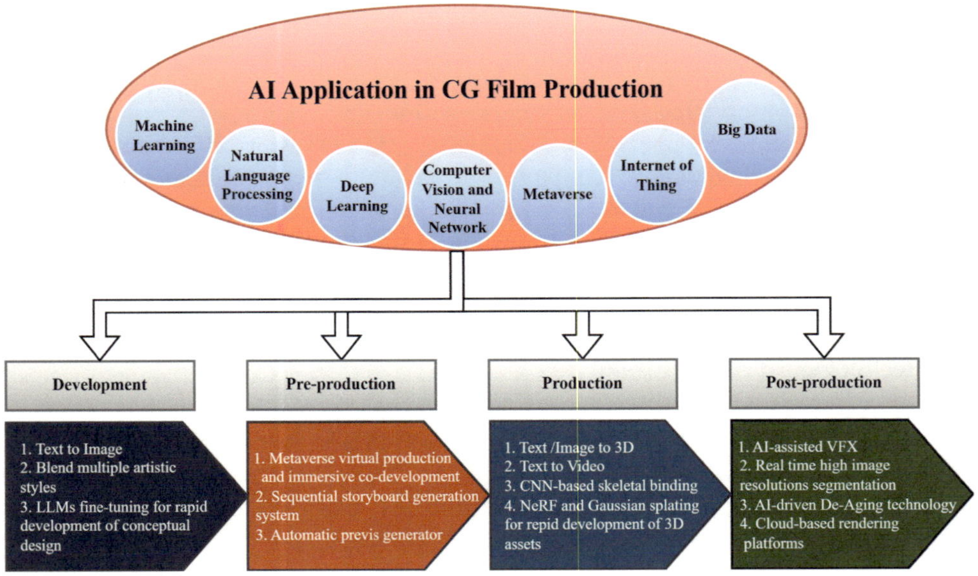

Figure 1.
Application of AI in filmmaking subprocesses.

that emphasizes multilevel, multivolume, and multistyle experiences, a key challenge emerges: How to achieve a balance between the objective efficiency gains brought about by technological reconfiguration and the subjectivity required for artistic expression. This topic has become a key development direction in advancing the application of AI in CG film production. In addition, the practical implementation of AI technologies still faces critical challenges in terms of industry adaptation. As CG film production increasingly integrates with the development of the Metaverse, industry professionals have raised concerns about the commercialization of AI. These concerns extend beyond the accuracy and consistency of generated content to include issues related to data privacy and ethical considerations. Within this context, whether AI can serve as a driving force for a paradigm shift in content creation within the virtual, collaborative environments enabled by the Metaverse will largely depend on the depth and scope of its technological integration. The extent to which AI can be effectively deployed will determine its future role and position in the CG film production industry.

In light of the numerous opportunities and challenges brought by AI in CG film production, this review aims to explore future technological pathways for AI from multiple perspectives. Focusing on the effective utilization of AI technologies from the standpoint of industry practitioners, the study re-examines the technical pipeline of CG film production. Through direct conversations with visual effects artists and technical professionals, it identifies and summarizes the key challenges of AI integration in current industry practices. The goal is to further advance the deep integration of technology and artistic expression, particularly within the evolving digital ecosystems shaped by the Metaverse.

The structure of this article is as follows: Sections 2–4 provide a detailed review of existing work within the production pipeline, including pre-production, production, and post-production stages, highlighting current AI trends and technical challenges; and Sections 5 and 6 discuss ethical considerations in AI applications and outline potential future directions for development.

2. Transformative applications of AI in the pre-production phase

The pre-production phase, also known as early-stage production, encompasses key steps such as scriptwriting, concept design, world-building, R&D, pre-visualization (Previs/Previz) [4], and even prototyping of digital assets, such as characters and environments [5]. In recent years, numerous applications have emerged within the industry, demonstrating the advantages of generative AI technologies in enhancing the efficiency of early-stage workflows. These technologies are reshaping traditional methods that relied heavily on manual expertise and iterative trial-and-error processes. By enabling semantically driven and multimodal content generation, AI is transforming the creative logic behind concept design, establishing novel pipelines that support transitions from text to image and from static elements to dynamic visualizations. Within the context of the Metaverse, where immersive world construction and rapid prototyping are increasingly essential, these innovations offer transformative potential for the future of CG film production.

The following section will elaborate on the development and application of AI in this stage from three perspectives.

2.1 From text to world: LLM-driven scriptwriting and world-building

One of the most prominent applications of generative AI is text generation powered by LLMs, which has brought transformative changes to both individual and commercial text-processing tasks. In the early-stage design phase, LLMs similarly demonstrate strong potential in supporting various text-related tasks. For large-scale CG film projects, concept development and world-building typically require textual materials exceeding hundreds of thousands of words [6]. Traditionally, this phase depends heavily on experienced narrative designers conducting extensive knowledge retrieval and background research, which is time-consuming and labor-intensive. The integration of LLMs has significantly streamlined this process. Trained on vast corpora of general-purpose and domain-specific creative content, LLMs possess advanced capabilities in both language comprehension and generation. Through natural language prompts constructed by users, these models can rapidly produce large volumes of coherent, stylistically consistent content tailored to project-specific needs. Furthermore, with the application of fine-tuning techniques, LLMs can be further adapted for personalized and professional-level outputs.

Current mainstream fine-tuning approaches include full-parameter fine-tuning, parameter-efficient techniques such as adapter modules, prompt tuning, and Low-Rank Adaptation (LoRA) [7]. Among these, LoRA has gained popularity due to its lightweight architecture and low computational cost, making it particularly suitable for customizing LLMs in terms of artistic style, cultural context, or historical setting [8]. Domain-specific fine-tuning via LoRA or prompt tuning enables LLMs to generate narrative content that aligns more precisely with the logic of immersive, interactive storytelling. Additionally, adapter-based fine-tuning allows for modular transfer across different genres and linguistic styles without altering the base model, thereby enhancing the model's generalization ability in multiproject and cross-platform scenarios.

A key challenge in utilizing LLM-generated content for CG film production lies in ensuring stylistic coherence and thematic consistency across the generated materials. Addressing this challenge requires the application of effective prompt engineering strategies. By carefully designing prompts, artists and screenwriters can guide the LLM to maintain alignment with the intended narrative theme throughout the content generation process, while minimizing the risk of outputs that conflict with predefined settings or creative intentions [9]. In addition to prompt construction, the ability to handle long-form contextual information is particularly critical when developing complex world-building frameworks. Recent advances in reasoning LLMs, such as OpenAI's GPT-01 and DeepSeek R1, have significantly improved long-context processing capabilities while preserving creative diversity [10]. These models enable the inclusion of extensive background information and intricate details, yielding world-building outputs that are not only rich in depth but also logically consistent across broad narrative scopes [11]. Despite the strong performance of reasoning LLMs in structured content generation tasks, they continue to face challenges related to AI hallucination when processing highly complex or multidimensional cross-domain information [12]. AI hallucination refers to the phenomenon where models generate outputs that appear coherent and plausible but are, in fact, fictitious, inaccurate, or logically inconsistent [13]. For instance, DeepSeek R1 has been observed to introduce quantum mechanics-related concepts or irrelevant metaphors during the world-building process, even when such elements are not contextually appropriate. These generated scripts may fail to provide meaningful inspiration for artists and, when repetitive patterns emerge, may even lead to user frustration or creative fatigue. Such issues often stem from memory overflow or knowledge transfer bias during long-context reasoning, particularly when prompt inputs are overly complex or span multiple domains [14]. Therefore, while generative models offer powerful tools for text-based ideation in CG film production, their outputs still require careful human review. Additionally, refining system-level prompt engineering is essential to mitigating hallucinations and ensuring that generated content remains coherent, relevant, and conducive to the creative workflow.

To conclude, enhanced by fine-tuning and long-context capabilities, LLMs have fundamentally transformed the efficiency and scope of textual creation in CG world-building. However, persistent issues such as AI hallucination and the reliance on meticulous prompt engineering underscore the technology's current limitations. Therefore, the optimal role for LLMs in this domain is not as autonomous authors but as sophisticated assistive tools that augment, rather than replace, human creativity and critical oversight.

2.2 From text to image: Generative AI-driven visual concept design

The application of generative AI in the creation of visual concept art has gained widespread recognition among professionals in the CG film production industry. AI technologies, especially deep learning-based image generation models such as DALL-E, Midjourney, and Stable Diffusion, have been extensively adopted for generating creative imagery. With minimal textual input, artists can rapidly obtain visual concepts that align with their creative needs, either as sources of inspiration or as finalized design references [15]. This not only broadens the creative scope but also significantly reduces the time and cost traditionally associated with manual sketching and iterative design processes.

One notable feature of generative AI is its capacity to blend multiple artistic styles, thereby offering a broader range of creative possibilities. Through prompt engineering, artists can specify and combine different visual styles, enabling the generation of unique concept images. This approach allows creators to explore a wide array of visual directions beyond the constraints of traditional design frameworks, thus enhancing both diversity and originality in visual development. Moreover, fine-tuning techniques such as LoRA, mentioned above, further support the maintenance of consistent visual style and artistic direction across AI-generated outputs [8]. While generative AI can rapidly produce varied designs, maintaining stylistic coherence and quality remains essential in professional workflows. By applying LoRA-based adaptation, artists can train models to conform to specific esthetic requirements, ensuring uniformity across multiple iterations of visual content. This not only enhances the personalization of the creative output but also empowers artists to express their unique artistic vision while leveraging the efficiency of AI-assisted design.

In brief, generative AI revolutionizes visual concept design by coupling rapid stylistic exploration with fine-tuned artistic control, thereby evolving from a mere source of inspiration into a sophisticated instrument for executing a specific creative vision.

2.3 From static to dynamic: AI-empowered Previs and virtual production

AI also holds strong potential in the Previs (pre-visualization) phase of CG film production, which is used to plan and simulate the visual outcomes of a film before actual production begins. In this stage, AI can simplify the generation, adjustment, and layout of complex camera moves, character actions, and scene compositions. One of the most widely adopted Previs tools in current CG film production is Unreal Engine [16], which allows artists to render low-fidelity preview shots and accelerate design iteration rapidly. AI technologies further enhance this process by optimizing the efficiency of scene setup, lighting configuration, and camera control. Evin et al. developed Cine-AI, a system capable of generating virtual cinematic sequences in the style of human directors [17], while CinePreGen leverages state-of-the-art video generation models and integrates with real-time rendering engines to address challenges in camera manipulation and dynamic control during Previs [18]. The Previs process typically begins with storyboard design and layout planning for camera work. From a technical perspective, several advanced applications have already started transforming this process. For example, Rao et al. proposed a system capable of efficiently generating sequential storyboards from screenplays [19]. While many academic efforts have developed tools to support workflow reconfiguration, these tools still lack sufficient industry adoption, making their practical implementation in commercial pipelines an urgent direction for future exploration. In the layout stage, AI technologies are being employed to automate shot composition, with several promising attempts already reported [20, 21].

In recent years, empowered by a range of emerging tools, virtual production technologies have begun to restructure traditional linear workflows in CG film production, blurring the boundaries between early-stage pre-production and final output [22]. Within the evolving context of the Metaverse, where real-time collaboration, immersive environments, and high-quality digital assets are becoming central to content creation, virtual production serves as a critical enabler for bridging artistic ideation and technical realization. At this stage of the pipeline, the primary objective is to leverage a suite of virtual tools to generate virtual shots and sequences that support direct artistic exploration, iterative creative refinement, and strategic planning of final production decisions within a shared digital environment. In contemporary film and television projects, directors, cinematographers, and producers are increasingly able to visualize near-final shots in immersive or hybrid spaces earlier in the production timeline, significantly reducing iteration cycles and associated costs while enhancing cross-functional collaboration across distributed teams.

Traditional workflows in the stages outlined above are often characterized by repetitive, labor-intensive iterations. As these processes occur in the pre-production phase, they inherently demand rapid prototyping and agile revision cycles to meet fast-evolving creative requirements. Within the broader framework of the Metaverse, where immersive collaboration, real-time iteration, and persistent digital environments are reshaping production paradigms, such demands are further amplified. Insights from industry professionals interviewed indicate that achieving high precision and photorealism at this stage is generally unnecessary for internal iterative development purposes. Rather, there is a growing need for intelligent, AI-assisted tools capable of generating draft-level visual previews swiftly and adaptively, thereby expediting early-stage concept development. Digital artists expressed strong interest in adopting AI-driven virtual production technologies to enhance workflow flexibility, support geographically distributed creative teams, and align more effectively with the real-time, iteration-centric production logic characteristic of Metaverse-oriented CG pipelines.

As discussed above, current AI enhances the Previs phase by automating visual prototyping, aligning with the industry's shift toward virtual production. The crucial demand is not for photorealism but for speed and agility, enabling rapid creative iteration. Thus, AI's optimal role in this context should be positioned as a flexible, low-fidelity tool that accelerates creative decision-making within modern, dynamic production environments.

3. AI-powered reconstruction in the mid-production phase

3.1 Generative AI-based asset creation

Amid the growing influence of the Metaverse in reshaping digital content production, mid-stage workflows in CG film production are undergoing significant technological transformation. This phase typically includes critical tasks such as digital asset creation, character rigging and animation, and physical simulation. Traditional pipelines in these areas are heavily reliant on manual labor and complex multisoftware coordination, often lacking the agility and scalability needed to support real-time, immersive, and stylistically diverse content demanded by Metaverse-driven virtual environments.

In this context, the integration of generative AI has begun to reveal substantial potential. Following the paradigm of semantic interpretation, automated generation, and dynamic refinement, AI enables greater creative flexibility and accelerates asset iteration cycles. For instance, artists can now utilize natural language or image-based prompts to produce preliminary 3D assets, significantly lowering the barrier to entry for asset creation and allowing for rapid exploration of multiple stylistic variants [23]. Conventional 3D modeling workflows often require artists to spend several weeks sculpting high-fidelity assets manually. In contrast, neural-network-based 3D reconstruction techniques offer a more efficient alternative. NVIDIA's GET3D, for example, introduces a high-performance 3D generative model capable of synthesizing object textures and meshes directly from training data, streamlining downstream asset development [24]. When combined with style-transfer models such as StyleGAN-NADA [25], the generated meshes can be stylized through natural language prompts, satisfying the personalized artistic requirements of CG film production in Metaverse scenarios. However, current generative AI still faces key challenges related to controllability in terms of output precision and consistency, which continue to hinder its seamless integration into commercial production pipelines.

In summary, while generative models significantly accelerate the initial ideation and prototyping stages of 3D assets, their current limitations in output controllability and geometric precision restrict their direct application to production-grade content that demands stringent quality standards.

3.2 Emerging favorite for 3D scene representation

Recent advancements in Neural Radiance Fields (NeRF) and 3D Gaussian Splatting (3D GS) have further explored the representation and creation of 3D content, especially full-scene content. By implicitly representing the radiance (color and intensity) of each spatial point across different viewpoints via neural networks, NeRF enables the reconstruction of complex, high-fidelity environments within a continuous 3D space. It allows a single image to generate high-fidelity, multiangle continuous frames. Upon its emergence, it caused a sensation in the creative industry, with many digital artists diving into it and using NeRF for their creations. However, due to its implicit representation, it lacks editability, and, coupled with its enormous computational cost, its development in the CG field has been limited.

Unlike the implicit neural representation of NeRF, 3D GS explicitly represents 3D geometry using a collection of differentiable Gaussian distributions. This approach achieves an efficient balance between rendering quality and computational performance, making it highly suitable for creating environment assets in Metaverse applications, where real-time interactivity and high frame rates are essential.

A notable example is Magic3D, a pipeline that first generates a coarse 3D structure through a diffusion model and subsequently refines it using NeRF-based techniques to produce high-quality 3D models from textual input [26]. Such tools present new possibilities for asset modeling in CG film production, especially for rapid prototyping and concept iteration in early development stages. In the film *Creation of the Gods II: Demon Force*, visual effects engineers utilized Gaussian Splatting techniques to model expansive scenes, demonstrating the commercial feasibility of these emerging methods.[1] However, current NeRF- and Gaussian Splatting-based models still struggle to achieve the level of mesh granularity and geometric precision required for feature-grade visual effects in commercial film production. As a result, a more practical path forward for mid-stage AI-driven pipeline reconstruction may lie in establishing a hybrid workflow centered around AI-assisted generation and human refinement. In this framework, AI tools can efficiently generate low-precision assets such as draft props or environment blocks, which professional artists then refine to meet the visual and structural standards of final production. This human-in-the-loop model preserves artistic control while significantly improving production efficiency, aligning with the Metaverse-oriented vision of intelligent yet creatively empowered CG film production.

Consequently, although NeRF and 3D GS demonstrate novel scene-rendering capabilities, their current inability to produce assets with sufficient geometric precision for production confines their role to that of a preliminary assistive tool, tasked primarily with providing an initial structural framework for subsequent refinement by artists.

[1] This information is based on an unstructured interview conducted with VFX professionals involved in the production of *Creation of the Gods II* in February 2025.

3.3 AI-driven character animation and rigging

In the character rigging stage of CG film production, one promising approach involves leveraging neural networks to learn human pose patterns directly from video data, thereby enabling automated and accelerated skeletal rigging. In the fields of human pose estimation and automatic rigging, convolutional neural network (CNN)-based approaches have demonstrated effectiveness but are often limited in their ability to model complex temporal and spatial dependencies. Recently, transformer-based architectures have reshaped the landscape of pose estimation by significantly improving both accuracy and computational efficiency.

For example, PoseFormer abandons the CNN paradigm entirely in favor of a spatiotemporally optimized transformer architecture. This model captures intra-frame relationships among character joints as well as inter-frame temporal dynamics, ultimately producing precise 3D pose predictions for the center frame of a given video segment [27]. Such advances offer substantial theoretical efficiency gains compared to traditional manual rigging workflows, potentially reducing the time and labor required for the initial rig setup.

However, it is essential to note that the current generation of neural network-based rigging systems has yet to achieve the level of precision necessary for photorealistic or production-grade results. Despite encouraging progress in academic research, these methods are not yet widely adopted in commercial CG film production pipelines. As confirmed by industry practice, character animation for high-end productions still requires frame-by-frame manual adjustments by professional animators to meet the visual standards demanded in commercial environments. Therefore, while AI-driven rigging holds strong future potential, its practical application remains limited at present, serving more as a prototyping or assistance tool rather than a complete replacement for human expertise.

In practice, despite the significant theoretical potential for efficiency gains demonstrated by transformer-based methods, the precision of their current output does not yet meet the rigorous standards of commercial animation production, thus confining their present role to assistive functions or rapid prototyping in preliminary animation phases.

3.4 Pipeline integration and industrialization challenges

Despite the clear efficiency gains that AI can bring to mid-stage production workflows, its deployment in large-scale commercial projects still faces several challenges. Firstly, the development of high-performance AI models typically requires vast amounts of annotated training data. However, copyright restrictions within film studios often limit the availability of such datasets, thereby constraining the generalization capability of AI systems. In addition, assets generated via neural rendering techniques are prone to topological inconsistencies and mesh errors, necessitating manual intervention. Furthermore, physical effects such as fluid and deformation simulations in CG film production heavily rely on tools such as Houdini, which employ finite element-based iterative computation. These simulations are often computationally expensive, with a single run taking a very long time, sometimes even several days to complete. Given the complexity of the physical modeling involved, the application of AI in this domain remains constrained by the architectural limitations of current models and the high computational demands on hardware. As a result, whether AI can truly deliver net efficiency improvements, especially under production-grade constraints, remains an open question.

Through an in-depth investigation into current industry practices, we found that integration between AI-based tools and conventional digital content creation software, such as Maya or Blender, lacks standardized interfaces. The high cost of pipeline adaptation continues to pose a barrier to adoption. Notably, converting AIGC, which is often in nonstandard formats, into production-ready commercial formats remains one of the most significant unresolved technical hurdles in the current CG film production landscape.

4. Breakthroughs and challenges of AI in post-production

Unlike concept design and mid-stage asset development, animation, and effects – where creative ideation and technical generation are the primary focus – post-production in CG film production primarily centers on the compositing of all prior visual elements, followed by final rendering and stylization. In animation-specific workflows, post-production differs significantly from live-action filmmaking in that it does not require the compositing of live footage; however, it still involves a large amount of manual post-processing work, such as shot color grading, stylized processing, and lighting adjustments, where AI tools can offer substantial assistance.

4.1 The precision challenge in automated rotoscoping

Compared to the deployment challenges AI faces in mid-stage workflows, post-production has witnessed the emergence of several relatively mature AI applications. One of the most time-consuming and repetitive tasks in post-production is rotoscoping, which involves creating dynamic masks around objects in footage to isolate or modify them in the final composite. This process accounts for a significant portion of the labor load in animation and VFX workflows, prompting strong demand within the industry for AI-based solutions to improve efficiency. With AI-powered background matting and segmentation tools gaining popularity among general users, professionals in CG film production have begun integrating these technologies into real-world commercial animation projects. For example, Meta's Segment Anything Model, built on a transformer backbone, was described at its release as the "GPT moment" for image segmentation due to its near-instantaneous performance and imperceptible error margins for the human eye [28]. Despite these advances, current models still fall short of meeting the precision demands of theatrical film production. In professional rotoscoping for animated post-production, the acceptable error tolerance is typically below 10 pixels. While some recent models have approached this threshold in relatively simple scenes [29], they continue to struggle with complex materials such as fluid simulations, hair, and semi-transparent surfaces. These challenges often lead to noticeable visual artifacts, making such models unsuitable for theatrical-grade production. Moreover, real-time inference is not a strict requirement in post-production compositing pipelines, where artists prioritize accuracy and control over speed. As such, the near real-time performance advantage of advanced segmentation models cannot yet be fully exploited in this context. This highlights the gap between current AI segmentation capabilities and the rigorous quality standards required for high-end CG film production.

4.2 Application variances from facial effects to cloud rendering

In recent years, unlike the technical bottlenecks encountered in dynamic rotoscoping, AI-driven facial de-aging – the process of modifying an actor's apparent age using digital techniques – has emerged as a highly favored and increasingly mature application within the CG film production industry. One of the earliest and most widely recognized examples of this technology was in *Rogue One: A Star Wars Story*, where the facial likeness of a deceased character from the original trilogy was digitally rejuvenated to align the storyline with the broader franchise canon [30, 31]. Recent years have witnessed a proliferation of AI-based methodologies focused on facial image editing [32]. For instance, in Captain America: Civil War, the de-aging of the lead actor's face was achieved entirely through deepfake technology, producing highly realistic visual outcomes [33]. In the Chinese film industry, the use of deepfake-based facial de-aging has also reached a notable level of maturity. For example, in *The Wandering Earth* film series, facial de-aging of well-known actors was achieved by training AI models on two-dimensional facial datasets and replacing the original footage with synthetic outputs.[2] At the rendering stage, industry practitioners have also begun exploring the use of AI to enhance efficiency. Recent developments in cloud-based rendering platforms have integrated deep learning models to predict rendering hardware demands in real time, allowing for dynamic allocation of GPU cluster resources. While these systems offer clear performance benefits, they also raise concerns regarding data privacy and asset security. Despite claims from cloud rendering service providers about employing secure encryption protocols to protect user data, the need to upload proprietary and often confidential project files to third-party servers remains a critical issue. Consequently, for theatrical-level productions involving sensitive IP or trade secrets, many VFX studios continue to exercise caution or abstain from fully relying on cloud-based rendering solutions. This has sparked extensive discussions within the industry regarding data security and, more fundamentally, the ethical implications of AI.

In conclusion, AI demonstrates two distinct application prospects in post-production: On one hand, it has achieved successful production-level application in well-defined and data-accessible domains such as facial effects; on the other hand, its adoption in areas such as cloud rendering is primarily limited by nontechnical factors such as data security rather than by the performance of the AI technology itself.

---

[2] This information is based on an unstructured interview with VFX professionals involved in the post-production of The Wandering Earth, who described the pipeline and role of AI in facial de-aging for lead characters.

5. Ethical issues in AI applications

5.1 Privacy and data security

AI models often require extensive datasets for training, such as actors' facial data for animation modeling or copyrighted image assets for content generation, which raises significant privacy and security concerns. With the widespread adoption of deepfake technology in CG film production, some processes in post-production have become increasingly efficient. However, the collection, storage, and processing of highly sensitive actor-related data, particularly biometric data (e.g., facial recognition, motion capture, voice synthesis), amplify risks of data breaches and misuse. Additionally, AI-driven film recommendation systems enhance decision-making efficiency but introduce latent data security risks. Research indicates these systems are vulnerable to data poisoning attacks, wherein adversaries inject falsified user ratings into training data to manipulate outputs, leading to erroneous predictions or system malfunctions [34].

In other words, while AI applications in the film domain enhance operational efficiency across production and recommendation processes, they inherently introduce multifaceted privacy and security vulnerabilities. Unauthorized exposure or malicious exploitation of such data could severely compromise individual privacy and precipitate industry-wide trust crises [35]. These risks span from data collection to system integrity and demand urgent attention to safeguard individual rights and industry trust.

5.2 Fairness issues of box office analysis system

Warner Bros. partnered with the AI company Cinelytic to incorporate its AI-driven project management system, aimed at supporting data analytics and revenue forecasting during the "greenlighting" phase of film production [36]. The system is capable of rapidly assessing an actor's commercial value across different global markets and forecasting a film's expected box office and ancillary revenues across theatrical and streaming platforms within seconds. This technological integration significantly reduces the time that traditional executive teams would otherwise spend on repetitive, low-value-added tasks such as script evaluation, casting decisions, and scheduling. Simultaneously, it provides decision-makers with more quantitative and precise market reference data, enabling them to make more profit-driven choices in the packaging, marketing, and distribution strategies of films. However, learning models are often trained on datasets that contain inherent biases. These biases may arise from specific methodologies used during data collection, such as biased sampling strategies, where certain elements within a dataset are disproportionately weighted or emphasized, introducing distortions [37, 38]. According to research on bias and nondiscrimination in AI, if a machine learning system relies on demographic features such as race or gender during its predictive and decision-making processes, and this reliance leads to systematic disadvantage or discrimination against particular groups, then the system is generally considered to be unfair [39]. When biased sampling strategies are utilized, the resulting models may inherit and even amplify these biases, subsequently reflecting them in future predictions.

In the CG film industry, AI systems typically generate predictive analyses based on data such as actors' market value, audience preferences, and historical box office performance. However, if these training datasets systematically undervalue actors and narratives associated with certain races, genders, or cultural backgrounds, the AI may reinforce and perpetuate such biases in its recommendations. This may result in the prolonged marginalization of projects centered on underrepresented or minority groups during investment and production stages, thereby undermining fairness and diversity within the CG film industry.

5.3 The interpretability of black-box models

In recent years, methods that heavily rely on machine learning and deep learning models have been widely applied to tasks such as image generation, text creation, and content recommendation. These tasks are precisely the areas in which current AI is involved within CG film production. While these models have achieved remarkable results in terms of accuracy and efficiency, their highly complex internal structures and opaque reasoning processes make their decision-making difficult to interpret. As a result, they are often referred to as "black-box" models [40].

When referring to AI models, people first focus on their explainability, interpretability of decision-making processes, and structural transparency. Explainability typically refers to the ability of a model to explain or provide meaning to humans, while interpretability places more emphasis on the interactive interface between humans and decision systems, emphasizing whether the explanations of model outputs truly reflect the internal mechanisms of the model and are understandable to humans [41]. Transparency implies a certain degree of model explainability. In fields with high requirements for result controllability, such as film and television production, transparent models are more likely to be accepted by the industry. However, due to the unclear boundaries of these terms in practical applications, academia and industry often confuse them, leading to difficulties in the actual operations of model auditing and debugging [42]. For example, in the sentiment analysis of film reviews, since film ratings may not match the actual emotional tendencies, it is difficult for the model to judge whether the review is positive or negative, leading to incorrect predictions [43].

Transparency, explainability, and interpretability have become key factors in determining whether a model can be practically adopted and trusted. Creators often struggle to understand how AI arrives at specific results in screenplay generation, character settings, or visual effects, and they cannot determine whether these results are affected by biased data or violate creative intentions. Therefore, the interpretability of the model not only affects debugging and optimization during the development stage but also relates to responsibility attribution and content correctness after product release. When there are deviations in model output results, the explanation mechanisms of transparent models can help developers and content creators quickly locate the root causes of errors and ensure the auditability and traceability of the system, thereby avoiding the expansion of ethical and commercial risks.

6. The legal challenges faced by generative AI

6.1 The risk of data infringement in the training of AI models

In 2023, three major French publishing and authors' associations formally filed a lawsuit against Meta, accusing it of systematically scraping a large amount of copyrighted content, including French-language books, screenplays, and musical works, without authorization, for training its Llama series of LLMs [44]. This case exposes the lack of transparency in data utilization among current AI enterprises; in the absence of disclosure of data sources and authorization from rights holders, it is highly likely to infringe upon the legitimate rights and interests of original creators.

The use of unauthorized copyrighted works for training may constitute an infringement of the reproduction right, adaptation right, and the right to communicate through information networks of the original works. If the training data contain personal information, it further raises concerns about the risk to the data subject's right to data usage. According to Article 6 of the European Union's General Data Protection Regulation (GDPR), any data processing activity must have a legal basis, such as obtaining the consent of the data subject or satisfying legitimate interests [45]. However, the AI training process requires the ingestion of massive volumes of data, and in practice, enterprises or platforms find it difficult to obtain authorization for each individual piece of data; otherwise, they will face exorbitant costs and infringement risks. Moreover, variations in copyright identification, standards for fair use, and data protection laws across different countries and regions render the data involved in AI model training subject to complex legal obstacles.

6.2 The controversies over copyrightability and rights attribution

Regarding the artworks generated by AI, the issues of their copyrightability and rights attribution have become a focal point of widespread concern in legal and industrial circles. The emergence of AIGC has blurred the boundaries of the concept of human creation. Traditional copyright law systems generally require works to embody elements of human creation, emphasizing that the subject of creation is a natural person and that the work reflects the author's originality and intellectual labor achievements. However, existing copyright laws do not explicitly grant copyright protection to works created by nonhuman entities [46].

According to Article 3 of the *Copyright Law of the People's Republic of China*, a work referred to in the copyright law is defined as "an intellectual achievement in the fields of literature, art, and science that has originality and can be expressed in a certain form." Current laws and regulations do not explicitly stipulate the copyrightability of AIGC. Against this backdrop, certain judicial practices in China have gradually formed a consensus: If the AIGC generation process embodies the personalized choices and independent arrangements of natural persons, such content may be recognized as an original work, thereby qualifying for corresponding copyright protection [47].

Nevertheless, the United States Copyright Office has issued the *Copyright Registration Guidance: Works Containing Material Generated by Artificial*

Intelligence. It emphasizes that users do not have ultimate control over how AI systems interpret instructions or generate content; instead, AI systems independently determine how to execute instructions and present the final expression [48]. In other words, if an AI system exhibits a high degree of autonomy, the content it generates will be deemed to lack the directness and controllability of human creative behavior, thereby failing to meet the basic requirements for "works" under copyright law.

Whether user instructions belong to ideas or expressions, and the actual control users exercise over AIGC, remain key issues in current copyright disputes over AIGC. Relevant cases indicate that the law does not exclude the possibility of AIGC obtaining copyright protection when it meets the standard of originality, but this does not mean that all AIGC inherently possesses copyrightability. Whether AIGC meets the legal standard of originality should be judged comprehensively based on factors such as the user's personalized choices during the generation process, the degree of control over the generated results, and the originality characteristics of the content itself [49].

6.3 Career restructuring and the 3C principles

Recently, a coalition consisting of over 20 European and American animation workers' unions has declared a state of emergency regarding the application of AI in the animation industry [50]. The coalition issued a statement asserting that AI is exerting destructive impacts on the craftsmanship, commercial operations, and workers within the animation sector. It has called upon regulators and legislators to formulate laws safeguarding workers' rights and demanded that producers and related parties protect the creative culture rooted in human creation.

Generative AI demonstrates tremendous potential in enhancing the efficiency and creativity of film and television production. However, as emphasized by the coalition, generative AI not only encroaches on the livelihoods of human creators but also brings about numerous destructive consequences for the media and cultural industries. The 2025 research brief by the International Labor Organization (ILO) points out that generative AI not only transforms production processes but also permeates creative and decision-making links, exerting profound influences on occupations, skills, and employment. Among these, occupations such as actors, film directors, and producers fall into the category of low-to-medium exposure to AI [51]. This is because their work relies on capabilities that are difficult to replace with AI, including live performance, emotional expression, and creative decision-making, making the automation of their core tasks highly challenging. In contrast, occupations with medium exposure, such as graphic designers and photographers, have certain tasks that could potentially be executed by generative AI technologies. For instance, basic equipment debugging and simple graphic design can be handled by AI, yet core creative work and complex technical processes still require human leadership.

Based on the "3C principles" proposed by the ILO, the application of generative AI in film production should conform to three key ethical and legal guidelines [51]. Firstly, the principle of "Consent" mandates that the use of AI training data must obtain explicit consent from copyright holders. When utilizing AIGC in film and television production, if it involves the reference or use of elements from existing works, authorization from the original creators must also be secured. Secondly, the principle of "Compensation" requires that creators should receive fair and reasonable compensation when their works are used for AI training or when their creative ideas and styles are reflected in AIGC. Thirdly, the principle of "Control" stipulates that creators should have the right to govern the ways and scopes of their works' utilization in AI-related processes. They should be able to decide whether their works are used for AI training, as well as the application scenarios and extents of AI models developed from such training in film and television production. Collectively, these principles highlight the need for a regulatory and ethical framework that balances technological innovation with the protection of creators' rights. The unprecedented creative potential of generative AI in film production must be carefully weighed against the risks of copyright infringement, misappropriation of creative labor, and erosion of professional autonomy.

7. Future prospects

The rapid advancement of Metaverse and AI technologies continues to reshape the digital landscape. Within this context, AI tools are expected to further enhance CG film production and drive transformative changes in the film industry. Beyond the topics previously discussed, considerations from both technological development and regulatory perspectives suggest that prompt learning and accountability mechanisms are likely to emerge as key focal points in the near-future application of AI technologies in the CG domain.

7.1 Prompt learning for CG film production

Prompt learning, one of the new paradigms in modern natural language processing, enables researchers to effectively unlock the potential of pre-trained models through meticulously designed text prompts or examples, exhibiting significant advantages, particularly in low-data scenarios [52]. Unlike traditional model training, which relies on large volumes of labeled data, prompt learning guides models to output desired results by constructing "prompts" that align closely with task objectives. This approach has substantially lowered the barriers to AI applications and enhanced the generalization capability of models. In CG film production, this improved prompt-driven generation method holds enormous potential. For instance, by prompting language models to generate script excerpts or character settings, or utilizing text-to-image prompts to produce concept art and storyboards, AI systems can rapidly respond to creators' instructions and assist in iterating on content ideas. The quality of prompt design plays a decisive role in the effectiveness of generated content; thus, the role of AI prompt engineers has emerged as a critical link connecting human creativity and AI tools. Looking ahead, as model scales expand and application scenarios become more complex, research on prompt learning will continue to deepen. Key issues to be addressed include optimizing prompt structures, enhancing models' ability to comprehend complex intentions, and achieving precise control in multimodal generation tasks [53]. Concurrently, the professional and systematic training of prompt engineers will also become an important supporting direction for the practical implementation of AI technologies.

7.2 Accountability of AI systems

In the Metaverse era, as AI technology becomes deeply integrated into various stages of CG film production – from script generation and concept design to post-production compositing – the diversity and complexity of generated content have significantly increased, making the review and accountability mechanisms for AI systems an indispensable issue. At the level of AI regulation, the core of accountability mechanisms resides in the capacity to explicitly ascertain whether a decision conforms to predefined procedural and substantive standards, as well as to identify and hold responsible parties liable in instances where such standards are contravened [54]. UNESCO emphasizes that ethical reviews of AI systems should not only cover technical risks and benefits but also focus on the transparency of decision-making, fairness, and the clarity of the responsibility chain [55]. If regulatory mechanisms are improperly designed, they will not only fail to achieve genuine accountability but may also suppress many potentially beneficial applications of AI systems, hindering technological innovation and industry development. As important media for cultural communication, film and animation works require rigorous review and liability determination mechanisms to address potential risks of misleading, infringement, and discrimination posed by AIGC.

8. Conclusion

With the advent of the Metaverse era and advancements in AI technology, the CG film industry is encountering both opportunities and challenges. Particularly in terms of enhancing production efficiency and optimizing workflows, AI technology has demonstrated enormous potential, providing new ideas and methods for CG film creation. From early-stage concept design to mid-stage production, and further to post-production processes, AI technology has played a significant role in almost all aspects, driving the digital upgrading of the CG film industry. However, the application of AI in CG film production has also posed numerous challenges. Issues such as the controllability of AIGC, data privacy and security, fairness and nondiscrimination, transparency and interpretability, as well as intellectual property and legal problems, are all important aspects that require attention and resolution. These issues not only affect the healthy development of the CG film production industry but also relate to the fairness, justice, and cultural inheritance of society as a whole. By exploring human–machine collaboration models and optimizing technologies such as prompt learning, the auxiliary role of AI in creative generation can be further enhanced. Meanwhile, establishing and improving the accountability system for AI systems is crucial to ensuring the transparency and fairness of generated content, as well as the clarity of the responsibility chain, thereby addressing potential risks of misleading, infringement, and discrimination. Only by striking a balance between technological innovation and ethical–legal considerations can the benign interaction and sustainable development of AI and the CG film production industry be achieved.

Acknowledgments

The authors would like to express their sincere gratitude to Mr. Xin Wang and his team, Mr. Jia Ma and his team, Mr. Bin Li and his team, Mr. Xi Jin, Mr. Tianji Song, as well as the other CG artists who generously agreed to be interviewed and contributed invaluable perspectives to this study.

Author details

Zihan Deng[1†], Mingze Zhang[1†], Fei Zhao[2], Baijun Chen[3], Yihong Wang[1] and Nan Xiang[1*]

1 Xi'an Jiaotong-Liverpool University, Suzhou, China

2 Sanmu-Runde Culture Technology Co., Ltd., Beijing, China

3 Beijing University of Posts and Telecommunications, Beijing, China

† These authors contributed equally

*Address all correspondence to: nan.xiang@xjtlu.edu.cn

References

[1] Mohammad Mahdi Abootorabi, Omid Ghahroodi, Pardis Sadat Zahraei, Hossein Behzadasl, Alireza Mirrokni, Mobina Salimipanah, Arash Rasouli, Bahar Behzadipour, Sara Azarnoush, Benyamin Maleki, et al. Generative ai for character animation: A comprehensive survey of techniques, applications, and future directions. *arXiv preprint arXiv:2504.19056*, 2025

[2] Yunlong Tang, Junjia Guo, Pinxin Liu, Zhiyuan Wang, Hang Hua, Jia-Xing Zhong, Yunzhong Xiao, Chao Huang, Luchuan Song, Susan Liang, Yizhi Song, Liu, He, Jing Bi, Mingqian Feng, Xinyang Li, Zeliang Zhang, and Chenliang Xu. Generative ai for cel-animation: A survey, 2025

[3] Kunal Hossain and Jyotirmay Deb. A case study on integrating ai in making an animation movie. *International Journal For Multidisciplinary Research*, 7:2, 03 2025

[4] Hock Hian Wong. Previsualization: assisting filmmakers in realizing their vision. In *SIGGRAPH Asia 2012 Courses*, 1–20. 2012

[5] Wen-Fan Wang, Chien-Ting Lu, Nil Ponsa i Campanyà, Bing-Yu Chen, and Mike Y. Chen. Aideation: Designing a human-ai collaborative ideation system for concept designers. In *Proceedings of the 2025 CHI Conference on Human Factors in Computing Systems*, CHI '25, 1–28. ACM, April 2025

[6] Leah Zaidi. Worldbuilding in science fiction, foresight, and design. *Journal of Futures Studies*, **2**:12, 7 2019

[7] Ning Ding, Yujia Qin, Guang Yang, Fuchao Wei, Zonghan Yang, Yusheng Su, Shengding Hu, Yulin Chen, Chi-Min Chan, Weize Chen, Jing Yi, Weilin Zhao, Xiaozhi Wang, Zhiyuan Liu, Hai-Tao Zheng, Jianfei Chen, Yang Liu, Jie Tang, Juanzi Li, and Maosong Sun. Parameter-efficient fine-tuning of large-scale pre-trained language models. *Nature Machine Intelligence*, **5**(3):220–235, 2023

[8] Chenxi Liu, Towaki Takikawa, and Alec Jacobson. A lora is worth a thousand pictures, *arXiv preprint arXiv:2412*. 2024. 12048

[9] Yuying Tang, Haotian Li, Minghe Lan, Xiaojuan Ma, and Huamin Qu. Understanding screenwriters' practices, attitudes, and future expectations in human-ai co-creation, 2025

[10] Xiaoye Qu, Yafu Li, Zhaochen Su, Weigao Sun, Jianhao Yan, Dongrui Liu, Ganqu Cui, Daizong Liu, Shuxian Liang, Junxian He, Peng Li, Wei Wei, Jing Shao, Chaochao Lu, Yue Zhang, Xian-Sheng Hua, Bowen Zhou, and Yu Cheng. A survey of efficient reasoning for large reasoning models: Language, multimodality, and beyond, arXiv preprint arXiv:2503. 2025. 2161

[11] Alexander Gurung and Mirella Lapata. Learning to reason for long-form story generation, 2025

[12] Bakht Munir, Muhammad Zubair Abbasi, W Blake Wilson, and Allen Colombo Jr. Evaluating ai in legal operations: A comparative analysis of accuracy, completeness, and hallucinations in chatgpt-4, copilot, deepseek, lexis+ ai, and llama 3. *International Journal of Legal Information*, 1–12, 2025

[13] Lei Huang, Weijiang Yu, Weitao Ma, Weihong Zhong, Zhangyin Feng, Haotian Wang, Qianglong Chen, Weihua Peng, Xiaocheng Feng, Bing Qin, and Ting Liu. A survey on hallucination in large language models: Principles, taxonomy, challenges, and open questions. *ACM Transactions on Information Systems*, **43**(2):1–55, 2025

[14] Zijun Yao, Yantao Liu, Yanxu Chen, Jianhui Chen, Junfeng Fang, Lei Hou, Juanzi Li, and Tat-Seng Chua. Are reasoning models more prone to hallucination?, 2025

[15] Chaniporn Thampanichwat, Tarid Wongvorachan, Limpasilp Sirisakdi, Pornteera Chunhajinda, Suphat Bunyarittikit, and Rungroj Wongmahasiri. Mindful architecture from text-to-image ai perspectives: a case study of dall-e, midjourney, and stable diffusion. *Buildings*, **15**(6):972, 2025

[16] Epic. What is virtual production? 2024. [Accessed: 2025-June-12]

[17] Inan Evin, Perttu Hämäläinen, and Christian Guckelsberger. Cine-ai: Generating video game cutscenes in the style of human directors. *Proceedings of the ACM on Human-Computer Interaction*, **6**(CHI PLAY):1–23, 2022

[18] Yiran Chen, Anyi Rao, Xuekun Jiang, Shishi Xiao, Ruiqing Ma, Zeyu Wang, Hui Xiong, and Bo Dai. Cinepregen: Camera controllable video previsualization via engine-powered diffusion, *arXiv preprint arXiv:2408.17424*. 2024

[19] Anyi Rao, Linning Xu, and Dahua Lin. Shoot360: Normal view video creation from city panorama footage. In *ACM SIGGRAPH 2022 Conference Proceedings,* SIGGRAPH '22, New York, NY, USA, 2022. Association for Computing Machinery.

[20] Shiyuan Yang, Liang Hou, Haibin Huang, Chongyang Ma, Pengfei Wan, Di Zhang, Xiaodong Chen, and Jing Liao. Direct-a-video: Customized video generation with user-directed camera movement and object motion. In *Special Interest Group on Computer Graphics and Interactive Techniques Conference Conference Papers*, SIGGRAPH '24, 1–12. ACM, July 2024

[21] Zhouxia Wang, Ziyang Yuan, Xintao Wang, Tianshui Chen, Menghan Xia, Ping Luo, and Ying Shan. Motionctrl: A unified and flexible motion controller for video generation, In: *ACM SIGGRAPH 2024 Conference Papers* (pp. 1-11). 2024

[22] Daniel Silva Jasaui, Ana Martí-Testón, Adolfo Muñoz, Flavio Moriniello, J. Ernesto Solanes, and Luis Gracia. Virtual production: Real-time rendering pipelines for indie studios and the potential in different scenarios. *Applied Sciences*, **14**(6), 2024

[23] Jianyuan Wang, Minghao Chen, Nikita Karaev, Andrea Vedaldi, Christian Rupprecht, and David Novotny. Vggt: Visual geometry grounded transformer. In *Proceedings of the Computer Vision and Pattern Recognition Conference*, 5294–5306, 2025

[24] Jun Gao, Tianchang Shen, Zian Wang, Wenzheng Chen, Kangxue Yin, Daiqing Li, Or Litany, Zan Gojcic, and Sanja Fidler. Get3d: A generative model of high quality 3d textured shapes learned from images, *Advances in neural information processing systems*, **35**, 31841-31854. 2022

[25] Rinon Gal, Or Patashnik, Haggai Maron, Gal Chechik, and Daniel Cohen-

Or. Stylegan-nada: Clip-guided domain adaptation of image generators, *ACM Transactions on Graphics (TOG)*, **41**(4), 1-13. 2021

[26] Chen-Hsuan Lin, Jun Gao, Luming Tang, Towaki Takikawa, Xiaohui Zeng, Xun Huang, Karsten Kreis, Sanja Fidler, Ming-Yu Liu, and Tsung-Yi Lin. Magic3d: High-resolution text-to-3d content creation, *Proceedings of the IEEE/CVF conference on computer vision and pattern recognition*, (pp. 300-309), 2023

[27] Ce Zheng, Sijie Zhu, Matias Mendieta, Taojiannan Yang, Chen Chen, and Zhengming Ding. 3d human pose estimation with spatial and temporal transformers, In; *Proceedings of the IEEE/CVF international conference on computer vision* (pp. 11656-11665). 2021

[28] Alexander Kirillov, Eric Mintun, Nikhila Ravi, Hanzi Mao, Chloe Rolland, Laura Gustafson, Tete Xiao, Spencer Whitehead, Alexander C. Berg, Wan-Yen Lo, Piotr Dollár, and Ross Girshick. Segment anything, 2023

[29] Wenbin Li, Fabio Viola, Jonathan Starck, Gabriel J. Brostow, and Neill D. F. Campbell. Roto++: accelerating professional rotoscoping using shape manifolds. *ACM Trans. Graph*, **35**(4). 2016

[30] Wikipedia contributors. Ingvild deila — Wikipedia, the free encyclopedia. 2025. https://en.wikipedia.org/wiki/Ingvild_Deila [Accessed: 2025-June-17]

[31] Wikipedia contributors. Rogue one — Wikipedia, the free encyclopedia, 2025. https://en.wikipedia.org/wiki/Rogue_One [Accessed: 2025-June-17]

[32] Wenqing Wang, Haosen Yang, Josef Kittler, and Xiatian Zhu. Single image, any face: Generalisable 3d face generation, *arXiv preprint arXiv:2409* 2025

[33] Wikipedia contributors. Captain america: Civil war — Wikipedia, the free encyclopedia, 2025. [Accessed: 2025-June-17]

[34] Shuangyu Liu, Siyang Yu, Huan Li, Zhibang Yang, Mingxing Duan, and Xiangke Liao. A novel shilling attack on black-box recommendation systems for multiple targets. *Neural Computing and Applications*, **37**(5):3399–3417, 2025

[35] Hardeep Singh, Kamaljeet Kaur, Fakira Mohan Nahak, Sandeep Kumar Singh, and Sandeep Kumar. Deepfake as an artificial intelligence tool for vfx films. In *2023 7th International Conference on Computation System and Information Technology for Sustainable Solutions (CSITSS)*, 1–5. IEEE, 2023

[36] T. Siegel. Warner bros. signs deal for ai-driven film management system. The Hollywood Reporter.

[37] J Chen, H Dong, X Wang, et al. Bias and debias in recommender system: A survey and future directions. *ACM Transactions on Information Systems*, **41** (3):1–39, 2023

[38] Y Deldjoo, D Jannach, A Bellogin, et al. Fairness in recommender systems: research landscape and future directions. *User Modeling and User-Adapted Interaction*, **34**(1):59–108, 2024

[39] Fabian Lütz. Gender equality and artificial intelligence: Sdg 5 and the role of the un in fighting stereotypes, biases, and gender discrimination. In *Women's Empowerment and Its Limits: Interdisciplinary and Transnational Perspectives Toward Sustainable Progress*, 153–180. Springer, 2023

[40] V. Hassija, V. Chamola, A. Mahapatra, et al. Interpreting black-box models: A review on explainable artificial intelligence. *Cognitive Computation*, **16**(1):45–74, 2024

[41] Emrullah ŞAHiN, Naciye Nur Arslan, and Durmuş Özdemir. Unlocking the black box: an in-depth review on interpretability, explainability, and reliability in deep learning. *Neural Computing and Applications*, **37**(2):859–965, 2025

[42] Alejandro Barredo Arrieta, Natalia Díaz-Rodríguez, Javier Del Ser, Adrien Bennetot, Siham Tabik, Alberto Barbado, Salvador García, Sergio Gil-López, Daniel Molina, Richard Benjamins, et al. Explainable artificial intelligence (xai): Concepts, taxonomies, opportunities and challenges toward responsible ai. *Information fusion*, **58**:82–115, 2020

[43] Farzad Ahmed, Samiha Sultana, Md Tanzim Reza, Sajib Kumar Saha Joy, and Md Golam Rabiul Alam. Interpretable movie review analysis using machine learning and transformer models leveraging xai. In *2022 IEEE Asia-Pacific Conference on Computer Science and Data Engineering (CSDE)*, 1–6. IEEE, 2022

[44] K. Chan. Meta faces lawsuit over ai copyright claims in france.

[45] European Union. General data protection regulation (gdpr), article 6: Lawfulness of processing.

[46] Chawinthorn Watiktinnakorn, Jirawat Seesai, and Chutisant Kerdvibulvech. Blurring the lines: how ai is redefining artistic ownership and copyright. *Discover Artificial Intelligence*, **3**(1):37, 2023

[47] Junhe Law Offices. Analysis of five defensive strategies against aigc copyright infringement through four cases.

[48] US Copyright Office. Copyright registration guidance: Works containing material generated by artificial intelligence, 2023

[49] Wenlu Huang. Challenges and countermeasures of artificial intelligence to legal protection of intellectual property rights. *Dispute Settlement*, **10**(9):114–119, 2024

[50] International Coalition of Worker Unions. International coalition of worker unions declares emergency over ai use in animation.

[51] Janine Berg, Pawel Gmyrek, Margherita Licata, Tinovimbanashe Gwenyaya, and Martín Sánchez Freytes, Scaiano. Generative ai and the media and culture industry. Research brief, International Labour Organization. Research Department; International Labour Organization. Sectoral Policies Department, Geneva, 2025. Record Identifier: 995644832802676.

[52] Jules White, Quchen Fu, Sam Hays, Michael Sandborn, Carlos Olea, Henry Gilbert, Ashraf Elnashar, Jesse Spencer-Smith, and Douglas C Schmidt. A prompt pattern catalog to enhance prompt engineering with chatgpt. *arXiv preprint arXiv:2302.11382*, 2023

[53] Muhammad Uzair Khattak, Hanoona Rasheed, Muhammad Maaz, Salman Khan, and Fahad Shahbaz Khan. Maple: Multi-modal prompt learning. In *Proceedings of the IEEE/CVF conference on computer vision and pattern recognition*, 19113–19122, 2023

[54] Claudio Novelli, Mariarosaria Taddeo, and Luciano Floridi. Accountability in artificial intelligence: What it is and how it works. *Ai & Society*, **39**(4):1871–1882, 2024

[55] United Nations Educational, Scientific and Cultural Organization (UNESCO). Ethical impact assessment: a tool of the recommendation on the ethics of artificial intelligence, 2023

Chapter 18

Perspective Chapter: The Primacy of Poetics – Why Artists Will Build the Metaverse

Monica Storss

Abstract

This chapter interrogates dominant techno-deterministic narratives of metaverse development and advances a countervailing thesis: that the future of virtual economies will be shaped less by technical infrastructure than by cultural architectures of meaning. While automation and artificial intelligence rapidly commoditize once-scarce "hard skills" – coding, design, managerial oversight, financial analysis – the capacities resistant to computational replication – poetics, cultural intuition, narrative construction, culture-building, and meaning-making – emerge as the decisive vectors of value. To capture this shift, we introduce the figure of the synthesist: a hybrid professional archetype endowed with "bilateral fluency," the ability to operate across artistic-humanistic and technical-computational registers without translational loss. Drawing on case studies of failed corporate metaverse projects contrasted with thriving user-generated platforms, alongside neurocognitive research on creativity and integrative cognition, this chapter demonstrates that virtual environments achieve sustainability not through technical sophistication but through their ability to generate cultural resonance, participatory mythology, and affective engagement. Arguing that the metaverse economy is undergoing a paradigmatic transition from product-centered to meaning-centered organizational logics, necessitating antidisciplinary practice that exceeds conventional interdisciplinarity, such a reorientation foregrounds hybrid artist-leaders as the most strategically positioned actors to guide organizations through the transition. The implications are profound: educational curricula, talent pipelines, and governance structures must shift from skills-based replication toward creativity-centered innovation. Ultimately, the metaverse is not a technological frontier but a cultural epochal shift; its viability depends on recognizing artistry not as an ornamental supplement but as the infrastructural condition itself for value creation in virtual economies.

Keywords: metaverse economy, virtual worlds, future of work, artist, leadership, narrative and meaning-making

1. Introduction

The future of the metaverse will be driven by artists – and not in the way you may think. While conventional wisdom focuses on technical skills as the foundation of metaverse development, we're witnessing a fundamental inversion: every "hard skill" traditionally valued in corporate hierarchies – coding, graphic design, middle management, business systems, financial oversight – is rapidly becoming automatable through artificial intelligence (AI), robotic process automation (RPA), and other emerging tools. What remains irreplaceable are the intangible qualities that artists and humanities scholars possess: poetic vision, cultural intuition, meaning-making, and the ability to create experiences that resonate at a human level.

The future belongs to interdisciplinary thinking. As the boundaries between disciplines dissolve in virtual environments, success requires professionals who can navigate fluidly between creative vision, technical implementation, cultural understanding, and business strategy. The metaverse doesn't need specialists in isolation – it needs synthesists who can weave together multidisciplinary insights to create holistic experiences that serve diverse global communities.

Hybrid artists and creative leaders – visionary creatives, poets, and storytellers with technical literacy and leadership capabilities – will become the most valuable professionals in the metaverse economy. To meet this demand, our educational and organizational models must fundamentally shift from replaceable, skills-based hierarchies to creative-centered learning and innovation frameworks. The professionals who will thrive are those who refuse to be confined to single disciplines, instead developing the capacity to think across boundaries and integrate knowledge from multiple domains into coherent, meaningful experiences. This proposal outlines a fundamental paradigm shift essential for creating a meaningful and human-centered metaverse that builds global communities while advancing technological innovation. The transformation represents not merely an interesting trend but an evolutionary response to technological complexity that will determine which organizations and systems thrive in the age of the metaverse economy.

2. The metaverse paradox

The metaverse has been heralded as the next stage of human civilization, a digital twin of our social, economic, and cultural lives. Executives promised immersive universes where our avatars would work, shop, and socialize in frictionless synchrony. The money followed the rhetoric: Meta poured over $36 billion into Reality Labs from 2019 to 2022 alone [1]. And yet, in practice, the results are oddly... anticlimactic. Despite world-class engineering and vast financial investment, corporate metaverses feel flat and lifeless. Horizon Worlds – Meta's flagship project meant to entice millions – quickly earned a reputation as an empty lobby where even employees admitted they rarely wanted to log in.

Contrast this with amateur-built or community-driven platforms. Minecraft, designed initially by Markus Persson as a modest indie project, now sustains a sprawling cosmos of millions who build, socialize, and even host weddings and graduations [2]. Roblox, with its cartoonish avatars and simplistic physics, outpaces nearly every corporate attempt in terms of daily active users [3]. Second Life, far from dead, continues to serve as a cultural laboratory where users create art galleries, activist communities, and digital religions [4]. Those experiences aren't rich because of superior code; they're rich because someone understood character arc, dramatic tension, and emotional payoff.

Billion-dollar projects with photorealistic graphics and flawless infrastructures fail, while blocky, glitch-ridden, user-generated worlds thrive. The difference lies not in infrastructure but in meaning. Human beings do not flock to virtual spaces because their lighting engines simulate the reflection of neon across polished marble; they flock to them because they matter and create shared meaning. Virtual worlds that tell stories, generate belonging, and provide cultural resonance are the ones that last. Digital environments succeed when they become sites of identity play and storytelling, not when they replicate physical space.

Where the corporate metaverse obsesses over technical sophistication, the successful metaverse relies on poetics. Without artistry, virtual worlds are sterile simulations; with it, they become culture. The failure of corporate metaverse initiatives reveals a fundamental misunderstanding of how culture emerges in virtual spaces. Corporations approach virtual worlds with a manufacturing mindset, attempting to produce culture as if it were a product, rather than allowing it to emerge organically through human connection and shared meaning-making.

The metaverse rush has been driven by a push for quantifiable metrics – daily active users, engagement time, conversion rates – while remaining blind to the difficult-to-measure, intangible qualities that make virtual worlds meaningful: emotional resonance, narrative depth, and authentic community formation. Mistaking technical sophistication for cultural value, the corporate approach treats narrative as decoration rather than infrastructure, fundamentally misunderstanding that digital economies are powered not by scarcity but by story [5].

Successful virtual worlds allow users to cocreate participatory mythologies [4], yet corporate metaverses present prepackaged experiences designed to channel user behavior toward predetermined outcomes. This distinction between cultivation and control explains why amateur-built platforms sustain millions of engaged users, while billion-dollar corporate projects struggle to retain even their own employees.

Current corporate metaverse approach is trapped in an insurmountable paradox: requiring predictable outcomes and brand control, but authentic culture demands chaos, experimentation, productive failure, and genuine risk. This paradox manifests as systemic risk aversion that suffocates creativity before it can bloom.

The control imperative extends to user behavior management. UX teams design virtual spaces to direct users through predetermined pathways, measuring success by how effectively they can predict and monetize user actions. Yet, the magic of thriving virtual worlds emerges precisely from unexpected user creativity. These emergent behaviors are what corporations fear most and understand the least. When every feature must justify its return on investment before implementation, virtual worlds have been framed as extraction machines rather than expression platforms, designed to capture value from users rather than create value with them.

The metric-driven development process further compounds this problem. Quarterly earnings cycles demand immediate returns, but culture evolves at human speed, requiring patience and tolerance for apparent failure. Virtual worlds that don't demonstrate instant traction face swift abandonment, killed before nascent communities can form. This impatience with emergence creates a self-fulfilling prophecy: corporations abandon "failed" projects just as organic culture begins to take root, then cite their own failure to create authenticity as evidence that virtual worlds lack commercial viability.

3. Virtual economies are story economies

At the height of the NFT boom in 2021, a digital collage by the artist Beeple (Mark Winkelmann) sold for $69 million at Christie's. The image itself was infinitely replicable. Anyone with an internet connection could screen shot it, download it, copy it, share it, or print it on a t-shirt. What commanded value was not the file but the story – the narrative of digital art history, the mythology of blockchain ownership, and the cultural capital of being part of a pioneering moment [5].

For every NFT that soared, thousands languished unsold. The difference was not in technical architecture, which lived on blockchains of equal immutability, but in narrative gravity. Some NFTs were embedded in communities, memes, or esthetic movements; others were lonely tokens without a story to tell. The economics of NFTs are fundamentally the economics of narrative: a marketplace of cultural meaning rather than material scarcity.

This logic extends beyond speculative assets. Virtual real estate in platforms like Second Life and Decentraland derives its value not from geographic location (there is no "scarcity" in infinite code-space) but from its cultural placement. Parcels near popular clubs, art installations, or community hubs command higher prices because they are woven into collective narratives of belonging [4]. The same principle applies to virtual fashion: a pair of digital sneakers is valuable not for its pixels, but for the story it tells about identity, status, and affiliation.

Narrative value explains why some virtual worlds thrive while others collapse. The corporate metaverse often treats digital economies as technical infrastructure: design a marketplace, secure transactions, introduce scarcity mechanics, and the economy will flourish. But without stories – without cultural frameworks that give those transactions meaning – such marketplaces remain empty shells.

Humans are narrative animals. We do not simply consume media; we inhabit it, extend it, remix it, and embed it into the fabric of our lives. This is why Fortnite concerts, blending gameplay with celebrity performances, feel more compelling than sterile virtual conference halls. The former are participatory spaces of cocreation; the latter are digitized boardrooms.

Seen in this light, the metaverse is not primarily an economic project, but a storytelling project. Its economies rise and fall on the strength of the narratives that bind communities together. In virtual spaces, value is not stored in the blockchain ledger, but in the human imagination.

The global metaverse market size was estimated at USD 105.40 billion in 2024 and is projected to reach USD 936.57 billion by 2030 [6]. That growth won't come from operational excellence; it will come from creating experience engagements people didn't know they wanted or needed. The successful metaverse CEO won't optimize supply chains (AI will do that better); they'll create desire chains, narrative chains, and meaning chains. In an economy where digital tools lower costs and expand revenue opportunities, making global markets more accessible for individual creators [7], the competitive advantage isn't efficiency – it's imagination.

Look at who's actually creating value in the digital economy. AI is widely used in newsrooms, with 41% of news teams employing it to create illustrative art, 39% for social media content, and 38% for writing and generating articles [7]. What it can't do – yet – is create the narrative coherence, emotional resonance, and cultural significance that make the content matter.

The gaming segment held the largest market revenue share in 2024, driven by gaming applications that provide rich, interactive experiences [8] – and those experiences aren't rich because of superior code; they're rich because someone understood how narrative drives engagement, which builds community, which drives growth.

The metaverse is, at its core, a story-based economy. This is a wholly new kind of economics. To thrive in this landscape will require storytellers who build genuine community at the helm. Traditional economics rests on material limits: resources are finite, demand exceeds supply, and value derives from managing that imbalance. Virtual economies, however, operate on a very different logic. Here, scarcity is artificial – pixels can be endlessly reproduced. What gives a digital asset its value is not its rarity but its resonance. Digital economies themselves are powered less by scarcity but by story.

4. Middle-out compression: The great skills reversal

AI, RPA, and other emergent tools are eroding the scarcity value of technical skills. AI, with human oversight, can generate code at an industrial scale, graphic design is rapidly automatable, and financial systems increasingly rely upon algorithmic processes [9, 10]. This is not to say that these technologies are replacing humans – quite the contrary. If anything, AI and automation are augmenting human capability, allowing smaller teams and individuals to accomplish more, and any use of automation technology requires careful human stewardship. However, what was once a high-value corporate hierarchy of hard skills – software development, project management, systems optimization – is becoming susceptible to commoditization.

The narrative surrounding the metaverse has been dominated by technological determinism. Scholars and practitioners often describe metaverse futures in terms of infrastructure – distributed computing, blockchain economies, immersive headsets, extended reality (XR) interfaces, and AI [11, 12]. This vision, until recently, while impressive, emphasizes technical prowess: coding, modeling, optimizing, and managing digital architectures. Such extractive skills have been traditionally valorized in corporate and academic settings; they have been essential for value creation, building platforms, and maintaining infrastructures. However, the belief that these technical competencies will remain the cornerstone of metaverse development is increasingly untenable.

4.1 Automation and the decline of technical scarcity

The automation of knowledge-work has fundamentally altered the relationship between technical expertise and organizational value. Brynjolfsson and McAfee's [10] foundational work, The Second Machine Age, argued that digital technologies increasingly perform cognitive tasks once considered uniquely human. More recent studies confirm that AI is automating domains ranging from software engineering to financial analysis [9]. Even advanced programming tasks are no longer the exclusive domain of engineers, as tools like GitHub Copilot and OpenAI's Codex enable nonspecialists to produce functional code at speed and scale [13].

This erosion of technical scarcity challenges long-standing assumptions within corporate hierarchies – and this is a good thing. Traditionally, technical skill sets were gatekeepers to high-value roles in industries such as software, design, and management. As RPA and AI increasingly replicate these skills, their scarcity – and thus their value – diminishes [14]. Scholars of labor economics frame this as a process of "creative destruction," where old forms of expertise lose relevance as new paradigms emerge [15].

Not all skills are equally vulnerable. Sudies on task automation consistently emphasize that roles requiring contextual judgment, ethical interpretation, or cultural meaning-making resist computational replication [16, 17]. These findings align with arguments in media and cultural studies that emphasize the irreplaceability of narrative and aesthetic creation [18, 57, 69]. In the context of the metaverse, the automation of technical tasks foregrounds the value of intangible, human-centered capacities.

Human-centered design frameworks have long emphasized that technology succeeds not through its technical sophistication but through its capacity to align with human needs, emotions, and cultural practices [19, 47]. In the metaverse, this principle is even more pronounced: immersive environments fail if they do not resonate experientially with users [11].

Recent scholarship on XR emphasizes the role of embodiment, affect, and narrative in shaping user adoption. In his 2022 paper, "Metaverse: A Matter of eXperience," Luciano Floridi [20, 65] extended this argument by framing the metaverse as an "infosphere" – a socio-technical environment where ethical and cultural considerations are integral to system design. The politics of virtual worlds are inseparable from their cultural framings [21]. Empirical studies reinforce this view; XR learning environments show that users engage more deeply when experiences are infused with narrative coherence and cultural symbolism rather than when they are merely technically polished [22]. The lesson for metaverse design is clear: the meaningfulness of virtual experiences is grounded in artistry and cultural fluency, not technical execution alone.

Transdisciplinary research environments consistently outperform discipline-bound models in generating novel solutions. Innovation scholars increasingly highlight interdisciplinary creativity as the engine of breakthrough advances [23, 62]. Creativity does not emerge in isolation but in the cross-pollination of fields, where artistic sensibilities intersect with scientific rigor and technological experimentation.

In the metaverse, such interdisciplinarity is even more essential. Virtual worlds operate simultaneously as technological systems, cultural spaces, and economic platforms. Professionals who can synthesize across these dimensions are best positioned to steward, create, and deploy environments that are technologically sophisticated and culturally resonant.

Organizational research demonstrates that creativity is a core driver of competitive advantage. Amabile and Pratt's [24] "Dynamic Componential Model of Creativity and Innovation" shows how organizational cultures that support artistic exploration generate more sustainable innovation outcomes.

For much of the late twentieth century, professional advancement meant accumulating what were called "hard skills." Coding, business analysis, systems management, and financial modeling were treated as scarce commodities – the backbone of modern corporations and the ticket to secure, high-status employment [25]. The MBA became the credential par excellence, embodying the rationalized, technical approach to organizational life [26].

That logic is rapidly unraveling: GitHub Copilot can now translate natural language prompts into functional code [27]. Generative visual models like Stable Diffusion and DALL · E produce advertising-ready graphics in seconds [28]. Financial modeling, logistics coordination, and even middle-management duties are increasingly delegated to machine-learning systems [17]. As David Autor [16] argues, technological change is "hollowing out" the middle tiers of professional labor: highly routinized but well-compensated skills are the easiest to mechanize.

This is the great irony: the very "hard skills" once treated as essential are the most susceptible to automation. The engineer, the manager, the analyst – all find themselves slowly displaced by systems designed to perform their functions more cheaply and more efficiently.

What remains irreplaceable are precisely those capacities once devalued as "soft." Cultural intuition, poetic vision, the ability to create community and build resonance across communities are not programmable. An algorithm can generate an endless supply of narratives, but it cannot discern which one will break a heart, spark laughter, or capture the zeitgeist. A system can process text in hundreds of languages, but it cannot grasp the irony of a political cartoon or the pathos of a poem. These require the interpretive, imaginative faculties of the human mind [68]. So-called "soft" skills are revealing themselves to be the hardest of all – resistant to automation, indispensable to leadership, and central to the future of the metaverse. As Richard Florida [29] predicted in *The Rise of the Creative Class*, economies evolve toward privileging those who can innovate, narrate, and create cultural value.

These cases align with theoretical arguments that creativity is not simply an esthetic add-on but a strategic capability [29, 30, 50]. In the context of the metaverse, artistry functions as infrastructure: it is the very fabric of engagement, retention, and cultural legitimacy. What remains irreplaceable are the capacities associated with artistic, humanistic domains: poetic vision, narrative construction, cultural intuition, and the ability to create experiences that resonate at a deeply human level (**Figure 1**). These capacities are difficult to formalize or automate. They require context sensitivity, ethical judgment, and imaginative creativity that resist reduction to data-driven systems. If the metaverse is to succeed not as a novelty but as a meaningful cultural ecosystem, it must be designed and led by individuals who embody such capacities.

The professional figure of the future is not the narrow specialist but the synthesist – a hybrid creature who combines technical literacy with artistic imagination and cultural sensibility. This reversal is not a marginal shift; it is a paradigmatic reordering of value in the digital economy. The artist understands what the analysts miss: in virtual worlds, physics is negotiable, but narrative isn't. You can break the laws of gravity, but you can't break the laws of story. Meaning can not be automated.

5. The hybrid artist-leader: Rise of the synthesist

A virtual reality dev team just received playtest feedback with the directive to "make it feel more magical." The engineers want specifications – particle density,

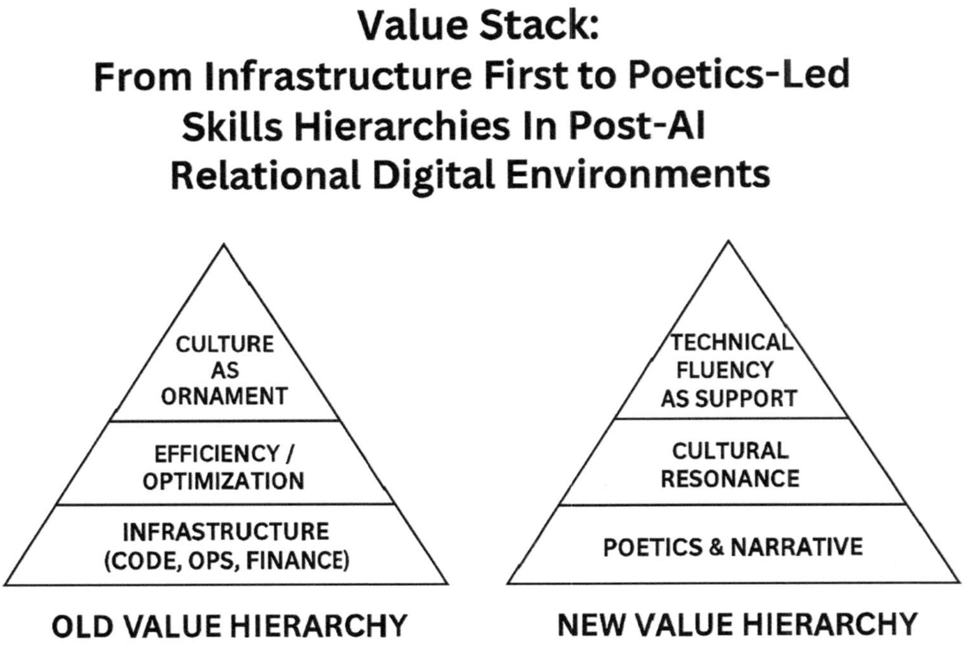

Figure 1.
Value shifts as automation reduces the scarcity of technical tasks. "Value Stack: From Infrastructure First to Poetics-Led Skills Hierarchies In Post-AI Relational Digital Environments," Monica Storss, 2025.

shader parameters, frame rate targets. The designers wave their hands and display their Miro, Figma, and Mural boards, speaking of "wonder" and "delight." The producers tap their watches, asking how many sprints "magical" will take. The meeting devolves into the Tower of Babel, each discipline speaking its own language, with no one able to translate.

Engineers, while possessing deep technical expertise, are trained to optimize within constraints rather than question whether those constraints should exist. Ask an engineer to make something "magical," and they'll optimize the hell out of your existing magic. But they won't ask whether magic is even the right word, or whether what you really want is "uncanny" or "liminal," "haunted" or "sublime."

Business leaders, educated in efficiency and optimization, struggle to imagine value beyond quantifiable metrics. They can tell you the ROI of "magical" but not why anyone would need magic in the first place.

Then someone speaks up – let's call them the synthesist. "Magical," they say, "means triggering memory and possibility – specific particle effects with randomized trajectories following a Perlin noise function, but weighted toward upward spirals. It means color palettes shifted toward violet with golden highlights triggered by proximity detection at 2.5 meters. It means sound design incorporating subliminal chimes at the edge of hearing, timed to the user's heartbeat if we can get biometric access. And it means interaction delays of exactly 0.3 seconds, which will be enough to build anticipation without frustrating flow."

The room goes quiet. Everyone just heard their own language, but somehow it all made sense together. They didn't just translate "magical" – they preserved the magic while making it buildable. This person isn't an interpreter between camps; they're something else entirely: the architect of impossible things, a composer of experiences that shouldn't exist. The synthesist isn't building features; they are building meaning. This emergent leader, artists and humanists who bridge worlds between technical fluencies and organizational stewardship, are the future leaders of the metaverse.

5.1 The cognitive architecture

The hybrid artist-leader possesses what Gardner [31] identifies as "synthesizing intelligence" – the capacity to integrate ideas from disparate sources into coherent, original amalgamations. This cognitive capability transcends traditional notions of interdisciplinarity, representing what Wagner [32] terms "creative intelligence": the ability to discover patterns across domains and transform these insights into innovative solutions.

Neuroscientific research reveals that individuals who engage regularly in both artistic and technical practices develop enhanced neural connectivity between brain regions typically specialized for different cognitive functions [33]. This neuroplastic adaptation enables what might be termed "cognitive ambidexterity" – the ability to shift fluidly between analytical and creative modes of thinking, or, more significantly, to engage both simultaneously.

The synthesist mindset reflects what McGilchrist [34] describes as the integration of left and right hemisphere processing – not the popular misconception of "left-brained" versus "right-brained" individuals, but rather the capacity to engage both the analytic-sequential processing associated with the left hemisphere and the holistic-contextual processing of the right hemisphere in dynamic interaction. This neurological integration manifests as the ability to perceive both the forest and the trees simultaneously – to grasp systemic implications while attending to granular details.

5.2 Bilateral fluency

The hybrid artist-leader possesses a "bilateral fluency"; they are native speakers of both creative and technical languages, requiring no translation between domains. This transcends the current model of "technical artists" or "creative technologists," who serve as interpreters between separate camps. Instead, these individuals think natively in both registers at once.

Research by Root-Bernstein et al. [35] on polymathic scientists reveals that Nobel laureates are twenty-two times more likely than average scientists to engage in artistic avocations. This correlation suggests not that art provides a break from scientific work, but that artistic practice develops cognitive capabilities essential for breakthrough innovation. The hybrid artist-leader embodies this principle professionally rather than avocationally.

5.3 How synthesists emerge

The artist-leader or synthesist is a chimera: they are an artist who is also technologically literate, a community builder who can speak both the language of art, poetics, philosophy and the language of code.

Artists can occupy a unique position in the knowledge economy. Unlike other professionals, who are rewarded for conformity to disciplinary norms [56], artists are rewarded for novelty and originality. Their métier is seeing what others cannot see and creating what does not yet exist. Engineers, while possessing deep technical expertise, are trained to optimize within constraints rather than question whether those constraints should exist. Business leaders, educated in efficiency and optimization, struggle to imagine value beyond quantifiable metrics. Scientists, despite investigative rigor, operate within paradigms that resist fundamental questioning.

If virtual economies run on stories and experience, then the future leaders of the metaverse will not be the spreadsheet wizards or the systems engineers. They will be the poets, the dramaturgs, the painters, the songwriters, the culture builders, and the designers of experience. Not artists in the old, romantic sense of a lone genius painting or writing in garrets; they are the refugees from disciplinary constraints – brilliant minds that don't fit in the existing boxes.

The synthesist may look like a failed startup founder whose products were beautiful but "ahead of their time" (translation: they built for meaning before market). Talent may be hiding in the art school dropout who couldn't afford tuition, so they taught themselves to code, or the open-source contributors whose Git repositories read like manifestos. They tried to color within the lines, but their work kept bleeding across boundaries. Traditional work, arts, and academia didn't know what to do with them. "Is this computer science or media studies?" "Is this engineering or art?" The answer was always "yes," and that was always the wrong answer – until now.

5.4 Cultural competency

If we are discussing the metaverse as a site of cultural production, we must also contend with its ethical dimensions. If virtual environments are to function as laboratories of imagination and belonging, the central question is not only who will build them but also for whom they are being built. The danger is that, without deliberate intervention, the metaverse simply replicates the exclusions, inequities, and blind spots of existing social systems under the guise of novelty.

The imaginative scaffolding of virtual worlds must be capacious enough to accommodate plural identities, languages, and ways of knowing, rather than defaulting to the homogenizing logics of dominant markets. Algorithmic infrastructures that govern avatars, content moderation, and recommendation systems are not neutral; they carry with them the potential to manifest bias, encoding exclusionary assumptions into the very texture of digital interaction. The ethical future of the metaverse depends on embedding these commitments into its very architecture, ensuring that it evolves not as a technosphere of exclusion but as a genuinely shared cultural commons.

The metaverse represents humanity's first truly global cultural space – not dominated by any single national or linguistic group but requiring navigation across all simultaneously. The hybrid artist-leader possesses what Earley and Mosakowski [36] term "cultural intelligence," the ability to function effectively in culturally diverse settings.

Virtual worlds complicate traditional notions of cultural competency. Physical world-cultures evolved over millennia within geographic and linguistic boundaries.

Virtual world cultures emerge rapidly, blend unpredictably, and evolve continuously. The synthesist must navigate not just existing cultures but emerging ones – digital native cultures that exist solely online, hybrid cultures that blend physical and virtual elements, and synthetic cultures created within specific platforms or communities.

Research on global virtual teams reveals that successful leaders develop what Jarvenpaa and Leidner [37] call "swift trust" – the ability to establish credibility and rapport quickly across cultural boundaries in digital environments. The hybrid artist-leader extends this concept, creating what might be termed "cultural bridges" – shared symbolic spaces that feel authentic to diverse communities without appropriating or diminishing any single culture.

Critically, hybrid artist-leaders bring cultural fluency to global communities. The metaverse is not a homogeneous space; it is a tangled network of subcultures, memes, and identity experiments. Leaders who can navigate these nuances – who understand irony, symbolism, and the delicate art of cultural translation – will outpace those who merely optimize processes. If culture is a "web of significance" spun by humans themselves, then in the metaverse, leadership means weaving those webs with intention.

This requires a deep understanding of how meaning varies across cultures: why certain colors, symbols, narratives, or interactions carry different significance in different contexts. But it also requires the creativity to imagine new cultural forms that don't yet exist. The hybrid artist-leader doesn't just respect existing cultures; they facilitate the emergence of new ones.

6. Cultural shifts and organizational transformation

6.1 From MBA to MFA: paradigm shift

While business schools are still teaching Porter's Five Forces and SWOT analysis, humanities graduates are being instructed in architecting cultural forces. They are being asked to turn in assignments that reimagine semiotics, epistemologies, and ontology itself. The MFA and degrees and programs like it, both in and outside of academia, teach what the MBA or MS cannot: how to create meaning itself. While engineering and business students learn to optimize existing systems, the MFA students learn to imagine systems that do not yet exist. They're being trained in the most crucial, inautomatable skills for the metaverse economy: naming the unnamable, making the intangible tangible, the invisible visible, and the impossible feel inevitable.

For most of the twentieth century, the MBA was the crown jewel credential for value creation. It signaled mastery over spreadsheets, organizational charts, and the ability to rationalize human behavior into manageable processes [26]. But in a world where AI increasingly performs those rationalizing functions, the MBA loses some of its luster. Enter the MFA – the Master of Fine Arts. What was once regarded as a quaint indulgence, suitable only for struggling novelists or theater directors, suddenly looks like a better predictor of resilience in the metaverse economy because its training cultivates precisely the capacities that resist automation.

The MBA asks: "How can we do this better?" The MFA asks: "What else can be?" In the metaverse economy, the second question is the one that matters.

Organizations that are able to identify and onboard the synthesist leader will have the competitive edge that will define the next trillion-dollar markets. Creative services exports surged to $1.4 trillion in 2022, marking a 29% increase since 2017 [7, 49], while traditional industries stagnate. The metaverse is viewed as a massively creative space that facilitates experimentation and the development of ideas in the digital domain that can then transcend into the physical domain [38]. Yet, we are still promoting spreadsheet jockeys to run companies that are trying, quite literally, to create entirely new realities. Second Life and VR Chat were not built by McKinsey consultants – they were built by people who understood that humans like efficiency but crave connection and experience.

Metaverse leadership demands cognitive diversity, not credentials conformity. New leadership in the metaverse economy will look very different from the current HR recruiter table. You're looking for creatives with technical backgrounds and leadership skills. The ideal candidate isn't someone with a traditional pedigree but someone with cognitive range. As Epstein [39] argues in *Range: Why Generalists Triumph in a Specialized World,* the most innovative problem-solvers are those who integrate knowledge from multiple domains. In practical terms, this means prioritizing candidates with unconventional educational and lived-experience combinations.

Perhaps most challenging, organizations must evolve cultures that value questions over answers, exploration over efficiency, and meaning-making over traditional metrics. This cultural shift requires tolerance for ambiguity, comfort with creative failure, and patience for emergence.

The prevailing models of business and education in the West remain rooted in twentieth-century industrial logic: isolate skills, quantify outcomes, and standardize performance. Such models are fundamentally incompatible with the demands of a metaverse economy. Instead of training learners to perform predictable tasks, we must prepare them to navigate uncertainty, create from ambiguity, and build meaning within complexity.

Problem-Based Learning and Project-Based Learning models champion the inversion of the skills-based model, instead asserting that the necessary skills can be acquired; it is the mission alignment with a larger problem-solving creative scope that matters to invention. Innovation, too, must be redefined. Rather than equating novelty with technological breakthrough, we must ask: who is served by this system? Whose stories are included? What kinds of futures does this design make possible? In this reorientation, the artist is not an ornament or afterthought, but a primary architect of imaginaries.

6.2 Interdisciplinarity

Interdisciplinary work, while valuable, operates within existing structural constraints. When biologists collaborate with engineers in interdisciplinary projects, each maintains their disciplinary identity, vocabulary, and methodological approach. The collaboration occurs at interfaces – carefully negotiated boundaries where knowledge is translated between domains. This translation process, while enabling cooperation, inherently involves a loss of nuance and meaning.

Klein [40] identifies interdisciplinary work as "a means of solving problems and answering questions that cannot be satisfactorily addressed using single methods or approaches." However, this framework assumes that disciplines themselves remain valid organizational structures for knowledge – an assumption the antidisciplinary approach challenges.

6.3 Beyond interdisciplinarity: Antidisciplinary

While interdisciplinary approaches combine existing disciplines, the hybrid artist-leader operates in what is termed "antidisciplinary" space – territories that exist between and beyond established fields [41, 66]. Interdisciplinary work accepts disciplinary boundaries while seeking connections; antidisciplinary work questions whether such boundaries should exist at all. The hybrid artist-leader doesn't merely bridge disciplines; they operate in spaces where disciplinary distinctions become meaningless.

In an increasingly specialized economic landscape, the term "antidisciplinarity" emerges as a crucial concept for understanding and addressing complex and novel challenges. While often confused with related ideas like interdisciplinarity and multidisciplinarity, antidisciplinarity represents a distinct and more radical approach to knowledge and value creation. Rather than simply combining existing fields, it seeks to work in the "white spaces" between them, deliberately operating outside established disciplinary boundaries to forge entirely new methods, frameworks, and fields of inquiry.

The concept of antidisciplinarity, articulated by Joi Ito during his tenure as director of the MIT Media Lab (2011–2019) [49, 66, 67], represents a radical departure from traditional academic and professional frameworks. Interdisciplinary work is when people from different disciplines work together. An antidisciplinary project isn't the sum of a bunch of disciplines but something entirely new – the word defies easy definition [42]. This distinction proves crucial for understanding emerging leadership models.

To fully grasp the meaning of antidisciplinarity, it is essential to first differentiate it from its more common counterparts. Multidisciplinarity involves juxtaposing multiple disciplines to address a problem, with each field retaining its own methods and perspectives. A historical project, for example, might incorporate the study of economics, but the economist and historian would still work within their respective disciplinary confines. Interdisciplinarity, a more integrated approach, aims to synthesize knowledge and methods from different disciplines to create a more holistic understanding. A new field like neuroeconomics, which merges neuroscience and economics, is an example of interdisciplinarity in action.

Antidisciplinarity goes a step further. It is not about connecting existing dots but about exploring the uncharted territory where no dots yet exist [42, 53, 67]. This approach is not hostile to disciplines; rather, it acknowledges their limitations and seeks to operate in the conceptual gaps they leave behind. In the metaverse economy, this is where value creation lies.

One of the most prominent arenas for antidisciplinary practice has been at the intersection of technology, design, and art. The MIT Media Lab was founded on the principle of providing a home for "misfits" and thinkers who did not fit into traditional departments. Here, an artist might work with a computer scientist, not simply to create digital art but to develop new algorithmic tools that fundamentally change the way art is created and experienced. This collaboration may lead to novel methods that are neither strictly "art" nor "computer science," but something entirely new. This freedom from disciplinary tradition allows for a "radical collaboration" that can lead to truly unique and disruptive breakthroughs.

The benefits of embracing an antidisciplinary mindset are profound, particularly in a world grappling with multifaceted issues of high-risk, high-reward thinking, as researchers become more willing to explore unconventional hypotheses that might otherwise be dismissed by a peer review process rooted in disciplinary norms.

The antidisciplinary approach emerged from the recognition that, as we engage in tackling harder and harder problems that require many fields and perspectives, the separation of disciplines appears to be causing more and more damage [42, 67]. This damage manifests particularly in complex systems work, where artificial boundaries between fields prevent holistic understanding and innovation. The metaverse is, in itself, an antidisciplinary space. Modern problems require modern solutions.

6.4 Talent development: Specialization versus speculation

The question isn't whether you need artist-leaders; the question is whether you'll land them before your competition does.

Identifying talent will require cultural pivots in organizational, hiring, and educational cultures, with many of the frameworks already starting to take root. We already see the emergence of degrees in "Creative Technology" and "Narrative Engineering" that train learners to think synthetically rather than sequentially. Organizations seeking to develop hybrid artist-leaders must recognize that these capabilities can emerge from outside traditional professional development programs. Instead, they require what might be termed "cognitive cross-training" – deliberate exposure to both artistic and technical practices in contexts that encourage synthesists to engage in capacious reimagining, rather than specialization.

Organizations must adapt structures to accommodate leaders who don't fit traditional categories [50, 56]. This might involve creating new C-suite positions – Chief Creative Technologist, Chief Narrative Officer, Chief Experience Architect – that explicitly recognize synthesis as core organizational capabilities. Reporting structures for the metaverse may need to evolve beyond traditional functional hierarchies. Hybrid artist-leaders might simultaneously oversee technical development, creative direction, and cultural strategy. Traditional organizational charts, with neat categorical divisions, may need to give way to network structures where influence flows through expertise and vision rather than formal authority. The next generation of hybrid artist-leaders might emerge from entirely new pathways that refuse disciplinary categorization from the start.

6.5 Moving away from siloed work: From artist-in-residence to the C-suite

Currently, most corporate artist-in-residence programs are essentially expensive decoration – bring in an artist, have them make something pretty for the lobby, serve wine and cheese at an opening, and feel cultured. The artist-in-residence model that works for the metaverse doesn't treat artists as consultants but as leaders with actual decision-making power. Many organizations implement artist-in-residence programs that fundamentally misunderstand the artist's potential contribution, treating creative professionals as consultants who provide esthetic enhancement rather than strategic direction.

Effective artist-in-residence programs grant artists what Ann Balsamo [43] terms "decisional authority" – genuine influence over product development and strategic direction. Recentering artists as synthesists and leaders taps into previously unexplored value creation, unique to the metaverse economy. Microsoft's Artist-in-Residence program demonstrates the transformative potential of properly structured creative integration. When artists received authority to influence product development decisions, including veto power over features that violated esthetic or narrative coherence, user engagement metrics increased by 34% [43]. This improvement resulted not from superficial esthetic enhancements but from a fundamental reimagining of user experience through artistic perspectives.

Adobe's Creative Residency program has generated measurable value exceeding $50 million through innovations emerging from resident projects [44]. However, the program's true value transcends financial metrics, manifesting in organizational cultural transformation. Engineers develop artistic sensibilities, marketers embrace narrative thinking, and executives adopt creative director mindsets. "Cognitive contagion" [45] refers to the spread of creative thinking patterns through organizational networks. When artists embed within technical teams, the result exceeds improved esthetics; technical solutions become more innovative. When technologists integrate with creative teams, efficiency improvements combine with entirely novel expressive forms.

Empirical evidence supports the economic value of creative leadership. Organizations with artists in leadership positions demonstrate 23% higher innovation metrics compared to traditionally led firms. The creative economy generates $2.25 trillion globally, with 9% annual growth, exceeding overall GDP growth rates [46]. The metaverse market's projected growth to $936 billion by 2030 [6] will likely favor organizations that prioritize narrative coherence over technical optimization.

For the metaverse economy, one of the most impactful things an organization can do doesn't start with product; it starts in HR: stop hiring for roles, start hiring for range. Create spaces where boundaries dissolve. Measure meaning alongside metrics that are based on boundary crossing, not ladder climbing.

7. Conclusion: The synthesist imperative

The future of the metaverse will not be written in code alone; it will be authored in meaning. What corporations have mistaken for a design problem is, in fact, a cultural one: virtual worlds fail not because their polygons are insufficiently smooth, but because their meanings are insufficiently deep. The metaverse will not thrive as a sterile marketplace of transactions or a polished but empty showroom. It will thrive when it becomes a stage for stories, a space for connection, a laboratory for myth, and a commons for shared experience and collective imagination.

This requires a reevaluation of value itself. Technical expertise – the prized "hard skills" of the twentieth century – are increasingly abundant, automated, and commodified. What remains rare are the interpretive, imaginative, and connective capacities that cannot be programmed: the ability to conjure resonance, to hold paradox, and to cultivate belonging. What once was dismissed as "soft" now reveals itself to be the hardest skill of all.

The professionals who will shape the metaverse are not just engineers or analysts; they are synthesists – artist-leaders who inhabit antidisciplinary frontiers. They are translators of the ineffable into the buildable, able to articulate what "magic" means in terms of shader logic and story arc simultaneously. They are cartographers of emergent cultures, organically threading together strands of poetics, code, and community into woven tapestries that feel alive. They will not simply manage platforms but reimagine them, optimizing outcomes and experiences.

The paradigm shift is already underway. The hierarchy of skills is inverting. To ignore this is to risk building empty worlds that collapse under their own hollowness. To embrace it is to recognize that the metaverse is not only an economic frontier but a cultural, epochal shift, one that demands new forms of leadership and new architectures of learning, being, and doing.

If the twentieth century was defined by the engineer and the manager, the twenty-first will be defined by the synthesist. The question is no longer where artistry belongs in the metaverse; the question is whether organizations and institutions will recognize, before it is too late, that artistry is the metaverse's foundation.

The synthesist leader is not a luxury but a necessity. Without them, virtual environments risk becoming sterile, empty technospheres. With them, the metaverse becomes what it promises: a vibrant, lived world. The question facing organizations is not whether they need hybrid artist-leaders but how quickly they can identify and develop them.

The synthesist, a new kind of hybrid artist-leader, represents not a temporary adaptation but a fundamental evolution in professional capability for the metaverse. As the metaverse economy, built on story and meaning, matures, organizations that cultivate, recognize, and empower these synthesists will create virtual worlds that transcend functional utility to achieve cultural significance. The evidence suggests that traditional disciplinary boundaries actively impede innovation in virtual world development. The future belongs to those who refuse such boundaries – who think in code and color, algorithm and allegory, data and drama simultaneously. These hybrid artist-leaders don't merely bridge different worlds; they create entirely new ones where such bridges become unnecessary.

In economies increasingly defined by virtual experience and digital culture, the ability to synthesize creative vision with technical implementation, navigate cultural complexity while managing diverse teams, and translate imagination into reality becomes not merely valuable but essential. The hybrid artist-leader stands at the center of this transformation, building futures that are simultaneously technically sophisticated and deeply, meaningfully human. In the metaverse, the companies that win won't be the ones that understand the technology. They'll be the ones that understand the intangibles.

Author details

Monica Storss
Northeastern University, Boston, Massachusetts, USA

*Address all correspondence to: storss.m@northeastern.edu

References

[1] Dean G. Meta has pumped $36 billion into its metaverse and VR businesses since 2019. Business Insider [Internet]. 2022. Available from: https://www.businessinsider.com/charts-meta-metaverse-spending-losses-reality-labs-vr-mark-zuckerberg-2022-10 [Accessed: 2024-August-21]

[2] Niemeyer DJ, Gerber HR. Maker culture and Minecraft : Implications for the future of learning. Educational Media International. 2015;**52**(3):216–226. DOI:10.1080/09523987.2015.1075103

[3] Dionisio J, Iii WB, Gilbert R. 3D virtual worlds and the metaverse: Current status and future possibilities. ACM Computing Surveys. 2013;**45**(3):34. DOI:10.1145/2480741.2480751

[4] Boellstorff T. Coming of Age in Second Life: An Anthropologist Explores the Virtually Human. Princeton: Princeton University Press; 2008

[5] Dowling M. Fertile LAND: Pricing non-fungible tokens. Finance Research Letters. 2022;**44**:102096. DOI: 10.1016/j.frl.2021.102096

[6] Grand View Research. Metaverse Market Size, Share & Trends Analysis Report by Product, by Platform, by Technology, by Application, by End Use, by Region, and Segment Forecasts, 2024-2030 [Internet]. 2024. Available from: https://www.grandviewresearch.com/industry-analysis/metaverse-market-report [Accessed: 2024-August-21]

[7] Dwyer T, Perkins C, Redhead S, Sita J. Metaverse beyond the hype: Multidisciplinary perspectives on emerging challenges, opportunities, and agenda for research, practice and policy. International Journal of Information Management. 2022;**66**:102542. DOI: 10.1016/j.ijinfomgt.2022.102542

[8] United Nations Conference on Trade and Development. Creative economy outlook 2024 [Internet]. 2024. Available from: https://unctad.org/publication/creative-economy-outlook-2024 [Accessed: 2024-August-21]

[9] Eloundou T, Manning S, Mishkin P, Rock D. GPTs are GPTs: An early look at the labor market impact potential of large language models. ArXiv. 2023;2304.09919. DOI: 10.48550/arXiv.2303.10130

[10] Brynjolfsson E, McAfee A. The Second Machine Age: Work, Progress, and Prosperity in a Time of Brilliant Technologies. New York: W.W. Norton; 2014

[11] Mystakidis SM. Metaverse. Encyclopedia. 2022;**2**(1):486–497. DOI: 10.3390/encyclopedia2010031 [Accessed: 2024-November-06]

[12] Dwivedi YK, Hughes L, Baabdullah AM, Ribeiro-Navarrete S, Giannakis M, Al-Debei MM, et al. Metaverse beyond the hype: Multidisciplinary perspectives on emerging challenges, opportunities, and agenda for research, practice and policy. International Journal of Information Management. 2022;**66**:102542. DOI: 10.1016/j.ijinfomgt.2022.102542

[13] Vaithilingam P, Zhang T, Glassman EL. Expectation vs. experience: Evaluating the usability of

code generation tools powered by large language models. In: Extended Abstracts of the 2022 CHI Conference on Human Factors in Computing Systems; Apr 29-May 5; New Orleans. New York: Association for Computing Machinery; 2022. p. 1–7. DOI: 10.1145/3491101.3519665

[14] Frey C, Osborne M. The future of employment: How susceptible are jobs to computerisation? Technological Forecasting and Social Change. 2017;**114**:254–280. DOI: 10.1016/j.techfore.2016.08.019

[15] Schumpeter J. Capitalism, Socialism, and Democracy. New York: Harper & Brothers; 1942

[16] Autor DH. Why are there still so many jobs? The history and future of workplace automation. Journal of Economic Perspectives. 2015;**29**(3):3–30. DOI:10.1257/jep.29.3.3

[17] Susskind RE, Susskind D. The Future of the Professions: How Technology Will Transform the Work of Human Experts. Oxford: Oxford University Press; 2022

[18] Manovich L. 100 billion data rows per second: Media analytics in the early 21st century [Internet]. 2018. Available from: http://manovich.net [Accessed: 2024-August-21]

[19] Norman DA. Design of Everyday Things. Revised and Expand ed. New York: Basic Books; 2013

[20] Floridi L. Metaverse: A matter of experience. Philosophy & Technology. 2022;**35**:73. DOI: 10.1007/s13347-022-00568-6

[21] Gunkel DJ. Person, Thing, Robot: A Moral and Legal Ontology for the 21st Century and Beyond. Cambridge: MIT Press; 2023

[22] Makransky G, Lilleholt L. A structural equation modeling investigation of the emotional value of immersive virtual reality in education. Educational Technology Research and Development. 2018;**66**(5):1141–1164. DOI:10.1007/s11423-018-9581-2

[23] Sawyer RK. Explaining Creativity: The Science of Human Innovation. New York: Oxford University Press; 2019

[24] Amabile TM, Pratt MG. The dynamic componential model of creativity and innovation in organizations: Making progress, making meaning. Research in Organizational Behavior. 2016;**36**:157–183. DOI: 10.1016/j.riob.2016.10.001

[25] Ensmenger NL. The Computer Boys Take Over: Computers, Programmers, and the Politics of Technical Expertise. Cambridge: MIT Press; 2010

[26] Mintzberg H. Leadership and management development: An afterword. Academy of Management Executive. 2004;**18**(3):140–142

[27] Chen M, Tworek J, Jun H, Yuan Q, Pondé H, Kaplan J, et al. Evaluating large language models trained on code. ArXiv. 2021.abs/2107.03374 [Accessed: 2024-November-06]

[28] Ramesh A, Dhariwal P, Nichol A, Chu C, Chen M. Hierarchical text-conditional image generation with

CLIP latents. ArXiv. 2022. abs/2204.06125 [Accessed: 2024-November-6]

[29] Florida R. The Rise of the Creative Class: And How It's Transforming Work, Leisure, Community and Everyday Life. New York: Basic Books; 2002

[30] Howkins J. The Creative Economy: How People Make Money from Ideas. 2nd ed. London: Penguin Books; 2013

[31] Gardner H. Five Minds for the Future. Boston: Harvard Business School Press; 2007

[32] Wagner T. Creating Innovators: The Making of Young People Who Will Change the World. New York: Scribner; 2012

[33] Schlegel A, Alexander P, Fogelson SV, Li X, Lu Z, Kohler PJ, et al. The artist emerges: Visual art learning alters neural structure and function. NeuroImage. 2015;**105**:440–451

[34] McGilchrist I. The Master and His Emissary: The Divided Brain and the Making of the Western World. New Haven: Yale University Press; 2009

[35] Root-Bernstein R, Allen L, Beach L, Bhadula R, Fast J, Hosey C, et al. Arts Foster Scientific Success: Avocations of Nobel, National Academy, Royal Society, and Sigma Xi Members. Journal of Psychology of Science and Technology 2008; **1**:51–63

[36] Earley PC, Mosakowski E. Cultural intelligence. Harvard Business Review. 2004;**82**(10):139–146

[37] Jarvenpaa SL, Leidner DE. Communication and trust in global virtual teams. Organization Science. 1999;**10**(6):791–815. DOI:10.1287/orsc.10.6.791

[38] Leimeister JM, Turel O, Lowry PB, Zhang P, Benbasat I. Long live the metaverse: Identifying the potential for market disruption and future research. Journal of Management Information Systems. 2025;**42**(1):7–24. DOI:10.1080/07421222.2025.2455770

[39] Epstein D. Range: Why Generalists Triumph in a Specialized World. New York: Riverhead Books; 2019

[40] Klein JT. Interdisciplinarity: History, Theory, and Practice. Detroit: Wayne State University Press; 1990

[41] Ito J, Howe J. Whiplash: How to Survive Our Faster Future. New York: Grand Central Publishing; 2016

[42] Ito J. Antidisciplinary. Joi Ito's Web [Internet]. 2014 Oct 2. DOI: 10.31859/20141002.1939

[43] Balsamo A. Designing Culture: The Technological Imagination at Work. Durham: Duke University Press; 2011. DOI: 10.1215/9780822392149

[44] Adobe. The creativity dividend: How artistic leadership drives innovation. Forrester Consulting; 2014. Available from: https://www.americansforthearts.org/by-program/reports-and-data/legislation-policy/naappd/the-creative-dividend-how-creativity-impacts-business-results [Accessed: 2024-August-21]

[45] Burt RS. Structural holes and good ideas. American Journal of Sociology. 2004;**110**(2):349–399

[46] UNESCO. Re|shaping Policies for Creativity: Addressing Culture as

a Global Public Good. Paris: UNESCO; 2022

[47] NASA. JPL Creative Lab: Storytelling at the Frontier of Space Exploration [Internet]. 2020. Available from: https://www.jpl.nasa.gov/creative [Accessed: 2024-August-21]

[48] Newzoo. Global Games Market Report 2023. Amsterdam: Newzoo; 2023

[49] Ito J. Design and science. Journal of Design and Science. 2016. Available from: https://jods.mitpress.mit.edu/pub/designandscience [Accessed: 2024-August-21]

[50] Robertson BJ. Holacracy: The New Management System for a Rapidly Changing World. New York: Henry Holt and Company; 2015

[51] Haven K. Story Proof: The Science behind the Startling Power of Story. Westport: Libraries Unlimited; 2007

[52] Fjeldstad ØD, Snow CC, Miles RE, Lettl C. The architecture of collaboration. Strategic Management Journal. 2012;**33**(6):734–750

[53] Manovich L, Arielli E. Artificial aesthetics[Internet]. 2024. Available from: https://manovich.net/index.php/projects/artificial-aesthetics [Accessed: 2024-August-21]

[54] Sawyer RK. The iterative and improvisational nature of the creative process. Journal of Creativity. 2021;**31**:100002. DOI: 10.1016/j.yjoc.2021.100002

[55] Floridi L. Ethics, Governance, and Policies in the Digital Age. Cham: Springer; 2022

[56] Ito J. The antidisciplinary approach: IRI medal address. Research-Technology Management. 2017;**60**(6):20–23

[57] Ito J. Research statement[Internet]. PubPub. Available from: https://pubpub.ito.com/pub/researchstatement/release/2 [Accessed: 2024-August-21]

[58] Jenkins H. Convergence Culture: Where Old and New Media Collide. New York: New York University Press; 2006

[59] McWilliams G, Phillips D, McEvoy B, Phillips E, Lydon D, Chang JR, et al. Shaping the Metaverse: Policy Engagement with Immersive Technologies in the UK. Belfast: Queen's University Belfast; 2023

Chapter 19

Who Wants to Travel Digitally, and Why? – An Analysis of Personal Traits and Vicarious Sense of Place in a Virtual Environment

Ingvar Tjostheim and John A. Waterworth

Abstract

Who is interested in digital travel? In particular, what are the personal traits of individuals who use digital alternatives to physical travel? In this chapter, we aim to arrive at accurate answers to these questions. Our earlier work had shown that two characteristics distinguish people who are positive about digital travel versus those who are not: optimism, which we assessed using the Rosenberg self-esteem scale, and resistance to peer influence (RPI), which we assessed using the Steinberger and Monahan RPI-questionnaire. Our previous study took place during a time of travel restrictions introduced in response to the spread of the Covid-19 virus. To expand on those findings, we commissioned a new and larger national survey with 604 travellers to analyse whether these two characteristics can be used to identify those with a positive view of digital travel in general. This was conducted after Covid-19 restrictions had been removed. We asked our participants to express their views about travelling digitally by answering questions about the use of digital travel for guided tours, museum visits, and distant attractions. Our results showed that resistance to peer influence scores could indeed be used to predict the likelihood of users accepting digital travel technologies, but user optimism could not.

Keywords: digital travel, virtual tourism, personal characteristics, binary logistics, resistance to peer influence, user optimism

1. Introduction

There are several reasons why people might consider digital travel in place of physical travel. In some situations, it is not possible to travel [1]. Another reason is a concern for the environment, since physical travel worldwide uses large amounts of fossil fuels and other resources, adding to factors influencing global warming. In addition to such reasons, we wondered whether there is an emerging interest in visits to travel destinations with digital alternatives, possibly stimulated by the increased use of digital alternatives to travel during the pandemic. Many citizens plan their main holidays, including where to go and what to do, months before the vacation starts, often using digital devices to access online information about places and activities. In the future, will digital travel more significantly substitute for physical travel, or will it remain primarily a marketing tool promoting physical travel? Are there personality traits that can distinguish those who express an interest in and willingness to engage in digital travel?

In this chapter, we report and discuss findings from our most recent survey of travellers' views on digital travel. In addition to the questions raised above, the main research focus was the following: Can we identify factors that can identify those individuals who see travelling digitally (or using digital travel applications) as similar to (or as a substitute for) the experience of travelling physically, as opposed to those who do not see digital travel in this way? In addition to demographic characteristics, the survey included a self-esteem scale [2] and a resistance-to-peer-influence scale [3]. The chapter extends our earlier work reported in literature [4, 5, and 6] by examining personal characteristics as well as sense-of-place judgements for digital travel in greater detail and with a much larger, nationally representative panel of survey respondents.

2. Digital travellers and their characteristics

For this study, a group of survey participants in Norway was invited to give their views on digital travel applications and a virtual travel experience. A market research company recruited 600 respondents, using a representative sample of Norwegian citizens aged 16–69 years. The demographics of those taking part are presented in **Tables 1** and **2**.

Age in years	16–29	30–49	50–69
All participants (N = 604)	18%	38%	44%
Male (N = 283)	19%	30%	51%
Female (N = 321)	18%	45%	37%

Table 1.
Gender and age profile of the participants.

	Primary or secondary education	First degree (Bachelor)	Higher degree (Maser or higher)
All participants (N = 604)	47%	26%	27%
Male (N = 283)	50%	26%	24%
Female (N = 321)	45%	26%	29%

Table 2.
Educational profile of the participants.

Table 1 shows that there are fewer individuals in the age-group 16–29 years old compared to the other two groups. There is a small difference between the two other age-groups. We speculate that the oldest age group has more free time in which they might travel, take more lengthy vacations, and are on a firmer footing in terms of finances than younger participants in the study. Therefore, it was not a surprise that a slightly higher number of people in this age-group chose to participate in the travel survey.

Table 2 shows the level to which the participants were educated. Looking across society in general, the first group (having only primary or secondary education) is the largest. This is reflected by the fact that approximately 50% of our representative sample of the population belonged to this group.

As participants in the study were recruited from a large database representing the national population, we suggest that our results should have some generalisability.

2.1 Digital travel

As in our earlier study [4], for this study, we started the questionnaire with an explanation of what we meant by virtual tourism, digital travel products, and applications as follows:

> *The term virtual tourism is, by some, used to describe a digital visit – a digital experience of what the museums and tourist attractions have to offer. . . . For the next questions, we distinguish between these three: digital presentations or applications for museums or tourist attractions, activities for tourists, and guided tours.*

Travel and tourism companies have, as their guiding principle, the goal of encouraging individuals to become tourists, booking visits and making their way to a specific location – a destination. For this to happen, such companies are heavy users of direct advertising and other methods of marketing tourist locations. In this chapter, the term 'pre-taste' (of a destination and travellers' experiences there) is used to convey the sense that a digital presentation in an application, aimed at encouraging specific future travel, includes selected information for the user that allows the person to get a sense of the experience of actually visiting a particular place. A pre-taste is thus not merely a means to an end; its purpose is to create interest and influence the person to book a trip [6].

For this study, we created a two-minute video presenting Mexico as a travel destination. The aim was to inform our participants about the capabilities of virtual environments for exploring tourist locations such as ancient buildings, townships, and attractive natural areas. Recorded scenes from the game Forza Horizon 5 and photographic images of actual places were included in the video. As shown in **Figures 1–3**, places and archaeological sites are replicated in the game with a high level of photo-realism [7]. For further information, see the study by Tjostheim and Waterworth [5].

Using gaming and similar technologies can produce genuine 'as-if present' experiences in a place that is not their physical location, as seen in many video games. A few researchers have discussed this topic before in terms of the relationship between the sense of place and 'telepresence' – the sense of being in another place [8–10]. Slater and Sanchez-Vives [11] specifically considered virtual travel in this

Figure 1.
The Parque Municipal in Forza Horizon 5.

context, with reference to Cheong's [12] visions for virtual tourism in the mid-1990s. They write (p. 27):

> *'Perhaps, VR is not meant to be a substitute for real travel, but just another form of travel – no less valid in its own terms than all that physically boarding the real aeroplane entails'.*

A study by Tjostheim and Waterworth [6, 13, 14] demonstrated that ratings of both subjective telepresence and sense of place can be used to measure the user experience, intended activities, and relevant affordances in a virtual travel environment. According to Nam et al. [15], genuineness or authenticity has an impact on both the presence experience and satisfaction with the virtual visit, particularly for heritage sites. Sharma et al. [16] did not find a significant difference between a virtual tour and a physical tour in terms of authenticity, but VR exposure to a place enhanced the satisfaction of the subsequent physical visit. For further information about studies of VR in tourism and hospitality, we refer to the works by Calisto and Sarkar [17] and Di Dalmazi et al. [18].

2.2 Travellers' views on digital alternatives to physical experiences at tourist destinations

A traveller is someone who moves from one place to another. When the traveller arrives at the new place, the destination, they can explore the place and take part in activities. In the survey, we first conveyed the meaning of specific terms such as 'virtual tourism' and 'digital travel', while emphasising that these are digital and not physical visits. We asked the respondents to consider the digital presentation of a museum or attraction, a tourist activity, and a guided tour, responding in terms of the following alternatives:

Figure 2.
Uxmal in Forza Horizon 5.

Figure 3.
Heroica Mulegé (a) photo (b) Forza Horizon 5.

(1) The digital presentation is a marketing tool that can create an interest in (museum, activity, guided tour).

(2) A digital presentation can be a pre-taste of (museum, activity, guided tour), or it can substitute (museum, activity, guided tour). We also asked whether the digital experience was the same, or approximately the same, as the physical.

(3) Other, meaning: 'I disagree with the first two alternatives'.

Table 3 illustrates the proportions of participants who viewed different options for travelling digitally as pre-tastes of actual travel or as a substitute for travelling physically for specific purposes. **Table 4** shows how participants rated their experiences compared to how they perceived their experiences had they travelled physically to the location.

Table 3 shows that a small proportion of our 604 participants in the survey viewed the digital alternative as a substitute for a physical visit to the place. The preference for using digital products was, first, as a pre-taste, followed by for marketing purposes. Only a small segment of travellers indicated that they thought the digital presentation could be a satisfactory substitute for physically travelling to the place.

Table 4 illustrates the fact that most participants did not think that the experience in a virtual environment was the same as physical travel. However, there was a smaller number of participants who did. Of the three alternative purposes for digital travel, activities seem to be difficult to replicate digitally in an adequate way. According to the survey, only 2% chose this alternative.

It is possible to think that travelling digitally can provide an alternative to physically travelling even when the digital is not mimicking the physical in great detail or cannot substitute for the experience. We have identified a group we refer to

	Marketing	**Pre-taste**	**Substitute**	**Other = disagree with the first two or three descriptions**
Museum visit	33%	53%	6%	8%
Activity	41%	48%	2%	9%
Guided tour	44%	38%	8%	10%

Table 3.
Views of digital presentations for marketing, as a 'pre-taste' or as a substitute for physical travel.

	Approximately the same experience	**The same experience**	**Other = disagrees with the first two descriptions**
Visiting a museum or attraction	29%	12%	59%
Another activity	26%	7%	67%
A guided tour	30%	11%	59%

Table 4.
Views of digital experiences versus physical travel experiences.

as 'Travellers who see digital travel as a viable alternative to physical travel'. Of the 604 participants, we identified 168 respondents (28%) with this view.

Table 5 shows statistical details of the demographic profiles and the scales for personal characteristics of the respondents. We used measures of skewness and kurtosis to assess the shape of data distribution for each characteristic. As shown in the table, the values were less than ±2.0, indicating no problems with the way the data were distributed.

Both the Resistance to Peer Influence Scale and the Rosenberg Self-Esteem Scale are based on the subjective assessments by each of the respondents, assessing their personal traits on these dimensions. For further information about the two personal traits scales, the questions, and scoring methods, refer to literature [2, 3]. For further information about the Sense of Place Scale, see the study by Tjostheim and Waterworth [5].

There is not much existing research relating attitudes to travelling digitally, and virtual tourism generally, with the personal traits of prospective travellers, although demographic details are often provided. For instance, the article 'Would you enjoy virtual travel?' by Zhang et al. [19] lists several relevant factors but not personality traits or personal characteristics. Kim et al. [20] included optimism as a factor, but as a technology readiness type of optimism based on the work by Chung [21] and not a general personal trait. Dedeoğlu et al. [22] used a short 10-item scale for the five-factor personality traits developed by Gosling et al. [23] in interviews with visitors at a tourist destination, but not for virtual tourism or virtual travel.

As shown in **Table 6,** people who see digital travel as an alternative to physical travel scored lower on both the Resistance to Peer Influence Scale and the Rosenberg Self-Esteem Scale compared to the others. For vicarious sense of place, those who do view travelling digitally as an alternative to travelling physically scored more highly than the others. For vicarious sense of place, this is an expected result because, conceptually, vicariousness also has to do with the tendency to relate to the people living there, at the destination. Vicariousness is the experience of something indirectly or through others. Vicarious sense of place concerns not only the geographical place that someone can visit but also the people living there, the residents. 'Tourism involves a meeting of two populations: a better-known, stable population (the residents) and a generally ex-ante, less known and variable one (the tourists)' [24].

Table 6 shows that 48% of the respondents to our survey who experienced a vicarious sense of place (in that they had thoughts about the people living at the

	Min	Max	Mean	SD	Skewness	Kurtosis
Gender	1	2	1.53	0.50	−0.126	-1.99
Age	1	3	2.25	0.75	−0.45	-1.09
Education	1	3	1.80	0.84	0.39	-1.47
Optimism	1	3	2.16	0.92	−0.32	-1.73
Resistance to peers	1	3	2.35	0.73	−0.65	-0.90
Vicarious sense of place	1	3	2.16	0.81	−0.29	-1.40

Table 5.
*Descriptive statistics of the variables and measurements (*n = 604*).*

Resistance to Peer Influence Scale – RPIS (Steinberg & Monahan, 2007)			
	Low	**Medium**	**High**
Participants who did not view digital as an alternative to physical travel (N = 483)	10%	35%	54%
Participants who viewed digital as an alternative to physical travel (N = 121)	29%	32%	39%
The Rosenberg Self-Esteem Scale – RSES (Rosenberg, 1965)			
	Low	**Medium**	**High**
Participants who did not view digital as an alternative to physical travel (N = 483)	32%	9%	59%
Participants who viewed digital as an alternative to physical travel (N = 121)	44%	11%	45%
Vicarious Sense of Place (Relph, 1976, [25] Tjostheim & Waterworth, 2020)			
	Disagree	**Neither/nor**	**Agree**
Travellers who do not view digital travel as an alternative to physical travel (N = 483)	29%	32%	39%
Travellers who see digital travel as an alternative to physical travel (N = 121)	17%	35%	48%

Table 6.
Measurements of personal characteristics (n = *604).*

place in Mexico and the things that could be physically done there when visiting as a tourist) were positive towards digital travel, whereas 39% were not.

3. Analysis with binary logistics

We selected binary logistic regression for the investigation, utilising a dichotomous dependent variable. Binary logistic regression is applicable when the dependent variable is dichotomous, and the independent variables can be of any form. It may predict a categorical dependent variable based on continuous and/or categorical independent variables – in this case, whether an individual perceives a digital travel experience as analogous to or a substitute for real travel.

To juxtapose the present findings from our extensive national survey with our prior study [4], we reproduced the binary logistic regression technique employed in that earlier research. The percentages of individuals shown in bold in **Tables 3** and **4** were used as the criterion for classifying membership in the positive digital travel group. Travellers who perceived digital travel as an alternative to physical travel were assigned a Code of 1, while the others were assigned a Code of 0. We sought to determine if any of the assessed personal attributes or demographic variables effectively predicted our dependent variable – openness to digital travel. **Table 7** presents the binary logistic classification. The greater the proportion of accuracy, the more favourable the outcome; as shown in **Table 7**, the categorisation achieved 62% and 60% correctness.

Binary, 483 classified as 0 (percentage correct: 62% – in bold).	**301**	182
Binary, 121 classified as 1 (percentage correct: 60% – in bold)	48	73

Table 7.
Classification: the binary logistic prediction of the two groups.

	Independent variables	Beta estimates	SE	Wald	p (Sig)
Predictors in step 1 (the first model) – with the use of the backwards Wald procedure.	Constant	-0.045	0.545	0.007	0.934
	Male/female	0.151	0.218	0.484	0.487
	Age groups	-0.128	0.147	0.763	0.382
	Education 3 groups	-0.232	0.138	2.820	0.093
	Optimism, Rosenberg	0.045	0.127	0.123	0.726
	Resistance to peers	-0.711	0.151	22.145	0.001
	Vicarious sense of place	0.334	0.140	5.691	0.017

Table 8.
Binary logistic regression model – variables, first step.

We then computed which model variables made a significant contribution; see **Table 8**.

Nagelkerke R^2 is a pseudo R-square that can be used to assess model adequacy [26]. Similarly, the Hosmer and Lemeshow Test [26] can be used to assess goodness of fit. The score for the former in our calculation was 10.2%. The latter p-values were greater than the criterion of 0.05 for both models, confirming the use of the variables for making a prediction; see **Table 9**.

A lower score on the resistance to peers means conformity; that is, the person is, to a lesser degree, willing to go against their peers compared to those with a higher score on the resistance to peer questions. A high score on vicarious sense of place is the second predictor. We used backwards Wald to analyse the predictor variables and determine which predicted the most in relation to the dependent measure. The Wald statistic estimates shown in **Table 9** indicate that resistance to peers and vicarious sense of place were the only two significant predictors.

	Independent variables	Beta estimates	SE	Wald	p (Sig)
Predictors in step 5, the final model – with the use of the backwards Wald procedure	Constant	-0.443	0.449	0.971	0.324
	Resistance to peers	-0.767	0.138	30.877	0.001
	Vicarious sense of place	0.341	0.138	6.068	0.014
Model summary – final model	-2 Log likelihood	Cox and Snell R^2	Nagelkerke R^2	Hosmer and Lemeshow Test: Chi-square (Sig.)	
	564.872	0.064	0.102	10.402 (0.109)	

Table 9.
Variables in the final step and model summary.

4. Discussion and conclusions

For many, holidays are important. In Norway, most employees have five weeks of paid vacation per year, and many citizens can afford to go abroad or travelling to places in their own country. However, the concept of digital travel is new to many, which is why we started the survey with a short explanation about virtual tourism and digital travel before asking specific questions. We then asked our participants to give us their views on travelling digitally by using specific questions concerning visits to museums, attractions, and guided tours. To predict the acceptability of these applications and experiences for different types of users, we included personal traits of users in binary logistic models. The use of a large, nationally representative sample of respondents increases the likely generalisability of our findings compared to most other studies.

We found that resistance to peer influence was predictive of the likelihood of users responding positively to digital travel technologies. In addition to questions, a video of Mexico recorded from a computer game was presented to the respondents. The purpose was to illustrate digital travel and measure vicarious sense of place. The respondents watched the video and then answered questions about their vicarious sense of place. Since all participants viewed this video and thus had a direct experience of a realistic form of digital travel, we suggest that the study has higher ecological validity than a survey-question-only study.

Technologies are anticipated to significantly influence travel attitudes and behaviours by simulating visits to destinations and enhancing the ability of potential travellers to imagine themselves actually being there. The tourism industry leverages various media channels as means of attracting visitors. Although a virtual experience will often not fully satisfy a tourist compared to a physical visit, it can heighten the desire to see an actual place. For a large number of people, using digital applications to explore tourist sites or products serves as a primary motivation for travel. For many, evaluating a tourist site or product in advance of a possible visit is the main motivation for using a digital application [6, 27].

It is not always possible to travel physically. An example is the pandemic, with restrictions on physical travel imposed by the government. Our earlier study [4] was carried out during the pandemic, a time with travel restrictions. Comparing the results of the previous study with the national study presented in this chapter, we found little substantial difference in the pattern of responses. It should also be remembered that, for most people, digital travel is not seen as a substitute but rather a pre-cursor to physical travel. Taken together, these two factors might account for the lack of a noticeable difference between the two sets of ratings. We speculate that the experience of the pandemic restrictions, coupled with increased accessibility to high-fidelity interactive experiences of other places, may yet have a long-term positive effect on attitudes towards travelling via a digital application rather than travelling physically to a place. This is one area for further research on digital travel in the future.

As immersive technology continues to improve and become more affordable, the prevalence of convincing digital travel experiences is expected to increase in the future. '*Digital travel that closely simulates aspects of physical travel will perhaps not be an alternative or the first choice for most vacationers for their main holiday, but we envision that, for a segment of vacationers at least, digital travel will increasingly become a substitute for some physical travels to places and events, not just an add-on or pre-taste of them'* [4]. Currently, digital travel appeals to relatively few potential travellers. The main finding from our study is those potential travellers who will be willing to travel digitally in the future can, to some extent, be predicted according to their personal characteristics. This is an important finding relative to future tourism and travel generally, as well as to the design of innovative and relevant digital travel applications.

Author details

Ingvar Tjostheim[1*] and John A. Waterworth[2]

1 Hauge School of Management, NLA University College, Oslo, Norway

2 Umeå University, Umeå, Sweden

*Address all correspondence to: ingvar.tjostheim@gmail.com

References

[1] Zheng D, Luo Q, Ritchie B. The role of trust in mitigating perceived threat, fear, and travel avoidance after a pandemic outbreak: A multigroup Analysis. Journal of Travel Research. 2022;**61**(3):581–596

[2] Rosenberg M. Society and the Adolescent Self-image. Princeton, NJ, USA: Princeton University Press; 1965

[3] Steinberg L, Monahan KC. Age differences in resistance to peer influence. Developmental Psychology. 2007;**43**:1531–1543

[4] Tjostheim I, Waterworth JA. Tomorrow's digital travellers – Who are they? A study on travellers' views on digital travel experiences. In: Carvalho A, L, editors. Smart Innovation, System and Technologies, Advances in Tourism, Technology and Systems: Selected Papers from ICOTTS, Volume 1, Series ISSN. Singapore: Springer; 2023. p. 2190–3018

[5] Tjostheim I, Waterworth JA. Digital travel – a study of travellers' views of a digital visit to Mexico. In: Rocha Á, Ferrás C, Ibarra W, editors. Information Technology and Systems. ICITS 2023. Lecture Notes in Networks and Systems. Vol. **691**, Cham: Springer; 2023. p. 185–194. DOI: 10.1007/978-3-031-33258-6_17

[6] Tjostheim I, Waterworth JA. The Psychosocial Reality of Digital Travel: Being in Virtual Places. Cham: Palgrave Macmillan; 2022

[7] Comparing forza horizon 5 locations to real-life, Published 9 Nov 2021. Theodore Mc Kenzie, Senior Ed. https://80.lv/articles/comparing-forza-horizon-5-locations-to-real-life

[8] Turner P, Turner S. Place, sense of place, and presence. Presence: Teleoperators and Virtual Environments. 2006;**15**(2):204–217

[9] Turner P, Turner S, Carroll F. The tourist gaze: Towards contextualised virtual environments. In: Spaces, Spatiality and Technology. Dortrecht, The Netherlands: Springer; 2005

[10] Waterworth JA, Tjostheim I. Integrating the world of presence theory: Illusion, pretence, attending, and pretending. PsyArXiv. 2021;1–30. DOI:10.31234/osf.io/qbcfe

[11] Slater M, Sanchez-Vives M. Enhancing our lives with immersive virtual reality. Frontiers in robotics and AI. Published online 19 December 2016. https://doi.org/10.3389/frobt.2016.00074

[12] Cheong R. The virtual threat to travel and tourism. Tourism Management. 1995;**16**(6):417–422

[13] Tjostheim I, Leister W, Waterworth JA. Telepresence and the Role of the Senses. In: Berkich D, d'Alfonso M, editors. On the Cognitive, Ethical, and Scientific Dimensions of Artificial Intelligence. Philosophical Studies Series. Vol. **134**, Cham: Springer; 2019. p. 169–187. DOI: 10.1007/978-3-030-01800-9_9

[14] Tjostheim I, Waterworth JA. Virtual tourism in a game environment: Untangling judged affordances and sense of place. In: X. Fang. HCI in

Games. Cham, Switzerland: Springer; 2020. p. 202–217

[15] Nam K, Dutt CS, Baker J. 2023. Authenticity in objects and activities: Determinants of satisfaction with virtual reality experiences of heritage and Non-Heritage tourism sites. Information Systems Frontiers. **25** (3):1219–1237. DOI: 10.1007/s10796-022-10286-1

[16] Sharma I, Lim WM, Aggarwal A. Virtual reality as a sustainable alternative for authentic and satisfying tourism experiences. Tourism Recreation Research. 2025; Advance online publication. DOI: 10.1080/02508281.2024.2413832

[17] Calisto M, Sarkar S. A systematic review of virtual reality in tourism and hospitality: The known and the paths to follow. International Journal of Hospitality Management. 2024;**116**:103623. 10.1016/j.ijhm.2023.103623

[18] Di Dalmazi M, Mandolfo M, Guixeres J, Alca~niz Raya M, Lamberti L. 2024. How immersive technologies impact behavioral responses in destination marketing: The role of physiological arousal, presence, and age. International Journal of Contemporary Hospitality Management. **36**(11):3628–3650. DOI: 10.1108/ijchm-09-2023-1511

[19] Zhang SN, Li YQ, Ruan WQ, Liu CH. Would you enjoy virtual travel? The characteristics and causes of virtual tourists' sentiment under the influence of the COVID-19 pandemic. Tourism Management. 2022;**88**:104429

[20] Kim MJ, Lee CK, Preis MW. The impact of innovation and gratification on authentic experience, subjective well-being, and behavioral intention in tourism virtual reality. Telematics and Informatics. 2020;**49**:101349

[21] Chung N, Han H, Joun Y. Tourists' intention to visit a destination: The role of augmented reality (AR) application for a heritage site. Computers in Human Behavior. 2015;**50**:588–599

[22] Dedeoğlu BB, Okumus F, Xiaoli Y, Wenmin J. Do tourists' personality traits moderate the relationship between social media content sharing and destination involvement?. Journal of Travel & Tourism Marketing. 2019;**36** (5):612–626

[23] Gosling SD, Rentfrow PJ, Swann Jr WB. A very brief measure of the big-five personality domains. Journal of Research in Personality. 2003;**37** (6):504–528

[24] Bimonte S. The "tragedy of tourism resources" as the outcome of a strategic game: A new analytical framework. Ecological Economics. 2008;**67**(3):457–464

[25] Relph E. Place and Placelessness. London: Pion; 1976

[26] Hosmer W, Lemeshow S. Applied Logistic Regression. New York: Wiley; 1989

[27] Tjostheim I, Waterworth JA. Is There a Market for Digital Travel? Travellers' Views on Digital Travel and Willingness to Pay. In: Reis JL, Del Rio Araujo M, Reis LP, Dos Santos JPM editors, Marketing and Smart Technologies. ICMarkTech 2022. Smart Innovation, Systems and Technologies. Vol. **344**, Singapore: Springer; 2024. p. 635–645. DOI: 10.1007/978-981-99-0333-7_46